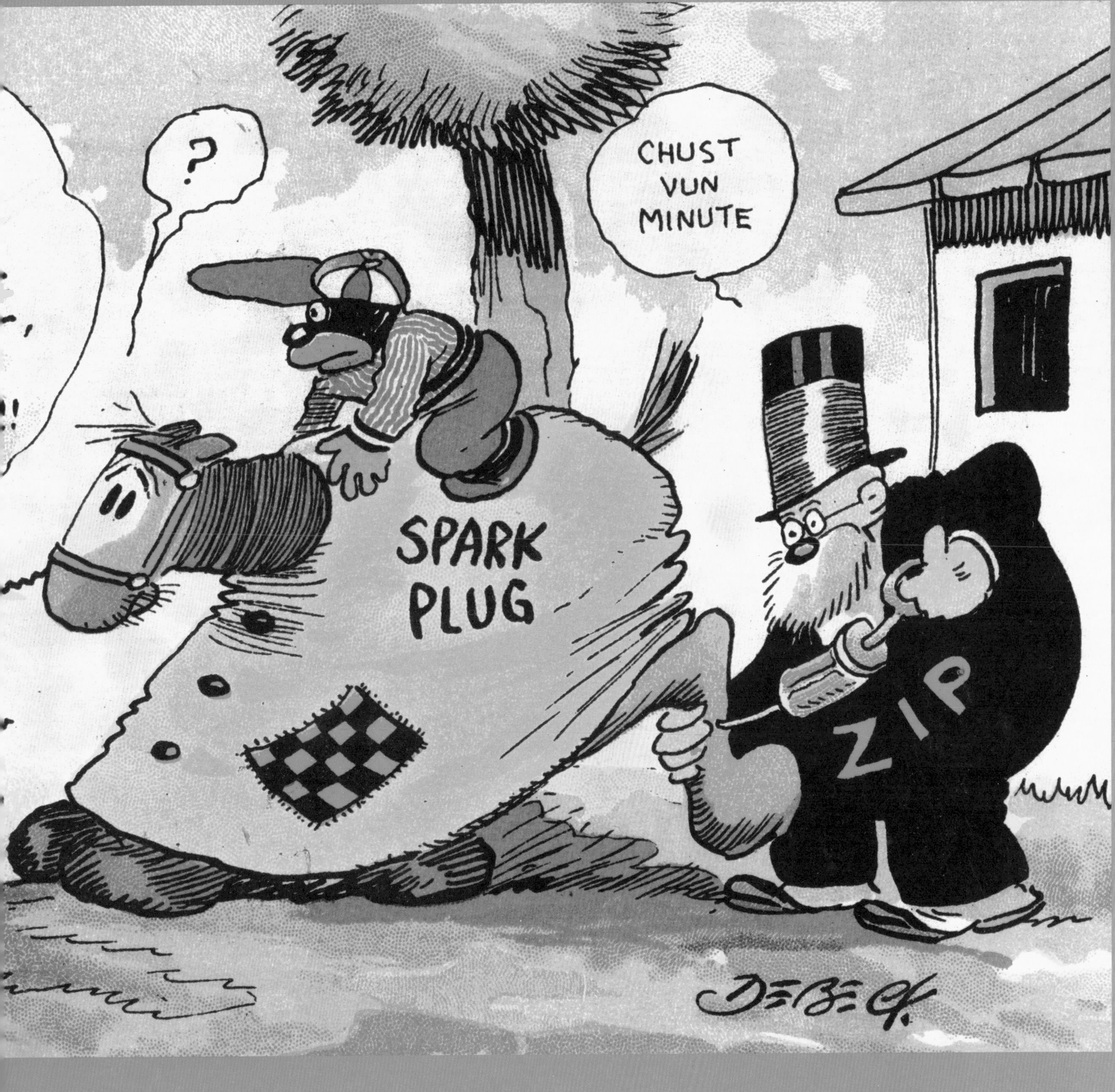
?
CHUST VUN MINUTE
SPARK PLUG
ZIP
DE BE CK.

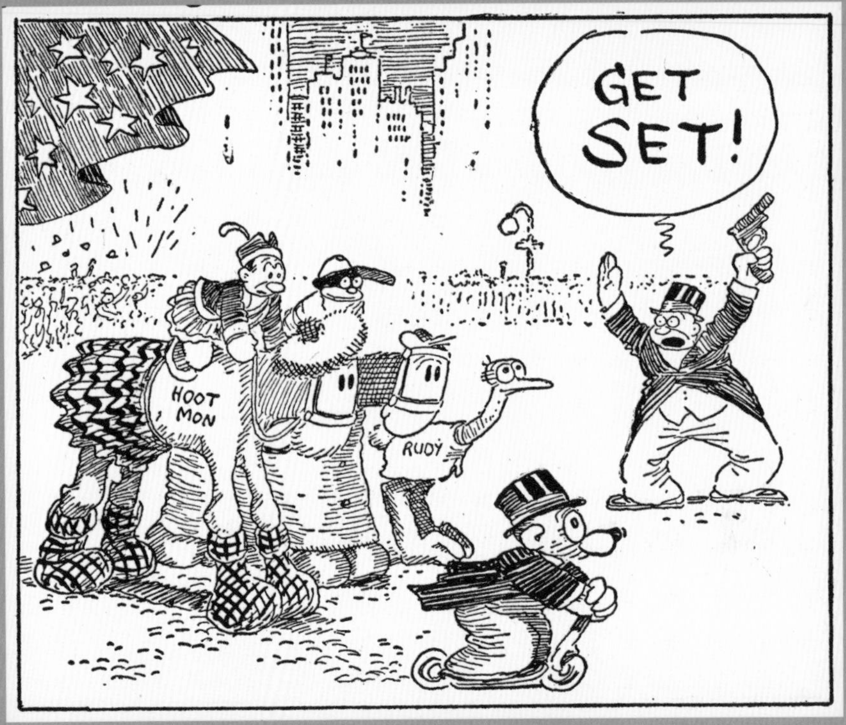
GET SET!
HOOT MON
RUDY

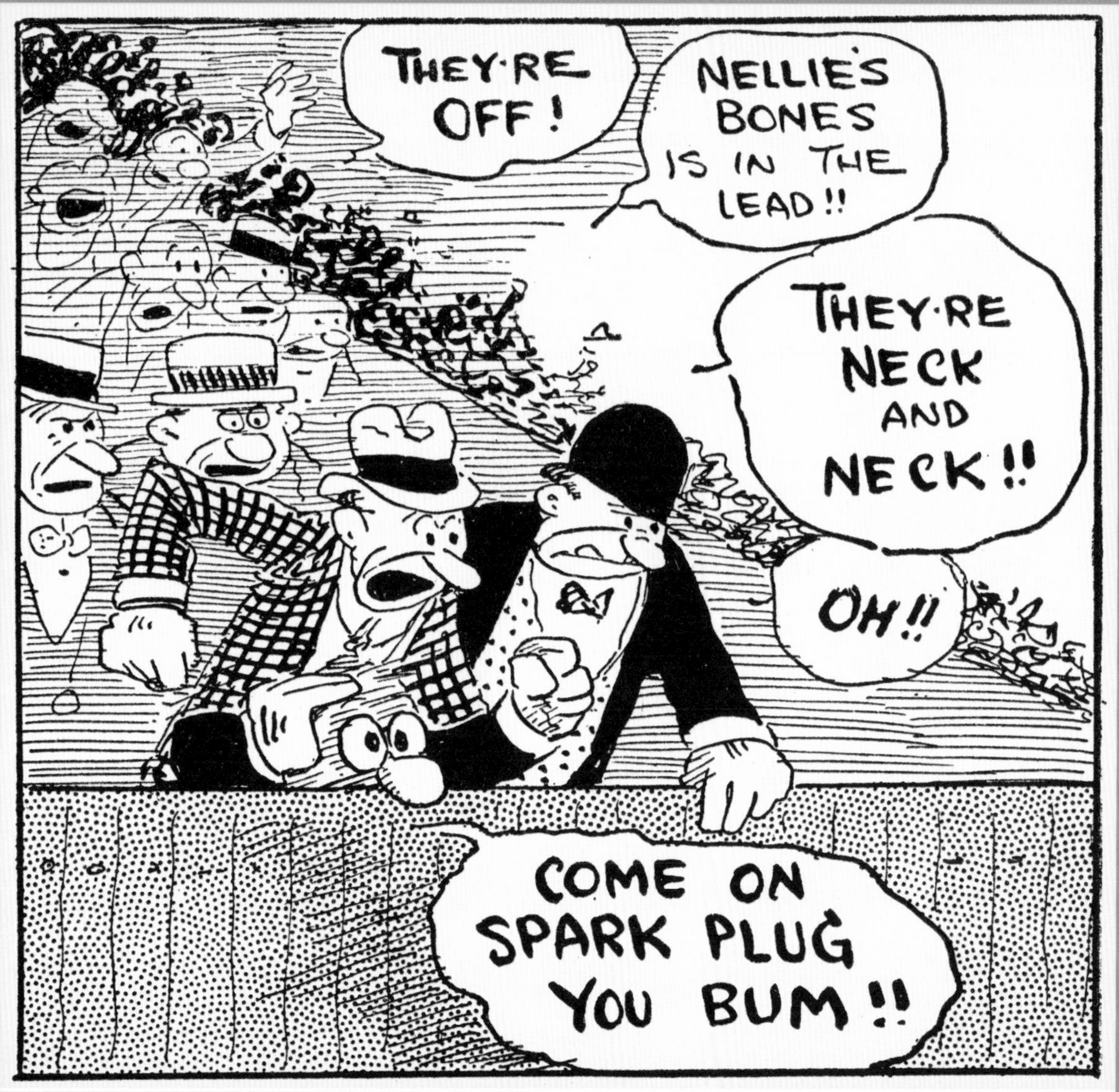
THEY'RE OFF!
NELLIE'S BONES IS IN THE LEAD!!
THEY'RE NECK AND NECK!!
OH!!
COME ON SPARK PLUG YOU BUM!!

DEDICATION

Clizia Gussoni
is a Sweet Mama, my Georgia Lee.

Clizia and this unpublished original artwork
are from the collection of the author.

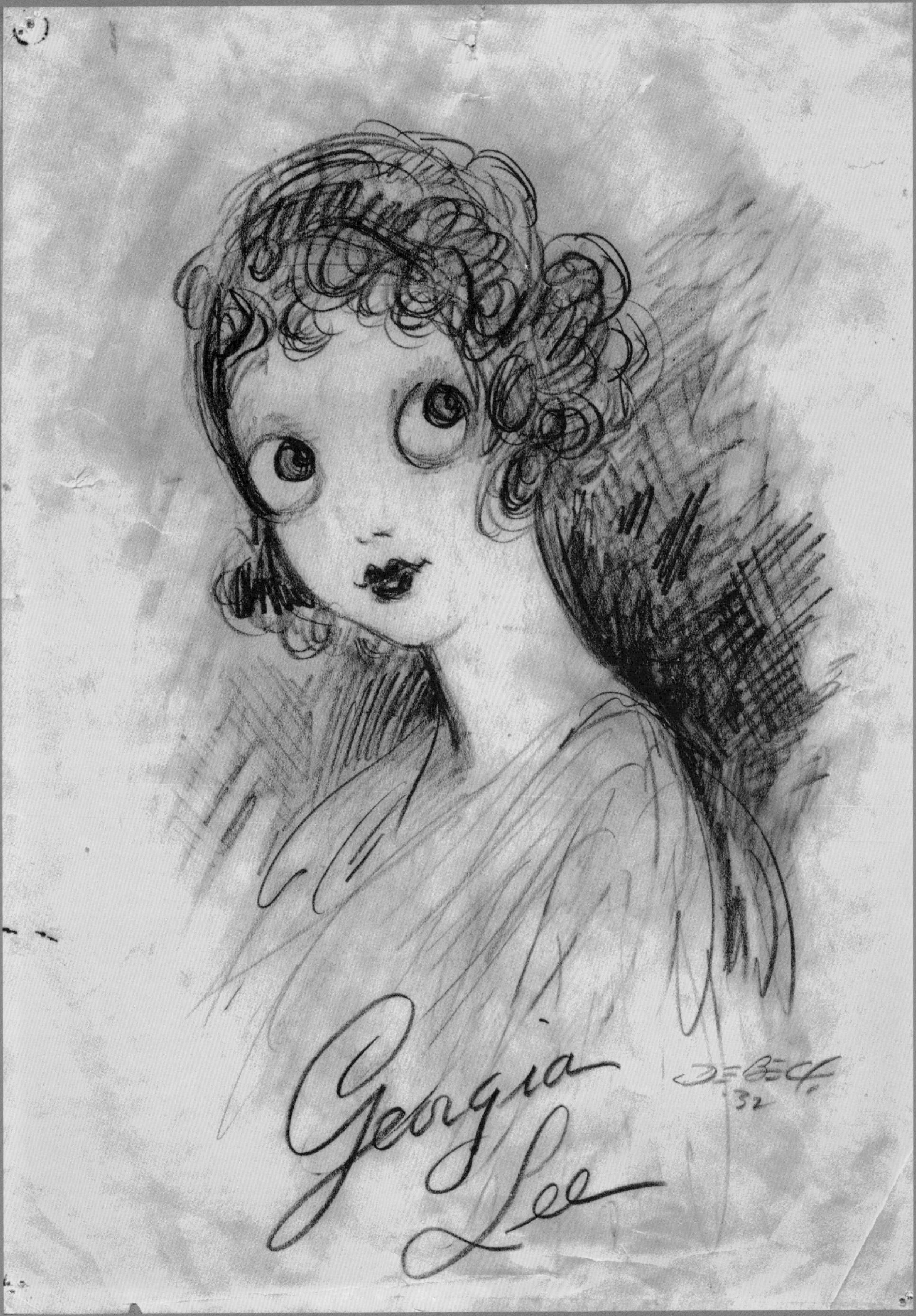
Georgia
Lee
DEBECK
'32

"If you like this book, order a few thousand of them and distribute them among your friends. If you want to make a great hit with the President of the United States, send him half a dozen copies. He can always use the pages for shaving paper and he may appoint you to a fine job."

—Billy DeBeck

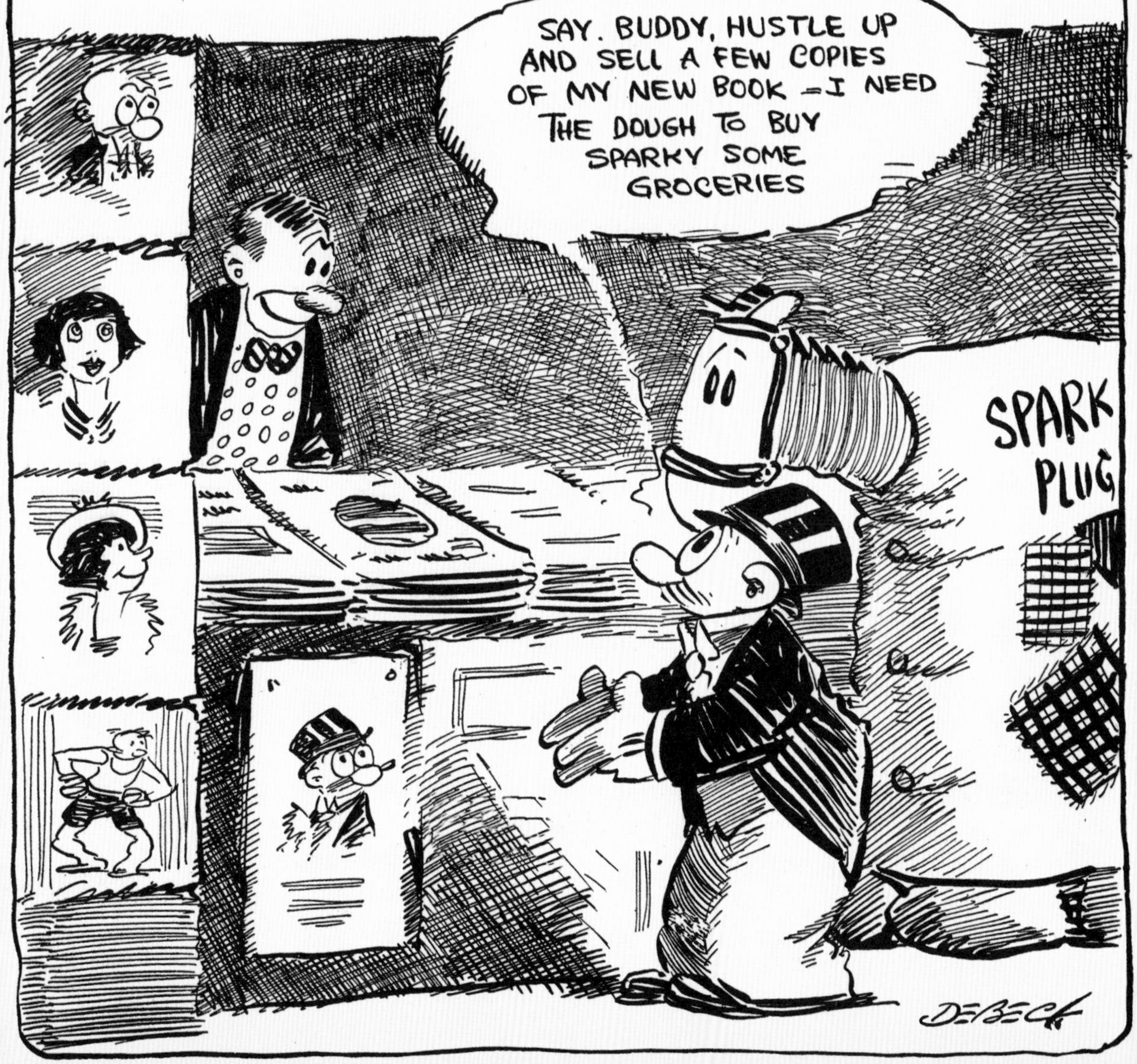
SAY. BUDDY, HUSTLE UP AND SELL A FEW COPIES OF MY NEW BOOK =I NEED THE DOUGH TO BUY SPARKY SOME GROCERIES
SPARK PLUG
DEBECK

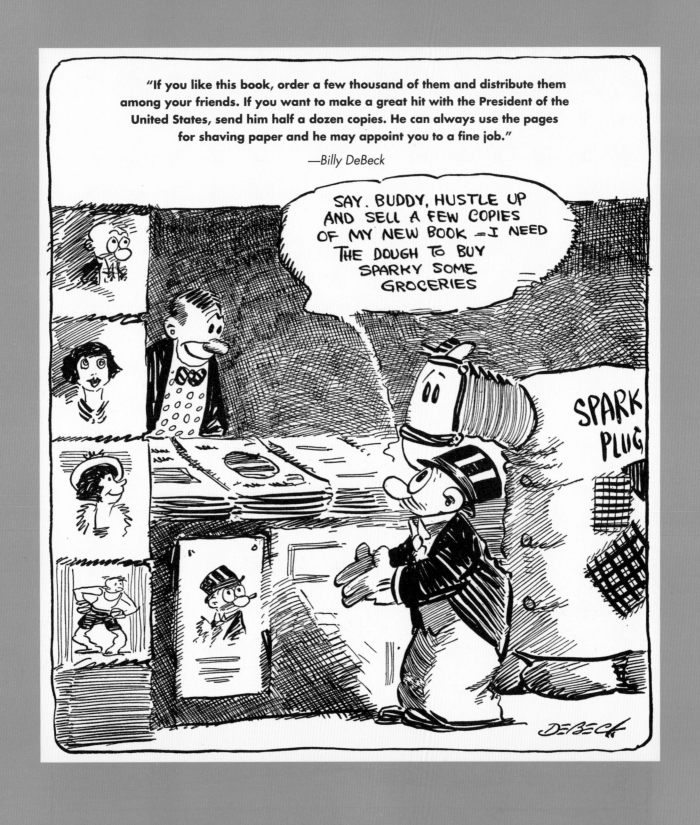

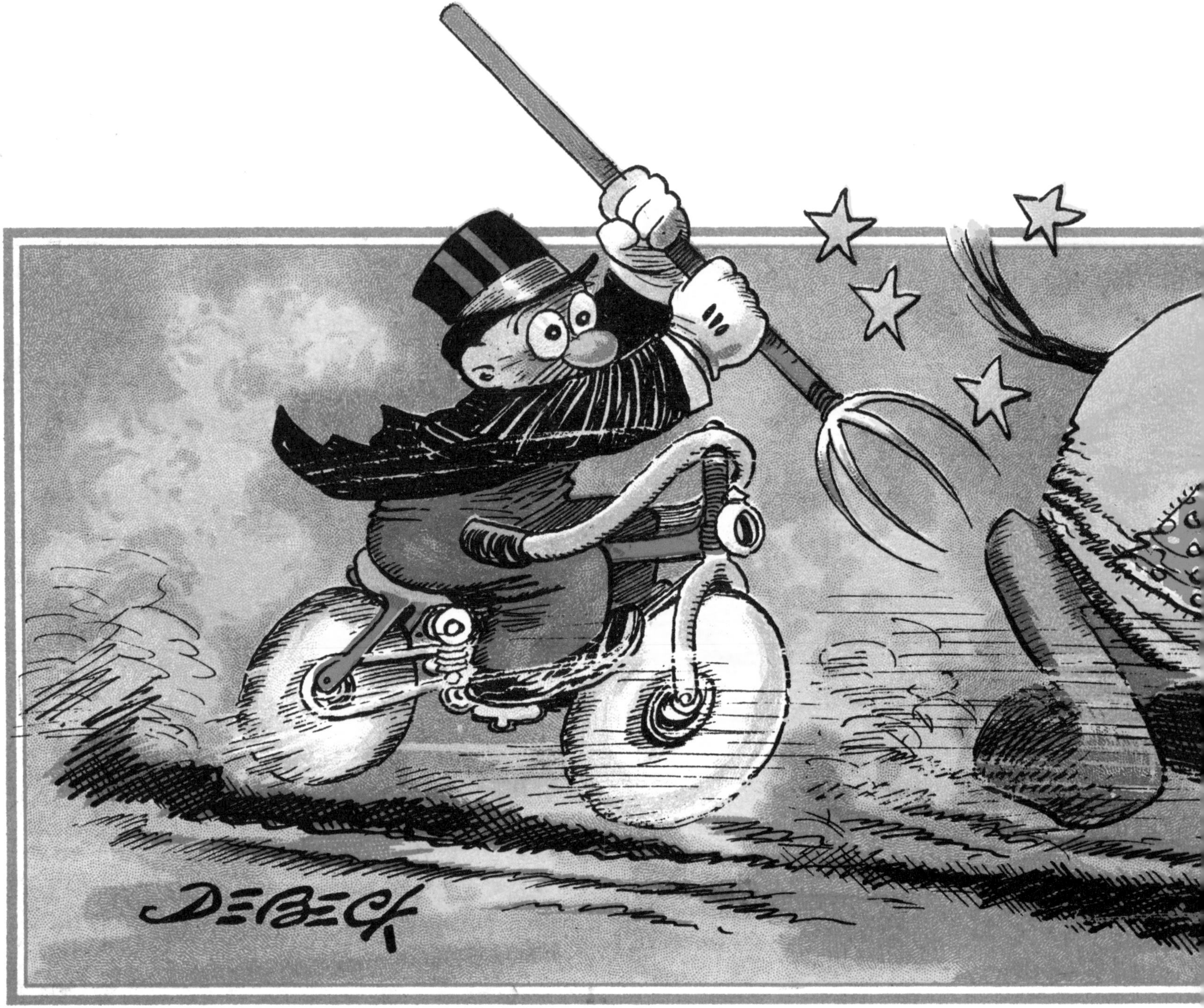
DEBECK

BARNEY GOOGLE

Edited & Designed by Craig Yoe • Produced by Clizia Gussoni • Foreword by Richard Thompson

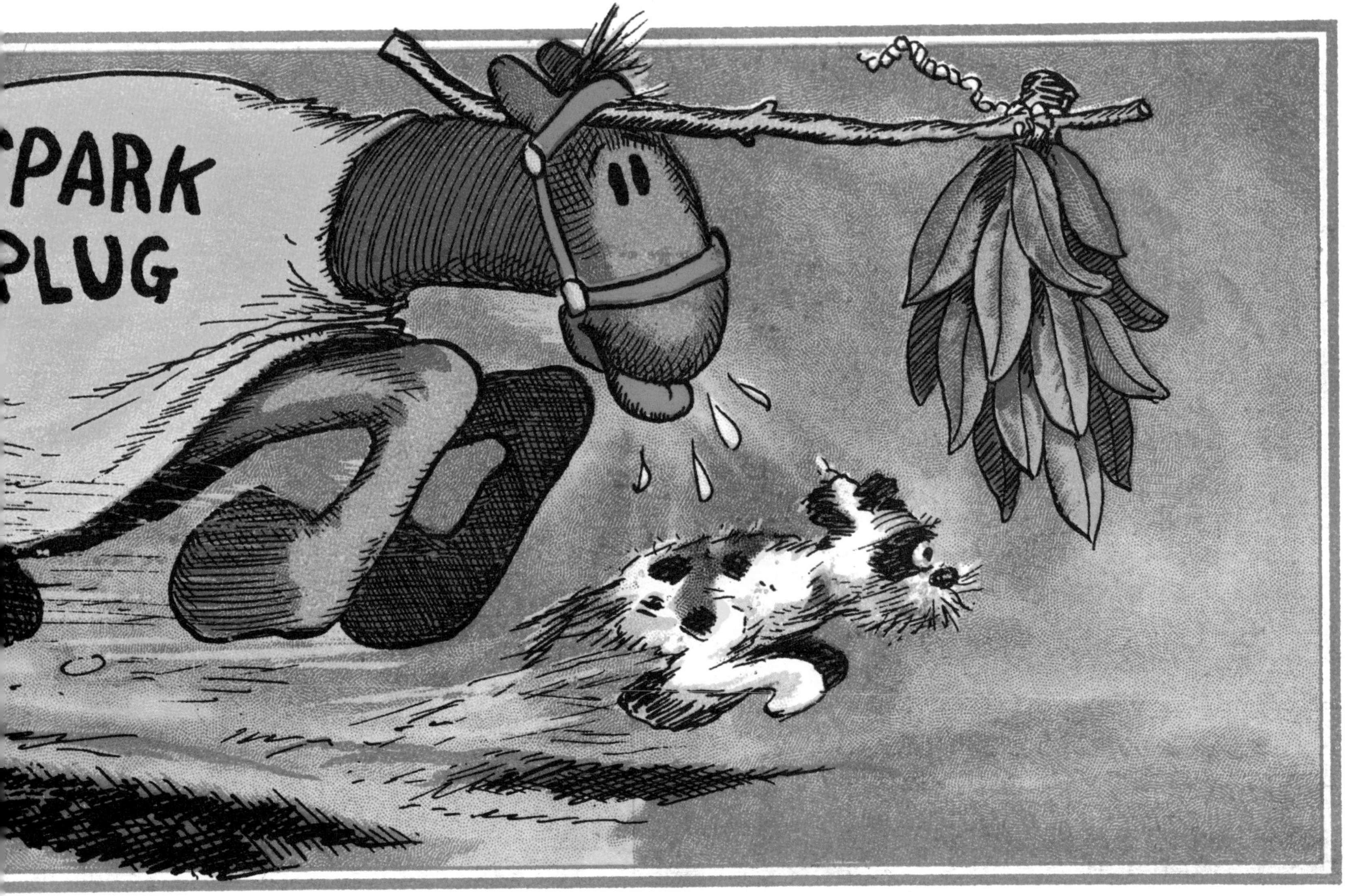
PARK
PLUG

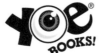

Yoe Books!
IDW PUBLISHING
San Diego, California

My deepest affection and gratitude to

David Scroggy,

my oldest friend and
a great patron of the arts.

Important Note: Cartoonists of the early 1900s often depicted races and ethnic groups in a way which we now recognize as demeaning and unacceptable. The strips herein are presented unaltered for historical purposes.

Above: A syroco-like sculpture done by YOE! Studio for Mike Richardson and David Scroggy (Dark Horse Comics). Front endpapers and pages 6 and 7: From the Barney Google and Spark Plug game, 1923. From the author's collection. Page 5: From *Barney Google and Spark Plug #4*, 1926. Page 23: From *Barney Google and Spark Plug #2*, 1924. Back endpapers: Courtesy of Heritage Auction Galleries.

ISBN: 978-1600106705
13 12 11 10 1 2 3 4

If you like this book, please blog, facebook, and tweet about it!
Visit the International Team of Comics Historians blog www.TheITCHblog.com.
Become a fan of YOE Books on Facebook, friend Craig Yoe on Facebook!

Future volumes of *Barney Google* are planned and we're soliciting rare strips, photographs, artwork, and ephemera.

The scope of this book is to present the daily comic strips which told the first Spark Plug story (and the strips that led up to it). Although stories in comic strips rarely came to an abrupt end, presented here is a natural stopping place.

A deep thanks to Richard Thompson for taking the time out of his busy schedule to create his delightful introduction.

This book was possible thanks to the generosity of collectors George Hagenauer and Merlin Haas, who provided three sets of strips to choose the best copies to be reproduced.

Much gratitude to the following "Sweet Mamas" without whom this book would not have been possible: Michael Barrier, Warren Bernard, Lee Binswanger, Brendan Burford, Steve Cottle, Ita Golzman, Cindy Jackson (James Branch Cabell Library, Virginia Commonwealth University), Bill Janocha, Cole Johnson, Mark Johnson, Chuck Johnston, Robert Kass, Terence Kean (Hake's Americana & Collectibles), Roger Langridge, Ulrich Merkl, Chris Thompson, Alex Winter (Hake's Americana & Collectibles), and Susan Allen Yonas.

Many thanks to the following individuals who were interviewed about DeBeck and generously provided invaluable information: Jerry Beck; R.C. Harvey; and the late Fred Lasswell, Billy DeBeck's assistant, who took over the reins.

For further information on Barney Google and Billy DeBeck, please refer to the enjoyable and exhaustive *Barney Google and Snuffy Smith: 75 Years of An American Legend* by Brian Walker with an introduction by Lucy Shelton Caswell (Comicana Books and Ohio State University Libraries).

YoeBooks.com
Operations: Craig Yoe & Clizia Gussoni, Chief Executive Officers and Creative Directors • Sandy Schechter, VP of Research • Design Associates: Nancy Bond, Mark Lerer • Media Associates: David Burd, Beth Davies, David Donihue, Tom Heintjes, J.J. Sedelmaier, Steven Thompson, Doug Wheeler

www.IDWPUBLISHING.com
Operations: Ted Adams, Chief Executive Officer • Greg Goldstein, Chief Operating Officer • Matthew Ruzicka, CPA, Chief Financial Officer • Alan Payne, VP of Sales • Lorelei Bunjes, Dir. of Digital Services • AnnaMaria White, Marketing & PR Manager • Marci Hubbard, Executive Assistant • Alonzo Simon, Shipping Manager • Angela Loggins, Staff Accountant • Cherrie Go, Assistant Web Designer • Editorial: Chris Ryall, Publisher/Editor-in-Chief • Scott Dunbier, Editor, Special Projects • Andy Schmidt, Senior Editor • Bob Schreck, Senior Editor • Justin Eisinger, Editor • Kris Oprisko, Editor/Foreign Lic. • Denton J. Tipton, Editor • Tom Waltz, Editor • Mariah Huehner, Associate Editor • Carlos Guzman, Editorial Assistant • Design: Robbie Robbins, EVP/Sr. Graphic Artist • Neil Uyetake, Art Director • Chris Mowry, Graphic Artist • Amauri Osorio, Graphic Artist • Gilberto Lazcano, Production Assistant • Shawn Lee, Production Assistant

July 2010. First printing. *Barney Google: Gambling, Horse Races, and High-Toned Women* is © 2010 Gussoni-Yoe Studio, Inc. All Rights Reserved, including the digital remastering of the material not held by copyright owners.
© 2010 King Features Syndicate and ™ Hearst Holdings, Inc.
Yoe Books™ is a trademark of Gussoni-Yoe Studio, Inc.

FOREWORD

Richard Thompson, *Cul de Sac's* Cartoonist, Sticks His Big Foot In His Mouth

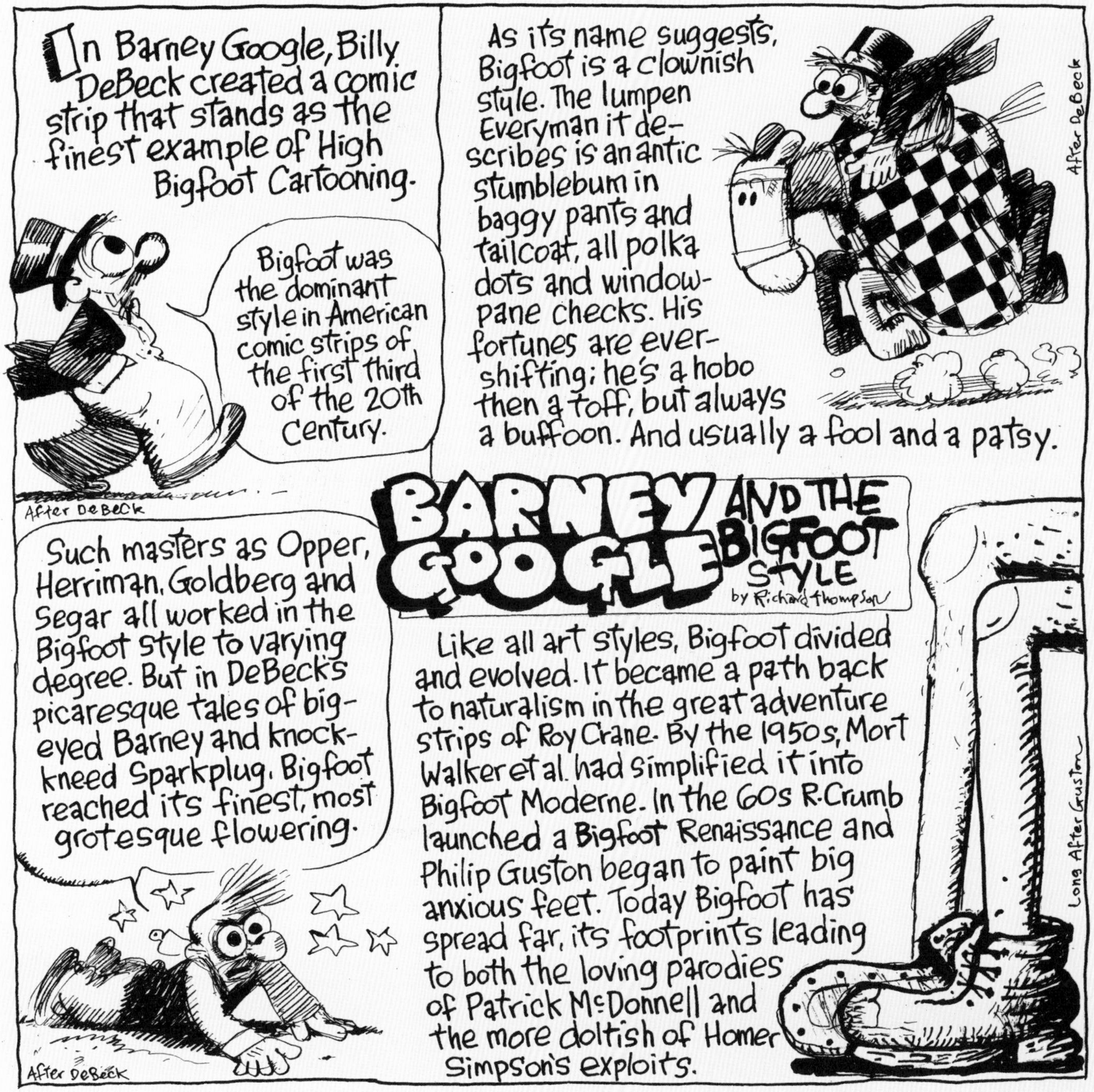
In Barney Google, Billy DeBeck created a comic strip that stands as the finest example of High Bigfoot Cartooning.
Bigfoot was the dominant style in American comic strips of the first third of the 20th century.
After DeBeck
As its name suggests, Bigfoot is a clownish style. The lumpen Everyman it describes is an antic stumblebum in baggy pants and tailcoat, all polka dots and windowpane checks. His fortunes are ever-shifting; he's a hobo then a toff, but always a buffoon. And usually a fool and a patsy.
After DeBeck
BARNEY GOOGLE AND THE BIGFOOT STYLE
by Richard Thompson
Such masters as Opper, Herriman, Goldberg and Segar all worked in the Bigfoot style to varying degree. But in DeBeck's picaresque tales of big-eyed Barney and knock-kneed Sparkplug, Bigfoot reached its finest, most grotesque flowering.
After DeBeck
Like all art styles, Bigfoot divided and evolved. It became a path back to naturalism in the great adventure strips of Roy Crane. By the 1950s, Mort Walker et al. had simplified it into Bigfoot Moderne. In the 60s R. Crumb launched a Bigfoot Renaissance and Philip Guston began to paint big anxious feet. Today Bigfoot has spread far, its footprints leading to both the loving parodies of Patrick McDonnell and the more doltish of Homer Simpson's exploits.
Long After Guston

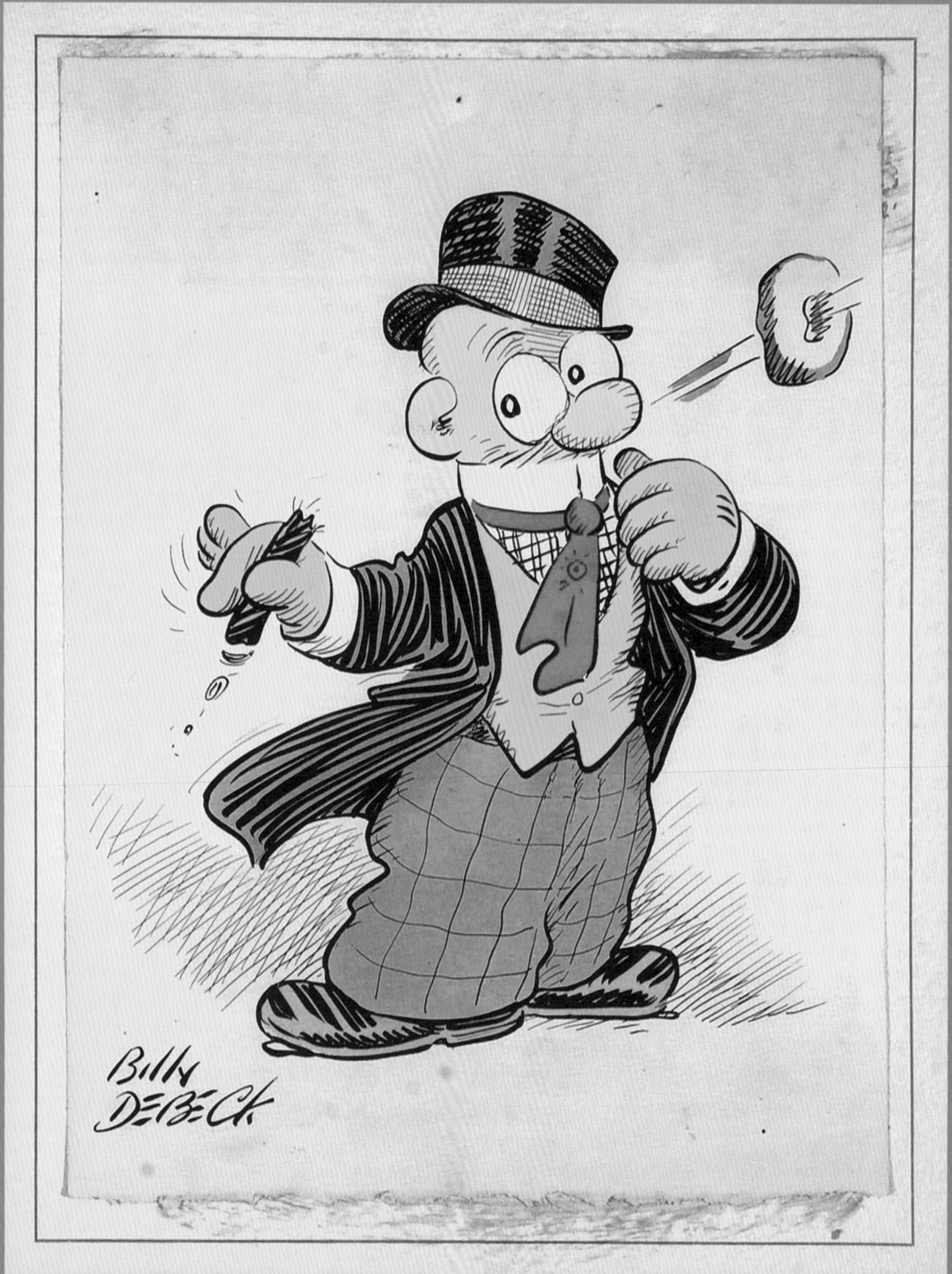
Billy
DeBeck

GOOGLE THIS!

Craig Yoe

The eyes have it—Barney Google Eyes. Google's creator Billy DeBeck (1890–1942) had an eye for great drawing. He was a master draftsmen, as amply demonstrated by the renderings of Mr. Barney Google, as well as his later hillbilly Snuffy Smith. DeBeck ranks with such greats as Frank Frazetta, Michelangelo Buonarroti, Heinrich Kley, Charles Dana Gibson, Reed Crandall, Edgar Degas, Lou Fine, David Ingres, and Milo Manara. Unlike those other masters, DeBeck drew funny. R. Crumb would be his closest equivalent, and the great Crumb himself has said DeBeck was an inspiration.

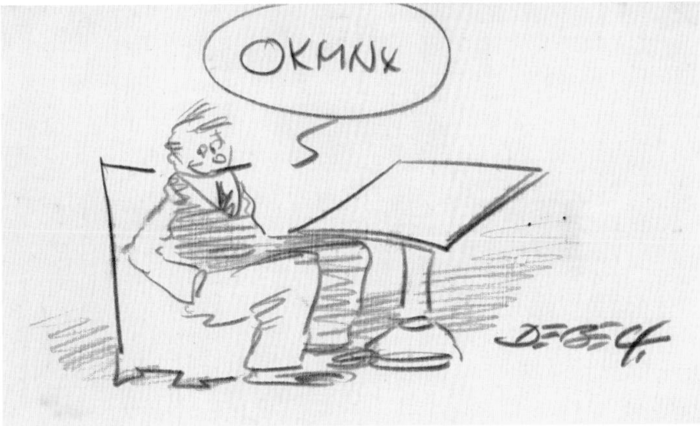
OKHNX

LEFT *A striking portrait of Mr. Barney Google. Courtesy of Hake's Americana & Collectibles.*

ABOVE *An unpublished DeBeck self-caricature. Translation, "OK, ham and eggs." From the collection of the author.*

Lucy Caswell, of the Billy Ireland Cartoon Library & Museum of the Ohio State University Libraries, has observed, "DeBeck's frenetic stories were well suited to the time of flappers and Prohibition."

Dr. John A. Lent, Ph.D. in Mass Communications, echoes, "The settings and language of *Barney Google* were those of city life—the race track, the nightclub, the sporting arena, and the street."

The title of DeBeck's strip started out long and ended up short, much like the character himself. Initially titled *Take Barney Google F'rinstance,* the strip first appeared in the *Chicago Herald and Examiner* sports page, on June 17, 1919. It featured a tall, lanky Barney. The title soon shrunk to just *Barney Google,* and the character contracted, too. He became a squat runt, maybe because he suffered the blows delivered by the very world he schemed to beat. Barney started as a Mutt and ended as a Jeff. Stephen Becker describes the Barney Google literary type as "the fool, the dupe, the pawn of society," in other words, everyman.

The new diminutive stature was certainly responsible for much of Barney's appeal, a weird kind of appeal. Barney was a rogue, sometimes a scoundrel, for sure a philanderer, and the ASPCA frowned upon horse kickers. But like lovable loser Homer Simpson or pilfering pirate Captain Jack Sparrow, we like and are rooting for Bad Boy Barney. DeBeck said of his creation, "I want to apologize for him. He isn't much to look at. He's a born lowbrow. He'd rather be with a stable-boy than with an emperor. And he's thoroughly irresponsible. But he isn't bad at heart. He's devoted to his wife. When the Sweet Woman gets on his nerves, he simply packs up and beats it. But he loves her just the same. And he always sees to it that, no matter how far away he is, she is well provided for. The further away he is, the more she gets."

We don't actually see a lot of Barney's matrimonial devotion to his henpecking "Sweet Woman." After substituting one nag (his wife) for another nag (his racehorse Spark Plug), Barney hooks up with his spouse only on rare occasions in the years that follow. Describing Barney's feelings for his pony, DeBeck shared, "Well, they change from time to time. When Spark Plug wins a race, Barney loves him like a brother. But when Sparky loses, Barney always figures out how much he could get for him at a glue factory."

The Barney Google fans were stuck like glue when a hot song about our little comic stripper was launched. Another

YASSUH, BOSS, YO' SHO' LOOK SWELL-BUT WOT ABOUT DIS CABLEGWAM YO' DIDN'T OPEN?
NOT NOW-NOT NOW- I MUST TODDLE ALONG-SO I LOOK SWELL, HUH- ??
SPARK PLUG
SNAP
OH, DEAR------ HERE COMES THAT MEAN OLD FLOORWALKER AGAIN---- YOU BETTER PRETEND YOU'RE BUYING SOMETHING, MR. GOOGLE--
?
?
?

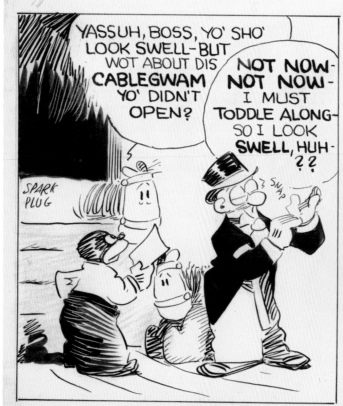

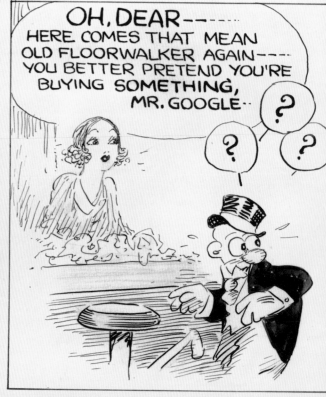

RIGHT *Barney Google, a Sweet Mama, and Spark Plug, all in one daily! October 23, 1931. From the collection of the author.*

creative christened Billy, this one Billy Rose, penned "Barney Google with the Goo-Goo-Googly Eyes." The song boomed and blared on every Jazz Age radio and record player, and the catchy tune was sung from every lip after its introduction in 1923. The hit status was no accident, but highly calculated by the Tin Pan Alley songwriter Rose. He wanted to write a smash and dug in the New York Public Library to study what was the common thread in number one songs.

Rose discovered that the "ooo" sound was the common denominator. Words like "moon" and "June" in tunes made folks croon and swoon. What better vehicle for Rose than Google with its long "oo"! Rose googled his tune. It became one of the biggest songs of all time. The tail wagged the dog—or horse, in this case—when the song made the strip with Barney Google and Spark Plug even more popular. The tune was recorded by many top musicians: from Billy Jones and Ernest Hare to Spike Jones. Here are some sample verses…

Barney Google with his goo-goo googly eyes
Barney Google had a wife three times his size
She sued Barney for divorce
Now he's living with his horse

AND THESE IS ALL HAND-STITCHED, YOU SAY?
BAH!!
ALMOST FOUR BUCKS !!✱!! SHOT !! **
DEBECK
OCT. 23
© 1931, King Features Syndicate, Inc., Great Britain rights reserved.

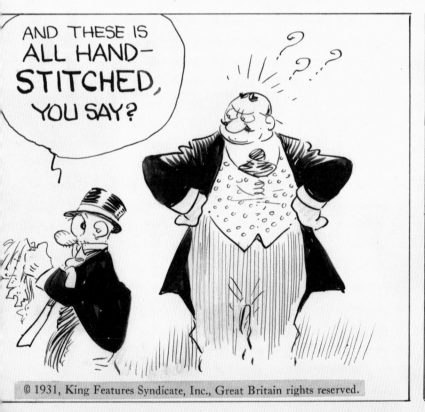

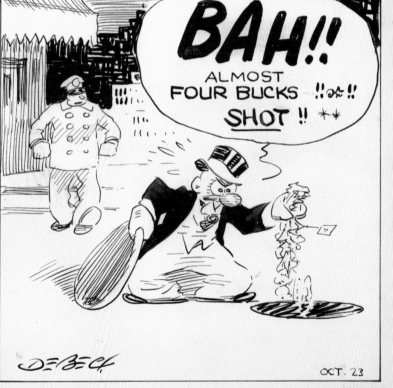

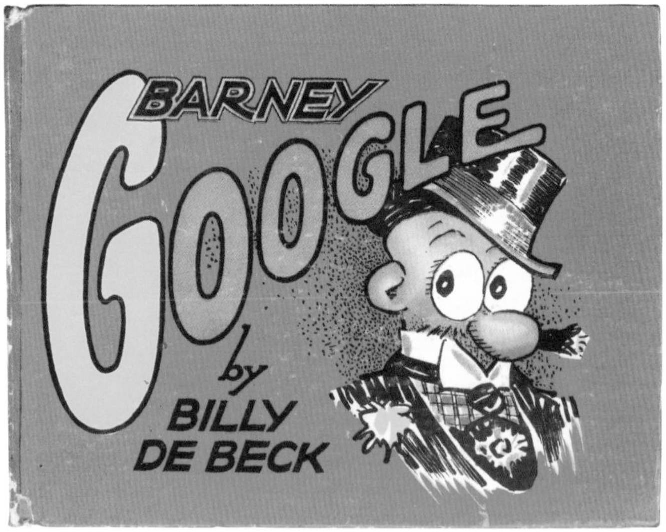
BARNEY
GOOGLE
by
BILLY
DE BECK

ABOVE *Cover to the Barney Google Little Big Book, Saalfield Publishing Company, 1935.*

Barney Google with his goo-goo googly eyes
Barney Google bet his horse would win the prize
He got odds of five to eight
Spark Plug came in three days late
Barney Google with his goo-goo googly eyes

Barney Google with his goo-goo googly eyes
Barney Google has a girl that loves the guys
Only friends can get a squeeze
The girl has no enemies
Barney Google with his goo-goo googly eyes

The music caught the public's fancy and the first Spark Plug story line reached top heights. Many more newspapers signed up to carry the feature, and comicker DeBeck found fame and fortune. A stable full of merchandise was produced and sold. *The Atlanta Constitution* reported, "The strip introduced the immortal Spark Plug, a squint-eyed racehorse, which in cash earnings outran Cavalcade, Gallant Fox, War Admiral, Seabiscuit, and many other turf stars." DeBeck responded, "Spark Plug, I am happy to say, has 'caught on.' All over the United States you find stuffed Spark Plugs, and Spark Plug games, and Spark Plug drums, and Spark Plug balloons, and Spark Plug tin pails. And there is a Spark Plug play on the road. The only thing that is lacking is a Spark Plug grand opera."

Not a grand opera, maybe, but DeBeck's work did make it into animation. First there was *Married Life,* which was part of a news reel realized by *The Seattle Sunday Times* in 1917. In an interview for this book, esteemed animation historian Jerry Beck explains, "Columbia Pictures made several deals to bring King Features comic strip characters to life on the movie screen in the 1930s and '40s. Their Charles Mintz studio had already been producing a popular series of *Krazy Kat* cartoons since the 1920s. In the 1930s, they released four Technicolor *Barney Google* cartoons. The first one, *Tetched In The Head,* brings Barney and Spark Plug to the Ozark Mountains, where they encounter Snuffy Smith and his wife Loweezy. They end up baby-sitting the couple's brood. The second film, *Patch Mah Britches,* has Barney bringing the entire Smith clan to the city for a banquet dinner and is padded with a series of tired 'eating gags.' The third film, *Spark Plug,* was a horse racing picture with Snuffy sleeping in the bleachers and Barney coaxing Spark Plug to the finish line. The final film was a parody of a *Major Bowes Amateur Hour,* the *American Idol* of its time. 'Major Google' gives the gong to Snuffy, Loweezy, and their clan. Snuffy gives a one-man performance of an 1890s melodrama and literally brings down the house."

Beck on DeBeck continues, "Though the animation was full and the drawings faithful to the strip, the cartoons themselves are bland affairs that did not create any demand for their con-

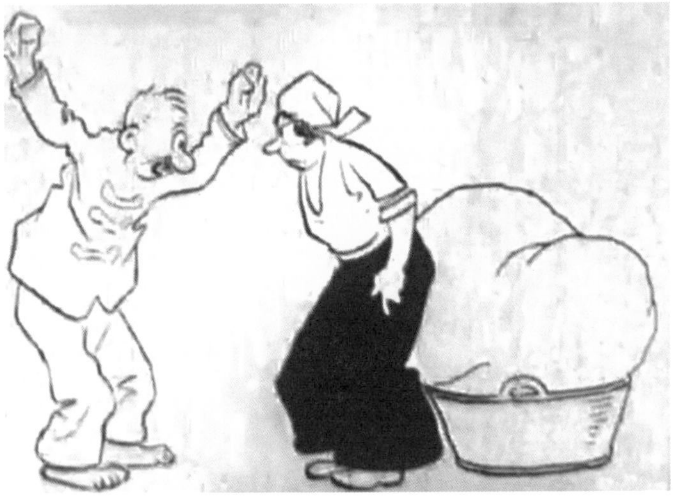

tinuation. These films have been out of circulation for decades, never shown on television, and existing only in edited silent home movie versions since their initial release. Recently, several prints have been located at the Library of Congress and in Columbia Pictures' vaults."

Later famed not for a yellow horse, but for a yellow submarine, producer Al Brodax was behind the 50 six-minute Barney Google and Snuffy Smith shorts of 1962 and 1963. Jerry Beck says, "These were generally a fun batch of TV cartoons, with several animated by 'cartoonist *extraordinaire*' Jim Tyer."

There were also *Barney Google* live action films. The first of a series starting in 1928 was *Horsefeathers,* starring Barney Hellum as Barney Google and Philip Davis as Spark Plug's jockey, Sunshine. It was said the makeup was so convincing that even DeBeck couldn't distinguish the real horse from his drawing. There were eleven or more films in the series, the last being *Slide, Sparky, Slide* in 1929.

Two DeBeck-derived feature films made it to the screen in 1942. Bud Duncan played Snuffy in *Private Snuffy Smith* and Cliff Nazarro joined him as Barney in *Hillbilly Blitzkrieg.*

The Barney Google song and the fame turned "goo-goo eyes" into a catchphrase. DeBeck's strip introduced or popularized many other phrases: "Horsefeathers," à la Milt

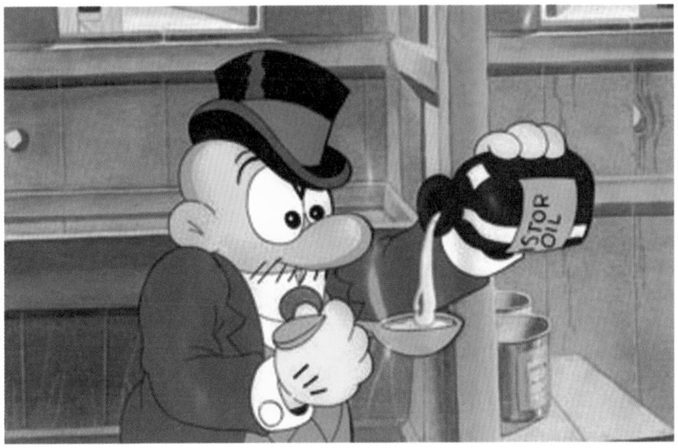
STOR
OIL

LEFT *Aleck and Pauline from* Married Life *exchange words in this 1917 silent short.*

ABOVE *A frame from* Tetched In The Head *(Columbia Pictures' Screen Gems, 1935). Courtesy of Jerry Beck, CartoonBrew.com*

Gross' "Banana Oil"; "hotsy totsy"; "jughaid"; "tetched in the haid"; "heebie jeebies"; "time's a-wasting"; "yardbird"; "shifless skonk"; "you're talkin' to a stranger"; "sweet mamas"; "yardbird"; "fotch me mah shootin' arn"; and—goodness gracious!—the great DeBeck introduced "balls o' fire"!

William Morgan DeBeck entered the race on April 16, 1890. Billy's father Louis was originally French (De Becque), while his mother Jessie Lee Morgan was Welsh/Irish. DeBeck got his classical art training at the Chicago Academy of Fine Arts, and beneath his humorous style, there was a strong ability to draw and compose. Fine Art's loss was The Funnies' gain in 1910, when the artist took a job drawing cartoons for *Show World,* a weekly theatrical publication.

Within months, DeBeck moved to the steel town of Youngstown, Ohio, where he drew political cartoons for the *Youngstown Telegram.* His weekly paycheck was the princely sum of $18. DeBeck moved one state over to Pennsylvania in 1912, where he became a staff cartoonist for the *Pittsburgh Gazette,* at over ten times the amount of his previous gig. Before taking another position, the artist tried freelancing for humor periodicals. In 1915, he even started his own cartooning correspondence course, with booklets titled *DeBeck Cartoon Hints* and *DeBeck Action Sketches.*

When freelancing didn't pan out, the cartoonist took the hint and returned to Chicago, where he developed the strip *Finn an' Haddie,* distributed by the Adams Syndicate. According to Brian Walker, author of the excellent *Barney Google and Snuffy Smith: 75 Years of An American Legend,* that strip never caught on and the artist landed a job with the *Chicago Herald* for $35 a week.

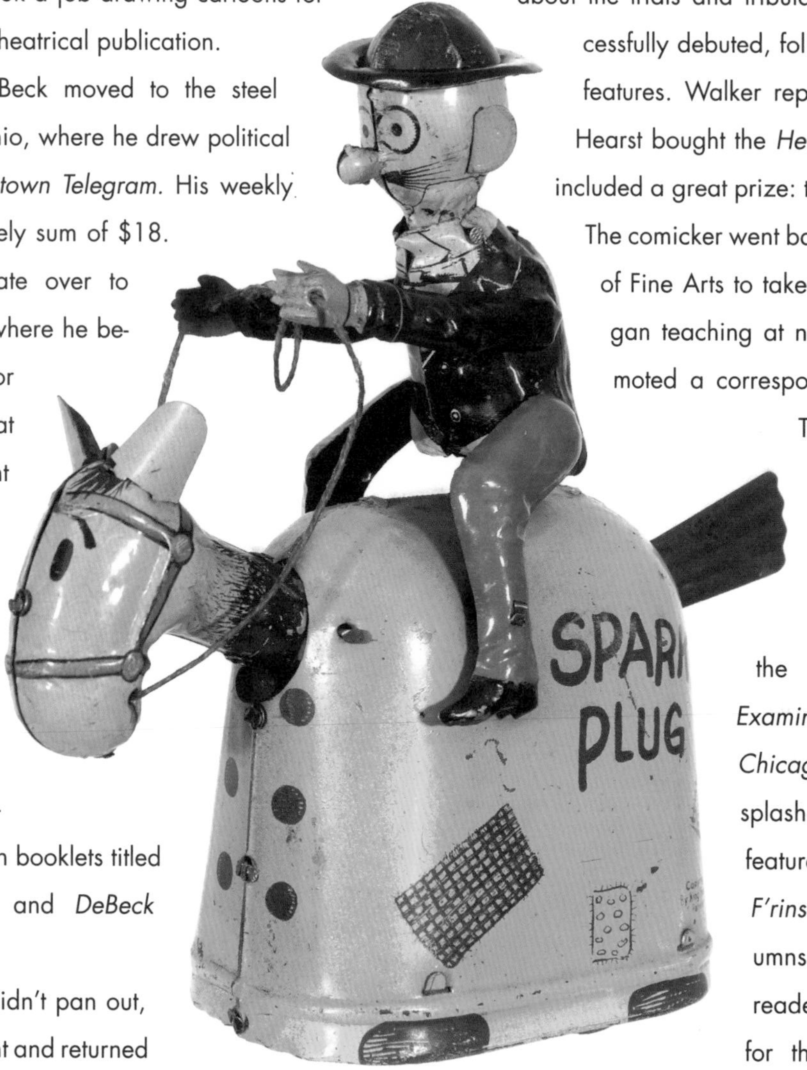
SPAR
PLUG

On December 9, 1915, DeBeck's *Married Life,* a strip about the trials and tribulations of wedded bliss, successfully debuted, followed by some single panel features. Walker reports that William Randolph Hearst bought the *Herald* in 1918. The purchase included a great prize: the comic artistry of DeBeck. The comicker went back to the Chicago Academy of Fine Arts to take some classes, but soon began teaching at night and the Academy promoted a correspondence course by DeBeck. The institution touted his tutelage to eager potential students in the pages of *Cartoons Magazine.*

When Hearst merged the *Herald* with his *Chicago Examiner,* the newly renamed *Chicago Herald and Examiner* splashed DeBeck's new comic feature *Take Barney Google F'rinstance* across all eight columns of the sports section. Male readers were the target audience for the antics of this pro-fight-following, pony-betting, poker-playing, henpecked carousing man. Before his shrinking act, Barney looked just like Aleck, the husband in the *Married Life* strip. DeBeck got bigger in status as the public took Barney Google to their hearts. Eventually, the artist moved to New York City, the reigning Capital of Cartoondom, where he resided in a plush Riverside Drive apartment.

In New York, DeBeck partied hard as he and his pals didn't believe in Prohibition, and the cartoonist had trouble keeping up with deadlines. The story goes that his frustrated editor locked DeBeck up without his pants in a hotel room, so he couldn't escape until he caught up with his work.

The artist's first wife, the "pretty and vivacious" Marian Shields, was less than successful in tempering his lifestyle. Billy married Marian for the first time in 1914, divorced her, and married her again in 1921. DeBeck's second wife, the former Mary Louise Dunne, was described as "a pretty, pert Irish girl with blue eyes and a doll-like figure." Mary brought him into a more low-key approach to living and encouraged him to socialize with less indulgent company. They were married from 1927 until his death from cancer in 1942.

The book and comic magazine publishing history of DeBeck's Barney Google started in 1922, the same year Spark Plug was introduced. Then, the inaugural Spark Plug episode was reprinted in *Comic Monthly,* "the first monthly newsstand comic publication," which was produced by Embee Distributing Company of New York. This series featured the likes of *Tillie the Toiler, Polly and Her Pals,* and *Little Jimmy.*

The tenth issue of *Comic Monthly* (October 1922), which was a Rube Goldberg *Foolish Questions* issue, announced, "They're Off! Readers of *Comic Monthly* may look forward to the funniest series of comic pictures ever published. The next issue of *Comic Monthly* will show that rollicking character Barney Google and his funny horse, Spark Plug, in a 24 act comedy entitled *The Abadaba Handicap.* You will see Spark Plug put through intensive training at great sacrifice to Barney

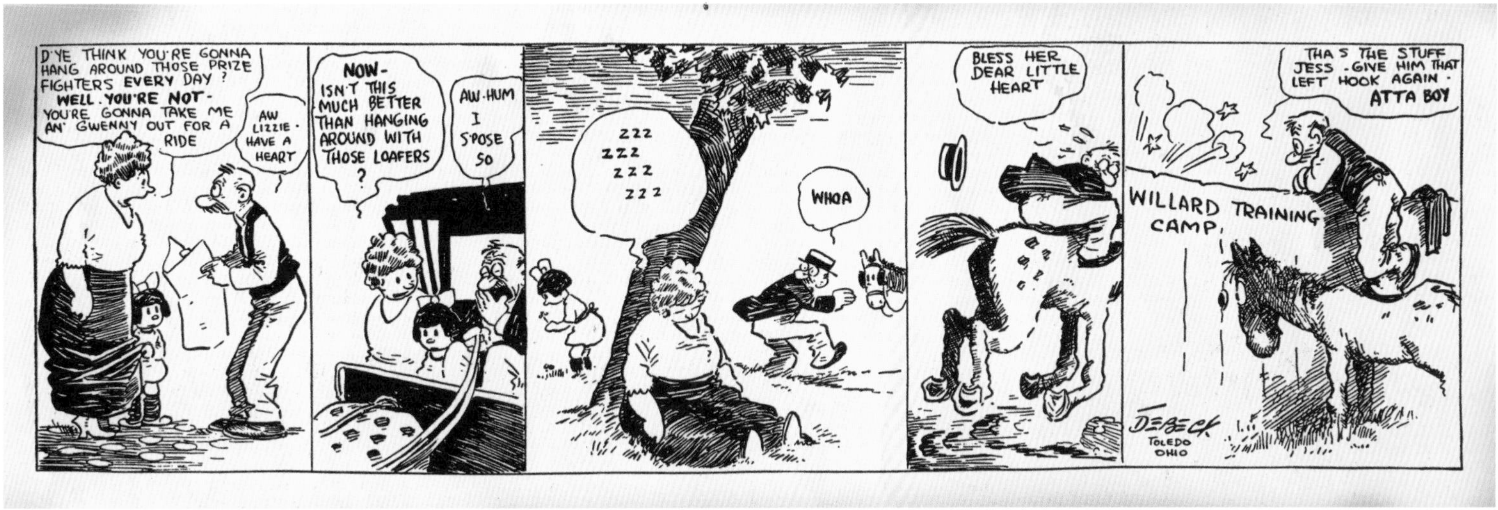
D'YE THINK YOU'RE GONNA HANG AROUND THOSE PRIZE FIGHTERS EVERY DAY? WELL. YOU'RE NOT- YOU'RE GONNA TAKE ME AN' GWENNY OUT FOR A RIDE
AW LIZZIE - HAVE A HEART
NOW- ISN'T THIS MUCH BETTER THAN HANGING AROUND WITH THOSE LOAFERS ?
AW-HUM I S'POSE SO
ZZZ ZZZ ZZZ ZZZ
WHOA
BLESS HER DEAR LITTLE HEART
THA'S THE STUFF JESS - GIVE HIM THAT LEFT HOOK AGAIN - ATTA BOY
WILLARD TRAINING CAMP.
DEBECK
TOLEDO OHIO

LEFT *Rare windup tin toy from Germany, dated 1923–1924, King Features Syndicate, U.S. patent #302947. Courtesy of Hake's Americana & Collectibles.*

BELOW *The first* Barney Google *strip from the* Chicago Herald and Examiner, *June 17, 1919. Note how tall Barney is. Underneath DeBeck's signature is "Toledo, Ohio." DeBeck was sent there to cover the training and the famous boxing match between Jess Willard and Jack Dempsey, fought on July 4, 1919.*

Disney + DeBeck

There's no hard evidence that Disney and DeBeck ever met, but they ran in the same circles.

Walt Disney (1901–1966) was a freshman at McKinley High School, Chicago, in 1917, his last year of formal education. At McKinley, Disney became the "junior art editor" and drew cartoons for his school's newspaper, *The Voice*. At that time, he was interested in a newspaper cartoonist career. One of Disney's anti-Kaiser cartoons even gives "apologies to Orr." Carey Orr (1890–1967) had been a student at the Chicago Academy of Fine Art. He used the money he had earned from being a baseball player to pay for his classes. After a job at small papers, Orr was hired at the *Chicago Tribune,* where his cartoons were showcased regularly on the front page. Orr would soon be awarded a gold medal from the U.S. Government for his stirring World War I cartoons. Disney, at age 16, forged his parents' signatures on documents to become a Red Cross ambulance driver in France in World War I.

Carl N. Werntz (1874–1944), a cartoonist at the *Chicago Record,* world traveler, painter, and photographer, had studied under Alphonse Mucha. In 1902, Werntz founded the Chicago Academy of Fine Arts, located at 81 East Madison Street. In addition to Fine Art the school had a heavy emphasis on applied arts, including cartooning taught by Werntz himself and fellow artists from the *Record*.

Billy DeBeck had attended the Academy after high school. Fresh back in Chicago from Pittsburgh, the artist returned to his alma mater as a student, in 1915, as reported in a *Cartoonist Magazine* article. According to Brian Walker, DeBeck was no longer a student by 1917. He taught evening classes at the Academy thanks to the success of his strip *Married Life* and his other cartooning. The school touted the now "celebrity" cartoonist in its ads (see page 39), promoting both their sessions and DeBeck's correspondence course in *Cartoons Magazine*. In the ads, the name of the institution was even called The Cartoon School of The Chicago Academy of Fine Arts or, alternatively, the Academarts Cartoon School. At this time, just before leaving for France to drive his cartoon-festooned ambulance, Disney enrolled in night classes at the Academy.

According to one Disney biographer, "to pay for his classes, Walt worked several additional hours a week in his father's jelly factory and took part-time jobs at the post office and as a station clerk on the Chicago El." While attending his hard-earned instruction at the Academy, Walter Disney, the future man behind the Mouse, most likely studied with William DeBeck, the soon to be creator of Barney Google. Maybe Billy even showed Walt the *Married Life* animation that *The Seattle Sunday Times* produced for its newsreel in 1917.

Pie-shaped eyes met goo-goo-googly eyes, hmm?

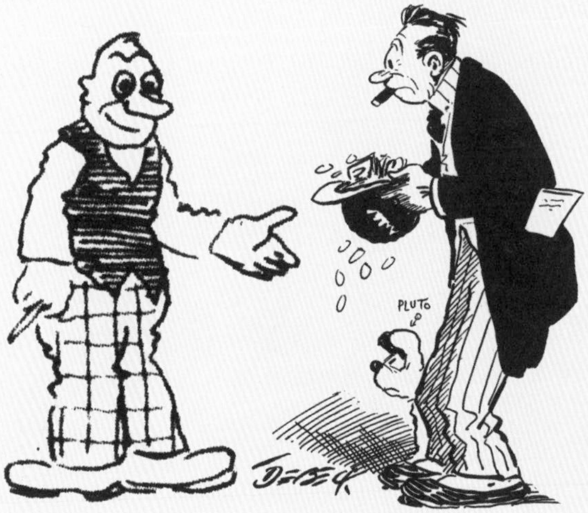
PLUTO

RIGHT *Walt draws an artist (note pencil) for his high school newspaper. Was it a self-portrait? 1917.*

FAR RIGHT *Definitely a self-portrait! DeBeck leaving Chicago for Florida—he's not going to Disney World! Coincidentally, Billy DeBeck's dog is named Pluto!*

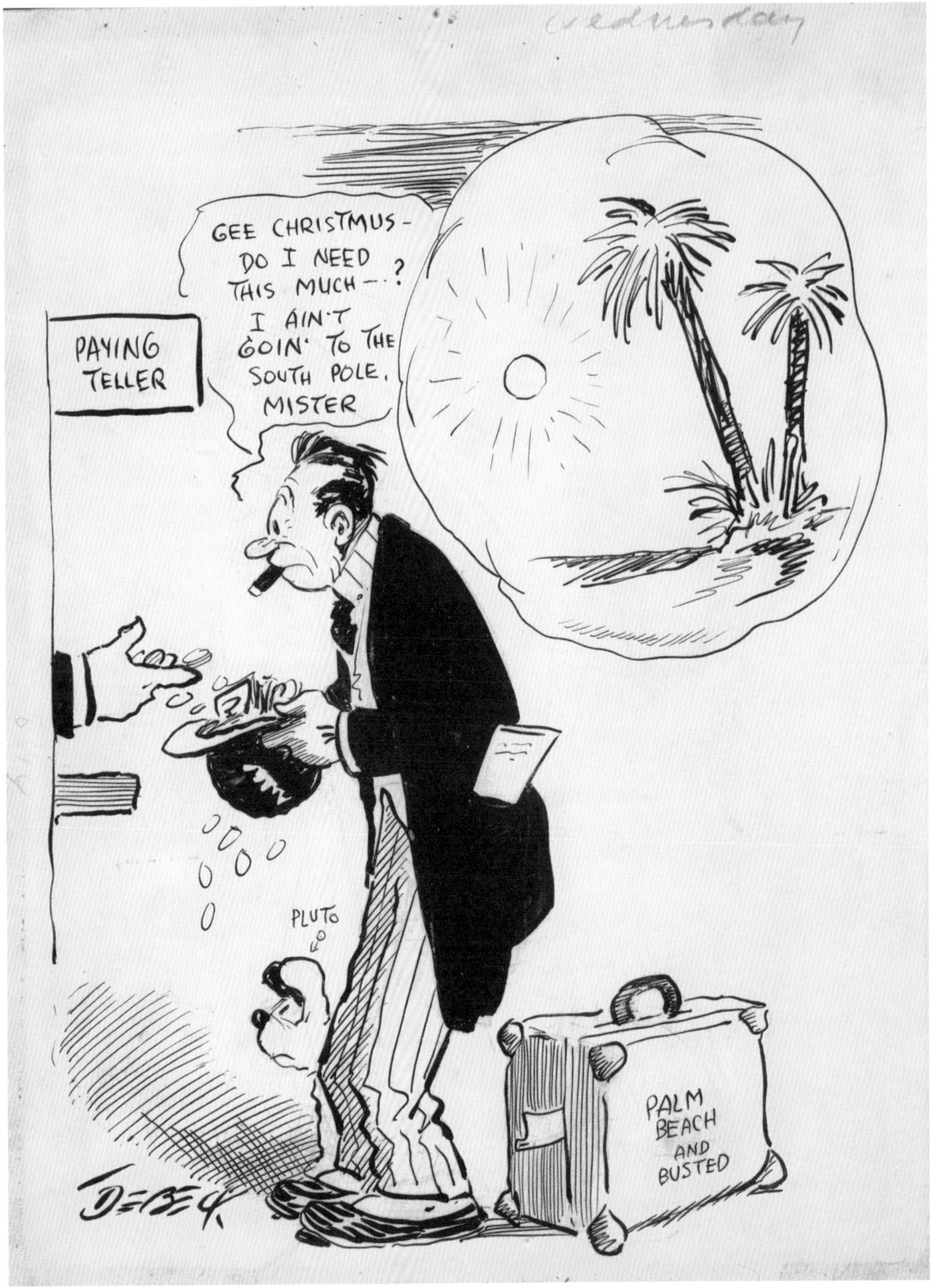
Wednesday
GEE CHRISTMUS-
DO I NEED
THIS MUCH--?
I AIN'T
GOIN' TO THE
SOUTH POLE.
MISTER
PAYING
TELLER
PLUTO
PALM
BEACH
AND
BUSTED
DEBECK

RIGHT *DeBeck gets advance money from the company teller to go to Palm Beach, Florida, for a vacation.* Chicago Herald and Examiner, *July 28, 1919. Printed from the original art from the author's collection. Thanks to Sandy Schechter.*

Google's pocket book. Does the noble steed make good and win a fortune for Barney Google?"

The back cover added a prediction, a warning, and an admonition: "The Spark Plug series will break all records for *Comic Monthly* sales and readers who fail to order in advance from their dealer will be disappointed. Tell your dealer NOW to get you a copy of the Spark Plug series of Barney Google."

The comic sported an original cover by DeBeck, but Spark Plug's first story in a "24 act comedy" meant they only reprinted 24 comic strips with some holes even in that small portion. The shading patterns on things like suit coats are inexplicably dropped.

BELOW *Billy DeBeck's personal Christmas card. The artwork from this card was engraved on the cigarette case that was the National Cartoonists Society's Billy DeBeck Award. From the collection of the author.*

Cupples and Leon Company Publishers of New York followed with four annual comic books, from 1923 to 1926. These also had wonderful DeBeck covers, featuring Spark Plug, but had many omissions within the stories.

Dell published a couple of regular-format comic books with Barney in the 1940s *Four Color* series, and Saalfield issued a Little Big Book in 1935. There were post-DeBeck stories featuring his characters published by Toby, Gold Key, and Charlton. They all featured comics by Fred Lasswell, DeBeck's talented assistant who had taken over the reins after the artist passed.

Presented in *Barney Google: Gambling, Horse Races, and High Toned Women* is Barney's first great adventure of many with his horse Spark Plug. The Spark Plug sequences show Barney at his best, i.e., his worst. He's an opportunist,

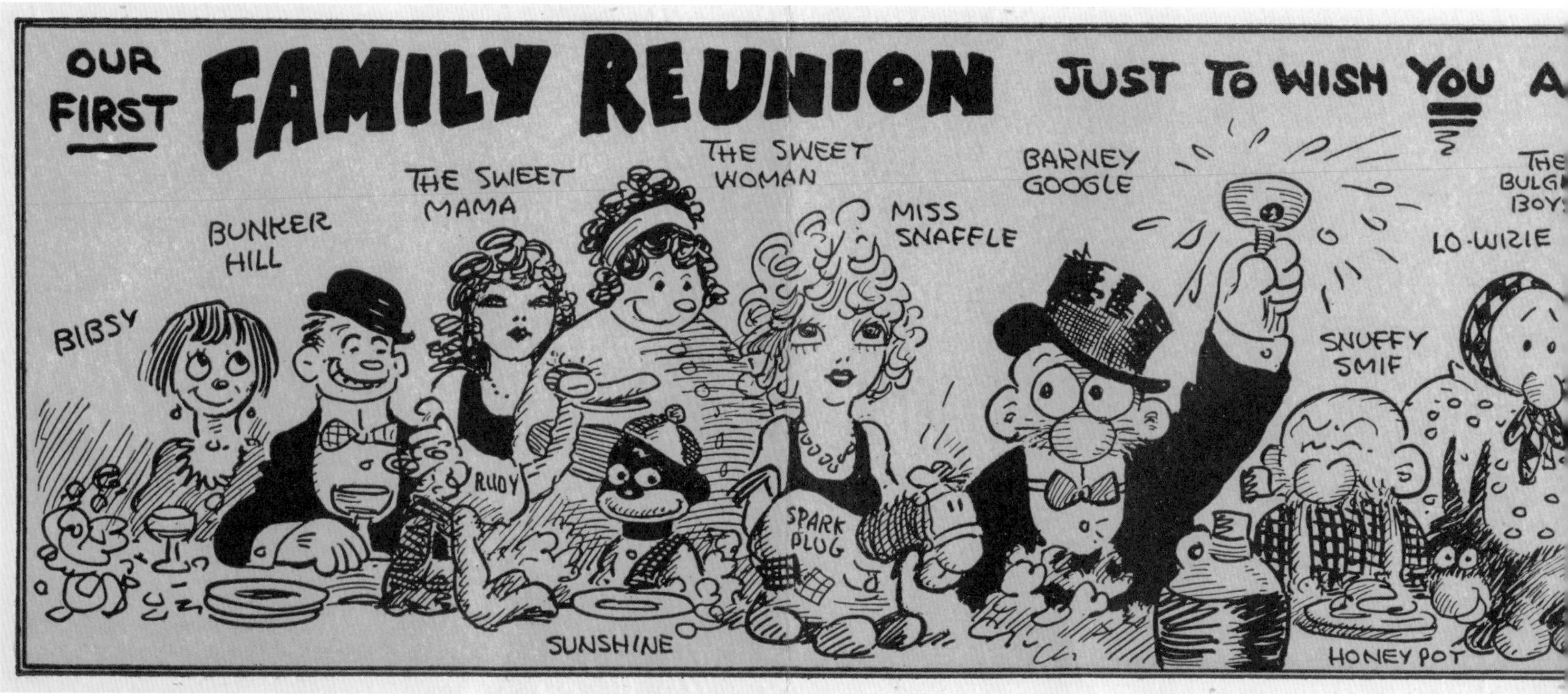
OUR FIRST
FAMILY REUNION
JUST TO WISH YOU A
THE SWEET WOMAN
THE SWEET MAMA
BUNKER HILL
MISS SNAFFLE
BARNEY GOOGLE
BIBSY
RUDY
SPARK PLUG
SNUFFY SMIF
LO-WIZIE
SUNSHINE
HONEY POT

a womanizing, blooey-eyed half-pint, and a friend of the fair weather variety to both man and beast. But the Lilliputian is still lovable to every last little cigar-chomping inch.

Barney Google: Gambling, Horse Races, & High Toned Women also presents the delightfully funny gag-a-day strips, which preceded Spark Plug's debut. As you read Barney Google's adventures, you'll cheer at the deftly composed and shaded pen-and-ink drawings with their big foot humor. There's plenty of booting of butts, bonking of head bones, and some sizzling sweet mama flappers.

DeBeck's captivating damsels—he was a fan of Charles Dana Gibson's girls—were coquettish and sexy, but they also had a cartoony flair. In his correspondence course, DeBeck wrote, "All women want to be pretty. No matter how homely a woman is, she always strives to make the best of it and will appear at her best. Therefore, it is obvious, that the artist, if he desires to please, will never take liberties, but will strive to make his women characters as they would have him make them—not as they seem to be."

Don't be seduced and distracted by DeBeck's pretty girls, because the hallmarks of the strip are action and humor. The artist pushed the idea of movement in his cartooning correspondence course: "When you draw the figure of a man, make him do something. Think carefully what you want to portray and plan out in your mind what the natural position of your figure would be while doing a certain thing and then exaggerate that action. The real humor comes in drawing a figure in action."

DeBeck's comic was held in the highest regard by his fellow cartoonists. When the artist passed, his widow established the Billy DeBeck Award for the National Cartoonists Society. As comics historian, critic, and cartoonist R.C. Harvey tells in an interview for this book, "On the evening of May 11, 1947, at the monthly dinner meeting of the National Cartoonists Society at the Society of Illustrators Clubhouse, *Terry and the Pirates* and *Steve Canyon's* Milton Caniff became the first cartoonist to be formally honored by the group as the Outstanding Cartoonist of the Year.

"The trophy was a handsome silver cigarette box, its lid engraved with pictures of Barney Google and Snuffy Smith. DeBeck's widow, Mary, had the idea of instituting an annual citation. She would furnish the prize, she said, if it could be awarded in the name of her late husband. Known officially as the Billy DeBeck Memorial Award, it was also briefly called the 'Barney'—in imitation of the film industry's

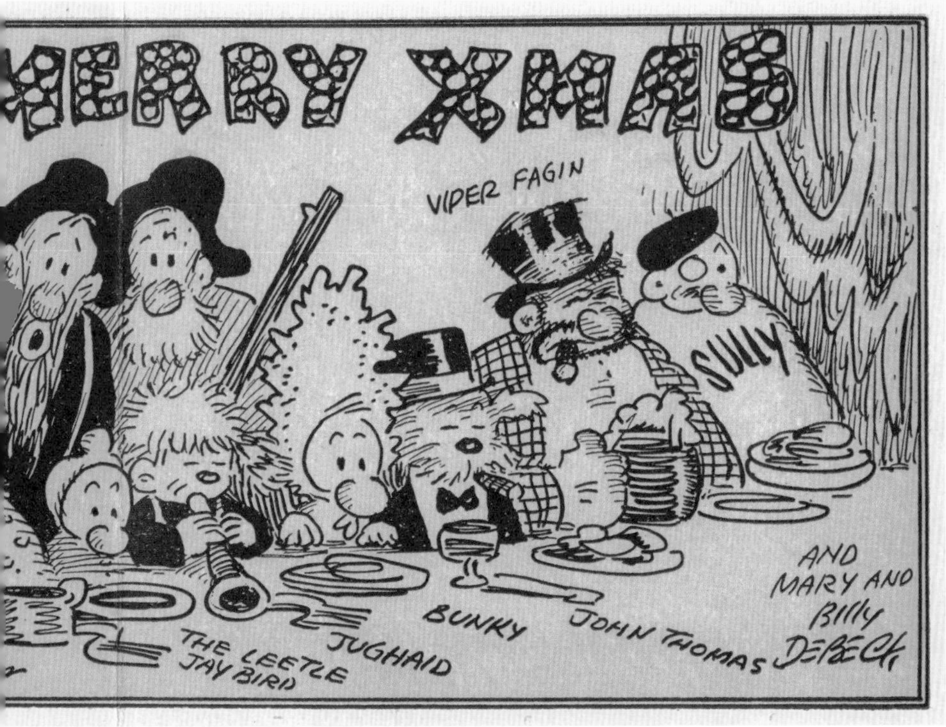

ERRY XMAS
VIPER FAGIN
SULLY
AND MARY AND Billy DEBECK
BUNKY
JOHN THOMAS
JUGHAID
THE LEETLE JAY BIRD

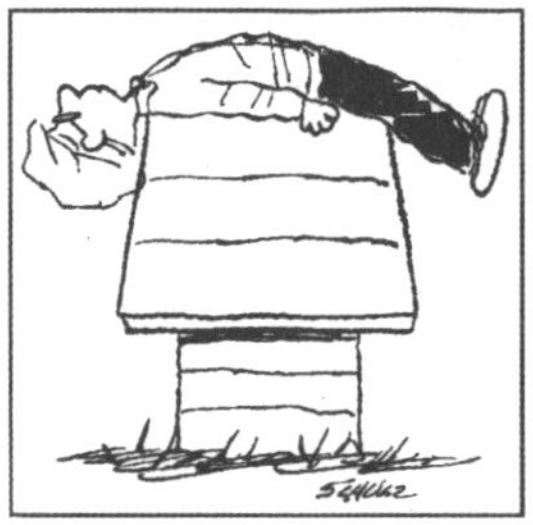

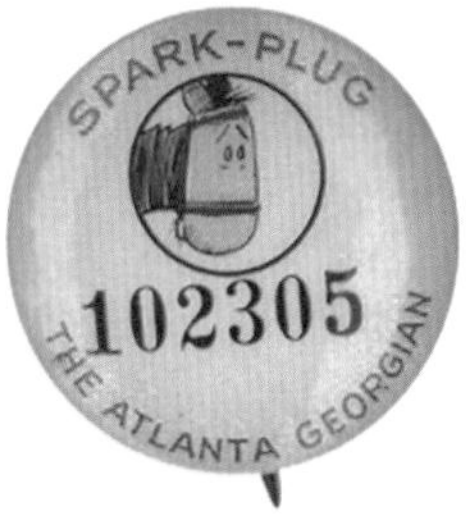
SPARK-PLUG
102305
THE ATLANTA GEORGIAN

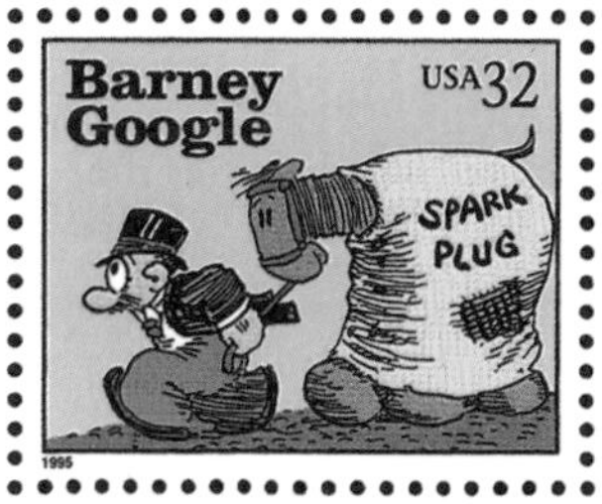
Barney Google
USA32
SPARK PLUG
1995

practice of referring to its most prestigious prize by an informal first name."

Harvey continues, "As long as DeBeck's widow lived, the selection of the 'cartoonist of the year' was made by a committee of one. 'Mrs. DeBeck arbitrarily decided who would win,' Caniff told me years later. 'I've never talked with anybody who was ever consulted about it. I'm not absolutely certain, of course; she may have consulted people, but no one I talked with knew of it if she did. She never consulted me—naturally, she didn't consult me on the first one. And never after that. She just made the choice and presented the Award, and that was that.'"

Harvey concludes, "In 1953, after the death of DeBeck's widow, the Barney was retired and replaced by the Reuben. It was named in honor of NCS's first president, Rube Goldberg."

DeBeck d'man was "one of the most likable, personable and talented cartoonists in the game," said comicker Chuck Thorndike, who interviewed him in 1935. Thorndike learned that DeBeck was "a complete golf nut and alternates between his summer homes in Great Neck, Long Island, to the one in Tampa, Florida." DeBeck's golf companions included Babe Ruth and Dizzy Dean.

Thorndike proclaimed, "*Barney Google* is easily among the top five of the best-known strips in the world, and to this writer, with the possible exception of Chic Young's *Blondie,* it is the funniest of all. Billy's sense of timing, his characters, expressions, and vernacular are, to me at least, tops in comedy in the strip field."

DeBeck himself said, "I hope you like Barney and his horse. You will find that Barney, with all his faults and weaknesses, is human, like the rest of us. And you've simply got to like Spark Plug." You certainly are going to be google-eyed at the wonderfulness that Billy DeBeck fills his panels with. But, why take Chuck Thorndike's, my, or even Mr. Billy DeBeck's word for it?

Saddle up and start reading—TIME'S A WASTIN'!

TOP, LEFT *Charles Schulz was cute as a button! The creator of* Peanuts *recounts, "The comics entered my world early. I was two days old when an uncle nicknamed me 'Sparky,' short for Spark Plug, Barney Google's horse in a popular strip of the time. And that name has stuck with me since."*

TOP, CENTER *Promotional button for* The Atlanta Georgian*, 1930s.*

TOP, RIGHT *In 1995, Barney Google was one of 20 characters included in the Comic Strip Classics series of commemorative U.S. postage stamps. Courtesy of Lee Binswanger.*

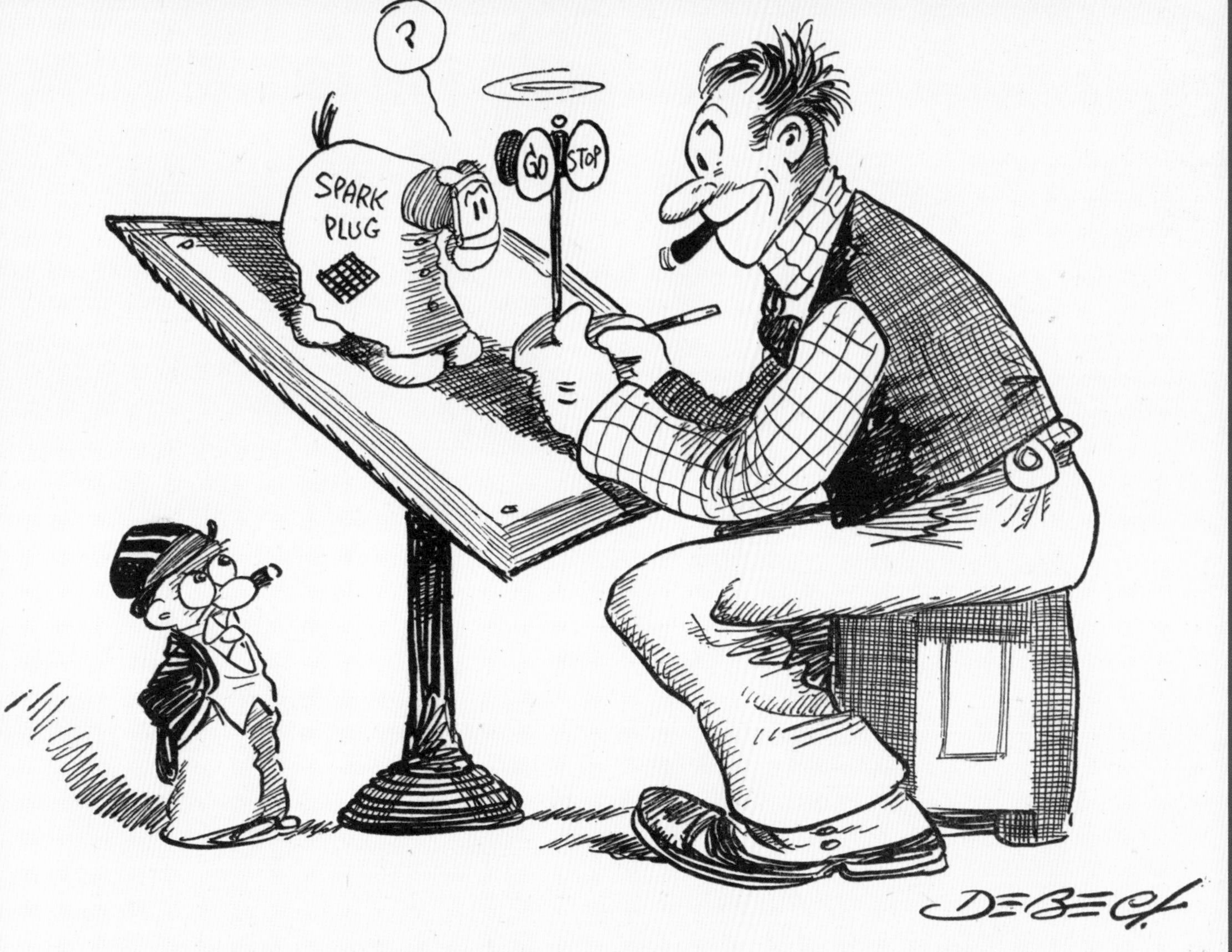
?
SPARK PLUG
GO
STOP
DEBECK

A BILLY DEBECK SCRAPBOOK

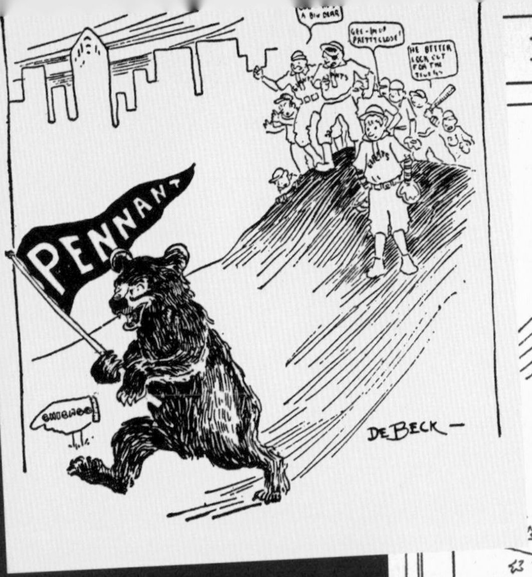
PENNANT
DE BECK

Above is a drawing DeBeck did when he was a student at the Chicago Academy of Fine Arts.

An early essay on his career by 'Will.' "Cartoons Magazine," April 1913.

Note DeBeck's raccoon "dingbat," as the political cartoonists of the day called their mascots.

DE BECK OF THE PITTSBURGH GAZETTE-TIMES

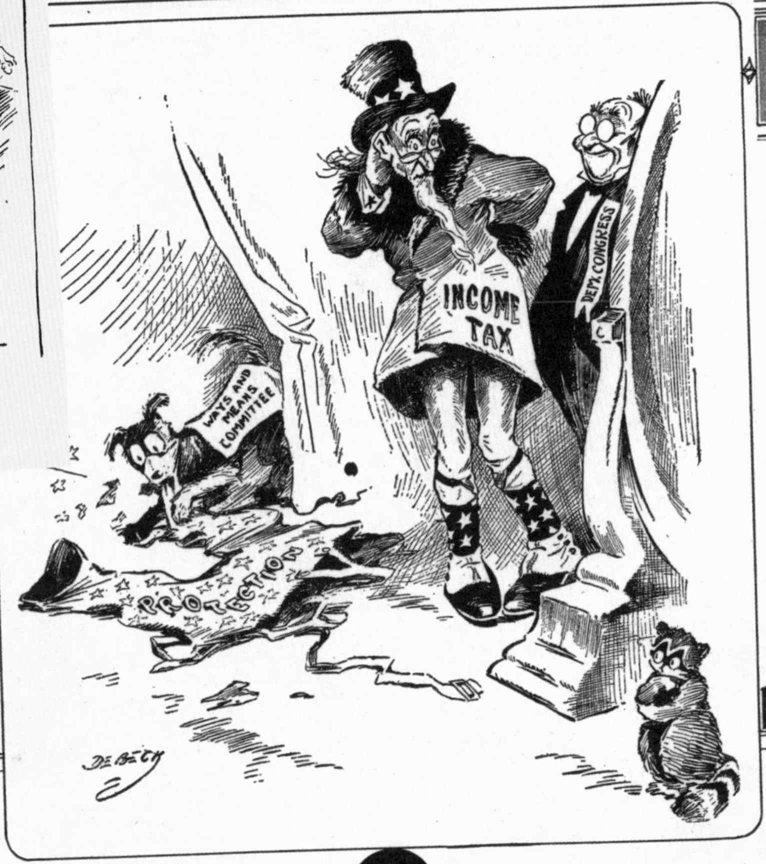
INCOME TAX
DEP'Y CONGRESS
WAYS AND MEANS COMMITTEE
PROTECTION
DE BECK

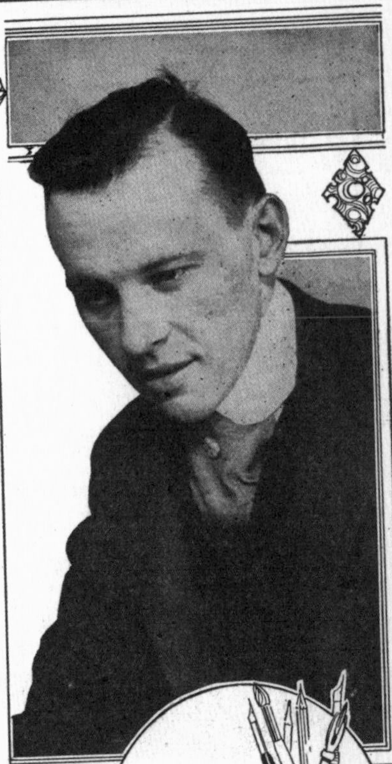

Will De Beck

THE chilly blasts of a belated March blizzard, sweeping in from Lake Michigan and whistling about the high buildings of Chicago, sent the few persons on the streets hurrying to shelter, and so intent was the population of Chicago on its own affairs that few were aware that I had on that day, April 16, 1890, arrived in their midst.

I don't remember much about the first few years, but later, when I was able to walk and talk and sit on the front porch and watch the passing throngs, I had day dreams. Yes, I dreamed and planned an imposing career. Moreover, it was not to become an artist. I never thought of that. In fact, I did not know that artists existed.

My dream was to become a milkman. To have full charge of a fine cart which contained innumerable bottles of the creamy fluid—without water added—to drive the streets, spring lightly from the wagon; and, carrying a wire basket containing several bottles, deposit the said bottles on the doorsteps and porches. No higher existence appealed to me, and I believed that if ever I grew up big enough to occupy such a position my happiness would be complete.

Then I was sent to the Chicago public schools, and here I obtained my first look at art. Along with the other things, I was taught drawing. I liked it but I developed an aversion to geography and spelling, but I managed to get through the graded schools and the Hyde Park high school. By this time my parents had decided to place me in the Academy of Fine Arts.

At the end of two years I secured a position in an engraving house and was paid two dollars a week. Six months was enough of this and I landed a place with the Show World. Then I learned of a place open on the Youngstown, Ohio, Telegram, and I hurried to Youngstown without writing to apply for the position. The next day I sent for my trunk and I remained in Youngstown two years. The two years were happy ones, and G. Frank Herrick, the managing editor, an excellent critic and an interested art student, by his untiring efforts to make me turn out good stuff, did much for me.

I came to Pittsburgh as the cartoonist for the Gazette-Times last fall, and this change pleased me greatly as it brought me again to work with pen and ink after the "dusty" years I had gone through drawing on chalk plates.

A spirited political cartoon from the "Pittsburgh Gazette-Times" titled "One People, One Country, One Flag," 1914.

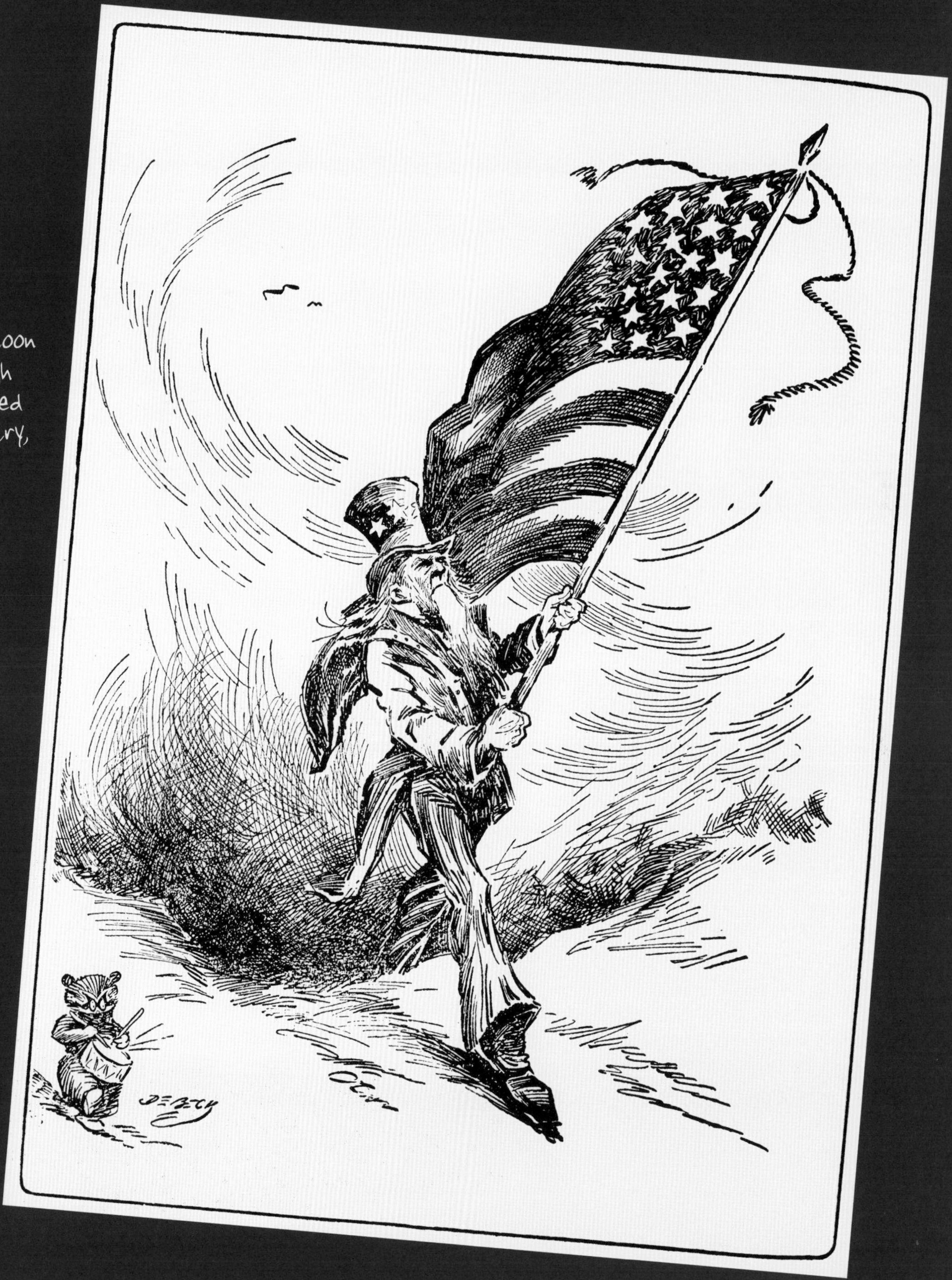

Far Left: From the collection of the author.
Left: Courtesy of Warren Bernard.
Right: From the collection of the author.

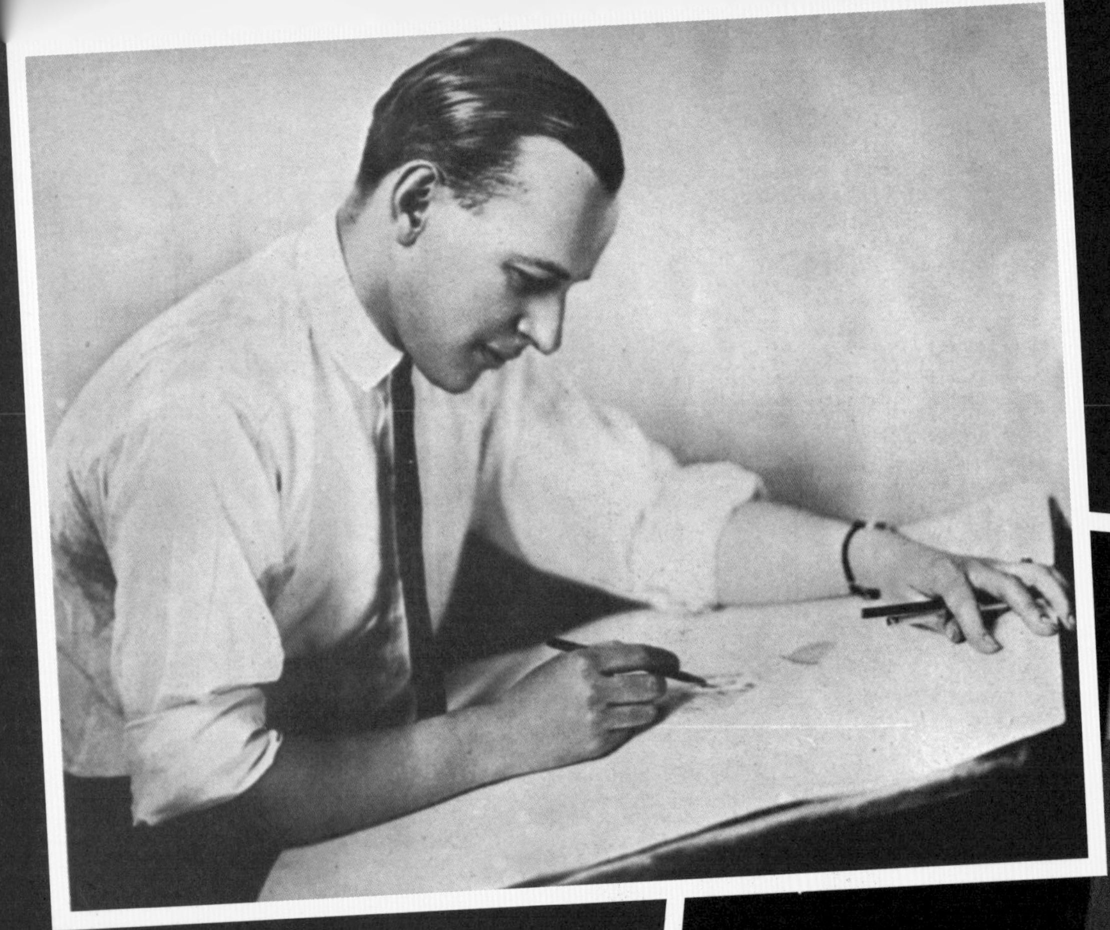

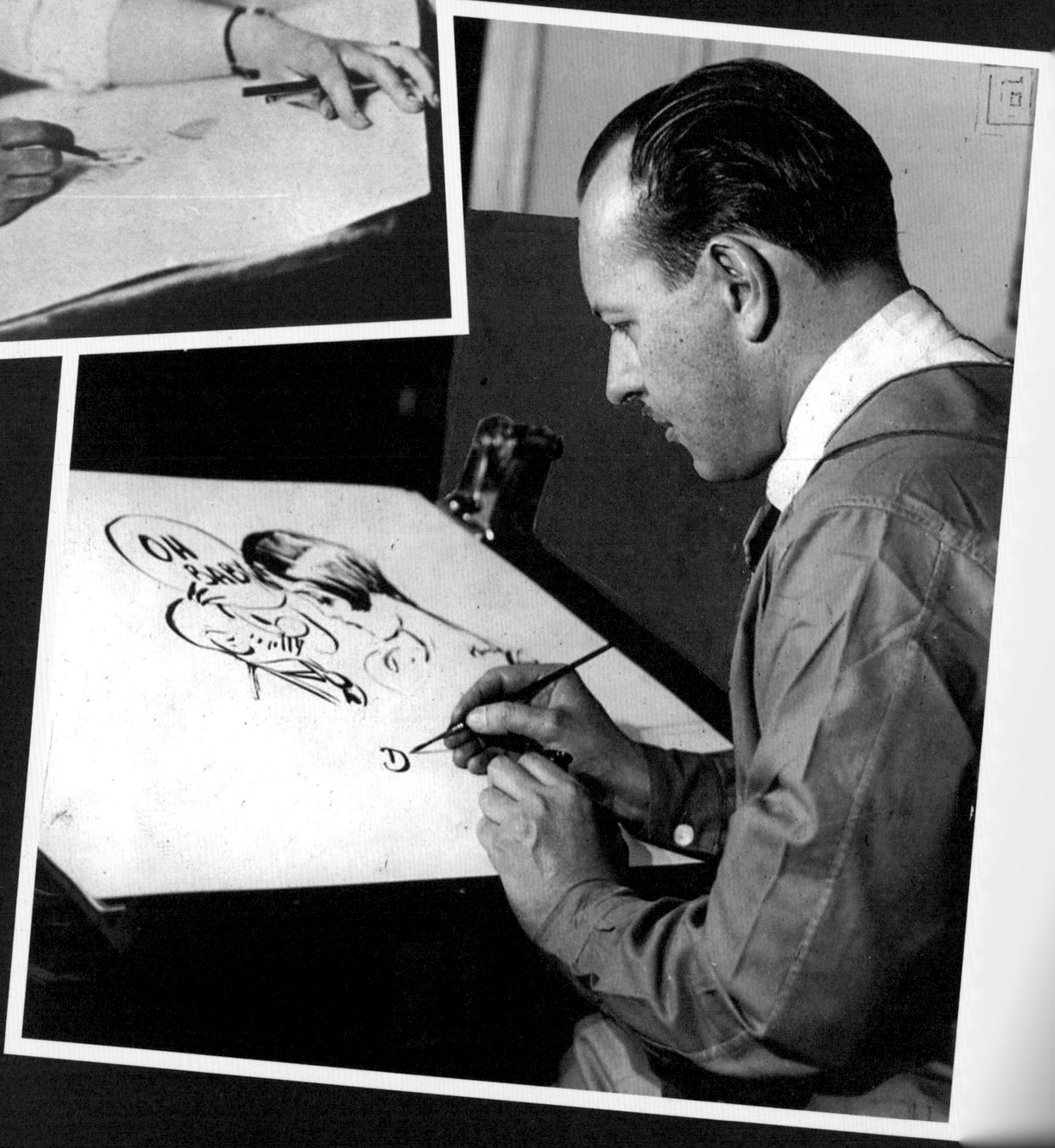

'Beck to the drawing board, and making cartooning look easel!

Billy DeBeck drawing away at different stages in his life. The first photo is dated 1923, the second 1929. In the photo on the far page, the artist is drawing Bunky, 1940.

Above: From the collection of the author.
Right: Courtesy of Ulrich Merkl.
Opposite: From the collection of the author.

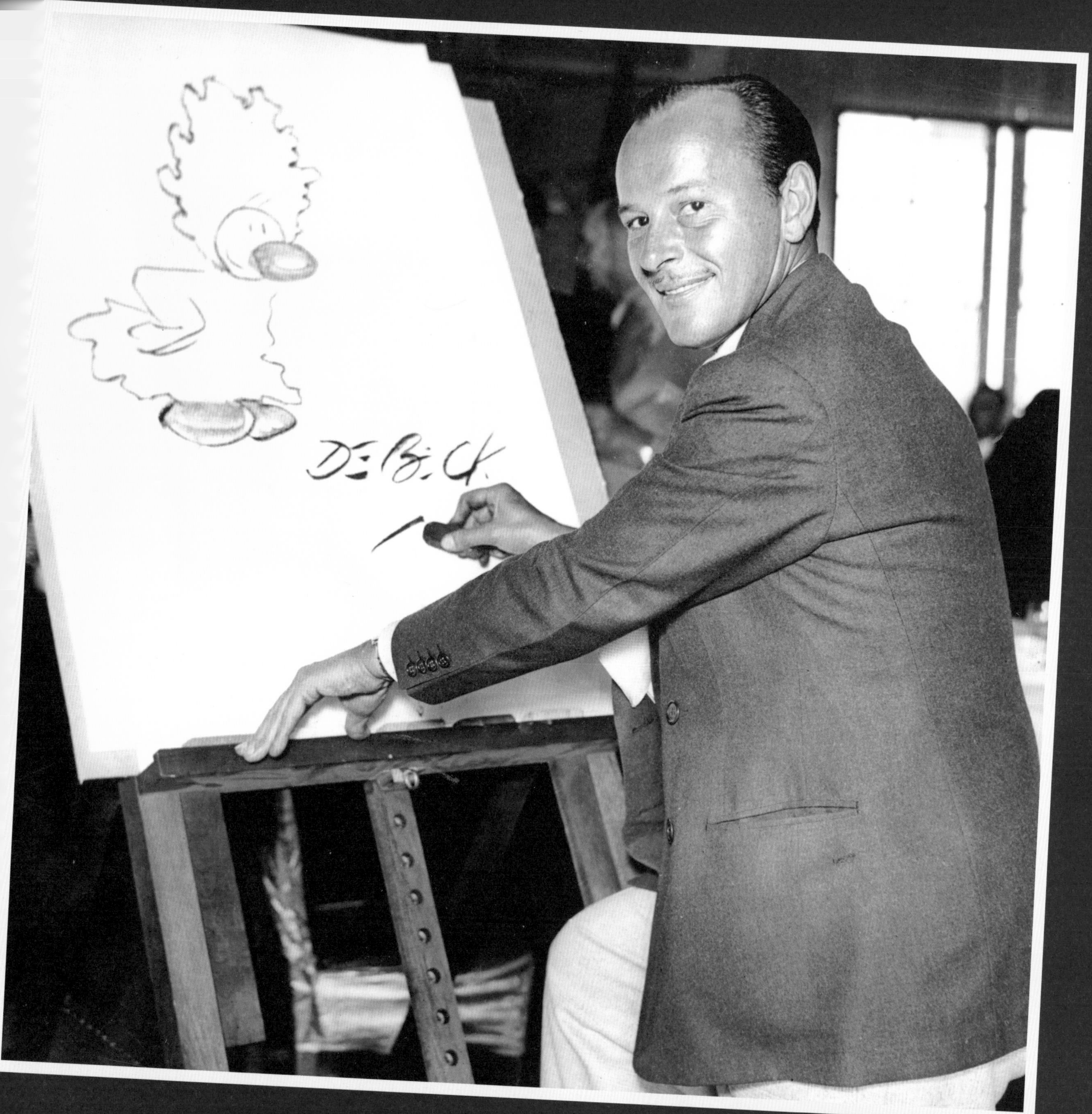

An April 17, 1928, newspaper photo of Marian. The handwritten notation on the back reads, "Divorced wife of Billy DeBeck, cartoonist, will marry Fidel LaBarba, ex-pugilist."

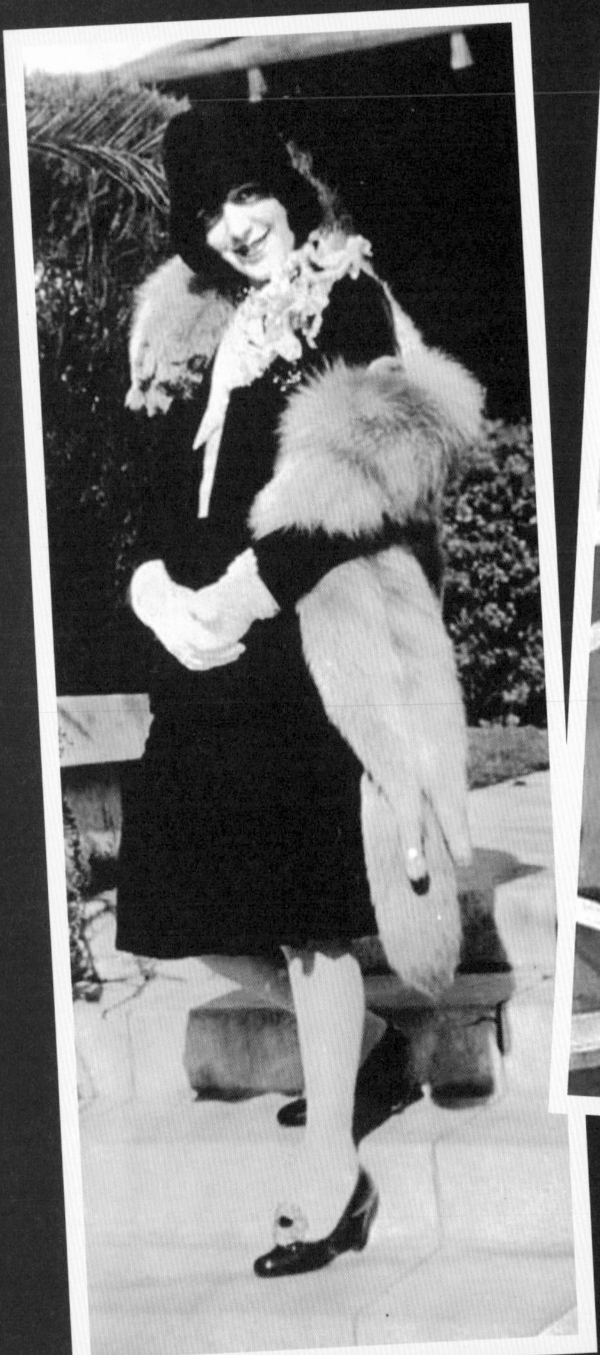

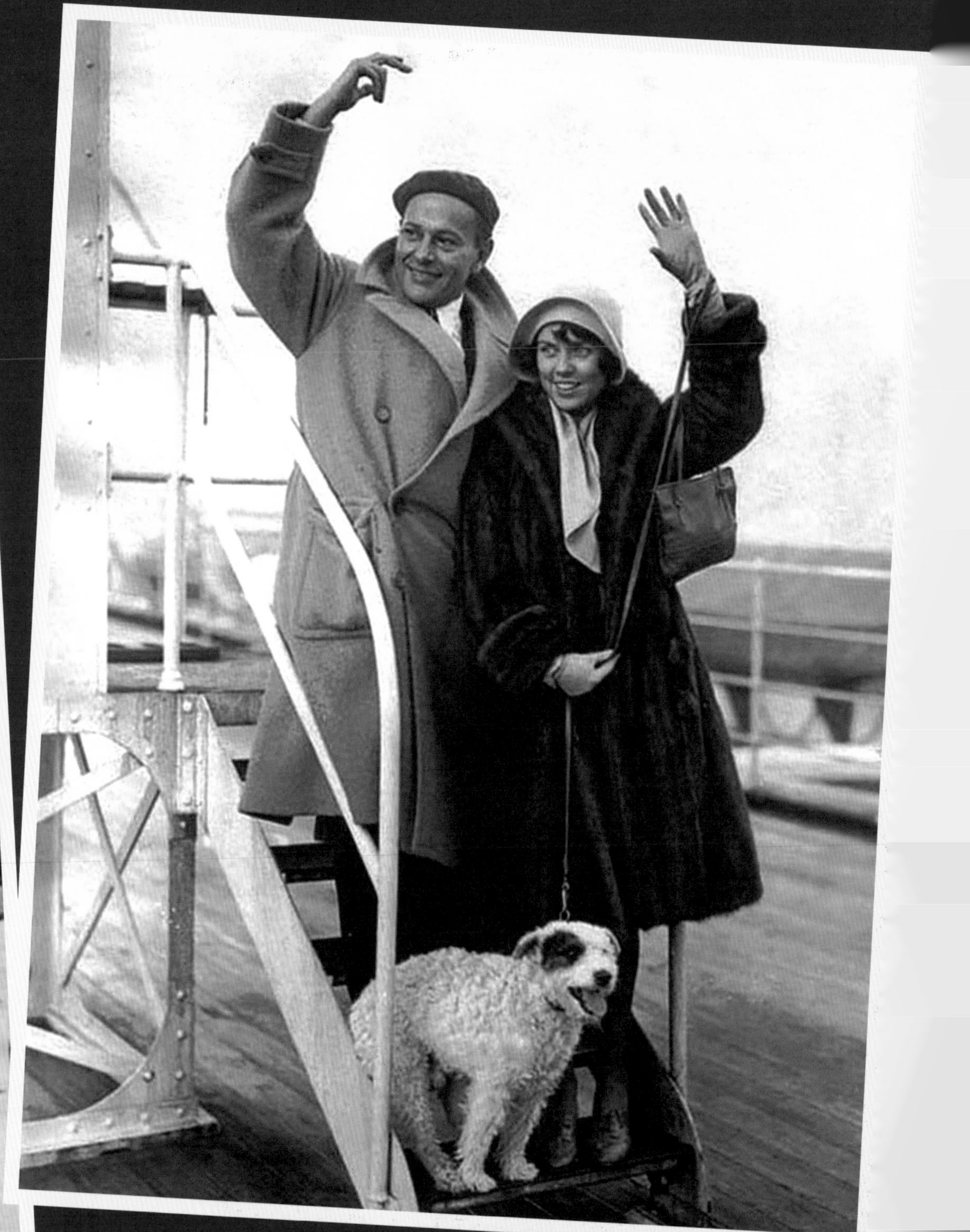

The back of this publicity photo reports, "New York—Billy DeBeck, famous cartoonist and creator of 'Barney Google,' is shown with [second] wife [Mary Louise] on their arrival aboard the Ile de Fra from Europe, where they spent a year touring the various countr Their pet, 'Sparky' is shown in the picture." November 11, 1929.

Above: Courtesy of Ulrich Merkl.
Opposite: From the collection of the author.

Two plates from "DeBeck's Cartoon Hints," 1915.
The artist was clearly inspired by the great
animal cartoonist T.S. Sullivant.

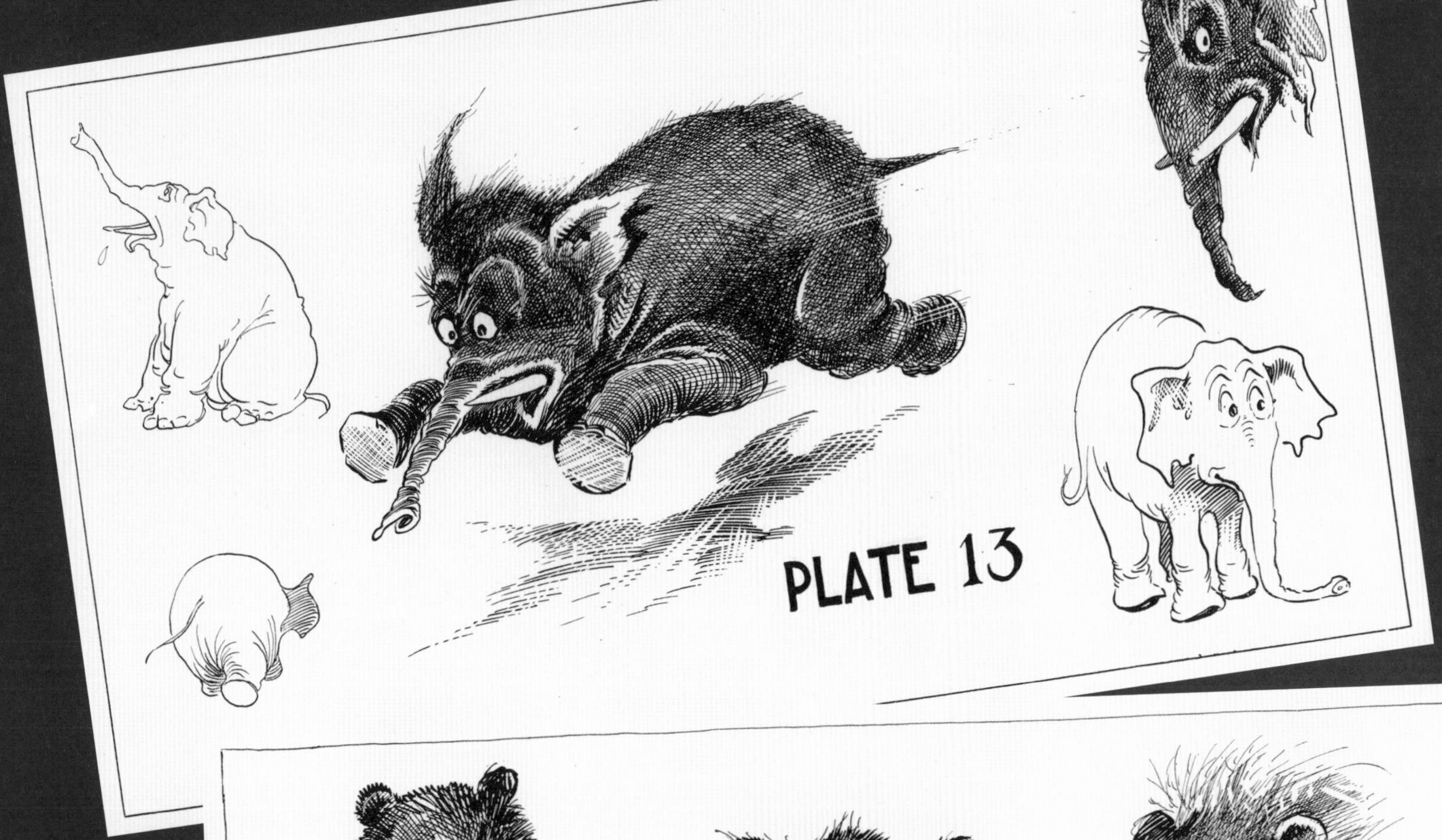
PLATE 13

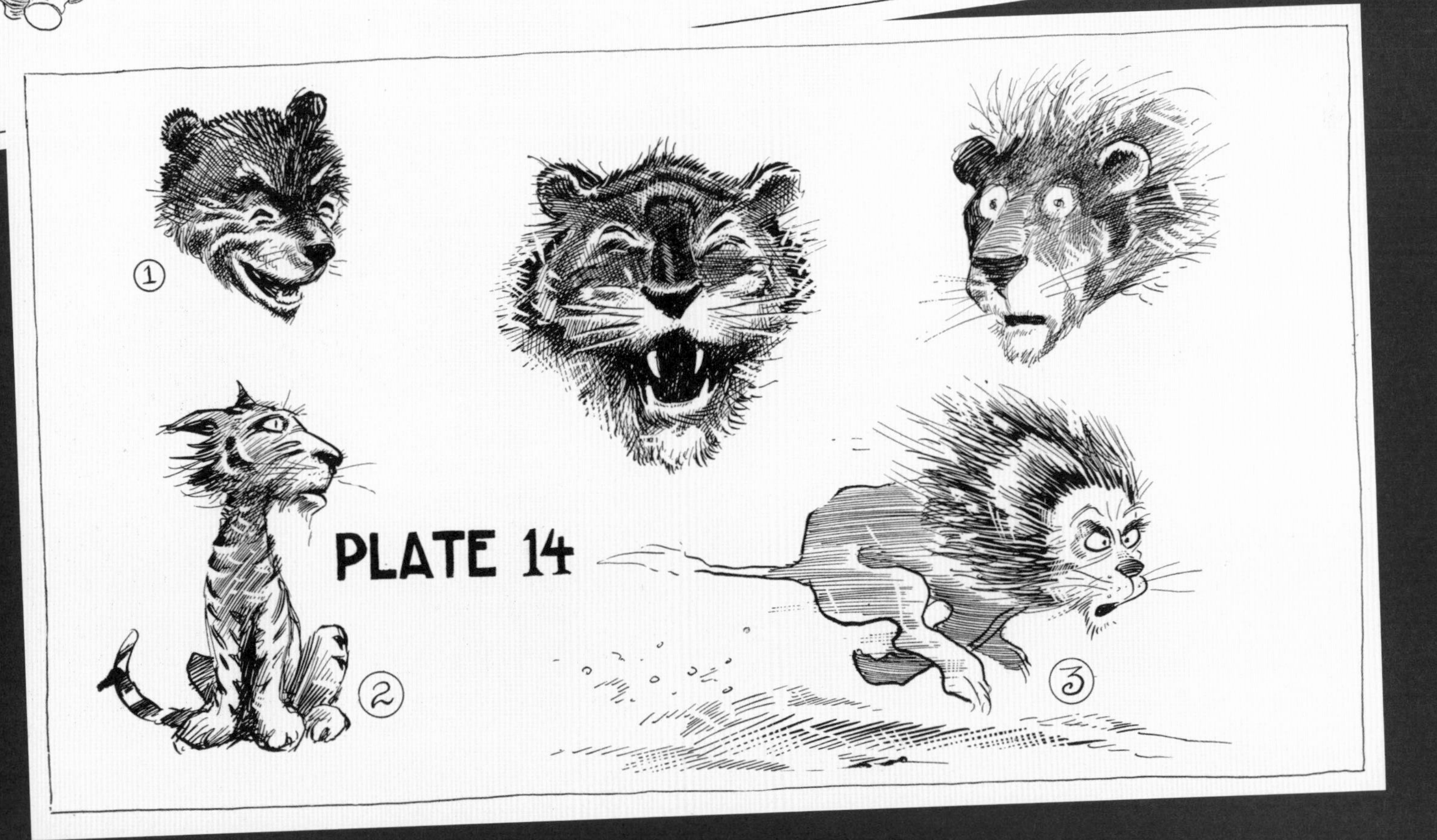
1
2
3
PLATE 14

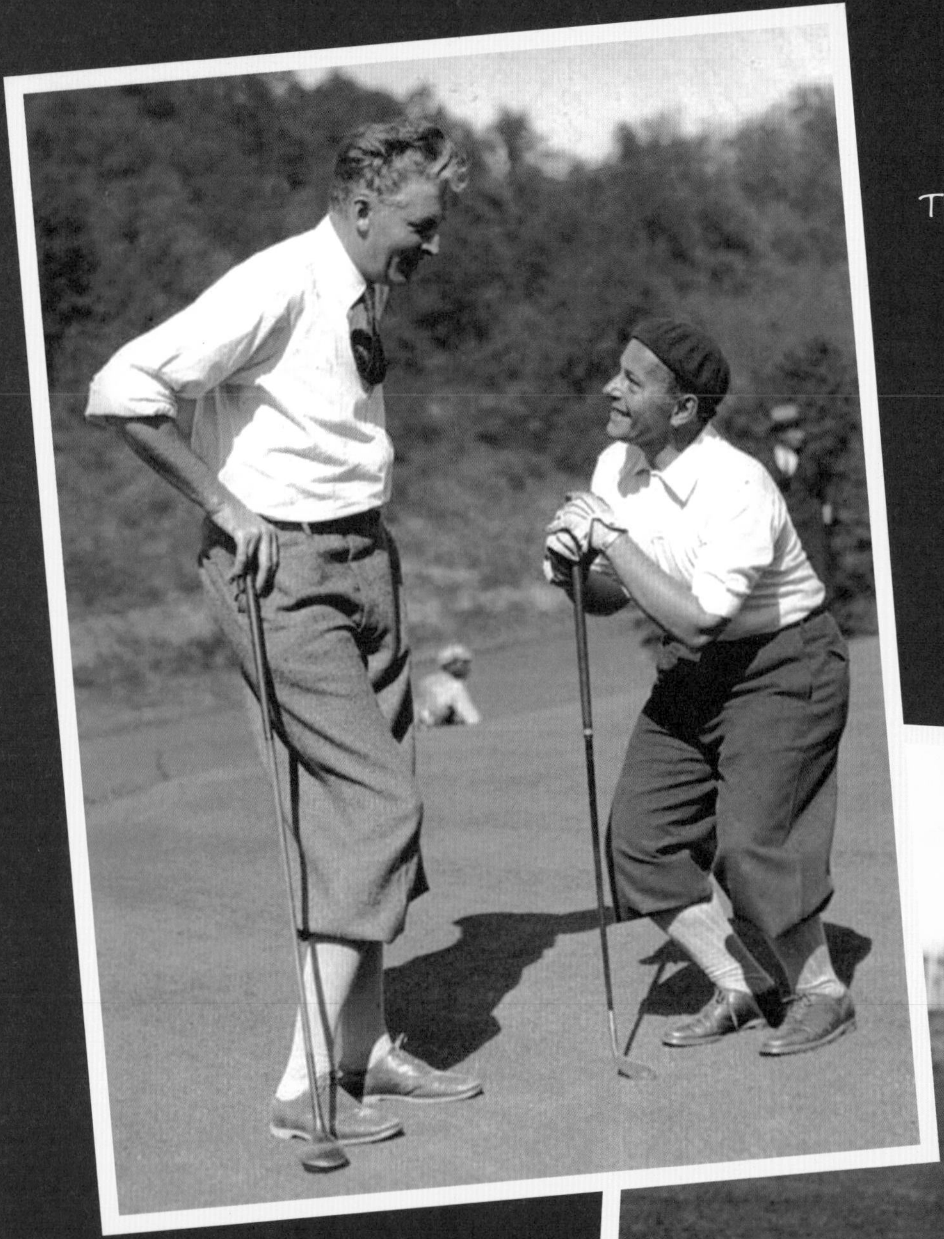

Billy and fellow cartoonist H.T. Webster poking fun at their opposite statures. The Artists and Writers Annual Tournament, Hot Springs, Virginia, October 13, 1931.

Rube Goldberg invents a human golf tee for duffer DeBeck, 1931.

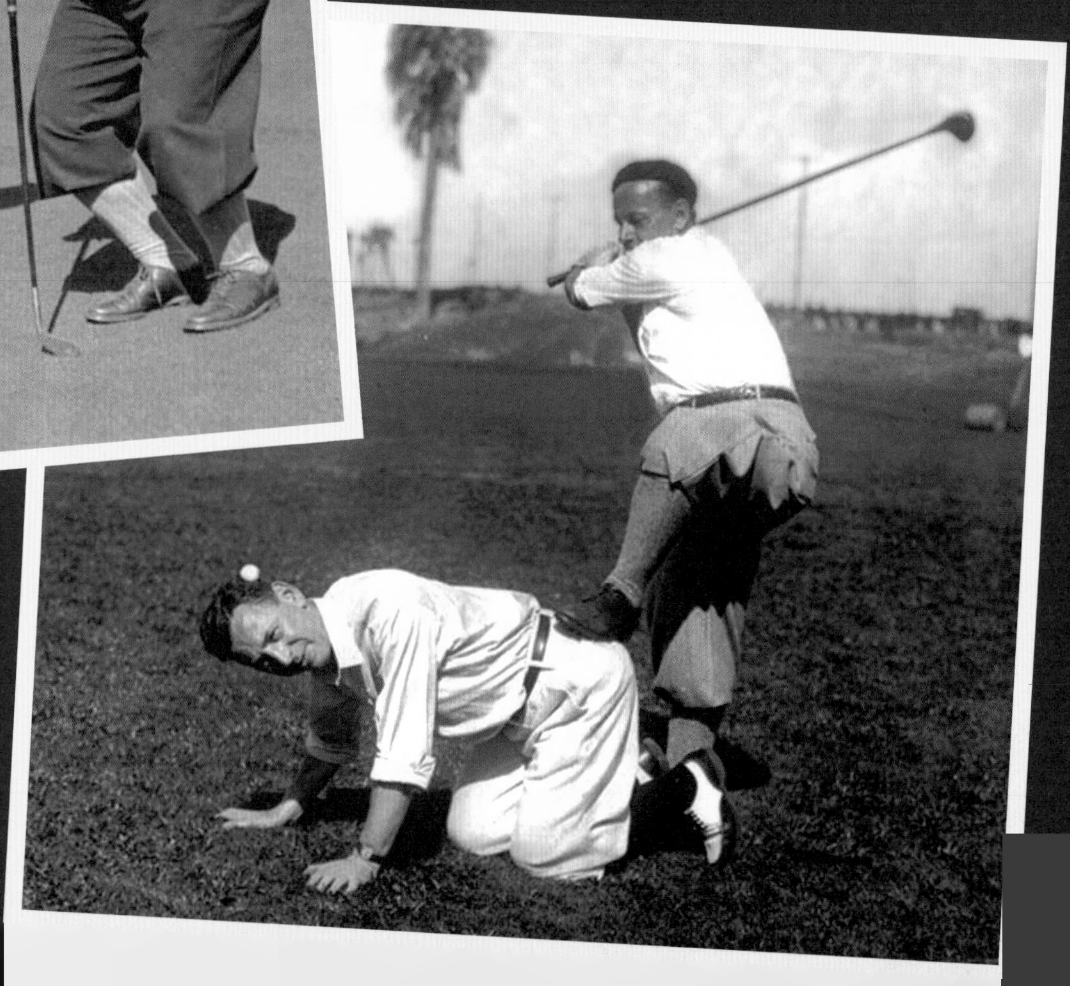

The artist was a big golf enthusiast, often playing with celebrities like Dizzy Dean, pitcher of the St. Louis Cardinals.

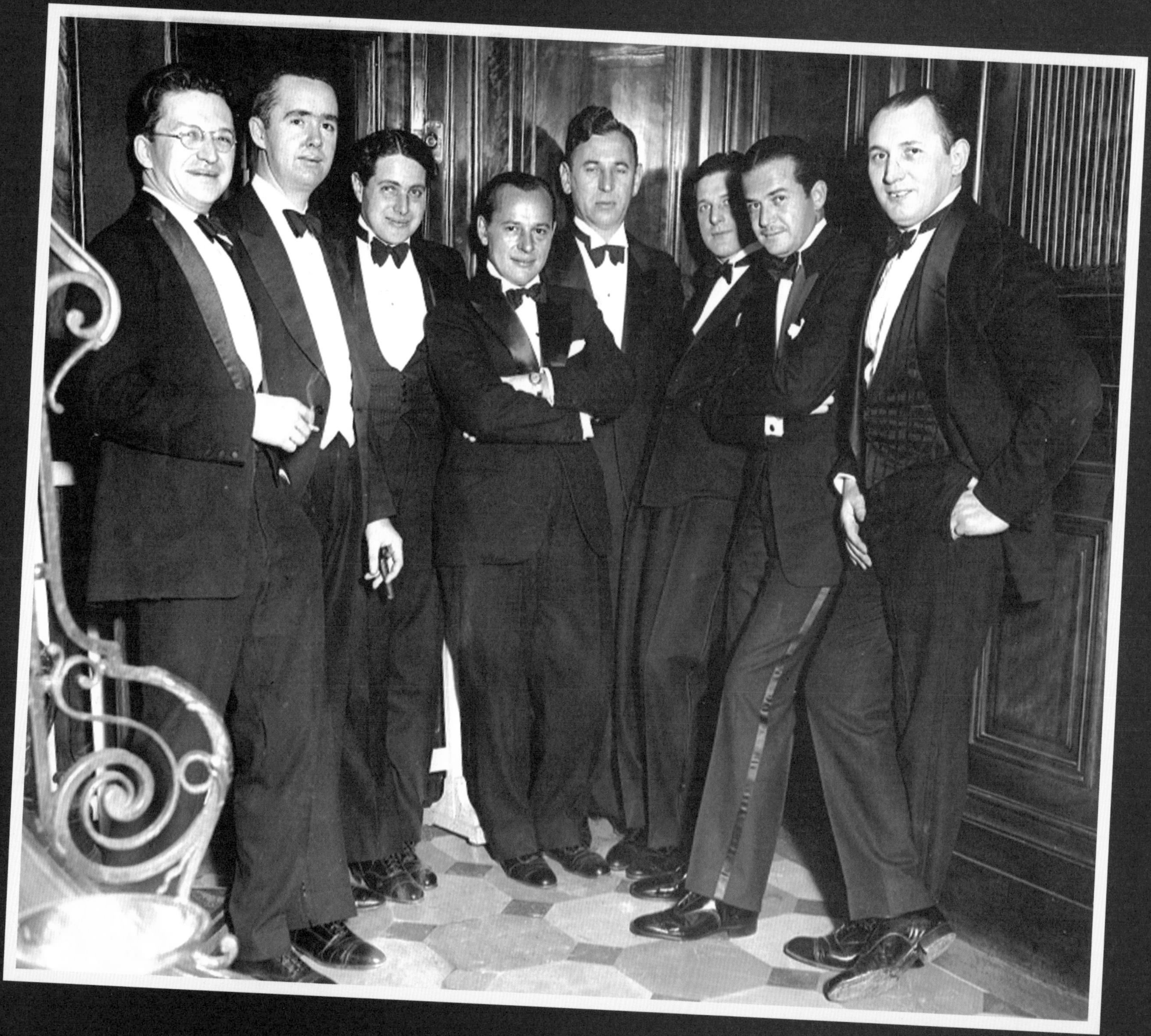

Dressed to impress on the Ile de France, DeBeck poses with Milt Gross at his right and Rube Goldberg at his left. That's Robert Ripley on Billy's farthest left, believe it or not!

Billy DeBeck and heavyweight champion of the world Jack Dempsey, in Los Angeles, July 12, 1923.

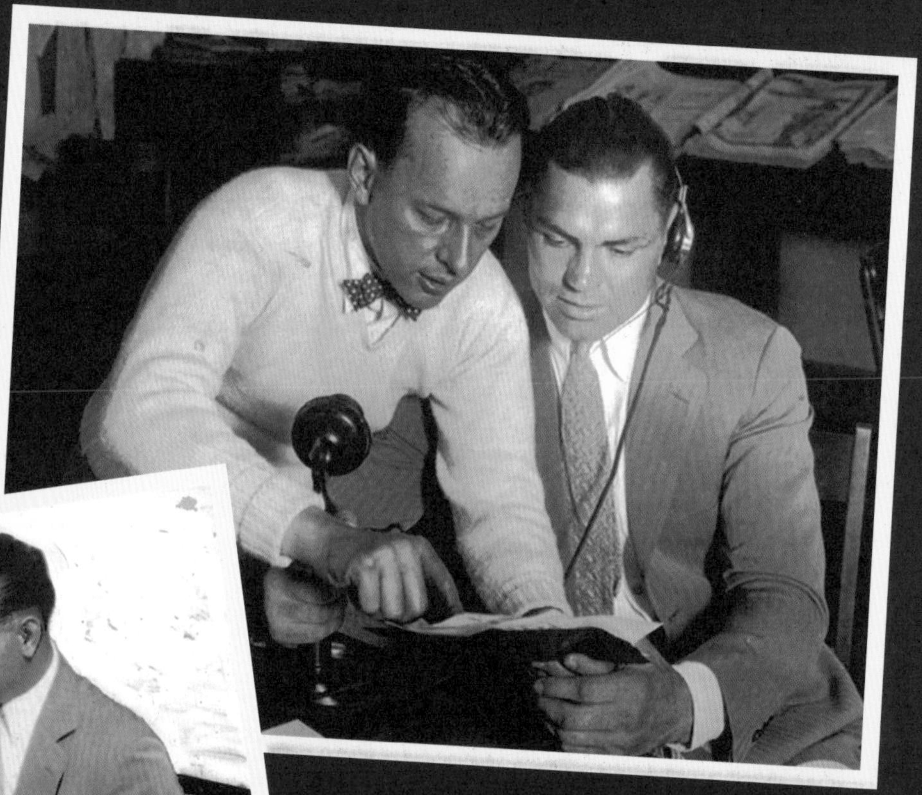

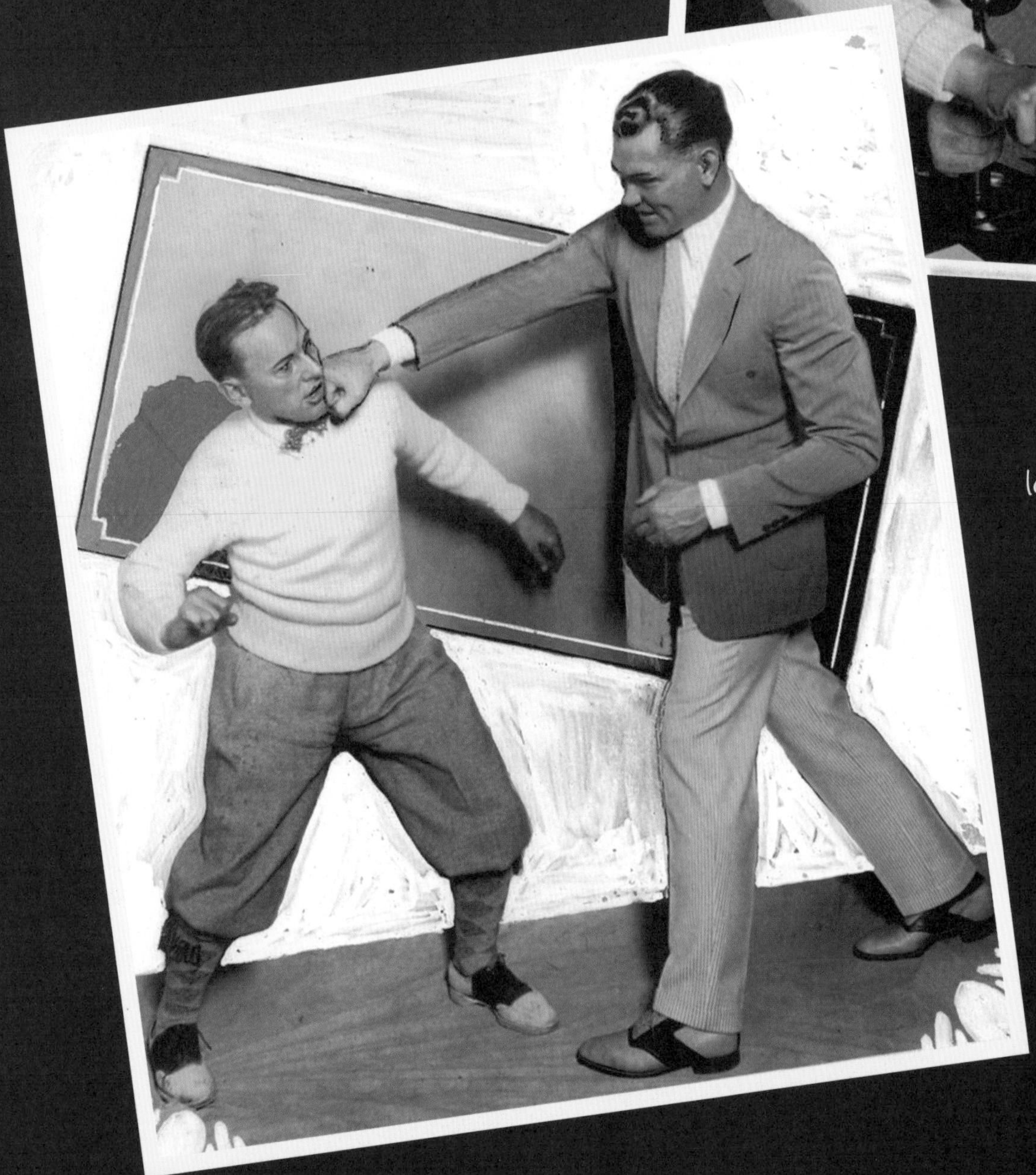

After listening to the famous Willard-Firpo fight on a special long-distance telephone to the ringside in Jersey City, New Jersey...

... the pen-and-inker and the pugilist ham it up!

ZIP ... POW!

Above and opposite: Courtesy of Ulrich Merkl.

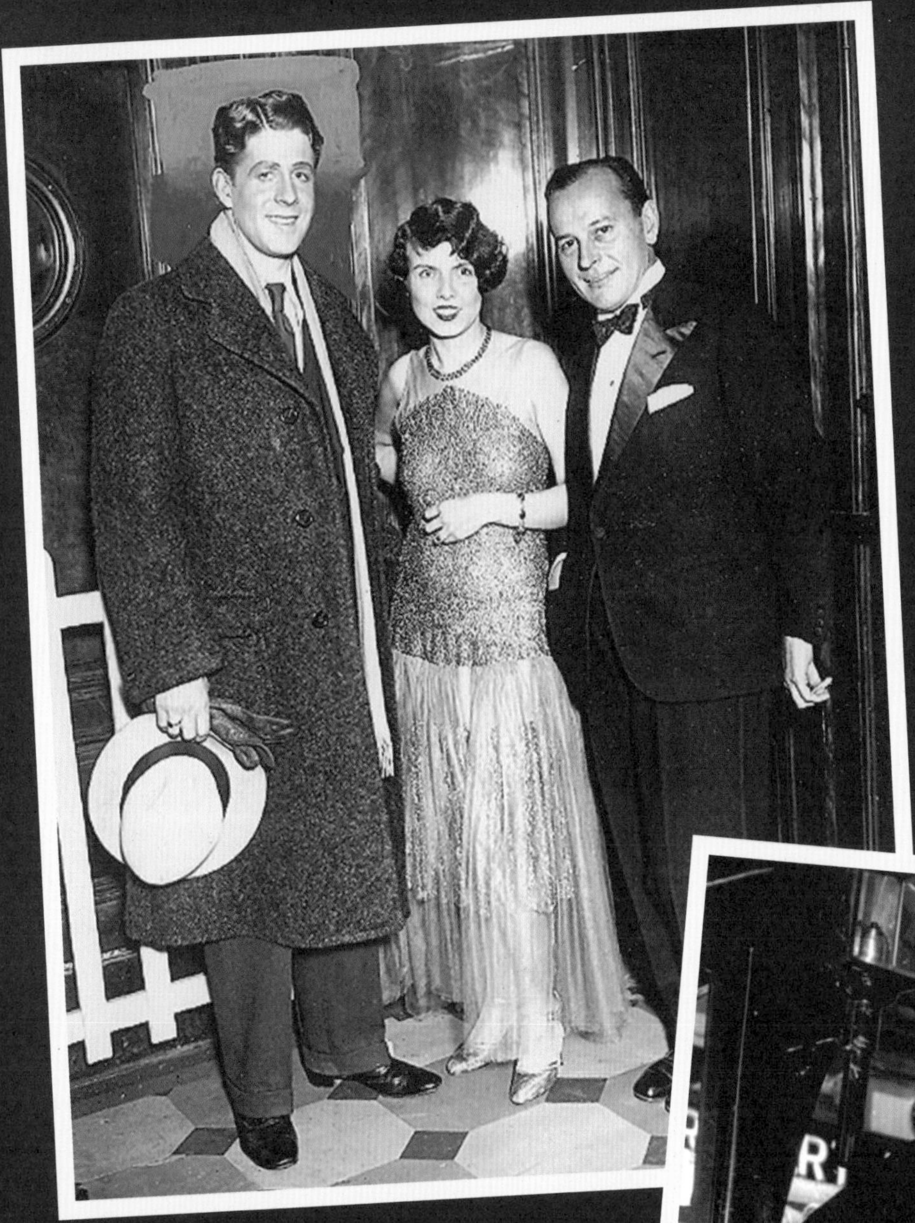

Billy hung with celebs. On the left, he and Mary Louise pose with singer Rudy Vallee on the Ile de France, 1929.

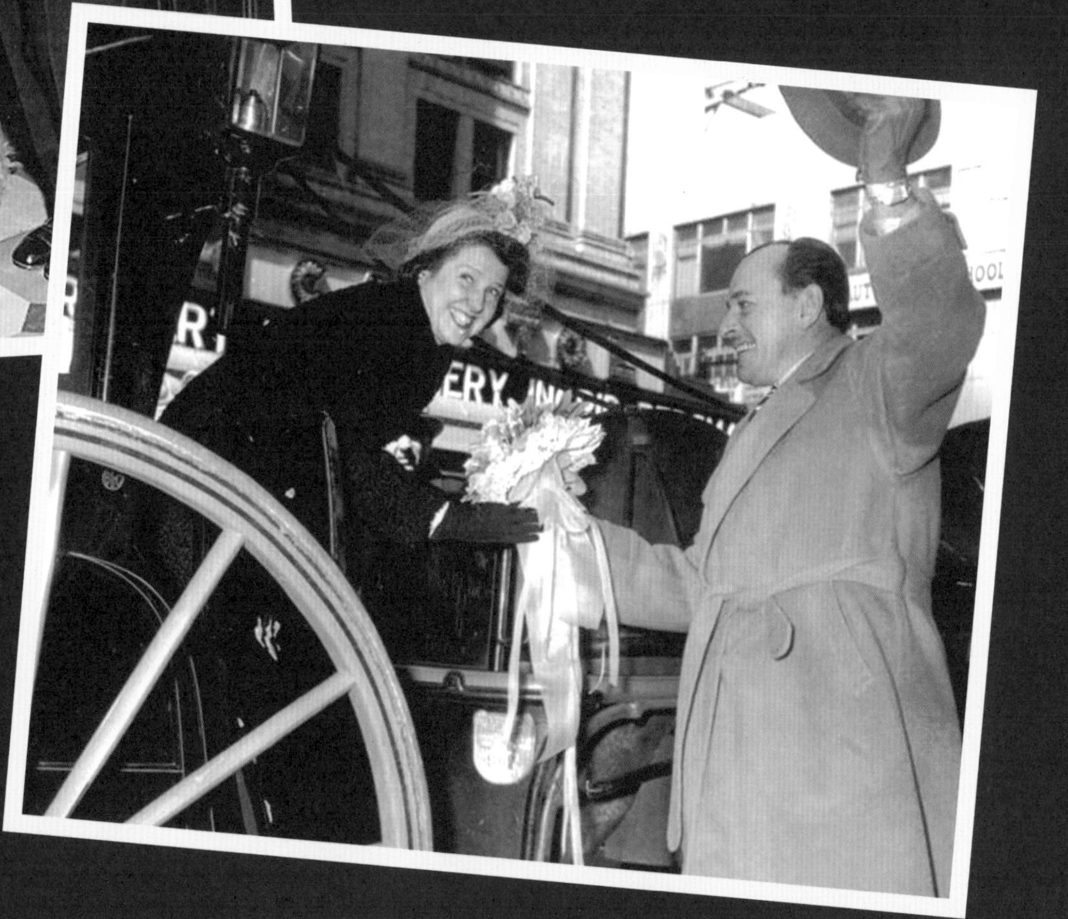
ERY

On the right, Billy escorts socialite and patron of the arts Gertrude Vanderbilt to a luncheon celebrating the 30th anniversary of the Winter Garden Theatre. New York, March 20, 1941.

Hollywood actor Lew Cody, who appeared in nearly 100 films, horsing around with the cartoonist. DeBeck's drawing has Barney saying to Spark Plug, "You bum! Get that Lew Cody expression offa your pan!"

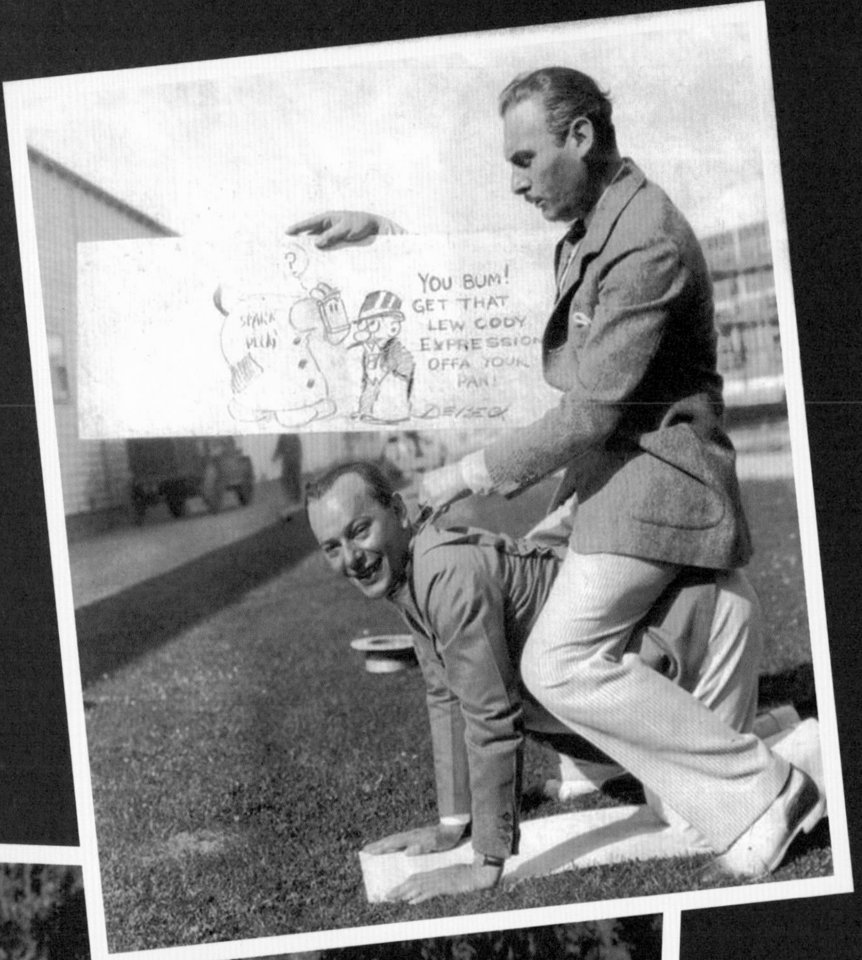
YOU BUM! GET THAT LEW CODY EXPRESSION OFFA YOUR PAN!
DEBECK

A publicity still of the crew and actors filming the 1928 Barney Google movie "Horsefeathers."

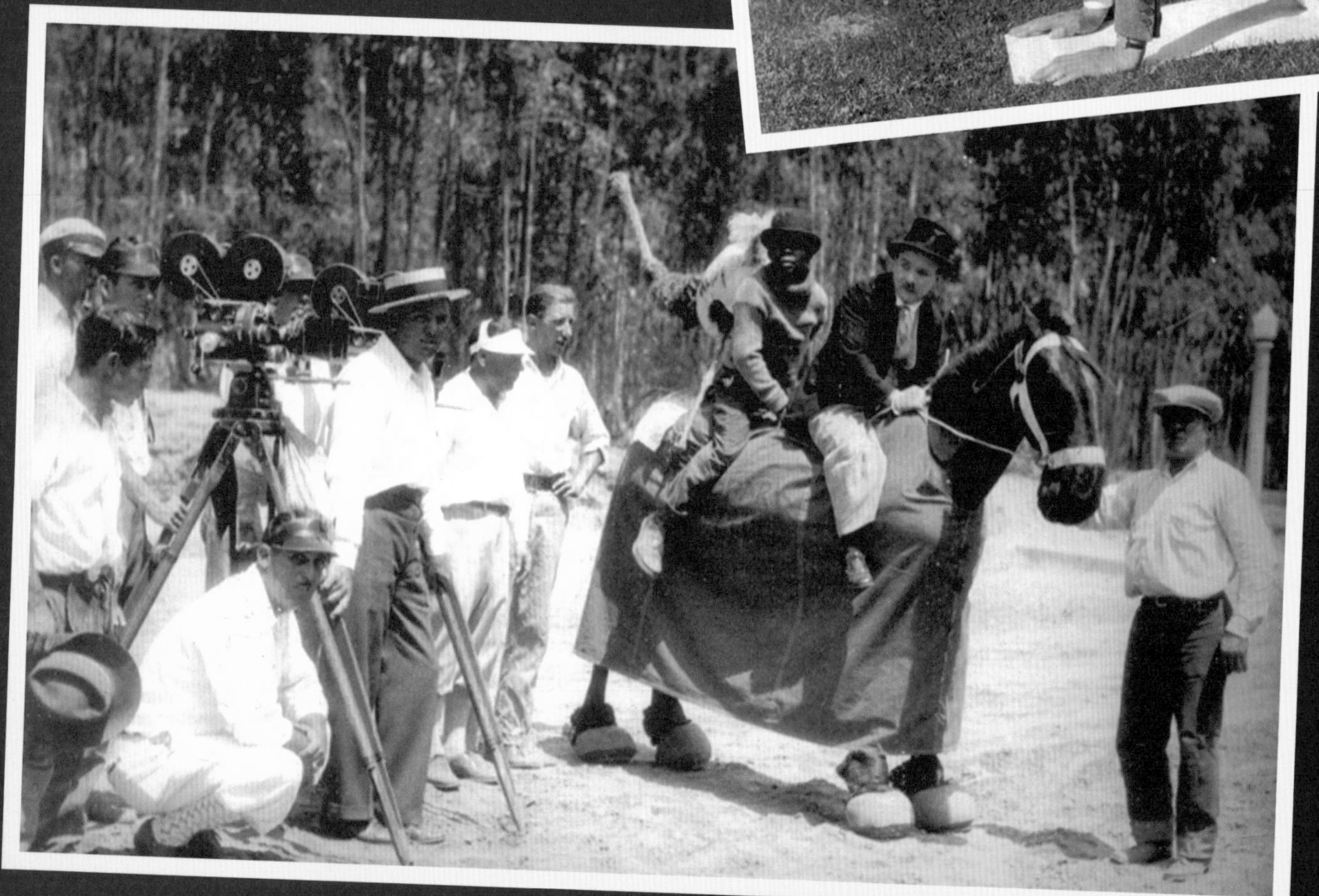

Above and opposite: Courtesy of Ulrich Merkl.

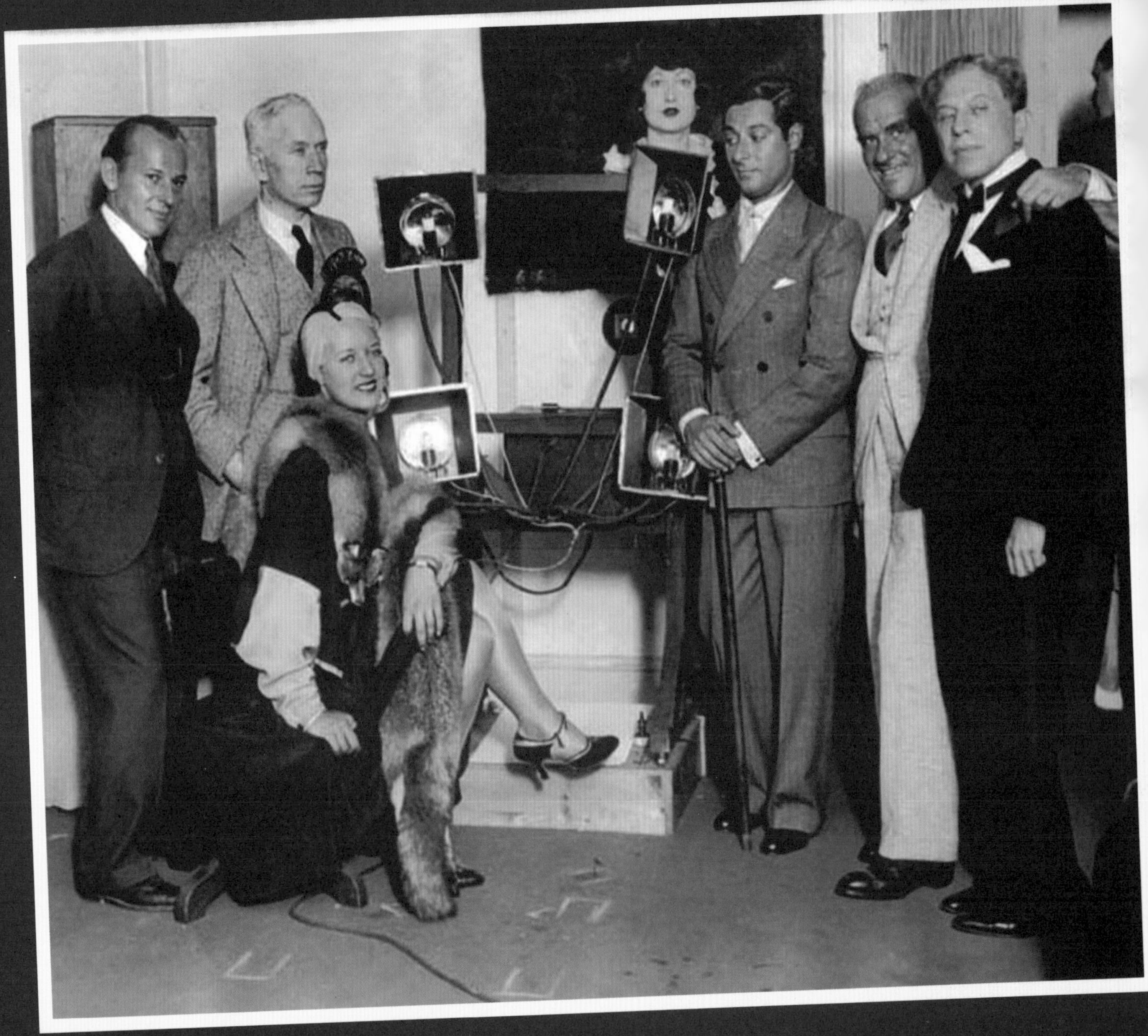

"The first radio-audio-vision public show" broadcast from the station of the Jenkins television corporation, Jersey City, New Jersey. The show was seen and heard by TV set owners on the Eastern part of the United States. The sponsors were the American Radio News and the "New York Evening Journal." September 1, 1930.

From the left: Billy DeBeck; Harry Hershfield, cartoonist of "Abie the Agent;" Diana Seaby, Broadway star; Rose Pelswick, movie critic; George Jessel, actor and Academy Award-winning movie producer; Arthur "Bugs" Baer, journalist and wit; and Sid Grauman, founder of the famed Grauman's Chinese Theatre in Hollywood.

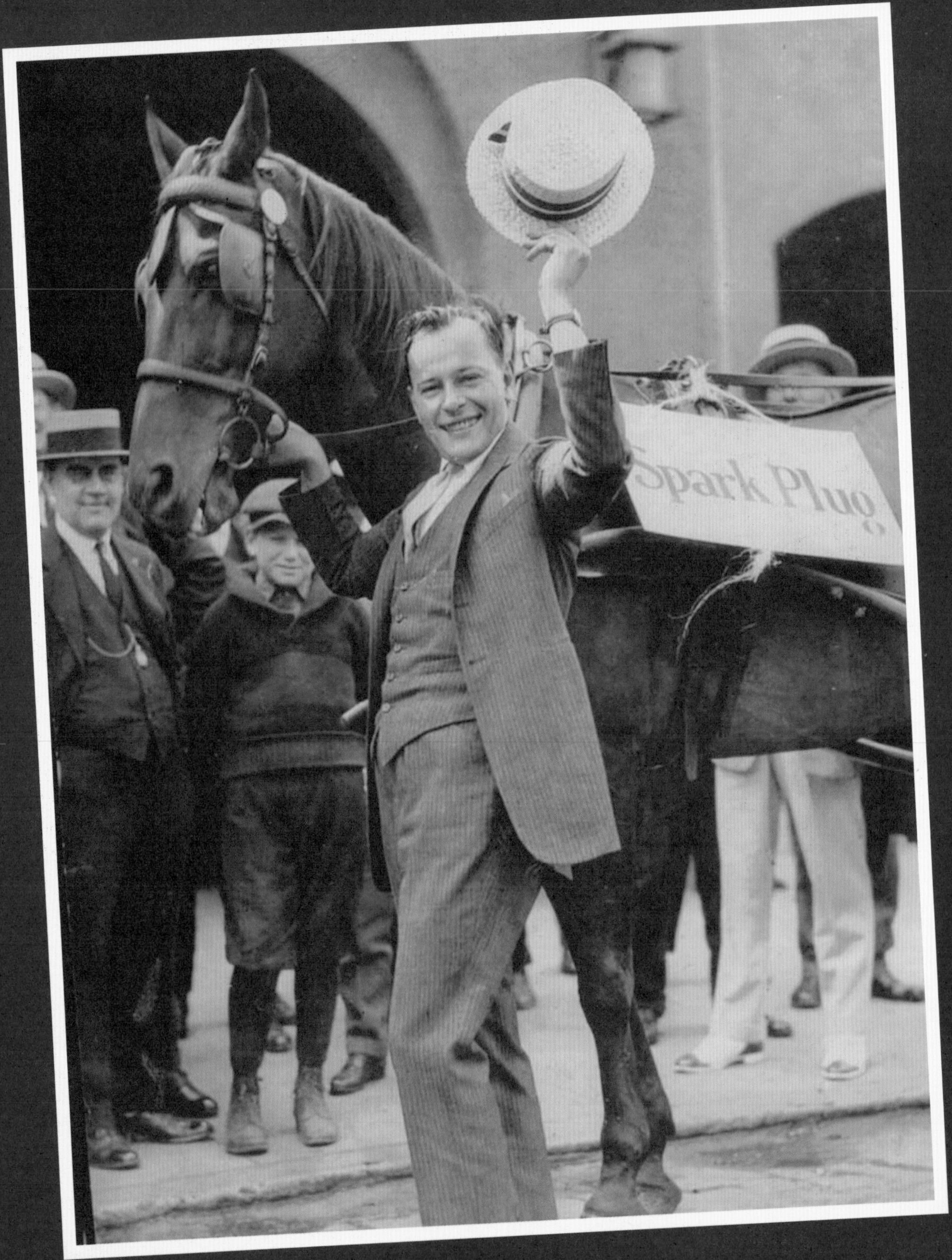
Spark Plug

Above: Courtesy of Ulrich Merkl.
Opposite: From the collection of the author.

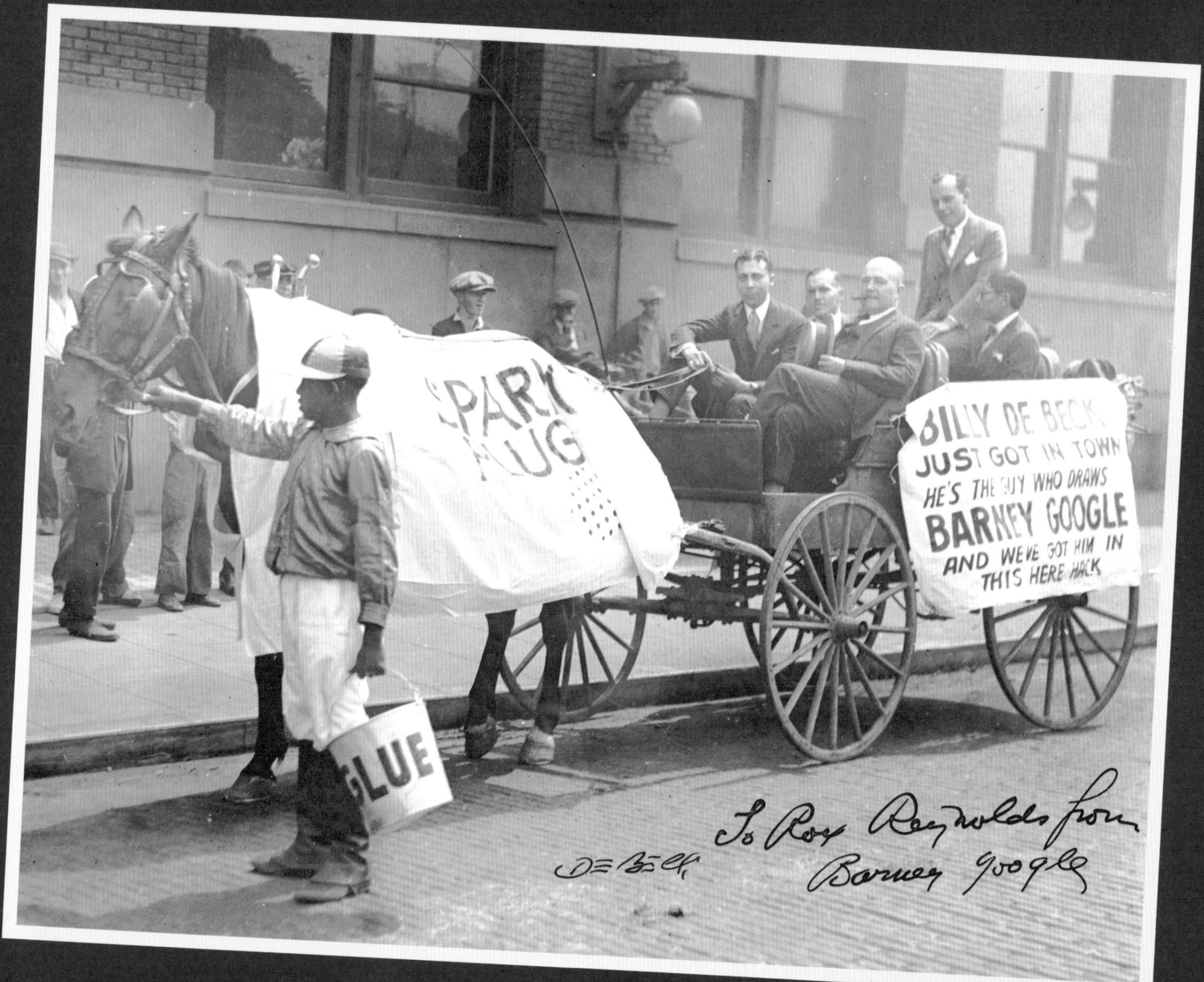
SPARK PLUG
BILLY DE BECK
JUST GOT IN TOWN
HE'S THE GUY WHO DRAWS
BARNEY GOOGLE
AND WE'VE GOT HIM IN
THIS HERE HACK
GLUE
To Roy Reynolds from
Barney Google
DeBeck

Above, in an autographed photo, Billy DeBeck sits tall on a publicity tour, escorted by the cigar-chomping Mayor of San Francisco, James Rolph, Jr.

In the far left picture, DeBeck with Spark Plug hails his crowd of admirers, 1923.

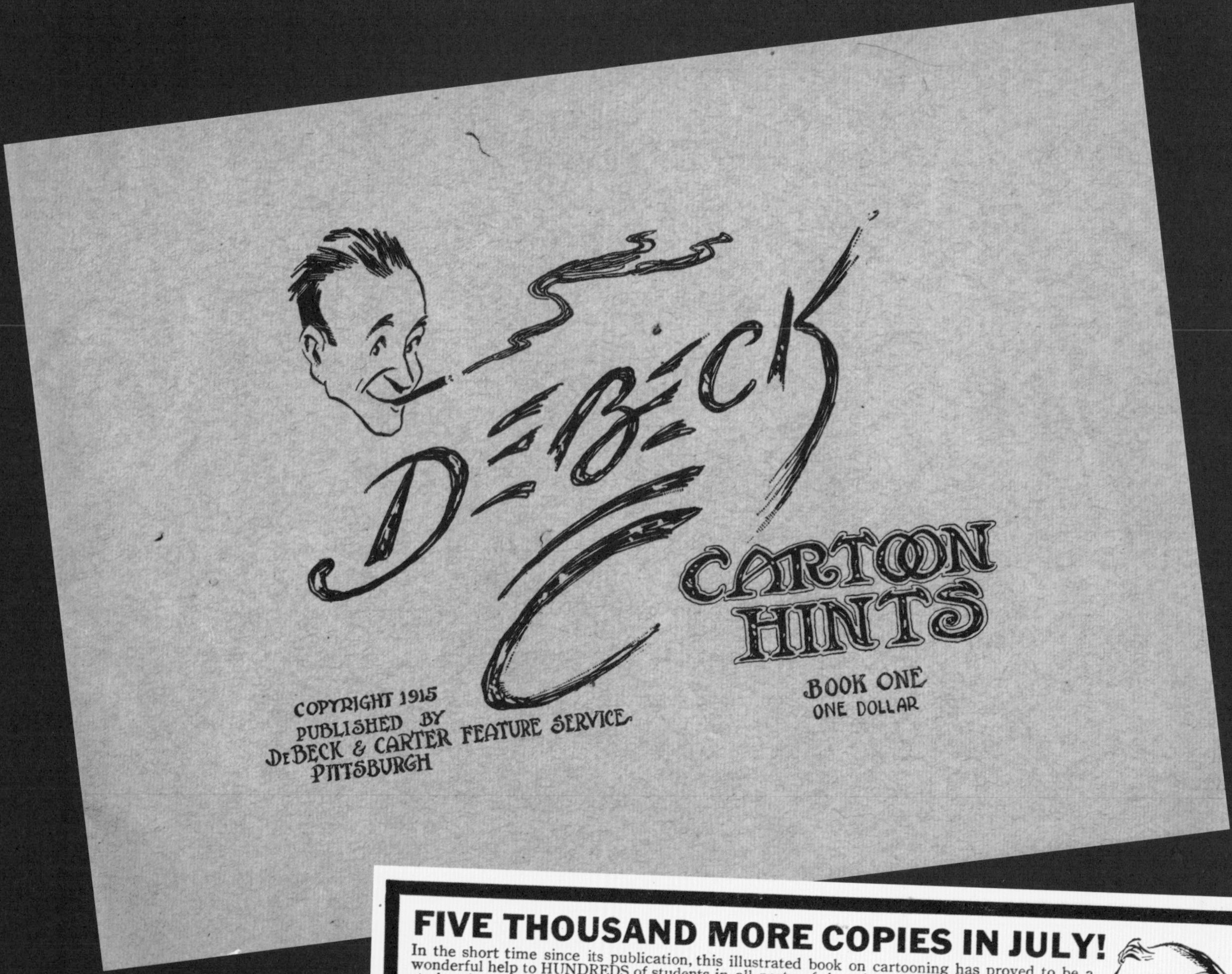
DeBECK
CARTOON HINTS
BOOK ONE
ONE DOLLAR
COPYRIGHT 1915
PUBLISHED BY
DeBECK & CARTER FEATURE SERVICE
PITTSBURGH

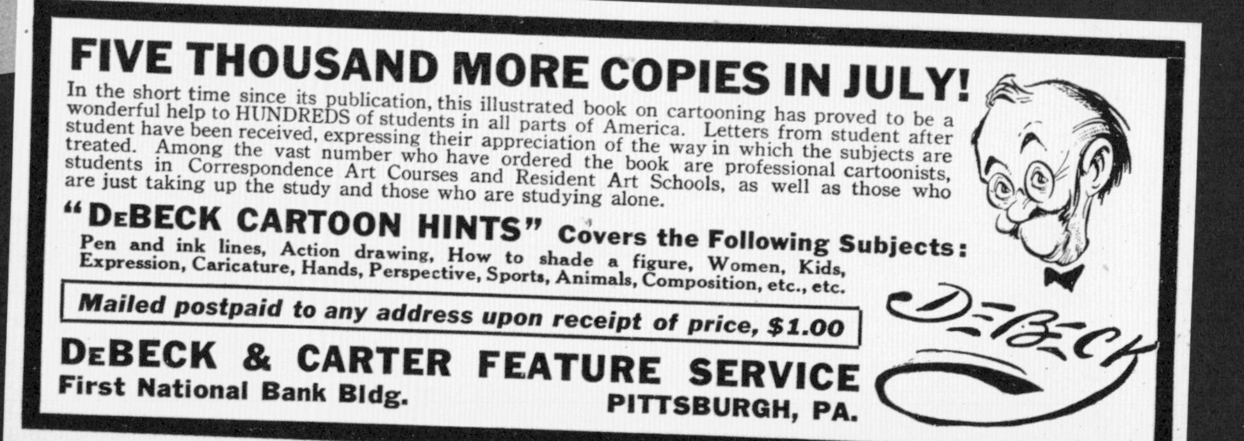
FIVE THOUSAND MORE COPIES IN JULY!
In the short time since its publication, this illustrated book on cartooning has proved to be a wonderful help to HUNDREDS of students in all parts of America. Letters from student after student have been received, expressing their appreciation of the way in which the subjects are treated. Among the vast number who have ordered the book are professional cartoonists, students in Correspondence Art Courses and Resident Art Schools, as well as those who are just taking up the study and those who are studying alone.
"DeBECK CARTOON HINTS" Covers the Following Subjects:
Pen and ink lines, Action drawing, How to shade a figure, Women, Kids, Expression, Caricature, Hands, Perspective, Sports, Animals, Composition, etc., etc.
Mailed postpaid to any address upon receipt of price, $1.00
DeBECK & CARTER FEATURE SERVICE
First National Bank Bldg.
PITTSBURGH, PA.
DeBECK

An ad touting the success of DeBeck's correspondence course. He marketed it while still in Pittsburgh, 1915.

Above and opposite: From the collection of the author.

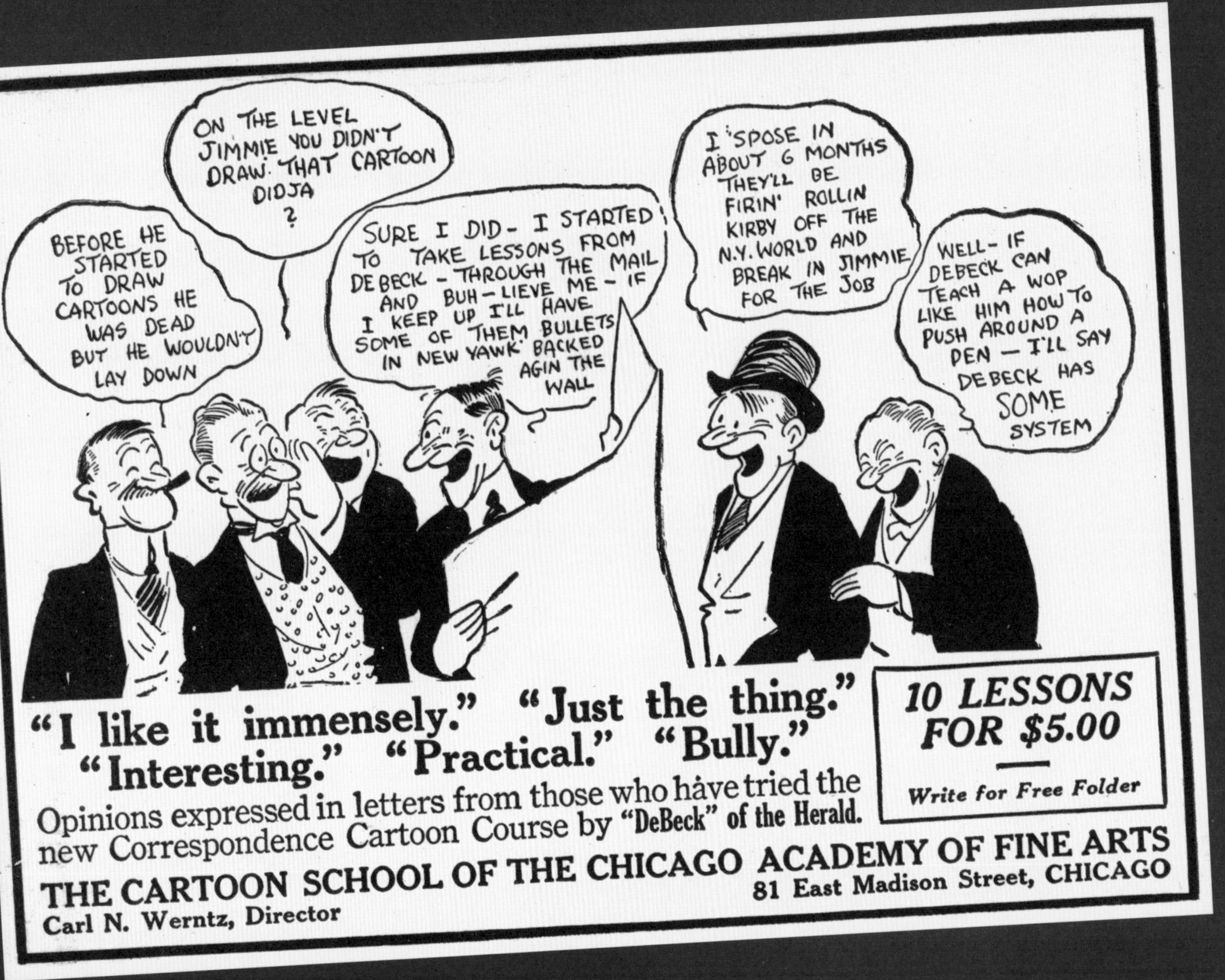
BEFORE HE STARTED TO DRAW CARTOONS HE WAS DEAD BUT HE WOULDN'T LAY DOWN
ON THE LEVEL JIMMIE YOU DIDN'T DRAW THAT CARTOON DIDJA ?
SURE I DID - I STARTED TO TAKE LESSONS FROM DEBECK - THROUGH THE MAIL AND BUH-LIEVE ME - IF I KEEP UP I'LL HAVE SOME OF THEM BULLETS IN NEW YAWK BACKED AGIN THE WALL
I SPOSE IN ABOUT 6 MONTHS THEY'LL BE FIRIN' ROLLIN KIRBY OFF THE N.Y. WORLD AND BREAK IN JIMMIE FOR THE JOB
WELL - IF DEBECK CAN TEACH A WOP LIKE HIM HOW TO PUSH AROUND A PEN - I'LL SAY DEBECK HAS SOME SYSTEM
"I like it immensely." "Just the thing." "Interesting." "Practical." "Bully."
Opinions expressed in letters from those who have tried the new Correspondence Cartoon Course by "DeBeck" of the Herald.
10 LESSONS FOR $5.00
Write for Free Folder
THE CARTOON SCHOOL OF THE CHICAGO ACADEMY OF FINE ARTS
Carl N. Werntz, Director
81 East Madison Street, CHICAGO

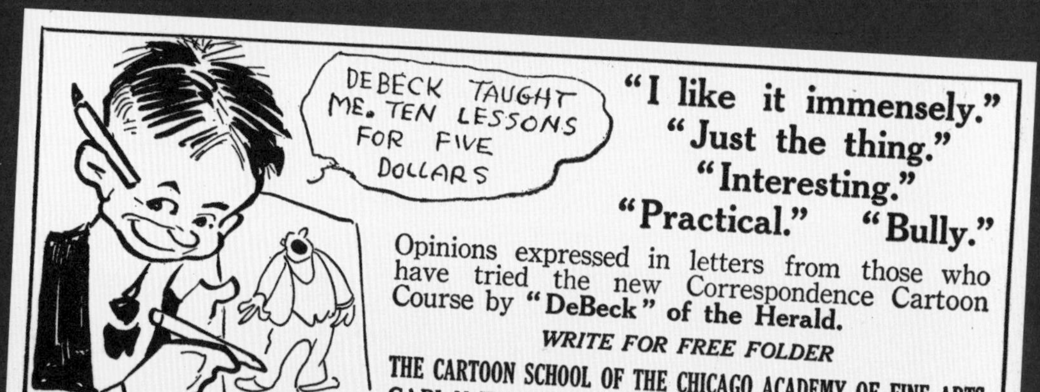
DEBECK TAUGHT ME. TEN LESSONS FOR FIVE DOLLARS
"I like it immensely." "Just the thing." "Interesting." "Practical." "Bully."
Opinions expressed in letters from those who have tried the new Correspondence Cartoon Course by "DeBeck" of the Herald.
WRITE FOR FREE FOLDER
THE CARTOON SCHOOL OF THE CHICAGO ACADEMY OF FINE ARTS
CARL N. WERNTZ, Director. 81 E. Madison St., CHICAGO

Ads in "Cartoons Magazine" for DeBeck's correspondence course.
Above, March 1919. Right, March 1917.

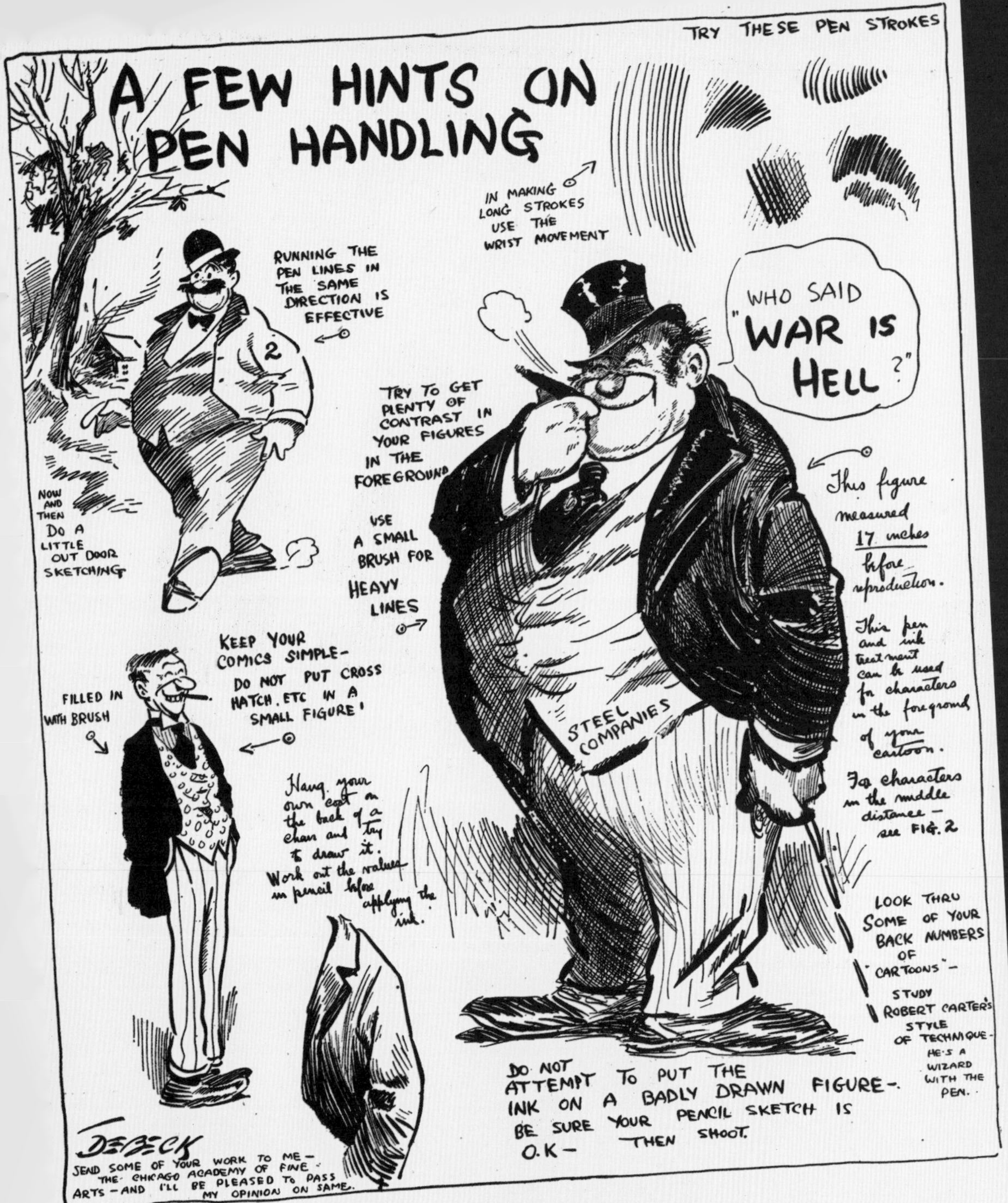
TRY THESE PEN STROKES
A FEW HINTS ON PEN HANDLING
IN MAKING LONG STROKES USE THE WRIST MOVEMENT
RUNNING THE PEN LINES IN THE SAME DIRECTION IS EFFECTIVE
2
WHO SAID "WAR IS HELL?"
TRY TO GET PLENTY OF CONTRAST IN YOUR FIGURES IN THE FOREGROUND
This figure measured 17 inches before reproduction.
NOW AND THEN DO A LITTLE OUT DOOR SKETCHING
USE A SMALL BRUSH FOR HEAVY LINES
This pen and ink treatment can be used for characters in the foreground of your cartoon.
KEEP YOUR COMICS SIMPLE - DO NOT PUT CROSS HATCH, ETC IN A SMALL FIGURE!
FILLED IN WITH BRUSH
STEEL COMPANIES
For characters in the middle distance - see FIG. 2
Hang your own coat on the back of a chair and try to draw it. Work out the values in pencil before applying the ink.
LOOK THRU SOME OF YOUR BACK NUMBERS OF "CARTOONS" - STUDY ROBERT CARTER'S STYLE OF TECHNIQUE - HE'S A WIZARD WITH THE PEN.
DO NOT ATTEMPT TO PUT THE INK ON A BADLY DRAWN FIGURE - BE SURE YOUR PENCIL SKETCH IS O.K - THEN SHOOT.
DEBECK
SEND SOME OF YOUR WORK TO ME - THE CHICAGO ACADEMY OF FINE ARTS - AND I'LL BE PLEASED TO PASS MY OPINION ON SAME.

THE PEN IS MIGHTIER THAN THE SWORD

Another Cartoon Lesson by DeBeck

That Is, If You Know How to Handle It Correctly. The Lines in the Upper Right-Hand Corner Are Not Thumb Marks, but Pen Strokes, Which You must Practice As a Musician Practices His Scales. Brush Work May Also be Used in a Pen-and-Ink Drawing Effectively. Try Out Some of These Hints for Yourself and Send the Result to Mr. DeBeck if You Appreciate Expert Criticism. DeBeck doesn't Care How Much Work You Make for Him—He Is a Glutton for It. Possibly You Are a Genius and Don't Know It

The Master Billy DeBeck gives a revealing lesson in penmanship in "Cartoons Magazine," September 1917. DeBeck rightly cites political cartoonist Robert Carter as one of the pen-and-ink greats.

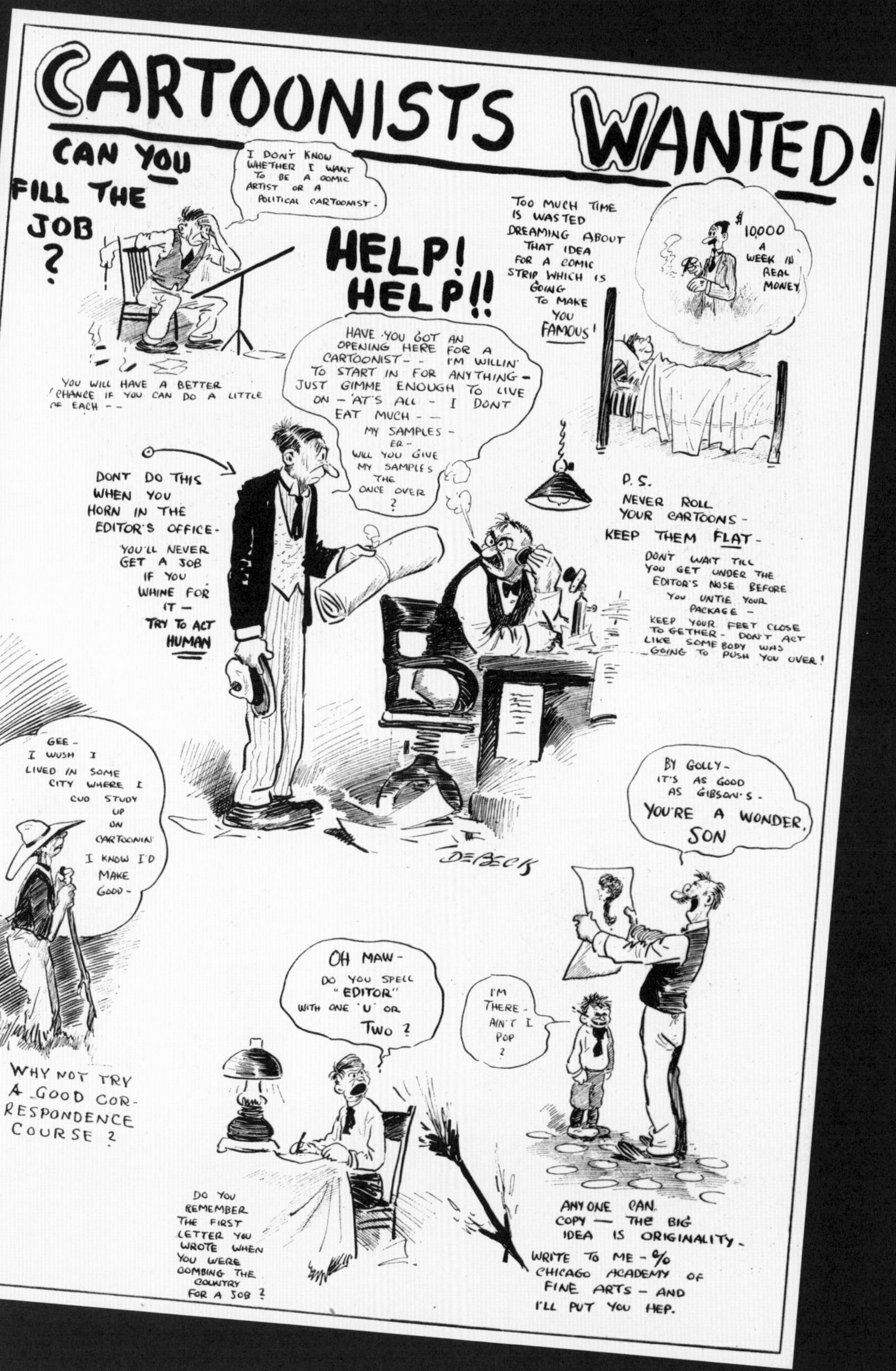
CARTOONISTS WANTED!
CAN YOU FILL THE JOB ?
I DON'T KNOW WHETHER I WANT TO BE A COMIC ARTIST OR A POLITICAL CARTOONIST -
YOU WILL HAVE A BETTER CHANCE IF YOU CAN DO A LITTLE OF EACH - -
HELP! HELP!!
TOO MUCH TIME IS WASTED DREAMING ABOUT THAT IDEA FOR A COMIC STRIP WHICH IS GOING TO MAKE YOU FAMOUS!
$10,000 A WEEK IN REAL MONEY
HAVE YOU GOT AN OPENING HERE FOR A CARTOONIST - - I'M WILLIN' TO START IN FOR ANYTHING - JUST GIMME ENOUGH TO LIVE ON - AT'S ALL - I DONT EAT MUCH - - MY SAMPLES - ER - WILL YOU GIVE MY SAMPLES THE ONCE OVER ?
DONT DO THIS WHEN YOU HORN IN THE EDITOR'S OFFICE - YOU'LL NEVER GET A JOB IF YOU WHINE FOR IT - TRY TO ACT HUMAN
P. S. NEVER ROLL YOUR CARTOONS - KEEP THEM FLAT -
DON'T WAIT TILL YOU GET UNDER THE EDITOR'S NOSE BEFORE YOU UNTIE YOUR PACKAGE - KEEP YOUR FEET CLOSE TO GETHER - DON'T ACT LIKE SOME BODY WAS GOING TO PUSH YOU OVER!
GEE - I WUSH I LIVED IN SOME CITY WHERE I CUD STUDY UP ON CARTOONIN' I KNOW I'D MAKE GOOD -
WHY NOT TRY A GOOD COR-RESPONDENCE COURSE ?
DEBECK
BY GOLLY - IT'S AS GOOD AS GIBSON'S - YOU'RE A WONDER, SON
I'M THERE - AIN'T I POP ?
OH MAW - DO YOU SPELL "EDITOR" WITH ONE 'U' OR TWO ?
DO YOU REMEMBER THE FIRST LETTER YOU WROTE WHEN YOU WERE COMBING THE COUNTRY FOR A JOB ?
ANY ONE CAN COPY — THE BIG IDEA IS ORIGINALITY.
WRITE TO ME - c/o CHICAGO ACADEMY OF FINE ARTS - AND I'LL PUT YOU HEP.

A DeBeck advertorial comic from "Cartoons Magazine," October 1917. The artist gives budding cartoonists practical advice, including no whining! In the bottom right vignette, DeBeck pays a tribute to Charles Dana Gibson's cartoon "The Eternal Question."

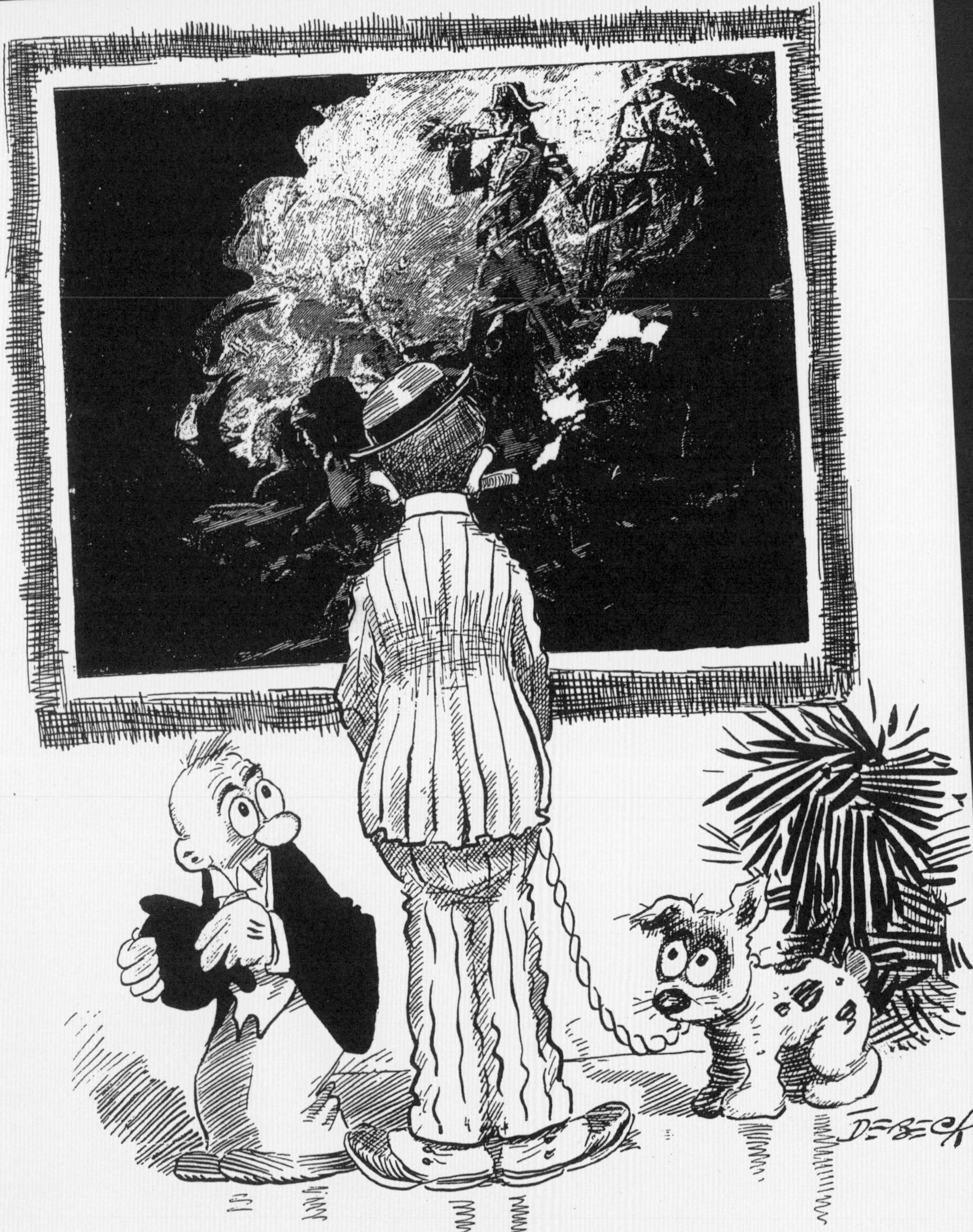
DEBECK

Barney: "Come on, Boss—I feel like a hoss in a garage!"

Billy DeBeck makes a wry comment about Fine Art in "Circulation Magazine," 1921.

Left: From the collection of the author.
Opposite: Courtesy of Bill Janocha.

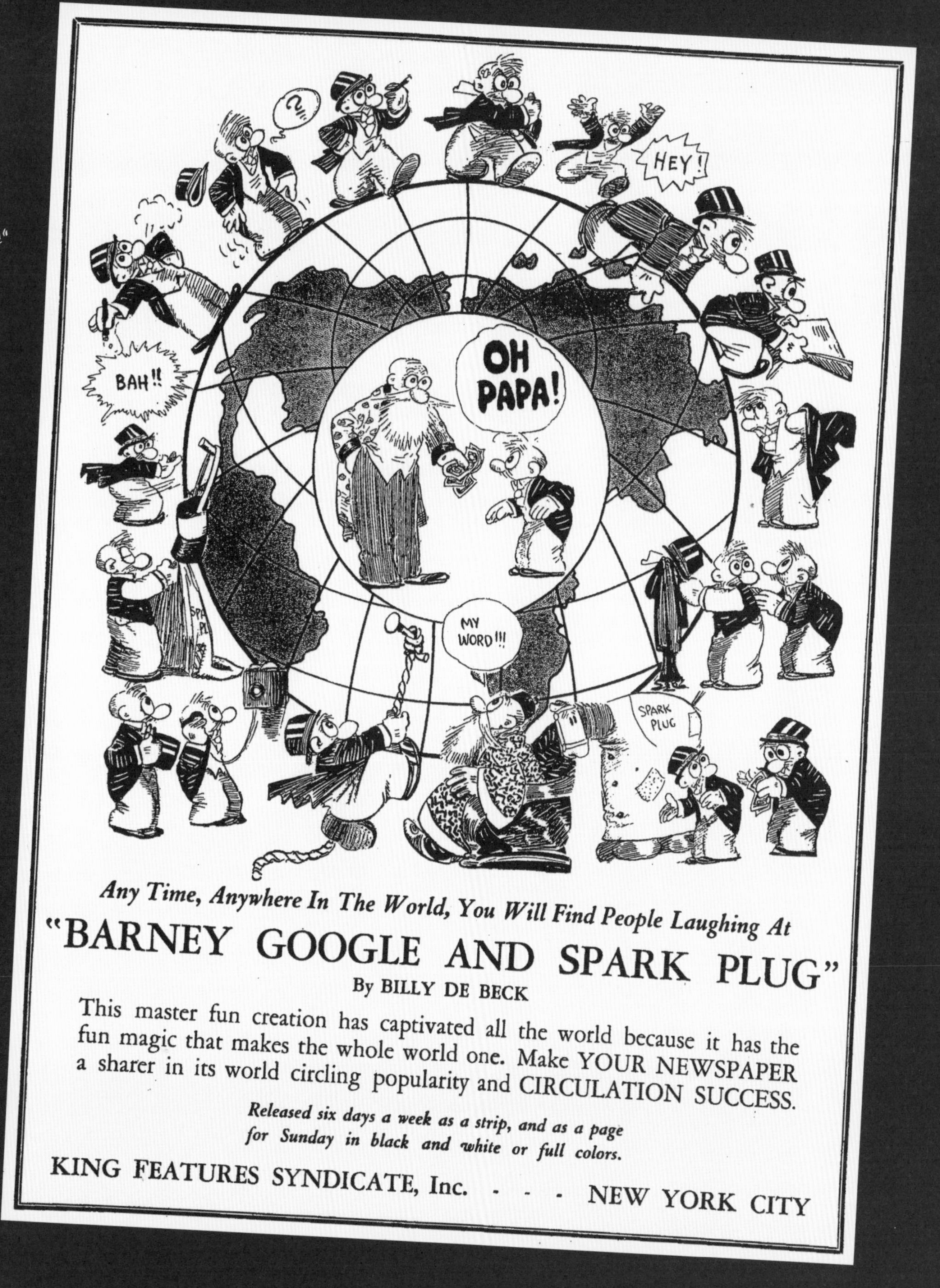
?
HEY!
OH PAPA!
BAH!!
MY WORD!!!
SPARK PLUG
Any Time, Anywhere In The World, You Will Find People Laughing At
"BARNEY GOOGLE AND SPARK PLUG"
By BILLY DE BECK
This master fun creation has captivated all the world because it has the fun magic that makes the whole world one. Make YOUR NEWSPAPER a sharer in its world circling popularity and CIRCULATION SUCCESS.
Released six days a week as a strip, and as a page for Sunday in black and white or full colors.
KING FEATURES SYNDICATE, Inc. - - - NEW YORK CITY

A "Circulation Magazine" ad from the 1920s.

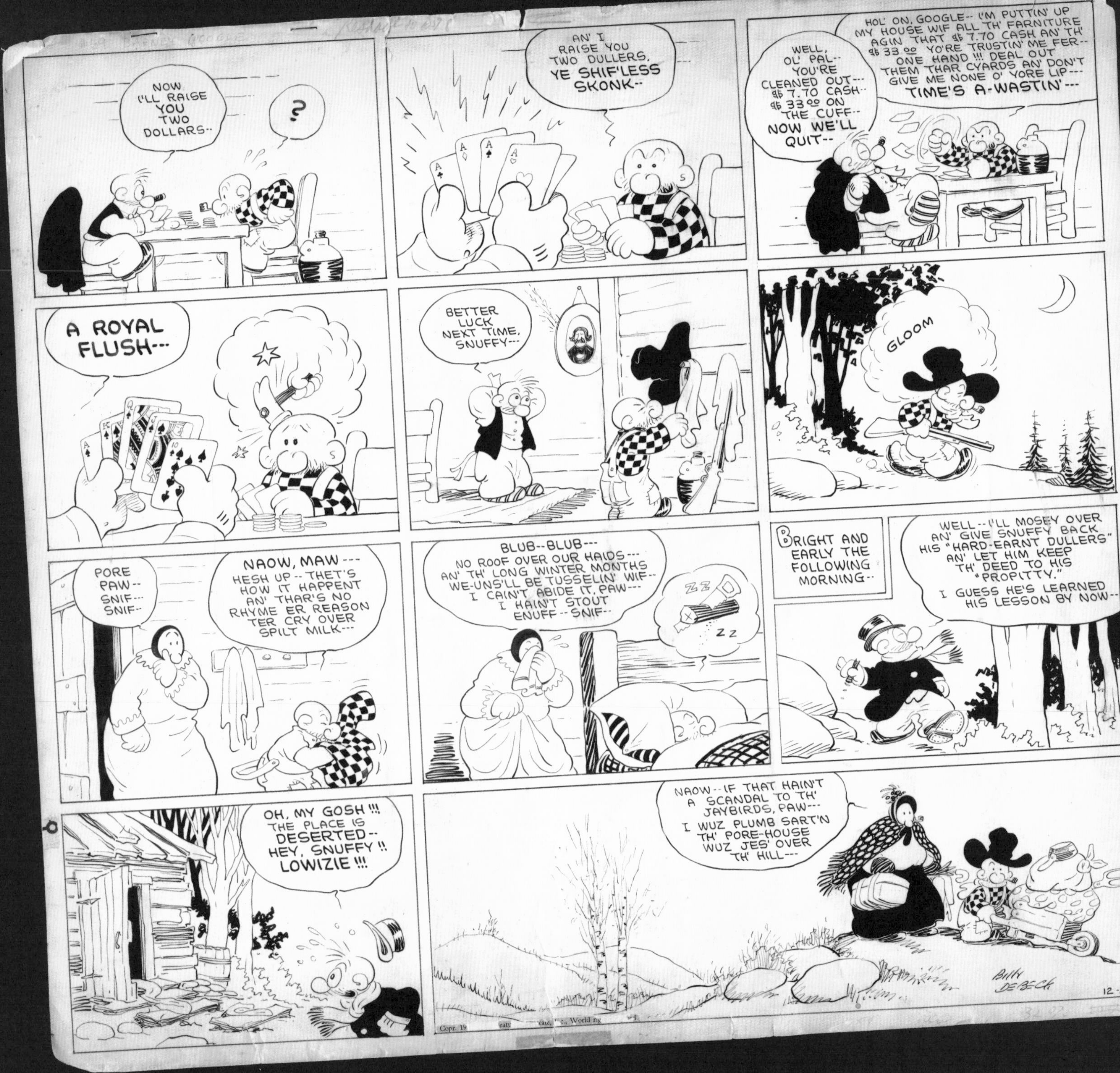
NOW I'LL RAISE YOU TWO DOLLARS--
?
AN' I RAISE YOU TWO DULLERS, YE SHIF'LESS SKONK--
WELL, OL' PAL-- YOU'RE CLEANED OUT--- $7.70 CASH-- $33.00 ON THE CUFF-- NOW WE'LL QUIT--
HOL' ON, GOOGLE-- I'M PUTTIN' UP MY HOUSE WIF ALL TH' FARNITURE AGIN THAT $7.70 CASH AN' TH' $33.00 YO'RE TRUSTIN' ME FER-- ONE HAND !!! DEAL OUT THEM THAR CYARDS AN' DON'T GIVE ME NONE O' YORE LIP--- TIME'S A-WASTIN'---
A ROYAL FLUSH---
BETTER LUCK NEXT TIME, SNUFFY---
GLOOM
PORE PAW-- SNIF--- SNIF--
NAOW, MAW--- HESH UP-- THET'S HOW IT HAPPENT AN' THAR'S NO RHYME ER REASON TER CRY OVER SPILT MILK---
BLUB--BLUB--- NO ROOF OVER OUR HAIDS--- AN' TH' LONG WINTER MONTHS WE-UNS'LL BE TUSSELIN' WIF-- I CAIN'T ABIDE IT, PAW--- I HAIN'T STOUT ENUFF--SNIF--
BRIGHT AND EARLY THE FOLLOWING MORNING--
WELL--I'LL MOSEY OVER AN' GIVE SNUFFY BACK HIS "HARD-EARNT DULLERS" AN' LET HIM KEEP TH' DEED TO HIS "PROPITTY." I GUESS HE'S LEARNED HIS LESSON BY NOW--
OH, MY GOSH !!! THE PLACE IS DESERTED-- HEY, SNUFFY !! LOWIZIE !!!
NAOW--IF THAT HAIN'T A SCANDAL TO TH' JAYBIRDS, PAW--- I WUZ PLUMB SART'N TH' PORE-HOUSE WUZ JES' OVER TH' HILL---
BILLY DEBECK
12-26

This 1937 newspaper strip appeared in the famous book "Comic Art in America" (1959). The caption there read, "A backwoodsy Barney Google of 1937. The city slicker outslicks himself. The last long panel is fine for both depth of field and humorous pathos." The above is reproduced from the original art.

Above: From the collection of the author.
Opposite: Courtesy of the Special Collections, James Branch Cabell Library, Virginia Commonwealth University.

It is reported that this image was painted on a door of one of Billy DeBeck's homes. It is now in a special archive at Virginia Commonwealth University.

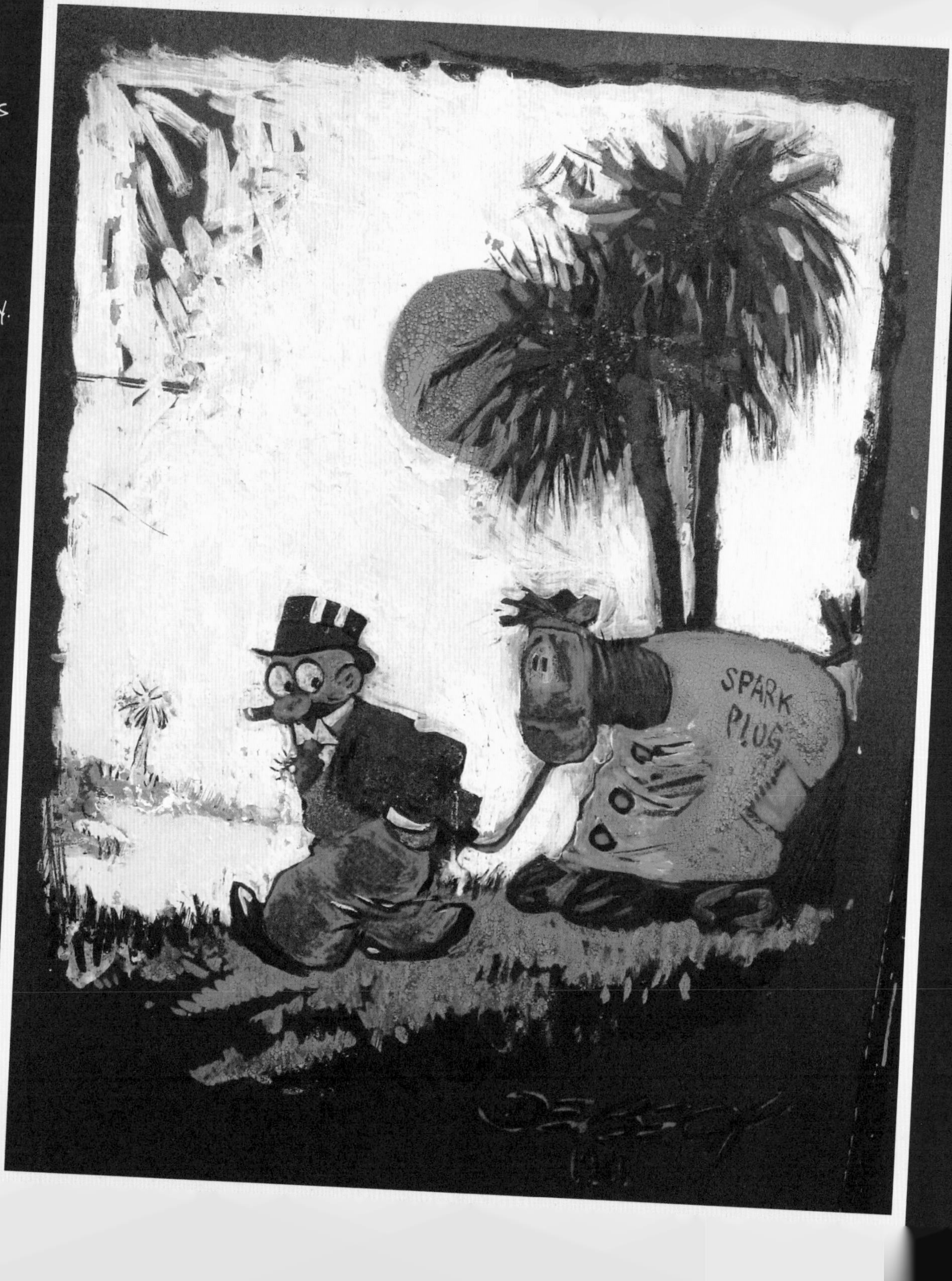
SPARK
PLUG

Waiting's the Easiest Thing Barney Can Do

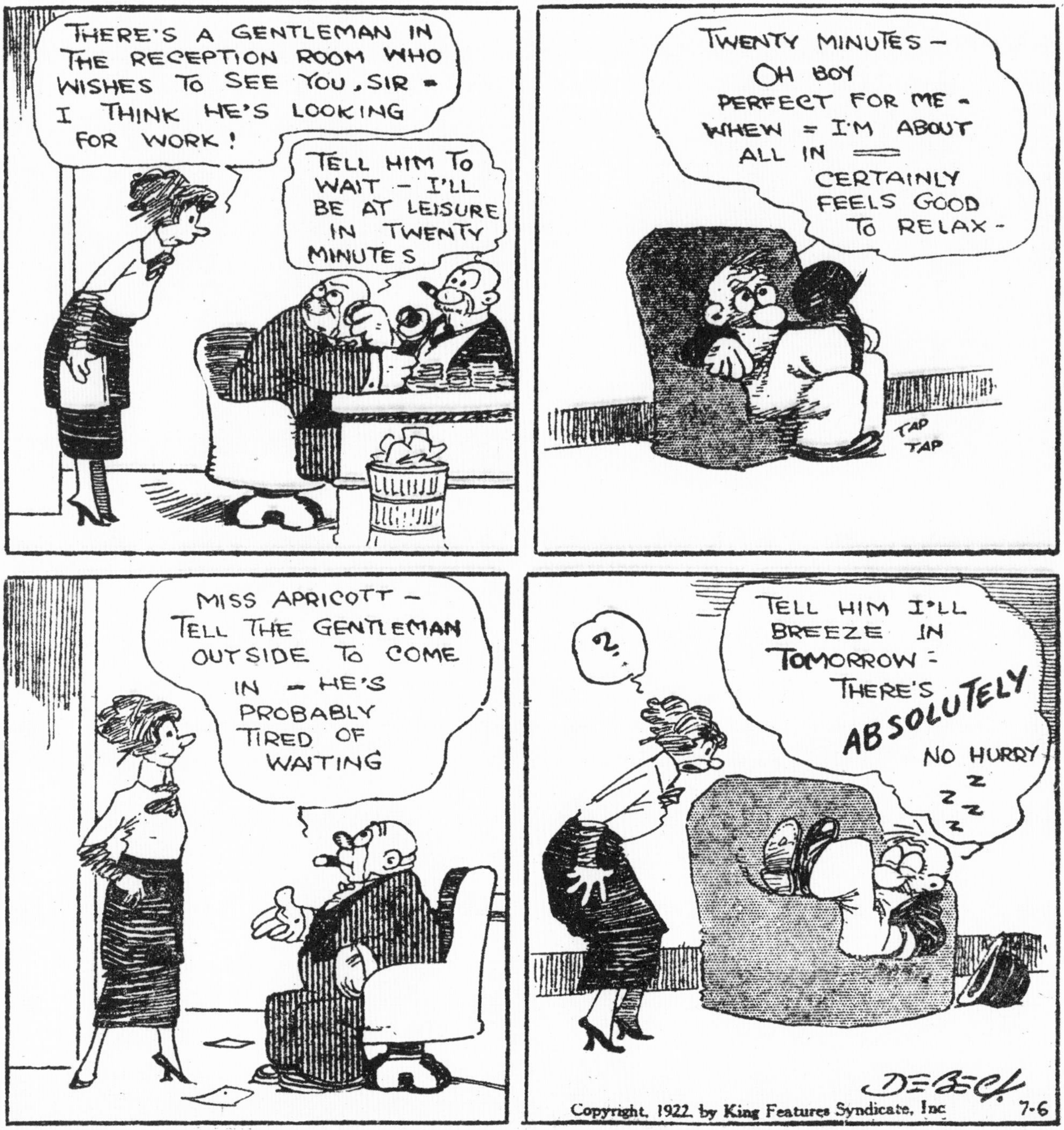
THERE'S A GENTLEMAN IN THE RECEPTION ROOM WHO WISHES TO SEE YOU, SIR - I THINK HE'S LOOKING FOR WORK!
TELL HIM TO WAIT - I'LL BE AT LEISURE IN TWENTY MINUTES
TWENTY MINUTES - OH BOY PERFECT FOR ME - WHEW = I'M ABOUT ALL IN = CERTAINLY FEELS GOOD TO RELAX -
TAP TAP
MISS APRICOTT - TELL THE GENTLEMAN OUTSIDE TO COME IN - HE'S PROBABLY TIRED OF WAITING
?
TELL HIM I'LL BREEZE IN TOMORROW - THERE'S ABSOLUTELY NO HURRY
Z Z Z Z
DEBECK
Copyright, 1922, by King Features Syndicate, Inc
7-6

If Barney Lives Long Enough There'll Be No Trouble About His Future

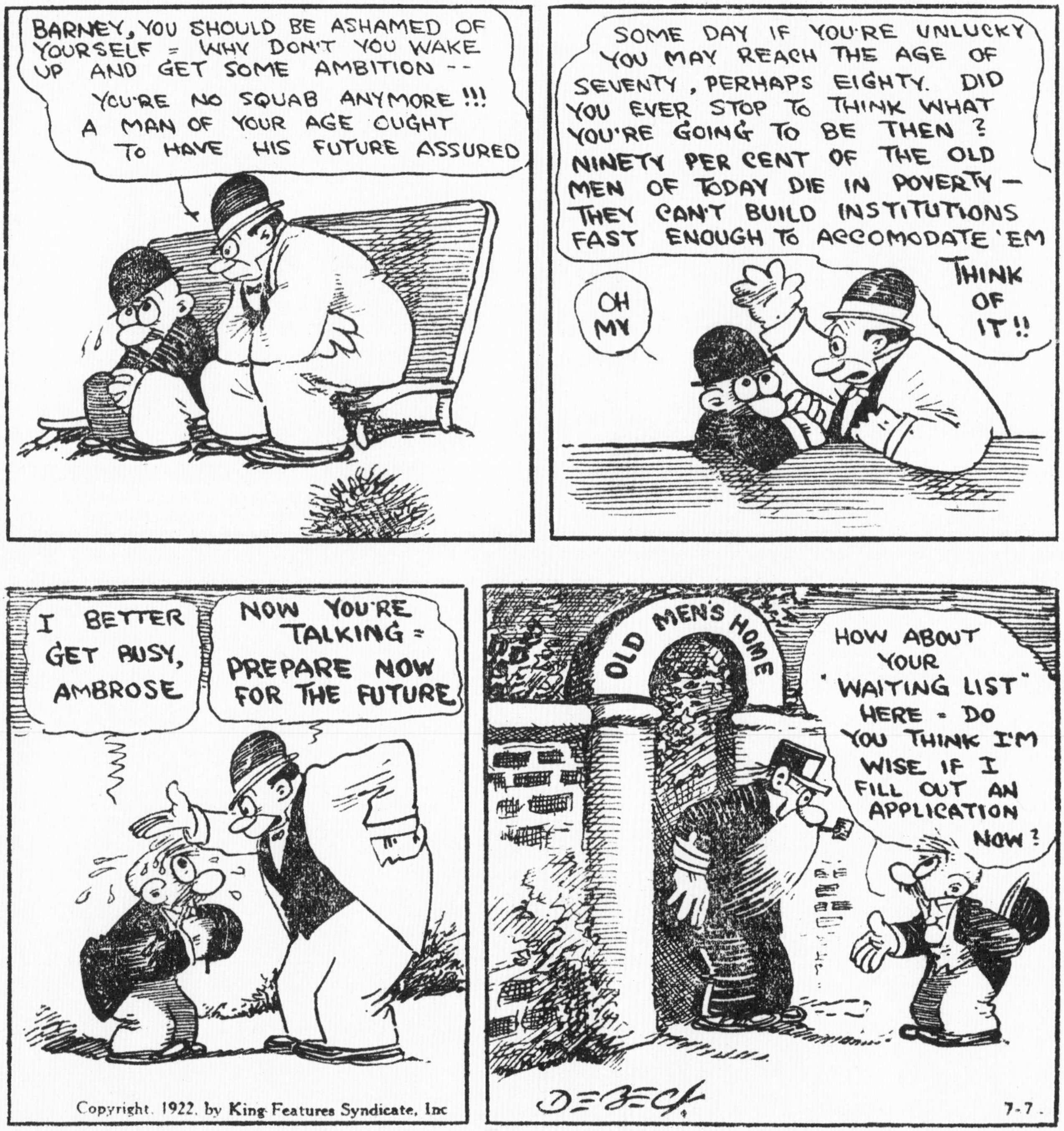

BARNEY, YOU SHOULD BE ASHAMED OF YOURSELF = WHY DON'T YOU WAKE UP AND GET SOME AMBITION -- YOU'RE NO SQUAB ANYMORE !!! A MAN OF YOUR AGE OUGHT TO HAVE HIS FUTURE ASSURED
SOME DAY IF YOU'RE UNLUCKY YOU MAY REACH THE AGE OF SEVENTY, PERHAPS EIGHTY. DID YOU EVER STOP TO THINK WHAT YOU'RE GOING TO BE THEN ? NINETY PER CENT OF THE OLD MEN OF TODAY DIE IN POVERTY - THEY CAN'T BUILD INSTITUTIONS FAST ENOUGH TO ACCOMODATE 'EM
OH MY
THINK OF IT!!
I BETTER GET BUSY, AMBROSE
NOW YOU'RE TALKING = PREPARE NOW FOR THE FUTURE
OLD MEN'S HOME
HOW ABOUT YOUR "WAITING LIST" HERE = DO YOU THINK I'M WISE IF I FILL OUT AN APPLICATION NOW ?
Copyright, 1922, by King Features Syndicate, Inc
DEBECK
7-7.

When It Comes to Betting Barney Always Goes the Limit

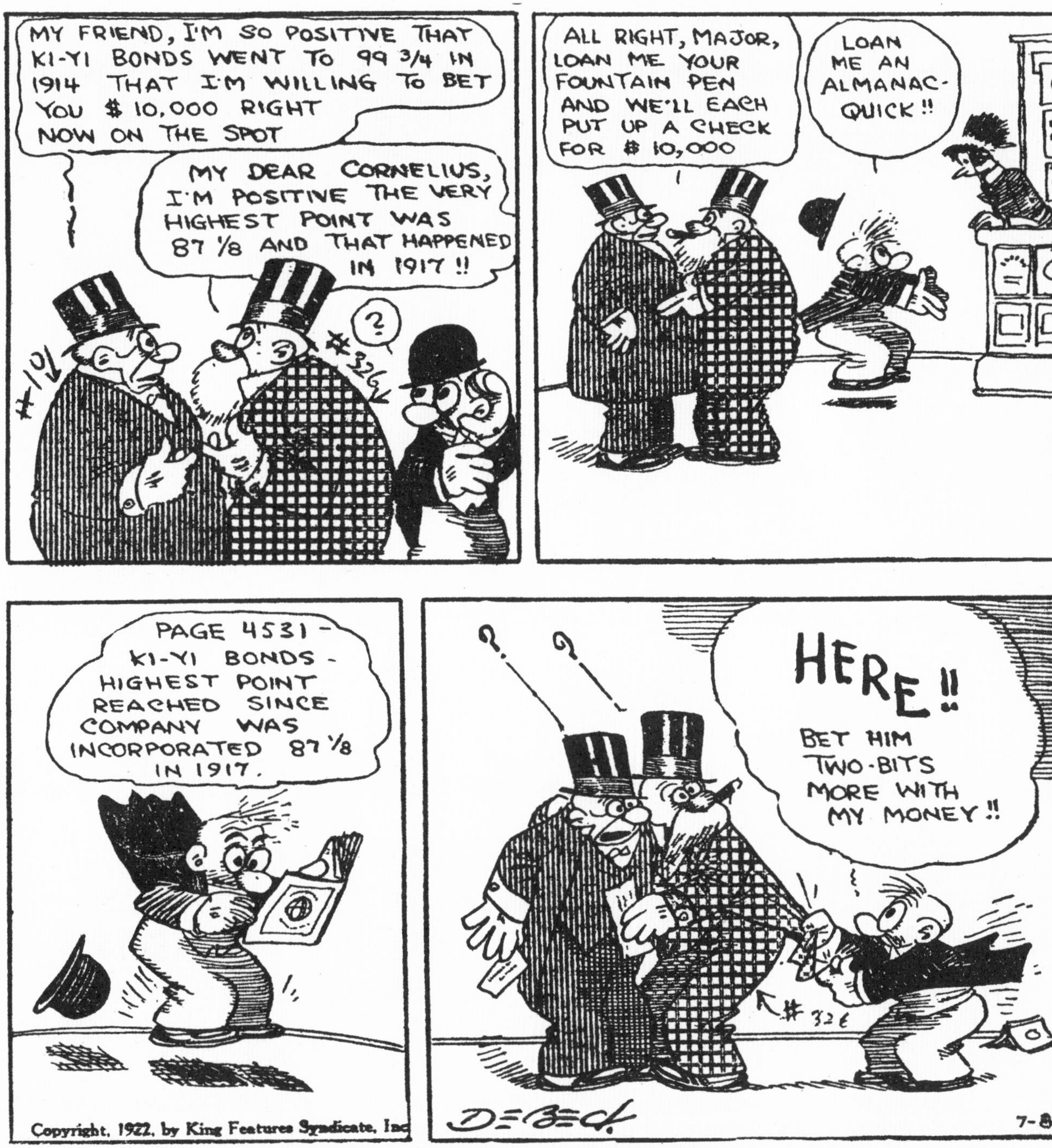
MY FRIEND, I'M SO POSITIVE THAT KI-YI BONDS WENT TO 99 3/4 IN 1914 THAT I'M WILLING TO BET YOU $ 10,000 RIGHT NOW ON THE SPOT
MY DEAR CORNELIUS, I'M POSITIVE THE VERY HIGHEST POINT WAS 87 1/8 AND THAT HAPPENED IN 1917!!
#1
?
#326
ALL RIGHT, MAJOR, LOAN ME YOUR FOUNTAIN PEN AND WE'LL EACH PUT UP A CHECK FOR $ 10,000
LOAN ME AN ALMANAC - QUICK!!
PAGE 4531 - KI-YI BONDS - HIGHEST POINT REACHED SINCE COMPANY WAS INCORPORATED 87 1/8 IN 1917.
Copyright, 1922, by King Features Syndicate, Inc
?
?
HERE!!
BET HIM TWO-BITS MORE WITH MY MONEY!!
#326
DEBECK
7-8

Well, Anyhow, Barney Gets His Wish

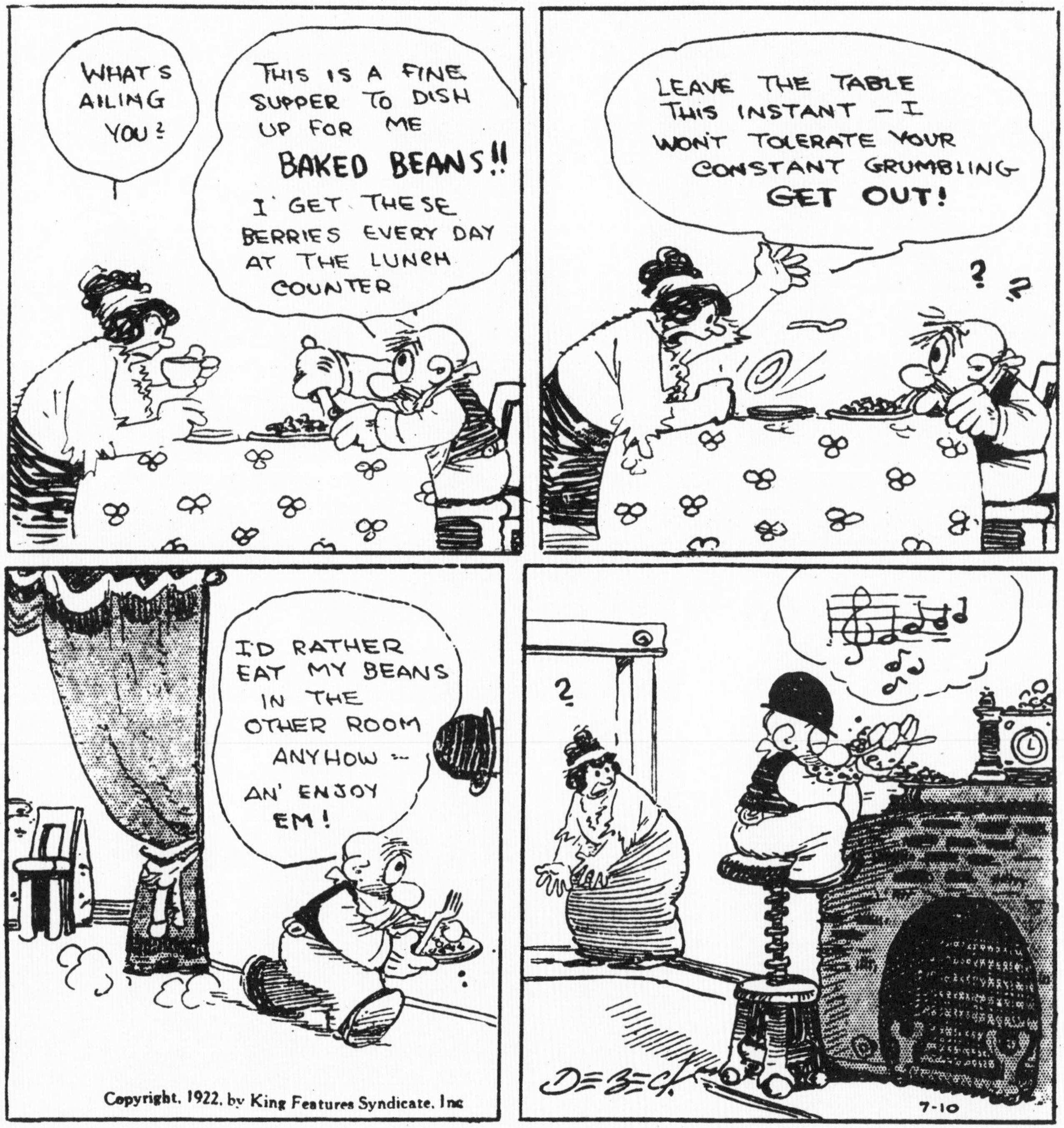

WHAT'S AILING YOU?
THIS IS A FINE SUPPER TO DISH UP FOR ME BAKED BEANS!! I GET THESE BERRIES EVERY DAY AT THE LUNCH COUNTER
LEAVE THE TABLE THIS INSTANT — I WON'T TOLERATE YOUR CONSTANT GRUMBLING GET OUT!
? ?
I'D RATHER EAT MY BEANS IN THE OTHER ROOM ANYHOW -- AN' ENJOY EM!
?
DE BECK
7-10

Barney Had to Figure Out Which One He Could Best Spare

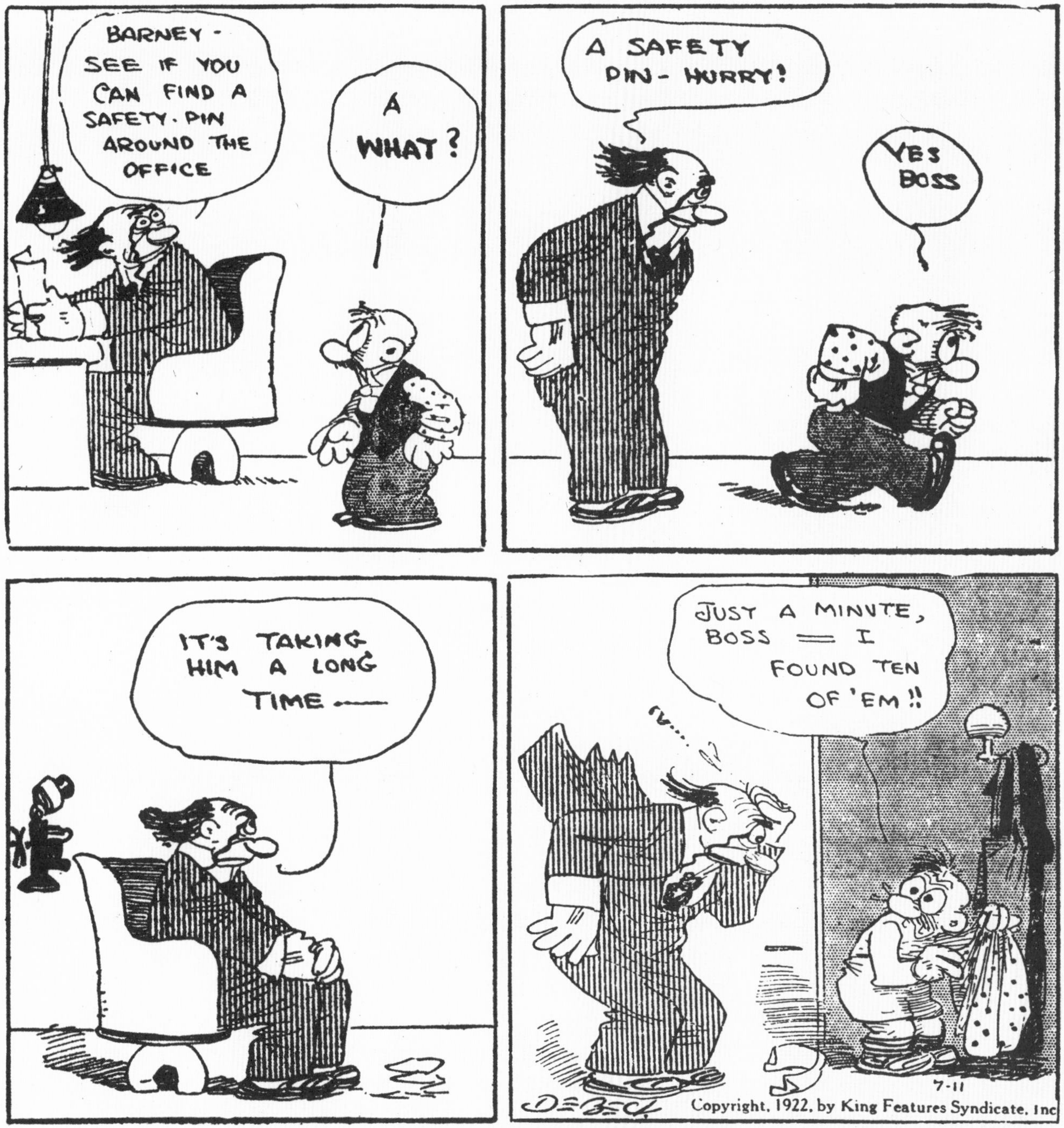
BARNEY - SEE IF YOU CAN FIND A SAFETY-PIN AROUND THE OFFICE
A WHAT?
A SAFETY PIN - HURRY!
YES BOSS
IT'S TAKING HIM A LONG TIME —
JUST A MINUTE, BOSS — I FOUND TEN OF 'EM!!
7-11
DE BECK
Copyright, 1922, by King Features Syndicate, Inc

Barney "Picks" a Good Place

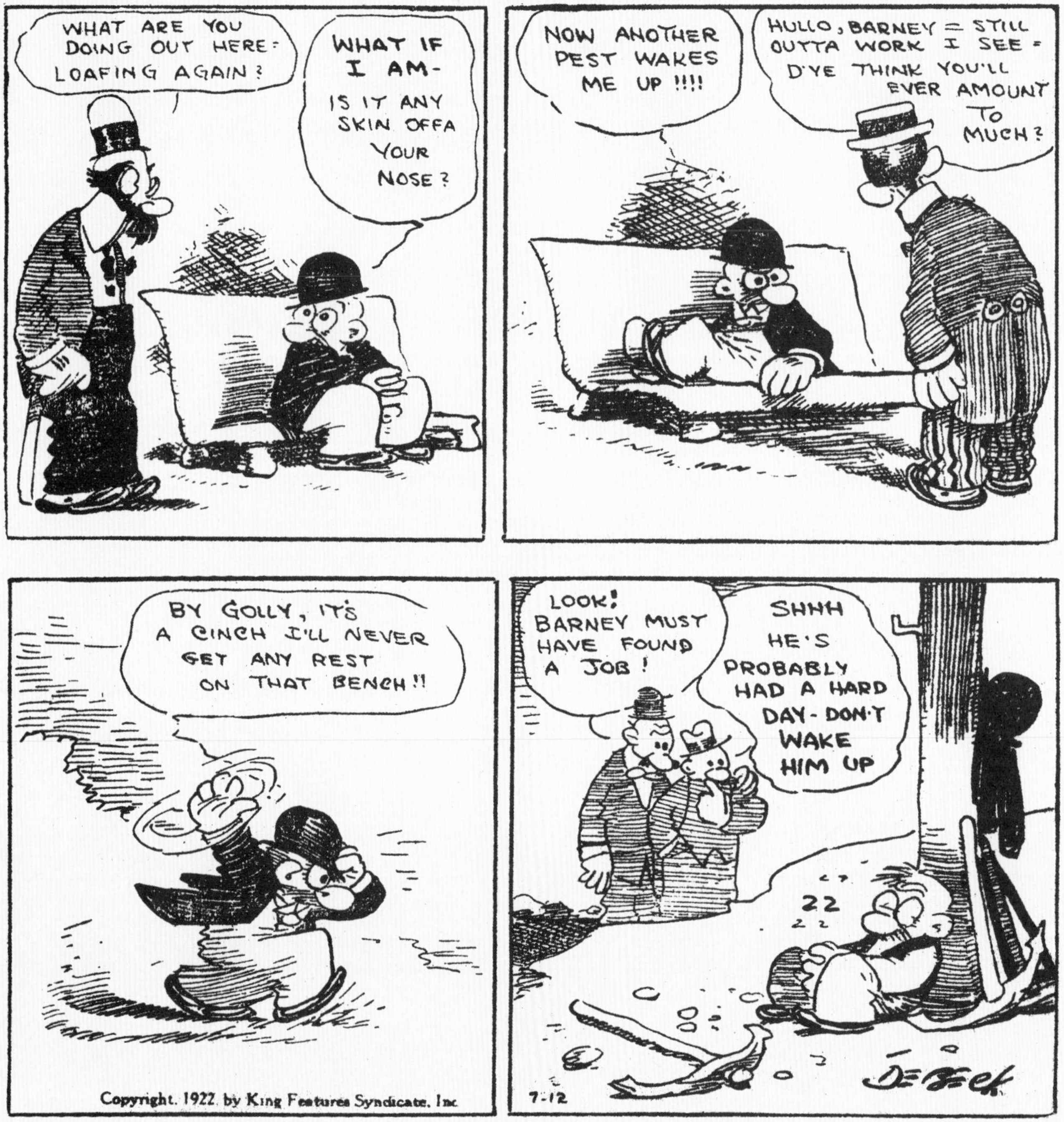
WHAT ARE YOU DOING OUT HERE= LOAFING AGAIN?
WHAT IF I AM- IS IT ANY SKIN OFFA YOUR NOSE?
NOW ANOTHER PEST WAKES ME UP !!!!
HULLO, BARNEY = STILL OUTTA WORK I SEE = D'YE THINK YOU'LL EVER AMOUNT TO MUCH?
BY GOLLY, IT'S A CINCH I'LL NEVER GET ANY REST ON THAT BENCH!!
LOOK! BARNEY MUST HAVE FOUND A JOB!
SHHH HE'S PROBABLY HAD A HARD DAY- DON'T WAKE HIM UP
ZZ
Copyright. 1922. by King Features Syndicate, Inc.
7-12
DE BECK

Barney'd Never Pass Up a Chance Like This

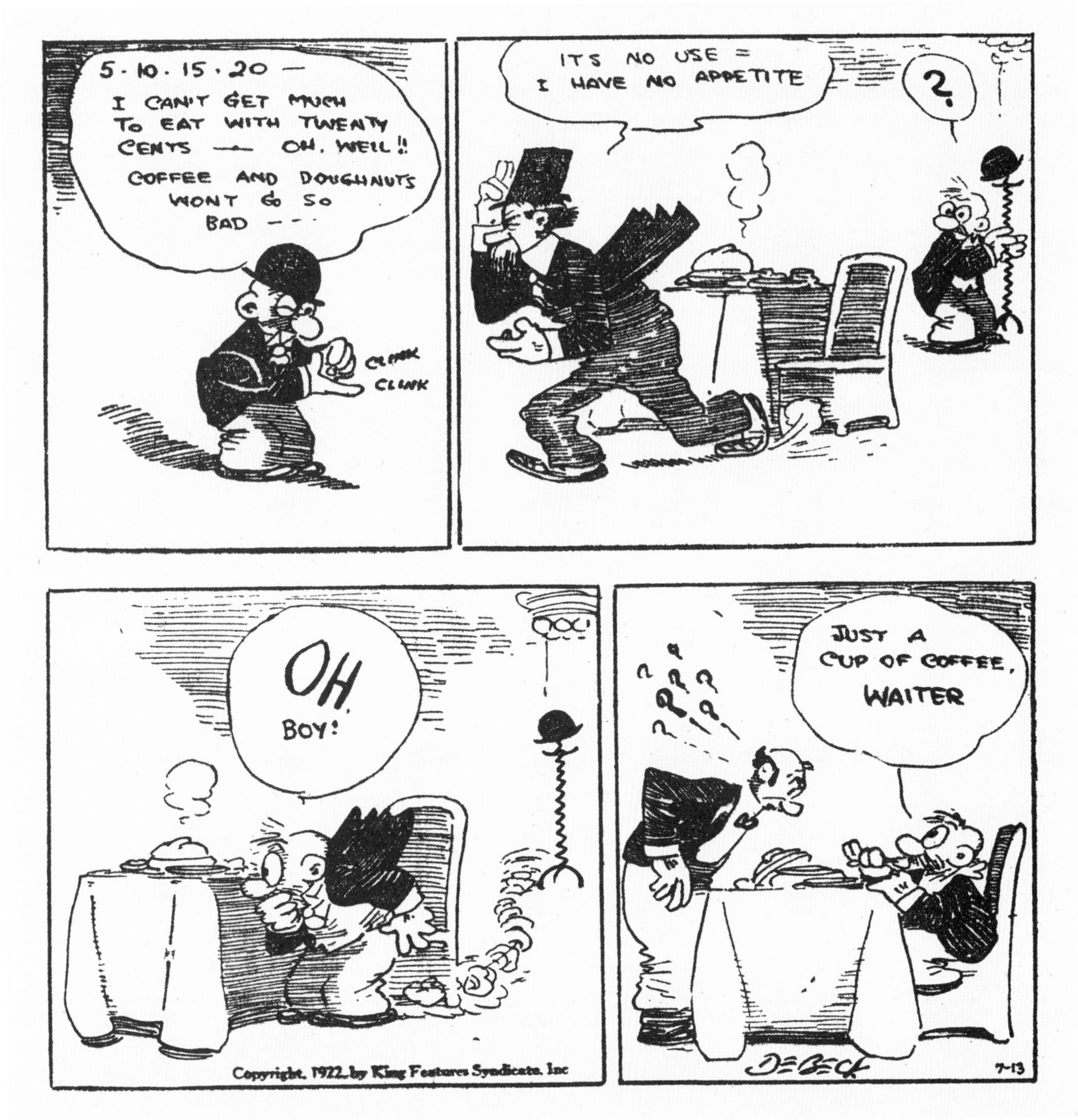
5 · 10 · 15 · 20 —
I CAN'T GET MUCH TO EAT WITH TWENTY CENTS — OH, WELL!! COFFEE AND DOUGHNUTS WONT GO SO BAD ---
CLINK CLINK
ITS NO USE = I HAVE NO APPETITE
?
OH. BOY!
JUST A CUP OF COFFEE, WAITER
Copyright, 1922, by King Features Syndicate, Inc
DEBECK
7-13

It Took All of Barney's Courage Even to Do This

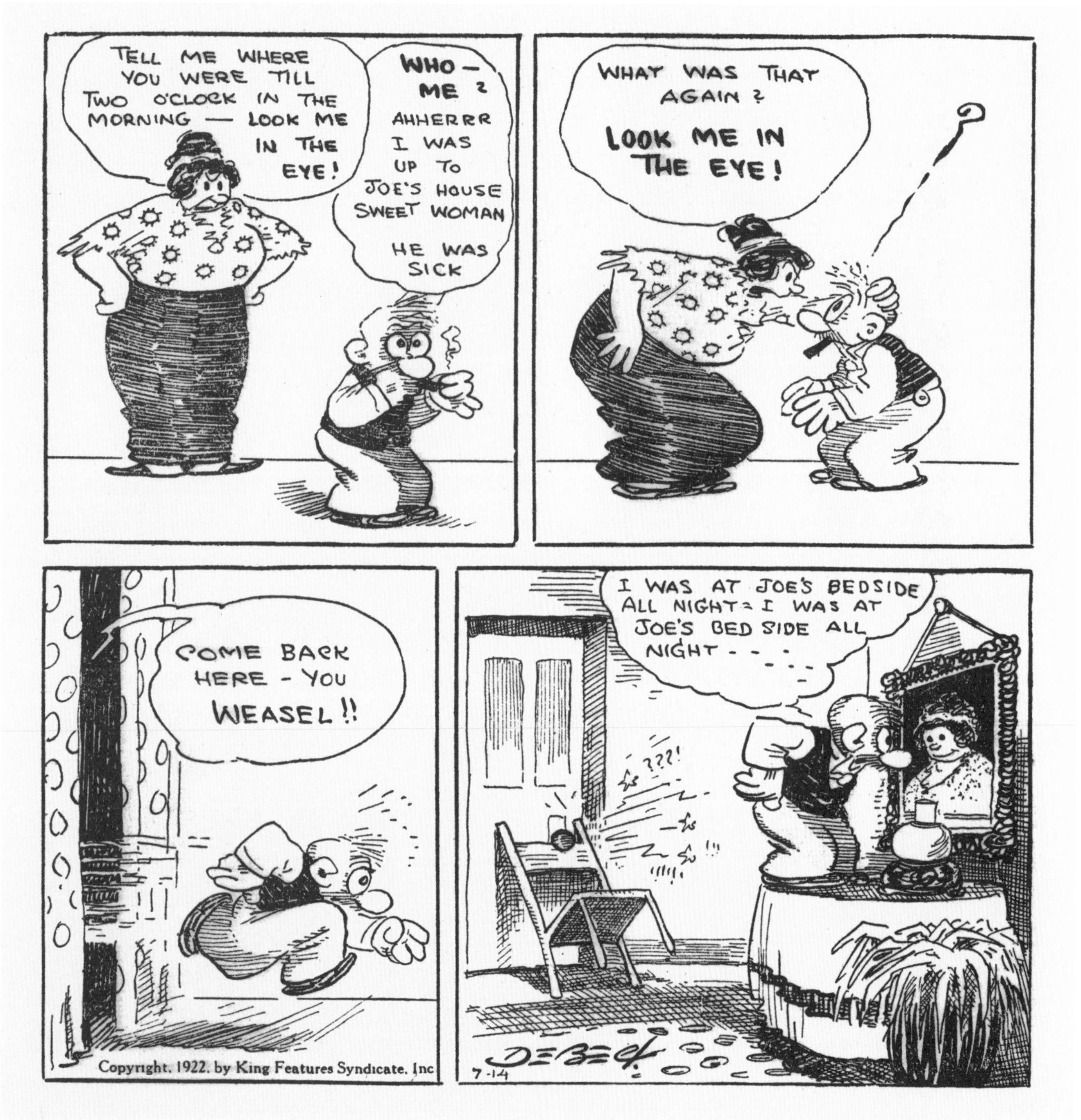
TELL ME WHERE YOU WERE TILL TWO O'CLOCK IN THE MORNING — LOOK ME IN THE EYE!
WHO — ME ? AHHERRR I WAS UP TO JOE'S HOUSE SWEET WOMAN HE WAS SICK
WHAT WAS THAT AGAIN ? LOOK ME IN THE EYE!
?
COME BACK HERE - YOU WEASEL !!
I WAS AT JOE'S BEDSIDE ALL NIGHT = I WAS AT JOE'S BED SIDE ALL NIGHT - - - - - -
???!
!!
Copyright, 1922, by King Features Syndicate, Inc
DE BECK
7-14

Barney Has an Eye to the Future

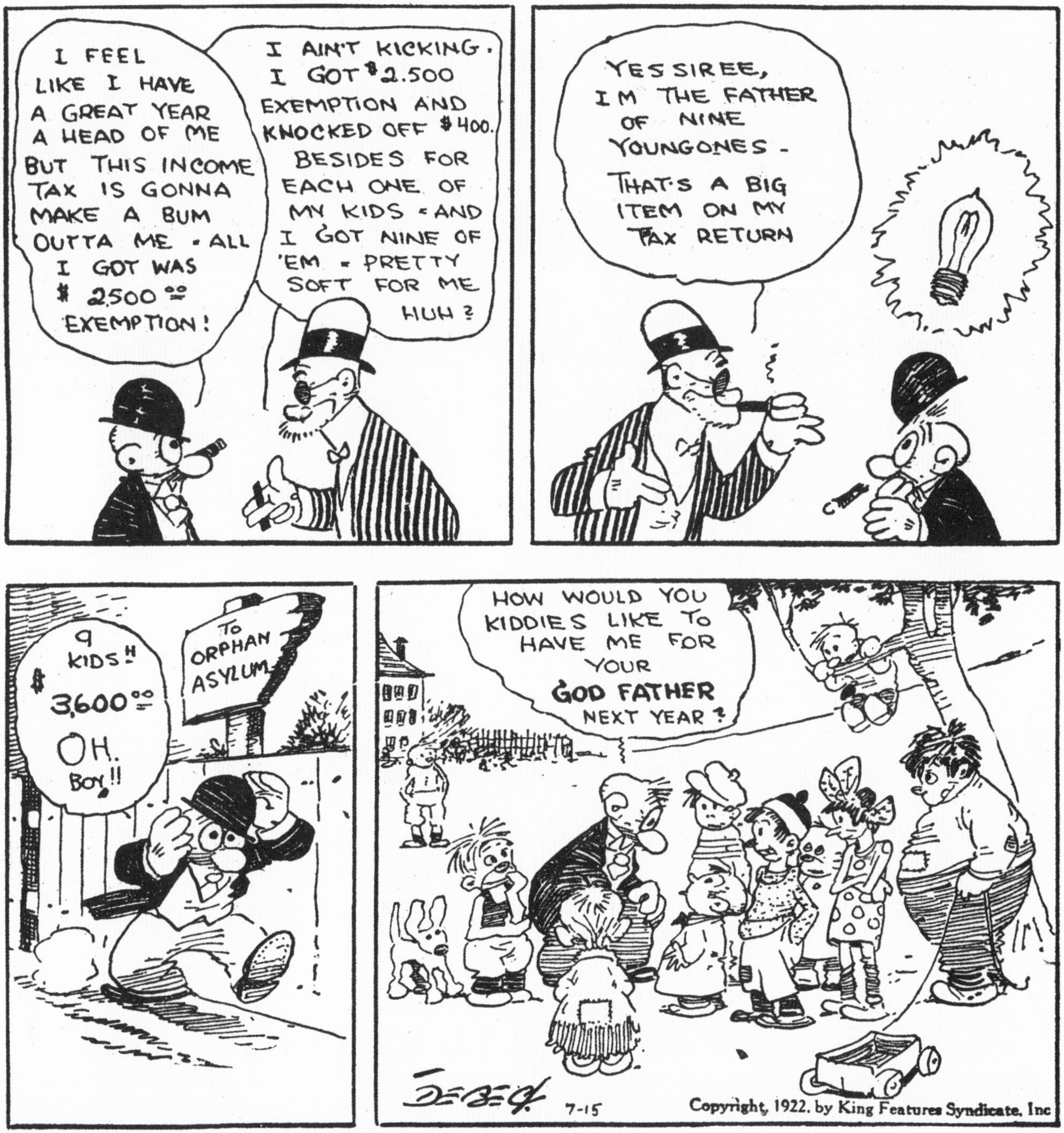
I FEEL LIKE I HAVE A GREAT YEAR A HEAD OF ME BUT THIS INCOME TAX IS GONNA MAKE A BUM OUTTA ME - ALL I GOT WAS $ 2500.00 EXEMPTION!
I AIN'T KICKING. I GOT $2.500 EXEMPTION AND KNOCKED OFF $400. BESIDES FOR EACH ONE OF MY KIDS - AND I GOT NINE OF 'EM - PRETTY SOFT FOR ME HUH?
YES SIREE, I'M THE FATHER OF NINE YOUNGONES - THAT'S A BIG ITEM ON MY TAX RETURN
9 KIDS!! $ 3,600.00 OH. BOY!!
TO ORPHAN ASYLUM
HOW WOULD YOU KIDDIES LIKE TO HAVE ME FOR YOUR GOD FATHER NEXT YEAR?
7-15
Copyright, 1922, by King Features Syndicate, Inc

Barney's Troubles Are Either Over—or Just Beginning

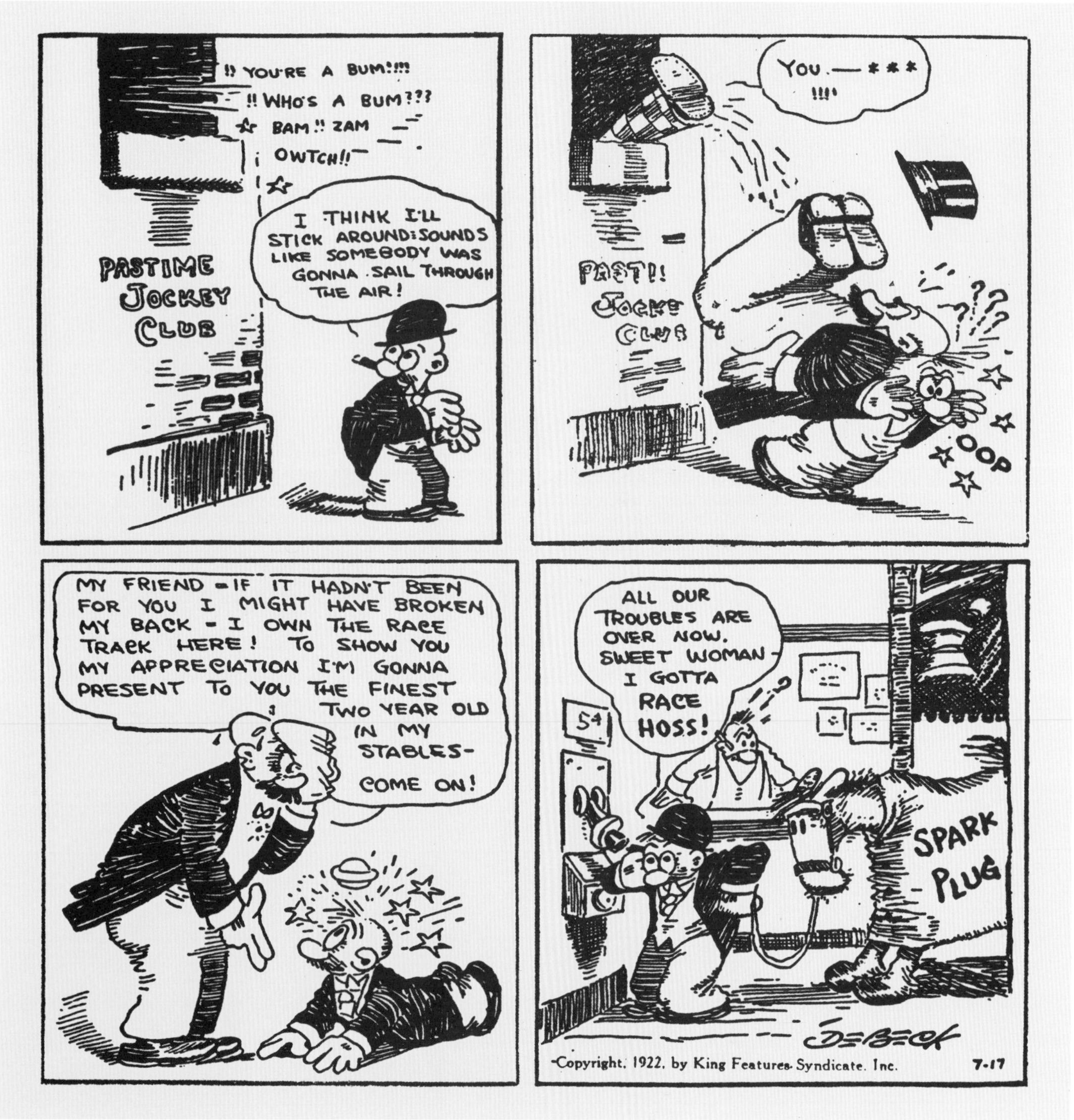
!! YOU'RE A BUM!!!!
!! WHO'S A BUM???
BAM !! ZAM
OWTCH!!
I THINK I'LL STICK AROUND: SOUNDS LIKE SOMEBODY WAS GONNA SAIL THROUGH THE AIR!
PASTIME JOCKEY CLUB
YOU. — * * * !!!'
OOP
MY FRIEND - IF IT HADN'T BEEN FOR YOU I MIGHT HAVE BROKEN MY BACK - I OWN THE RACE TRACK HERE! TO SHOW YOU MY APPRECIATION I'M GONNA PRESENT TO YOU THE FINEST TWO YEAR OLD IN MY STABLES - COME ON!
ALL OUR TROUBLES ARE OVER NOW, SWEET WOMAN - I GOTTA RACE HOSS!
SPARK PLUG
DE BECK
Copyright, 1922, by King Features Syndicate, Inc.
7-17

It's Three Bucks and Out for Barney and His Plug

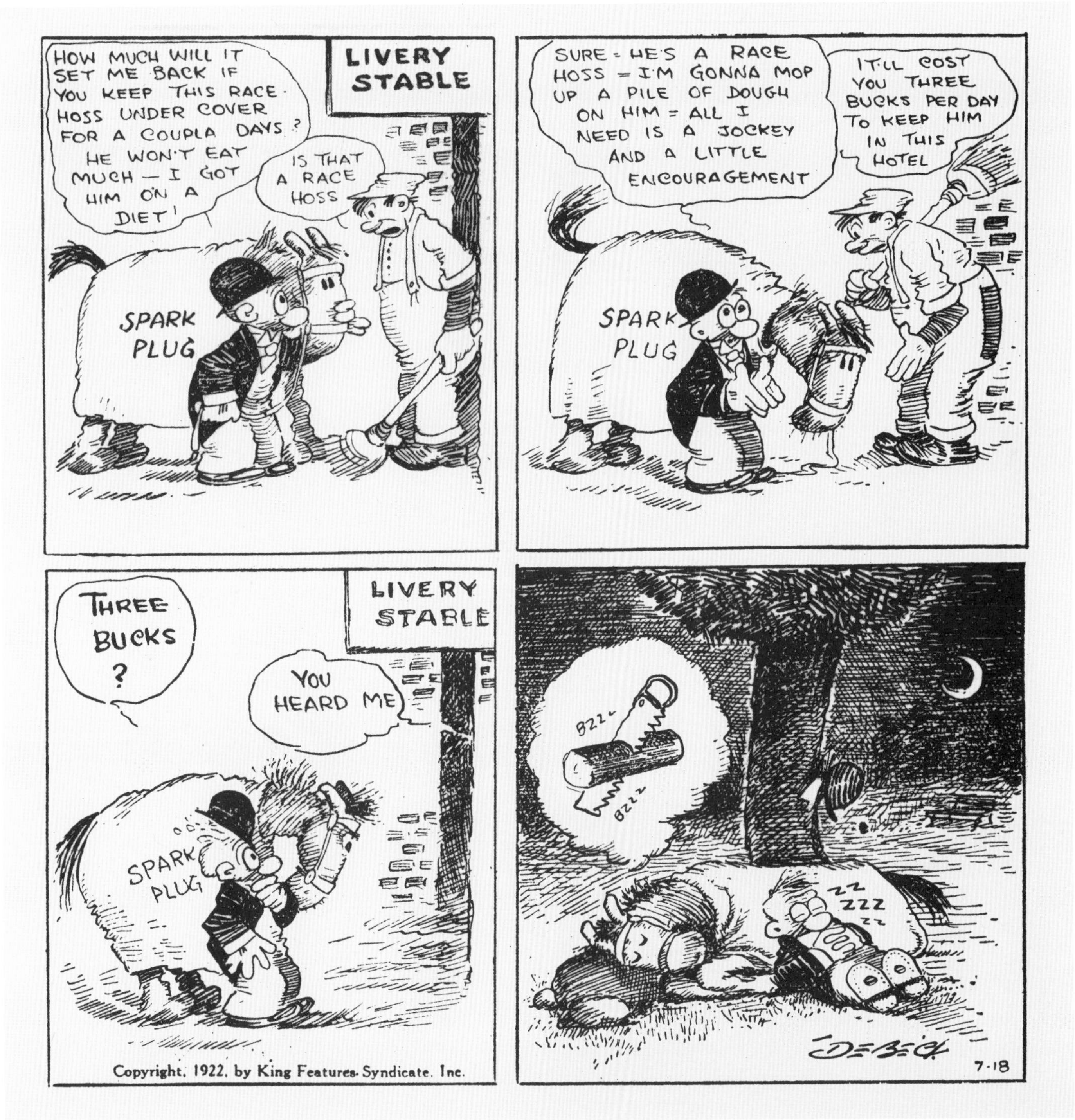
LIVERY STABLE
HOW MUCH WILL IT SET ME BACK IF YOU KEEP THIS RACE HOSS UNDER COVER FOR A COUPLA DAYS? HE WON'T EAT MUCH — I GOT HIM ON A DIET!
IS THAT A RACE HOSS
SPARK PLUG
SURE - HE'S A RACE HOSS - I'M GONNA MOP UP A PILE OF DOUGH ON HIM - ALL I NEED IS A JOCKEY AND A LITTLE ENCOURAGEMENT
IT'LL COST YOU THREE BUCKS PER DAY TO KEEP HIM IN THIS HOTEL
SPARK PLUG
LIVERY STABLE
THREE BUCKS ?
YOU HEARD ME
SPARK PLUG
BZZ
BZZZ
ZZ ZZZ ZZ
Copyright, 1922, by King Features Syndicate, Inc.
DE BECK
7-18

Barney Finds It Hard to Keep Cool

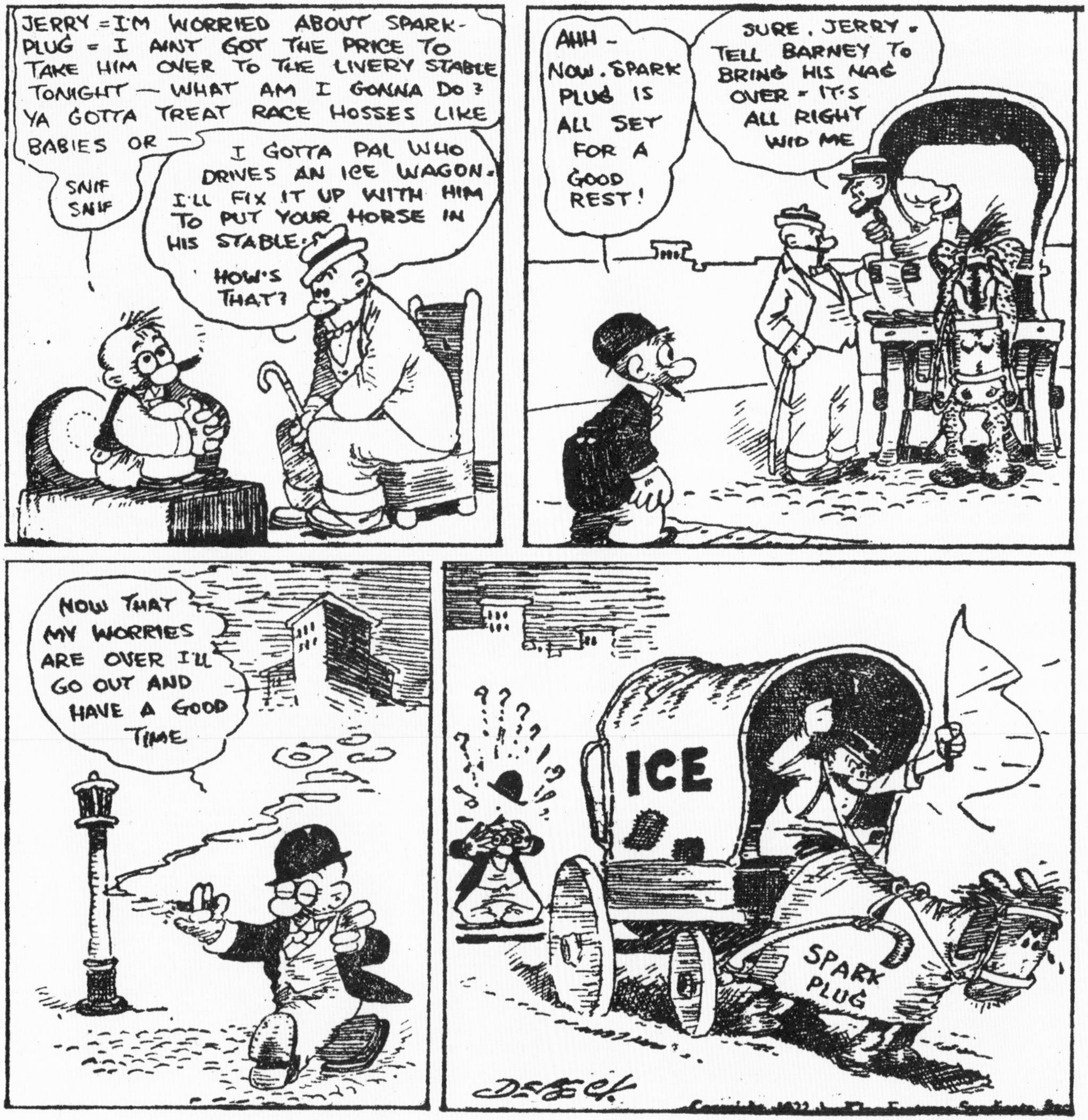

JERRY = I'M WORRIED ABOUT SPARK-PLUG = I AINT GOT THE PRICE TO TAKE HIM OVER TO THE LIVERY STABLE TONIGHT — WHAT AM I GONNA DO? YA GOTTA TREAT RACE HOSSES LIKE BABIES OR —
SNIF SNIF
I GOTTA PAL WHO DRIVES AN ICE WAGON = I'LL FIX IT UP WITH HIM TO PUT YOUR HORSE IN HIS STABLE = HOW'S THAT?
AHH — NOW, SPARK PLUG IS ALL SET FOR A GOOD REST!
SURE, JERRY = TELL BARNEY TO BRING HIS NAG OVER = IT'S ALL RIGHT WID ME
NOW THAT MY WORRIES ARE OVER I'LL GO OUT AND HAVE A GOOD TIME
ICE
SPARK PLUG

Barney and His Plug Are Due for a Trimming

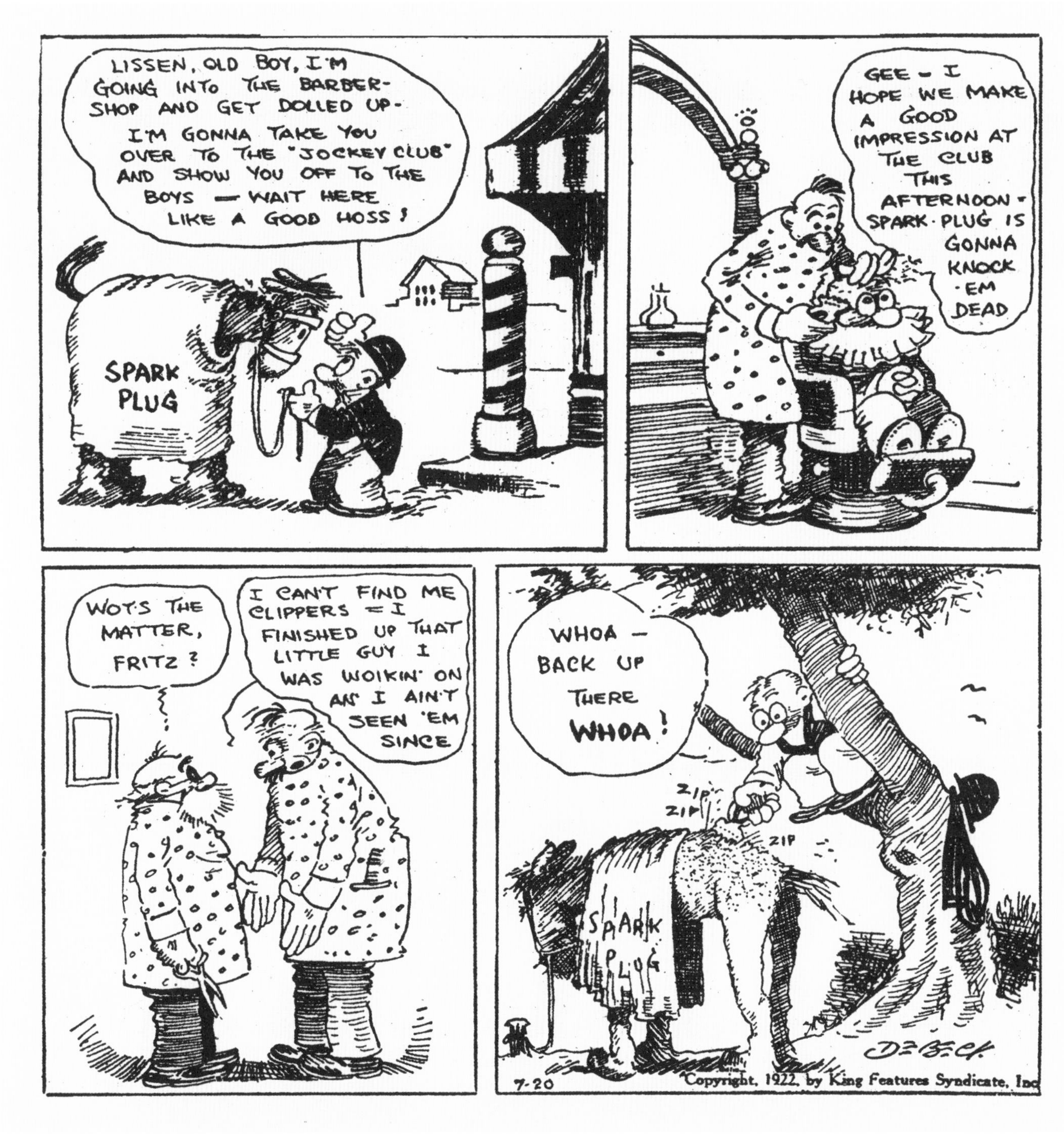
LISSEN, OLD BOY, I'M GOING INTO THE BARBER-SHOP AND GET DOLLED UP-
I'M GONNA TAKE YOU OVER TO THE "JOCKEY CLUB" AND SHOW YOU OFF TO THE BOYS — WAIT HERE LIKE A GOOD HOSS!
SPARK PLUG
GEE - I HOPE WE MAKE A GOOD IMPRESSION AT THE CLUB THIS AFTERNOON - SPARK PLUG IS GONNA KNOCK 'EM DEAD
WOT'S THE MATTER, FRITZ?
I CAN'T FIND ME CLIPPERS = I FINISHED UP THAT LITTLE GUY I WAS WOIKIN' ON AN' I AIN'T SEEN 'EM SINCE
WHOA - BACK UP THERE WHOA!
ZIP
ZIP
ZIP
SPARK PLUG
DeBECK
7-20
Copyright, 1922, by King Features Syndicate, Inc

Barney's Got Some Speedy Plug

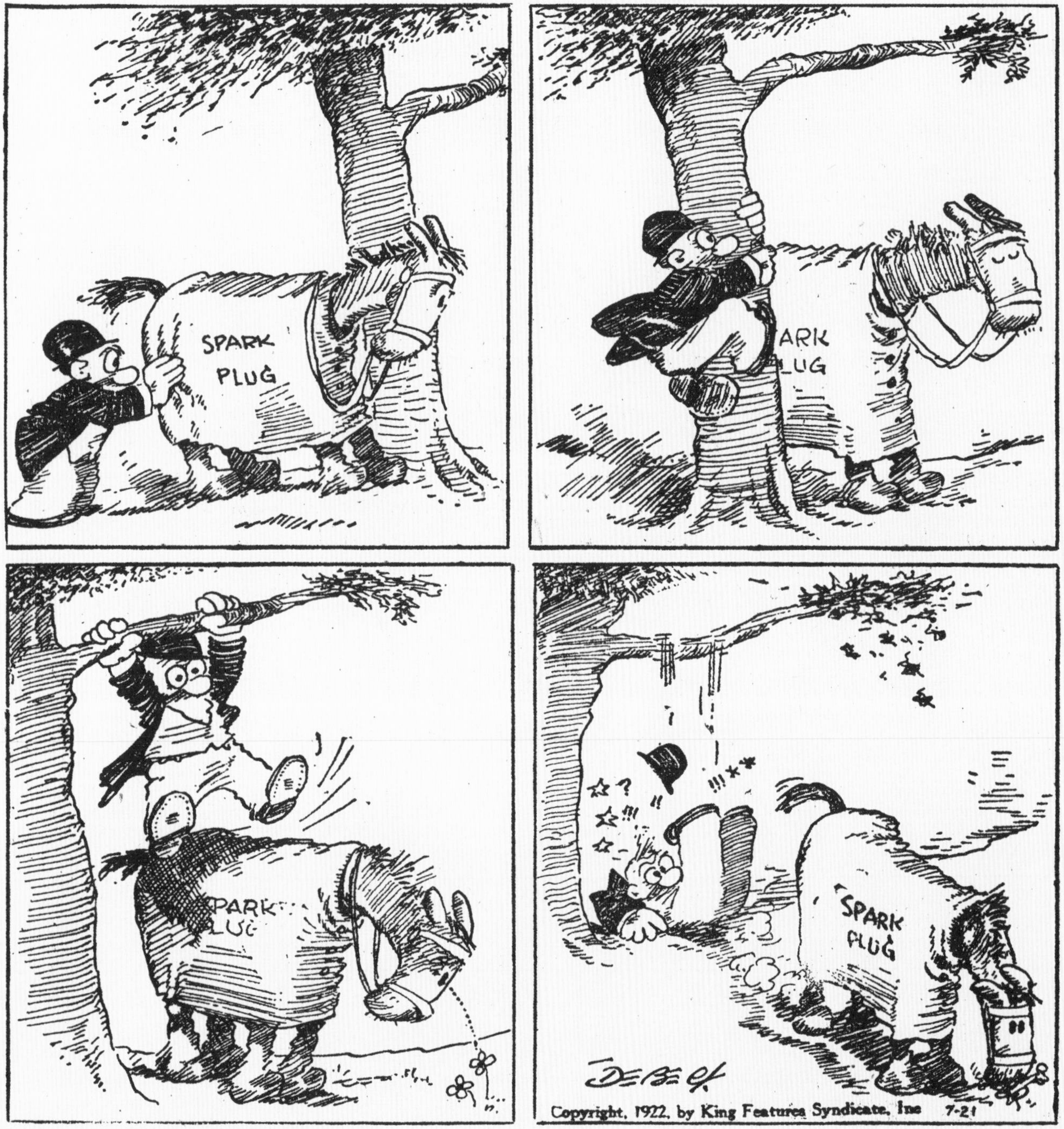
SPARK PLUG
ARK LUG
SPARK PLUG
SPARK PLUG
DE BECK
Copyright, 1922, by King Features Syndicate, Inc 7-21

Barney Sacrifices Speed for a Free Feed

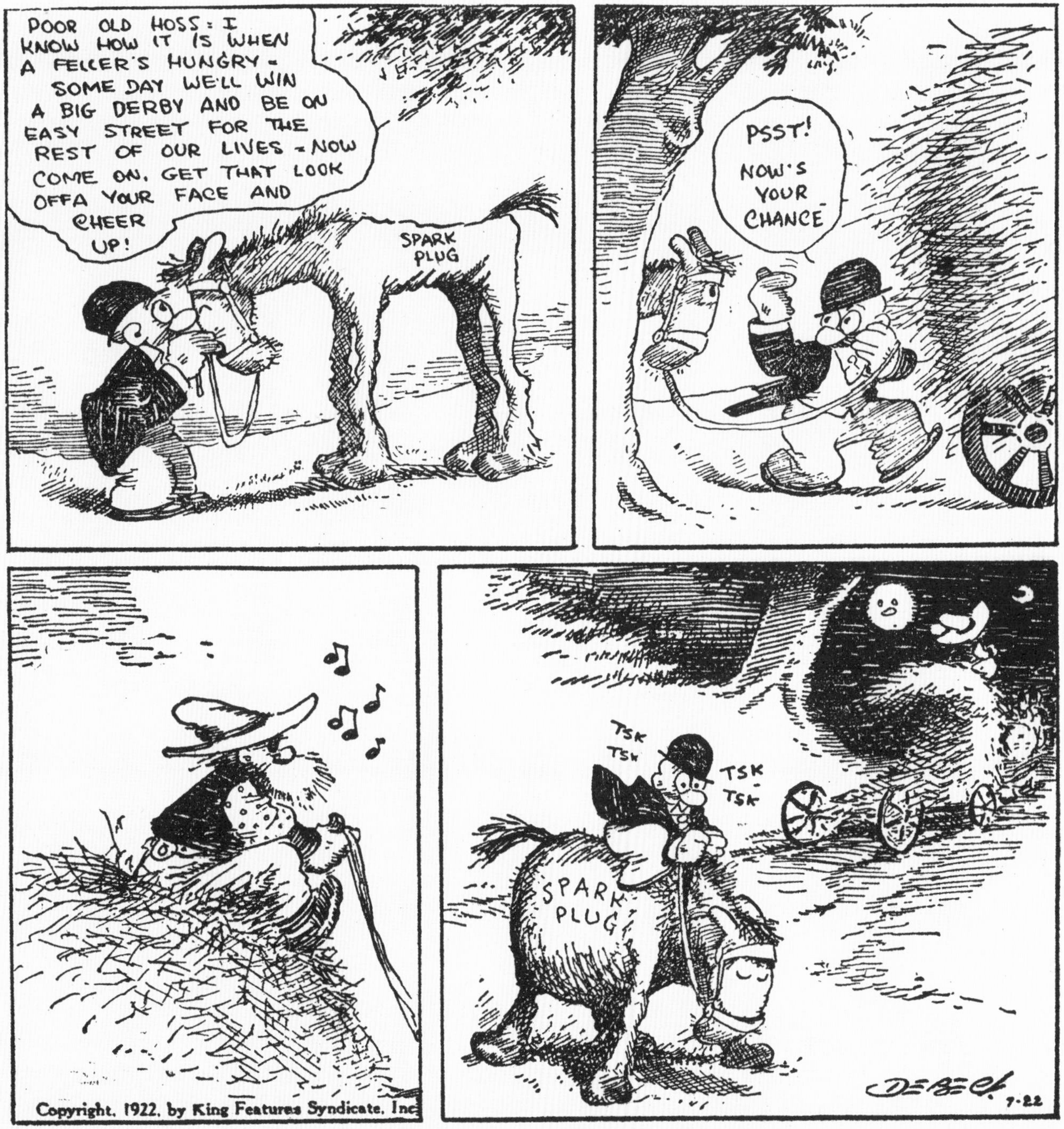

POOR OLD HOSS: I KNOW HOW IT IS WHEN A FELLER'S HUNGRY - SOME DAY WE'LL WIN A BIG DERBY AND BE ON EASY STREET FOR THE REST OF OUR LIVES - NOW COME ON, GET THAT LOOK OFFA YOUR FACE AND CHEER UP!
SPARK PLUG
PSST! NOW'S YOUR CHANCE
TSK TSK
TSK TSK
SPARK PLUG
DE BECK 7-22
Copyright, 1922, by King Features Syndicate, Inc.

Well, It's a Starter, Anyhow

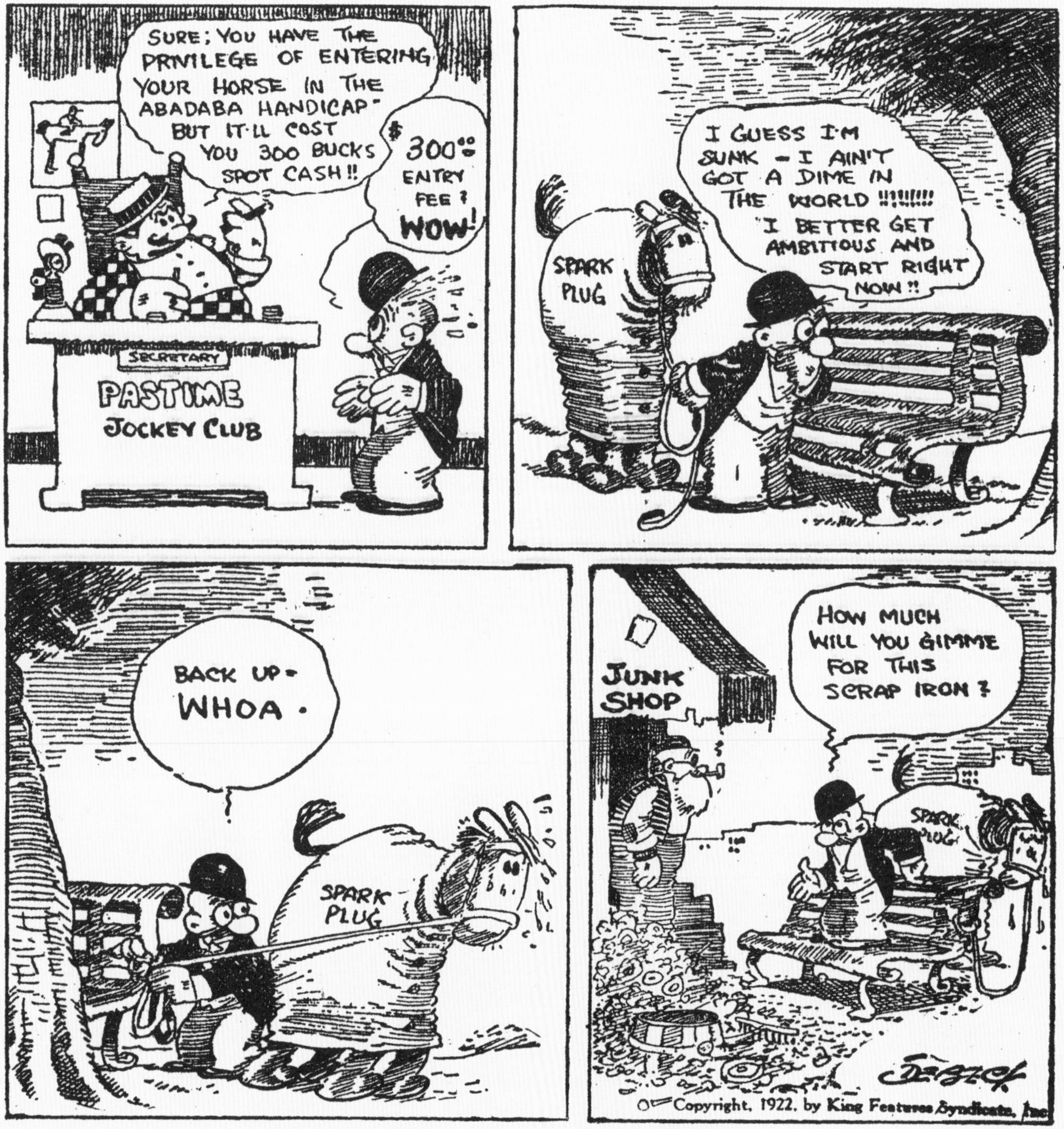
SURE; YOU HAVE THE PRIVILEGE OF ENTERING YOUR HORSE IN THE ABADABA HANDICAP" BUT IT'LL COST YOU 300 BUCKS SPOT CASH!!
$300.00 ENTRY FEE? WOW!
SECRETARY
PASTIME JOCKEY CLUB
I GUESS I'M SUNK - I AIN'T GOT A DIME IN THE WORLD !!!!!!!! I BETTER GET AMBITIOUS AND START RIGHT NOW!!
SPARK PLUG
BACK UP- WHOA.
SPARK PLUG
JUNK SHOP
HOW MUCH WILL YOU GIMME FOR THIS SCRAP IRON?
SPARK PLUG
Copyright, 1922, by King Features Syndicate, Inc.

Barney's a Bit Nearer the Goal

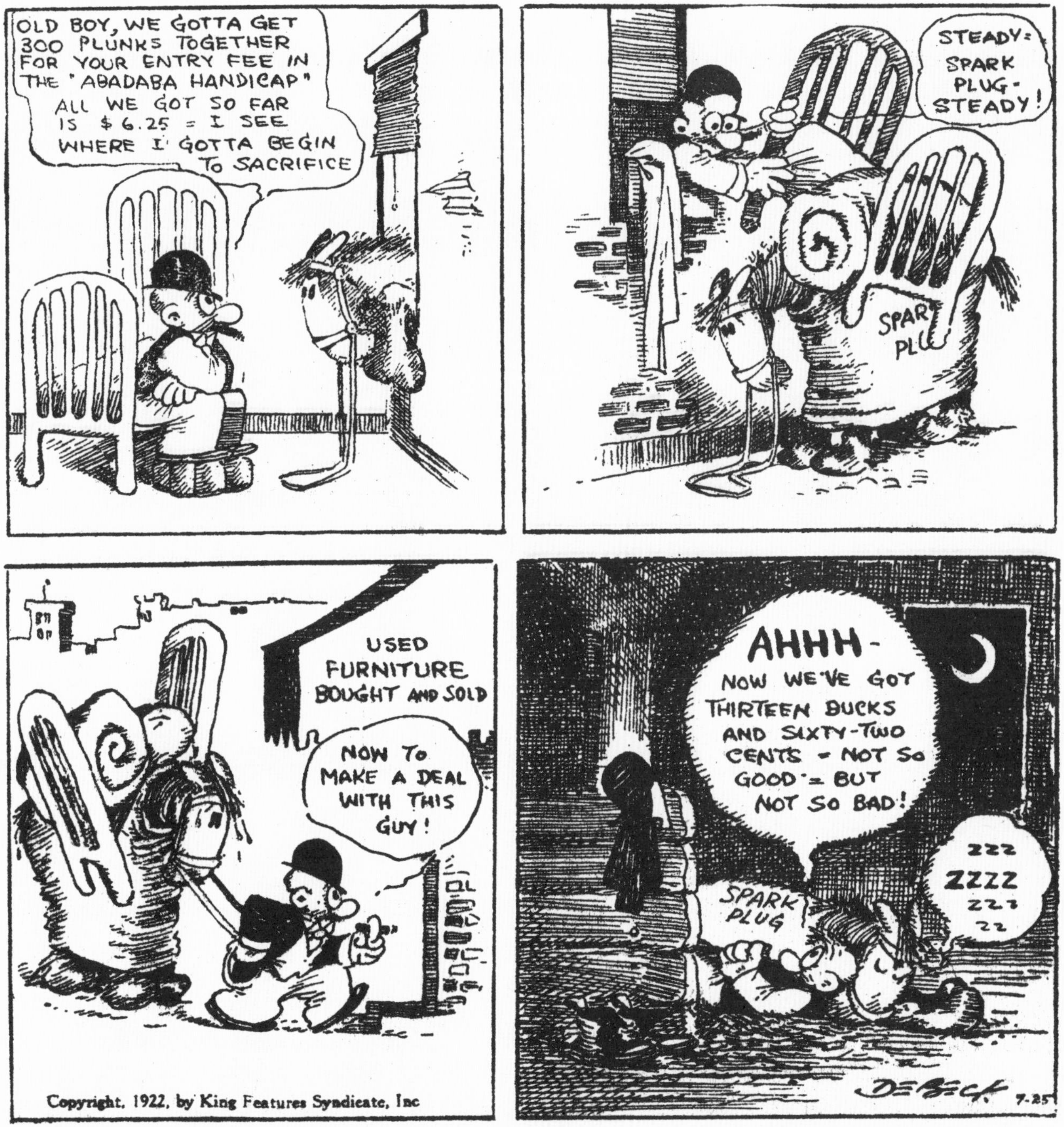
OLD BOY, WE GOTTA GET 300 PLUNKS TOGETHER FOR YOUR ENTRY FEE IN THE "ABADABA HANDICAP" ALL WE GOT SO FAR IS $6.25 = I SEE WHERE I' GOTTA BEGIN TO SACRIFICE
STEADY= SPARK PLUG- STEADY!
SPAR PL
USED FURNITURE BOUGHT AND SOLD
NOW TO MAKE A DEAL WITH THIS GUY!
AHHH- NOW WE'VE GOT THIRTEEN BUCKS AND SIXTY-TWO CENTS = NOT SO GOOD = BUT NOT SO BAD!
SPARK PLUG
ZZZ
ZZZZ
ZZZ
ZZ
DE BECK 7-25

Slow Work, But in the Right Direction

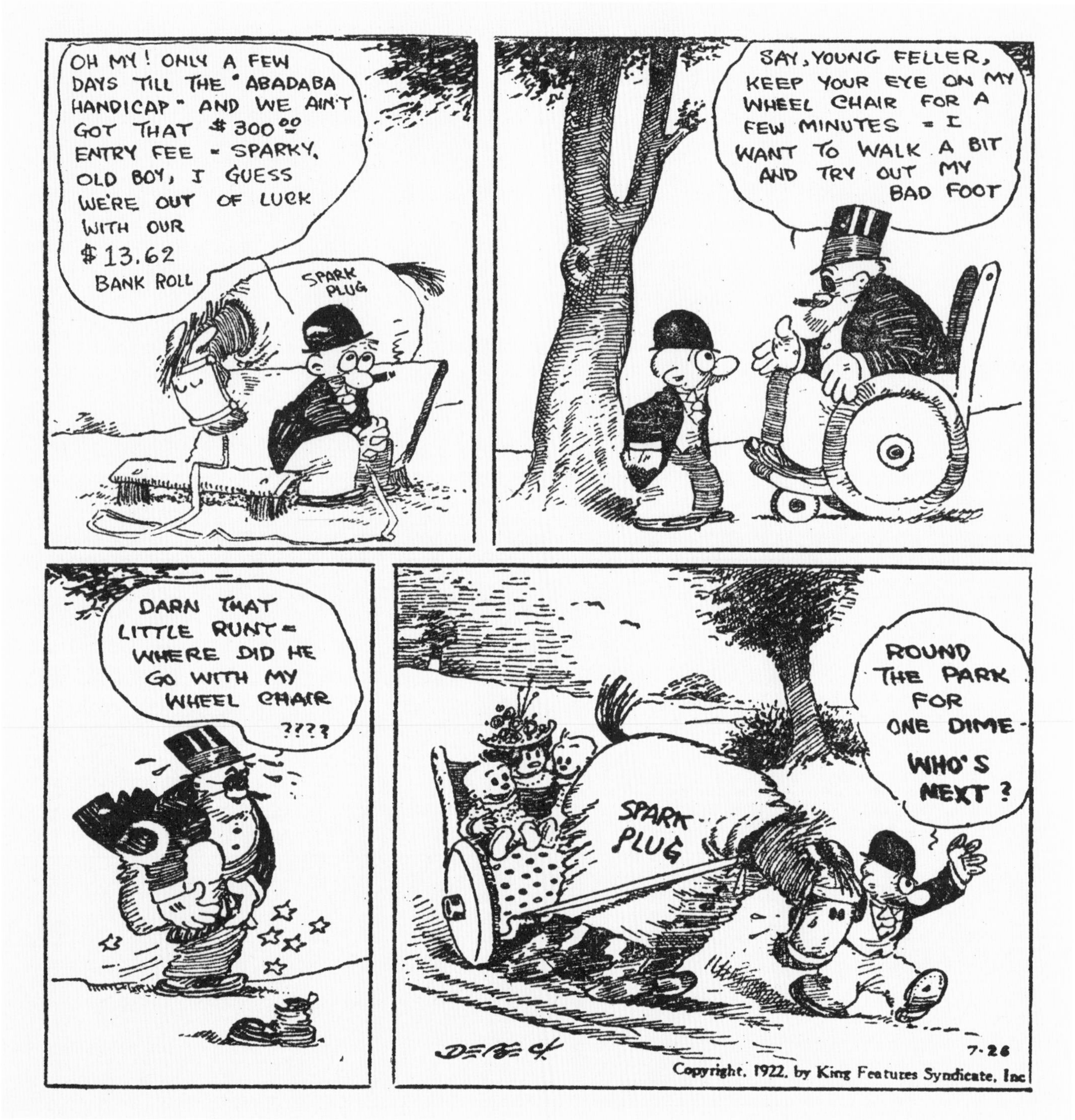

OH MY! ONLY A FEW DAYS TILL THE "ABADABA HANDICAP" AND WE AIN'T GOT THAT $300.00 ENTRY FEE - SPARKY, OLD BOY, I GUESS WE'RE OUT OF LUCK WITH OUR $13.62 BANK ROLL
SPARK PLUG
SAY, YOUNG FELLER, KEEP YOUR EYE ON MY WHEEL CHAIR FOR A FEW MINUTES - I WANT TO WALK A BIT AND TRY OUT MY BAD FOOT
DARN THAT LITTLE RUNT - WHERE DID HE GO WITH MY WHEEL CHAIR ????
ROUND THE PARK FOR ONE DIME - WHO'S NEXT?
SPARK PLUG
DEBECK
7-26
Copyright, 1922, by King Features Syndicate, Inc

Spark Plug's a Racer, Not a Truck Horse

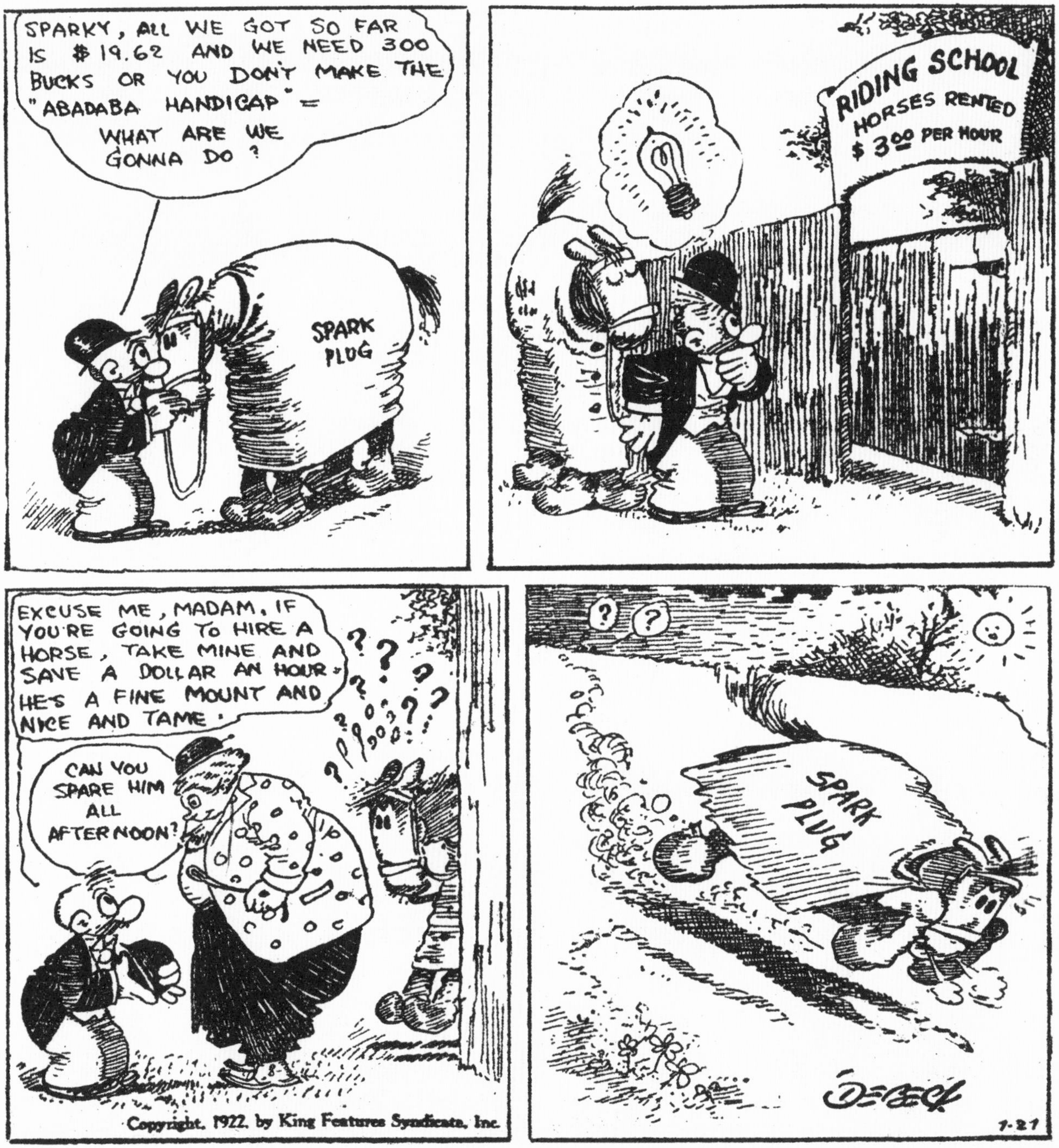
SPARKY, ALL WE GOT SO FAR IS $19.62 AND WE NEED 300 BUCKS OR YOU DON'T MAKE THE "ABADABA HANDICAP" = WHAT ARE WE GONNA DO ?
SPARK PLUG
RIDING SCHOOL
HORSES RENTED
$ 3.00 PER HOUR
EXCUSE ME, MADAM. IF YOU'RE GOING TO HIRE A HORSE, TAKE MINE AND SAVE A DOLLAR AN HOUR - HE'S A FINE MOUNT AND NICE AND TAME.
CAN YOU SPARE HIM ALL AFTERNOON?
Copyright, 1922, by King Features Syndicate, Inc.
SPARK PLUG
DE BECK
7-27

Well, Anyhow, Spark Plug Makes One Kind of a Speed Record

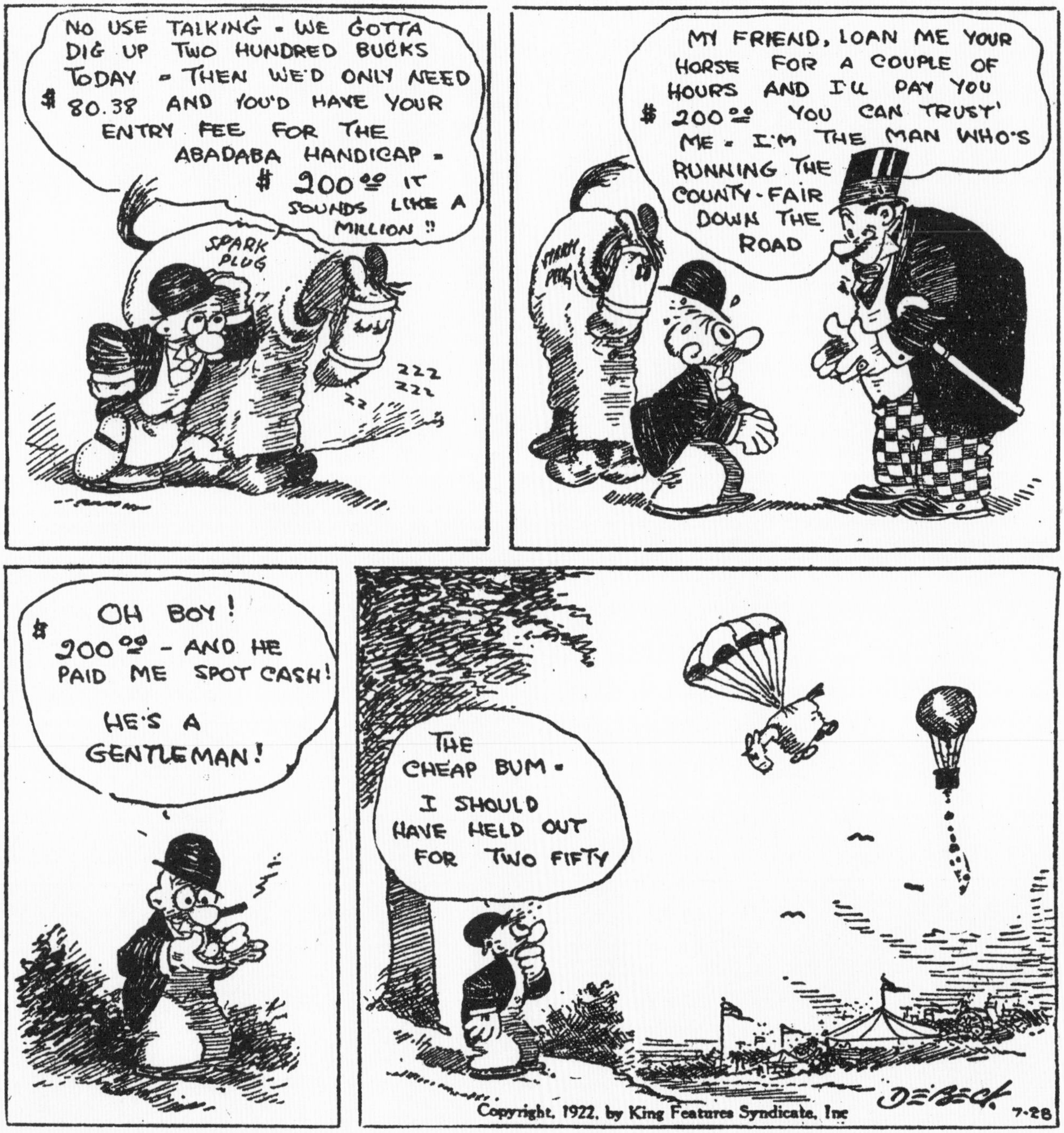
NO USE TALKING - WE GOTTA DIG UP TWO HUNDRED BUCKS TODAY - THEN WE'D ONLY NEED $80.38 AND YOU'D HAVE YOUR ENTRY FEE FOR THE ABADABA HANDICAP - $200.00 IT SOUNDS LIKE A MILLION !!
SPARK PLUG
ZZZ ZZZ ZZ
MY FRIEND, LOAN ME YOUR HORSE FOR A COUPLE OF HOURS AND I'LL PAY YOU $200.00 YOU CAN TRUST ME - I'M THE MAN WHO'S RUNNING THE COUNTY-FAIR DOWN THE ROAD
OH BOY! $200.00 - AND HE PAID ME SPOT CASH! HE'S A GENTLEMAN!
THE CHEAP BUM - I SHOULD HAVE HELD OUT FOR TWO FIFTY
DE BECK
7-28
Copyright, 1922, by King Features Syndicate, Inc

Money Means Nothing to Barney Without Spark Plug

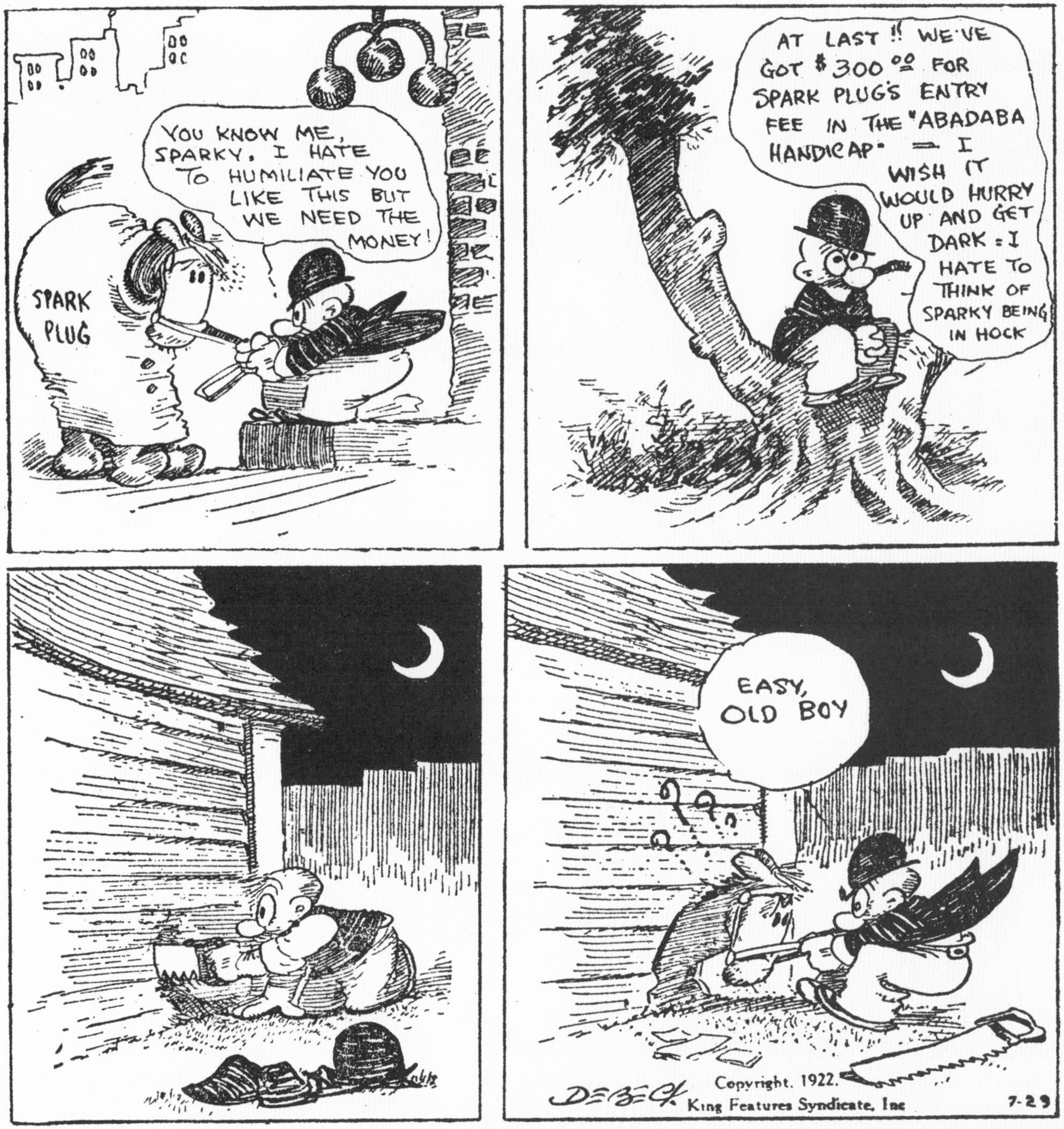
SPARK PLUG
YOU KNOW ME, SPARKY. I HATE TO HUMILIATE YOU LIKE THIS BUT WE NEED THE MONEY!
AT LAST!! WE'VE GOT $300.00 FOR SPARK PLUG'S ENTRY FEE IN THE "ABADABA HANDICAP" — I WISH IT WOULD HURRY UP AND GET DARK: I HATE TO THINK OF SPARKY BEING IN HOCK
EASY, OLD BOY
DE BECK
Copyright, 1922. King Features Syndicate, Inc
7-29

Now Spark Plug's Sure to Have a Nightmare

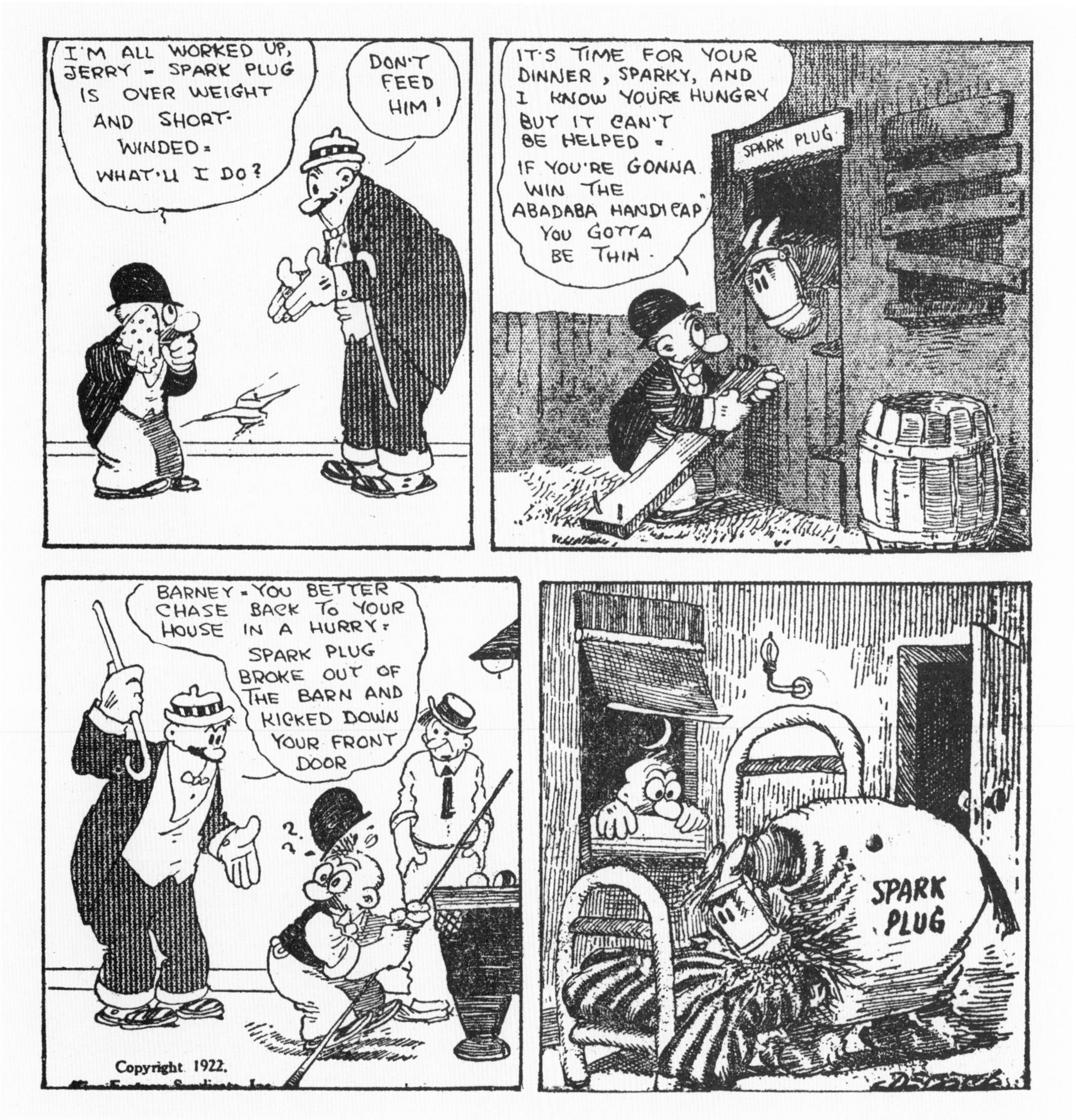
I'M ALL WORKED UP, JERRY - SPARK PLUG IS OVER WEIGHT AND SHORT-WINDED - WHAT'LL I DO?
DON'T FEED HIM!
IT'S TIME FOR YOUR DINNER, SPARKY, AND I KNOW YOU'RE HUNGRY BUT IT CAN'T BE HELPED - IF YOU'RE GONNA WIN THE "ABADABA HANDICAP" YOU GOTTA BE THIN.
SPARK PLUG
BARNEY - YOU BETTER CHASE BACK TO YOUR HOUSE IN A HURRY - SPARK PLUG BROKE OUT OF THE BARN AND KICKED DOWN YOUR FRONT DOOR
Copyright 1922.
SPARK PLUG

Well, Why Shouldn't It Work on a Horse?

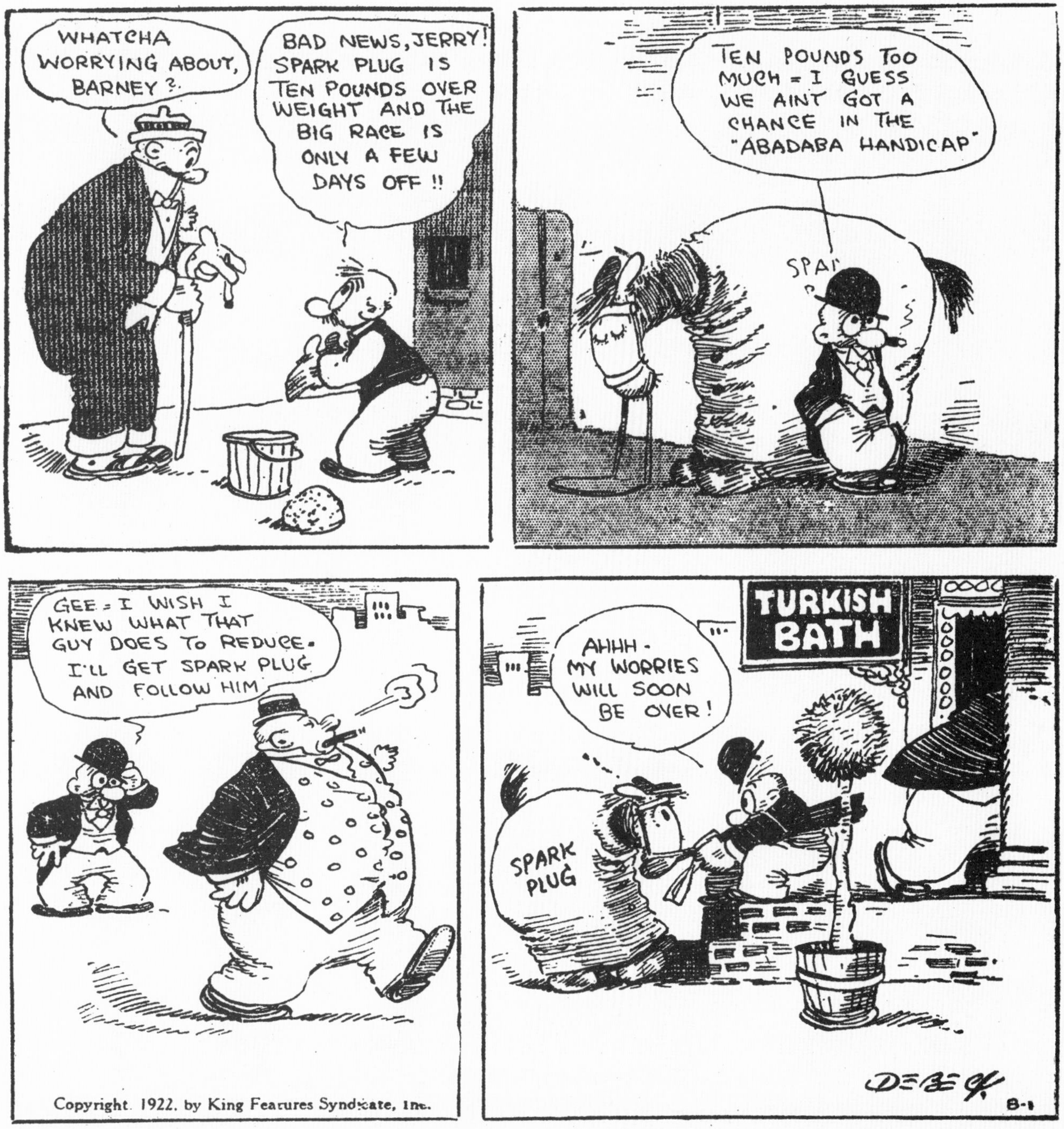

WHATCHA WORRYING ABOUT, BARNEY ?
BAD NEWS, JERRY! SPARK PLUG IS TEN POUNDS OVER WEIGHT AND THE BIG RACE IS ONLY A FEW DAYS OFF !!
TEN POUNDS TOO MUCH = I GUESS WE AINT GOT A CHANCE IN THE "ABADABA HANDICAP"
GEE = I WISH I KNEW WHAT THAT GUY DOES TO REDUCE. I'LL GET SPARK PLUG AND FOLLOW HIM
TURKISH BATH
AHHH - MY WORRIES WILL SOON BE OVER!
SPARK PLUG
Copyright. 1922, by King Features Syndicate, Inc.

It Certainly Looks Like Spark Plug's Going to Stick

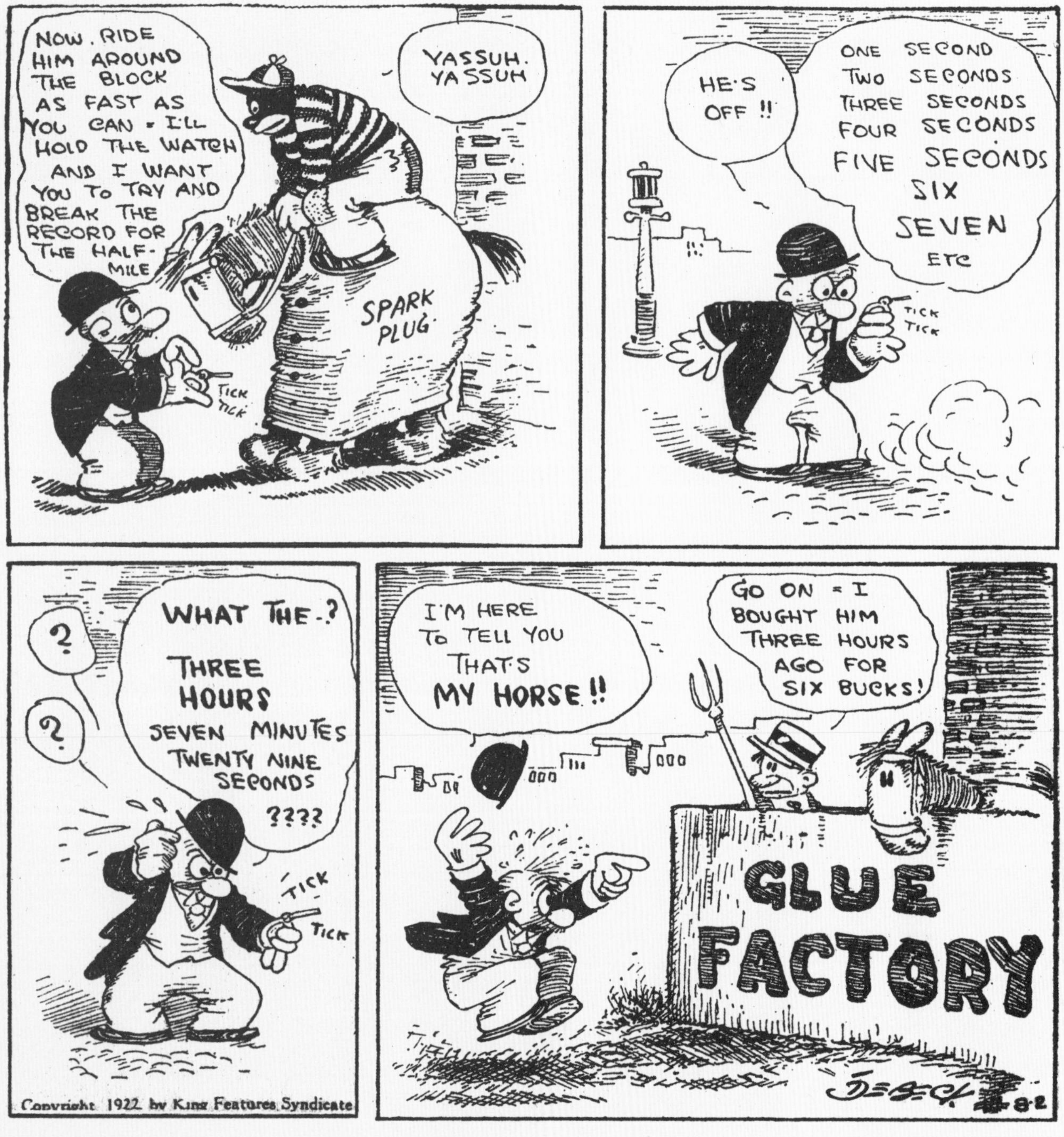
NOW, RIDE HIM AROUND THE BLOCK AS FAST AS YOU CAN - I'LL HOLD THE WATCH AND I WANT YOU TO TRY AND BREAK THE RECORD FOR THE HALF-MILE
YASSUH. YASSUH
SPARK PLUG
TICK TICK
HE'S OFF !!
ONE SECOND TWO SECONDS THREE SECONDS FOUR SECONDS FIVE SECONDS SIX SEVEN ETC
TICK TICK
?
?
WHAT THE-? THREE HOURS SEVEN MINUTES TWENTY NINE SECONDS ????
TICK
TICK
I'M HERE TO TELL YOU THAT'S MY HORSE !!
GO ON - I BOUGHT HIM THREE HOURS AGO FOR SIX BUCKS!
GLUE FACTORY
DE BECK 8-2

Well, Anyhow, Barney's Very Particular About Who's Valet to Spark Plug

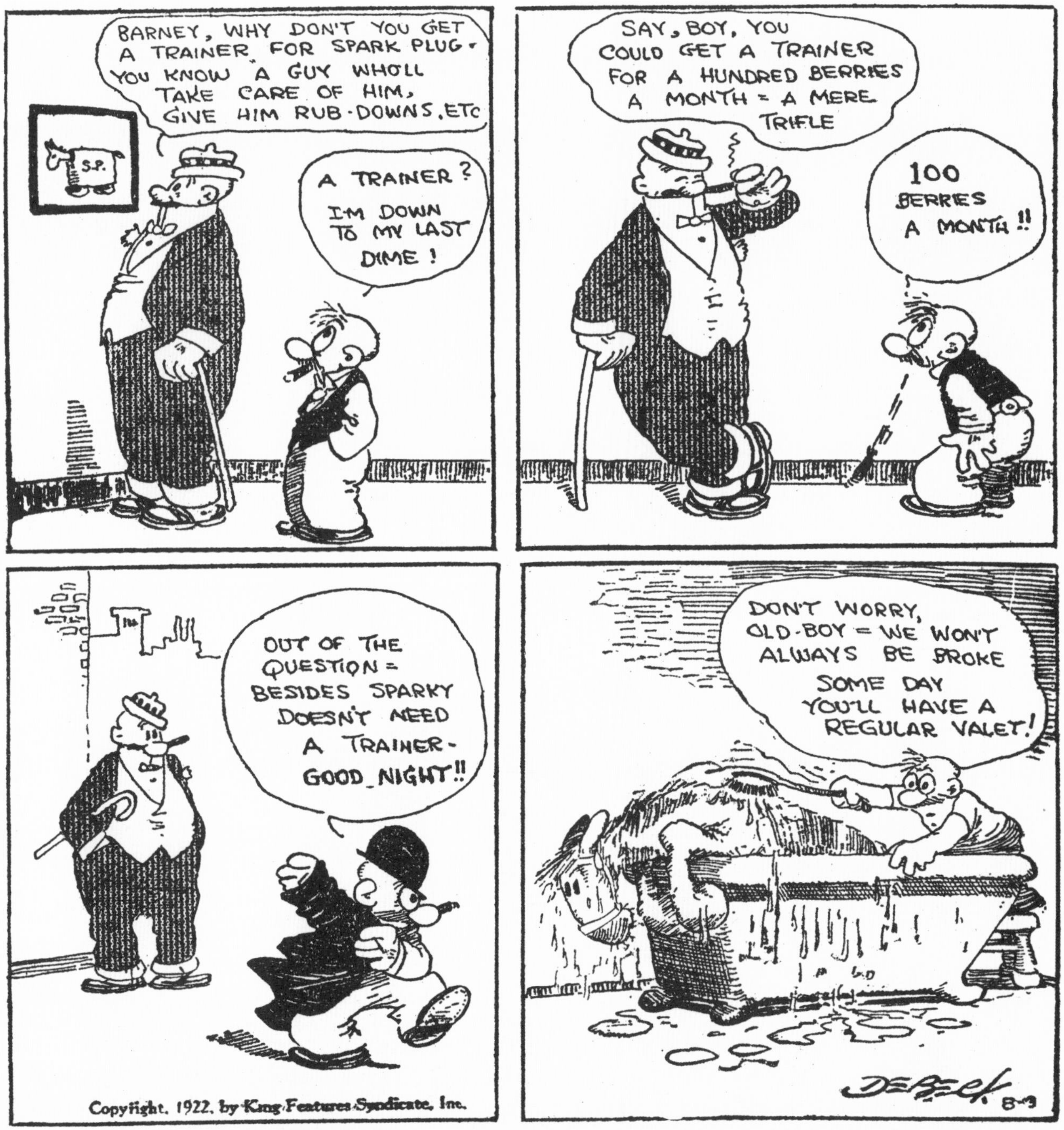

BARNEY, WHY DON'T YOU GET A TRAINER FOR SPARK PLUG - YOU KNOW A GUY WHO'LL TAKE CARE OF HIM, GIVE HIM RUB-DOWNS, ETC
S.P.
A TRAINER? I'M DOWN TO MY LAST DIME!
SAY, BOY, YOU COULD GET A TRAINER FOR A HUNDRED BERRIES A MONTH = A MERE TRIFLE
100 BERRIES A MONTH!!
OUT OF THE QUESTION = BESIDES SPARKY DOESN'T NEED A TRAINER - GOOD NIGHT!!
DON'T WORRY, OLD-BOY = WE WON'T ALWAYS BE BROKE SOME DAY YOU'LL HAVE A REGULAR VALET!
Copyright, 1922, by King Features Syndicate, Inc.
DEBECK 8-3

Well, Anyhow, It's Good Training for Spark Plug

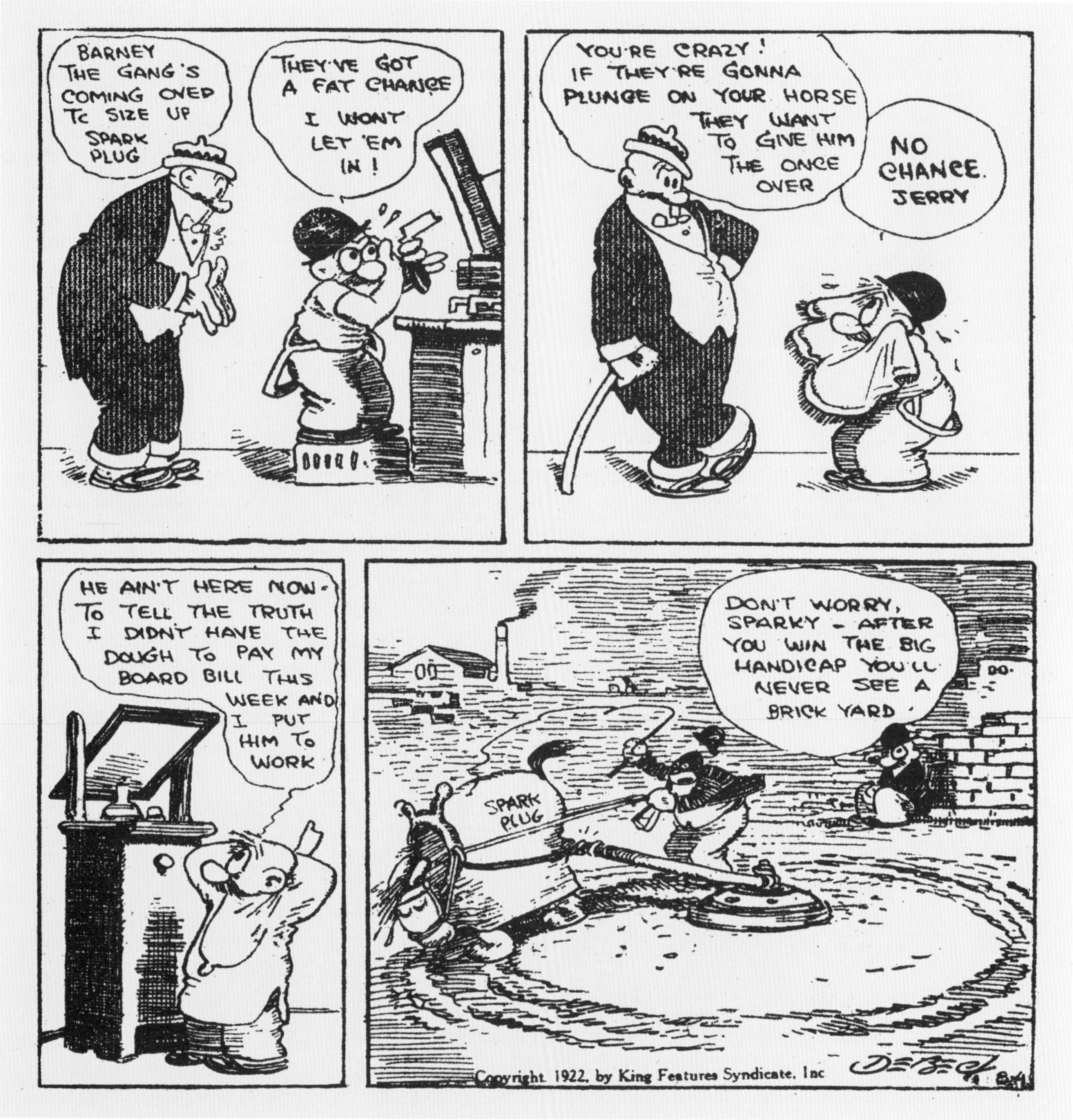
BARNEY THE GANG'S COMING OVED Tc SIZE UP SPARK PLUG
THEY'VE GOT A FAT CHANCE I WONT LET 'EM IN!
YOU'RE CRAZY! IF THEY'RE GONNA PLUNGE ON YOUR HORSE THEY WANT TO GIVE HIM THE ONCE OVER
NO CHANCE. JERRY
HE AIN'T HERE NOW - TO TELL THE TRUTH I DIDN'T HAVE THE DOUGH TO PAY MY BOARD BILL THIS WEEK AND I PUT HIM TO WORK
DON'T WORRY, SPARKY - AFTER YOU WIN THE BIG HANDICAP YOU'LL NEVER SEE A BRICK YARD.
SPARK PLUG
Copyright 1922, by King Features Syndicate, Inc
DE BECK

Looks Like a Skin Game May Cost Spark Plug His Hide

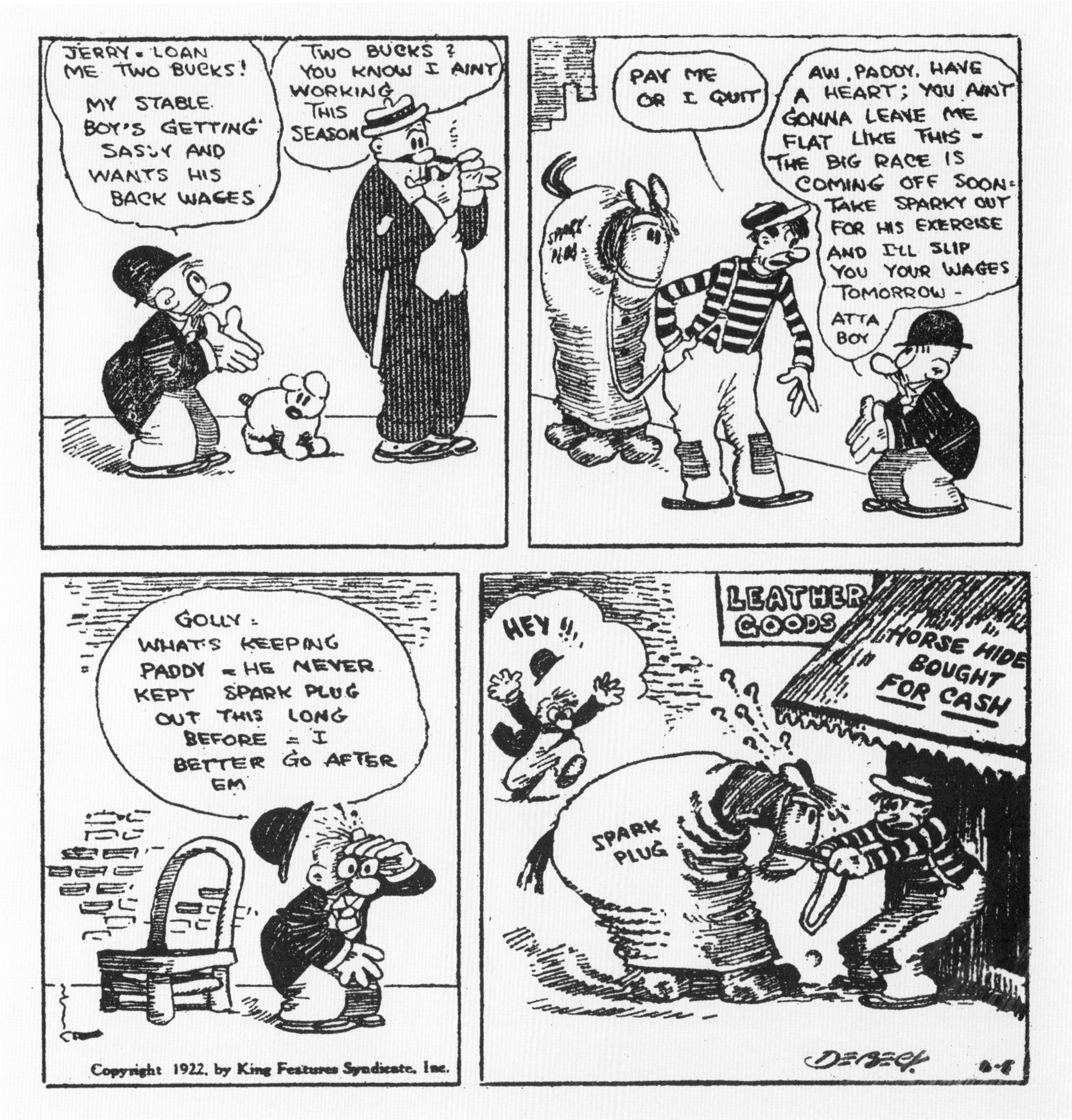
JERRY - LOAN ME TWO BUCKS! MY STABLE BOY'S GETTING SASSY AND WANTS HIS BACK WAGES
TWO BUCKS ? YOU KNOW I AINT WORKING THIS SEASON
PAY ME OR I QUIT
AW, PADDY, HAVE A HEART; YOU AINT GONNA LEAVE ME FLAT LIKE THIS - THE BIG RACE IS COMING OFF SOON - TAKE SPARKY OUT FOR HIS EXERCISE AND I'LL SLIP YOU YOUR WAGES TOMORROW -
ATTA BOY
GOLLY - WHAT'S KEEPING PADDY - HE NEVER KEPT SPARK PLUG OUT THIS LONG BEFORE - I BETTER GO AFTER EM
LEATHER GOODS
HEY !!
HORSE HIDE BOUGHT FOR CASH
SPARK PLUG
DE BECK
Copyright 1922, by King Features Syndicate, Inc.

It Looks Pretty Dark to Barney Just Now

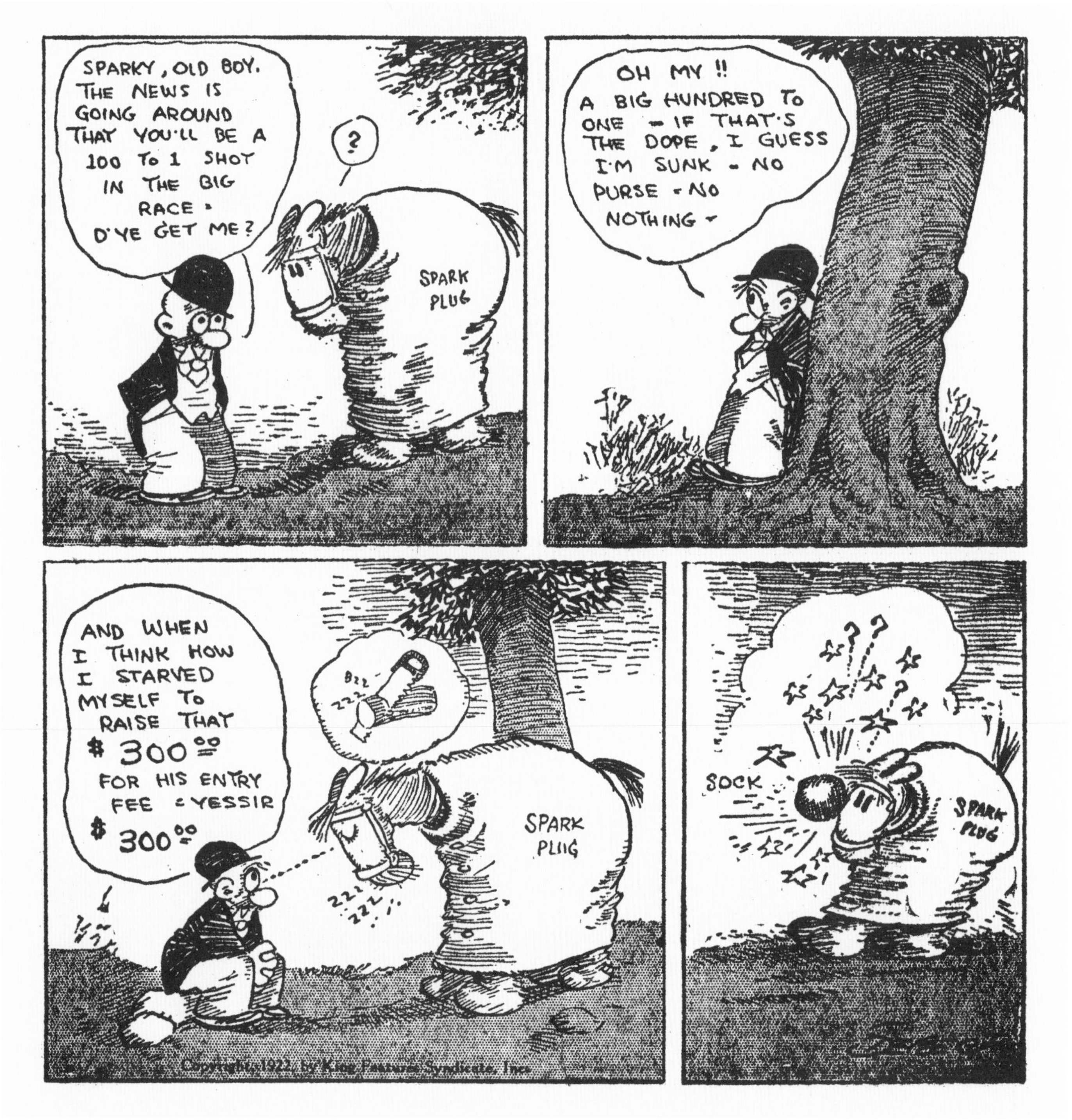

SPARKY, OLD BOY. THE NEWS IS GOING AROUND THAT YOU'LL BE A 100 TO 1 SHOT IN THE BIG RACE - D'YE GET ME?
?
SPARK PLUG
OH MY !! A BIG HUNDRED TO ONE - IF THAT'S THE DOPE, I GUESS I'M SUNK - NO PURSE - NO NOTHING -
AND WHEN I THINK HOW I STARVED MYSELF TO RAISE THAT $300.00 FOR HIS ENTRY FEE - YESSIR $300.00
SPARK PLUG
SOCK
SPARK PLUG
Copyright, 1922, by King Features Syndicate, Inc.

Barney Overlooks Just One Thing

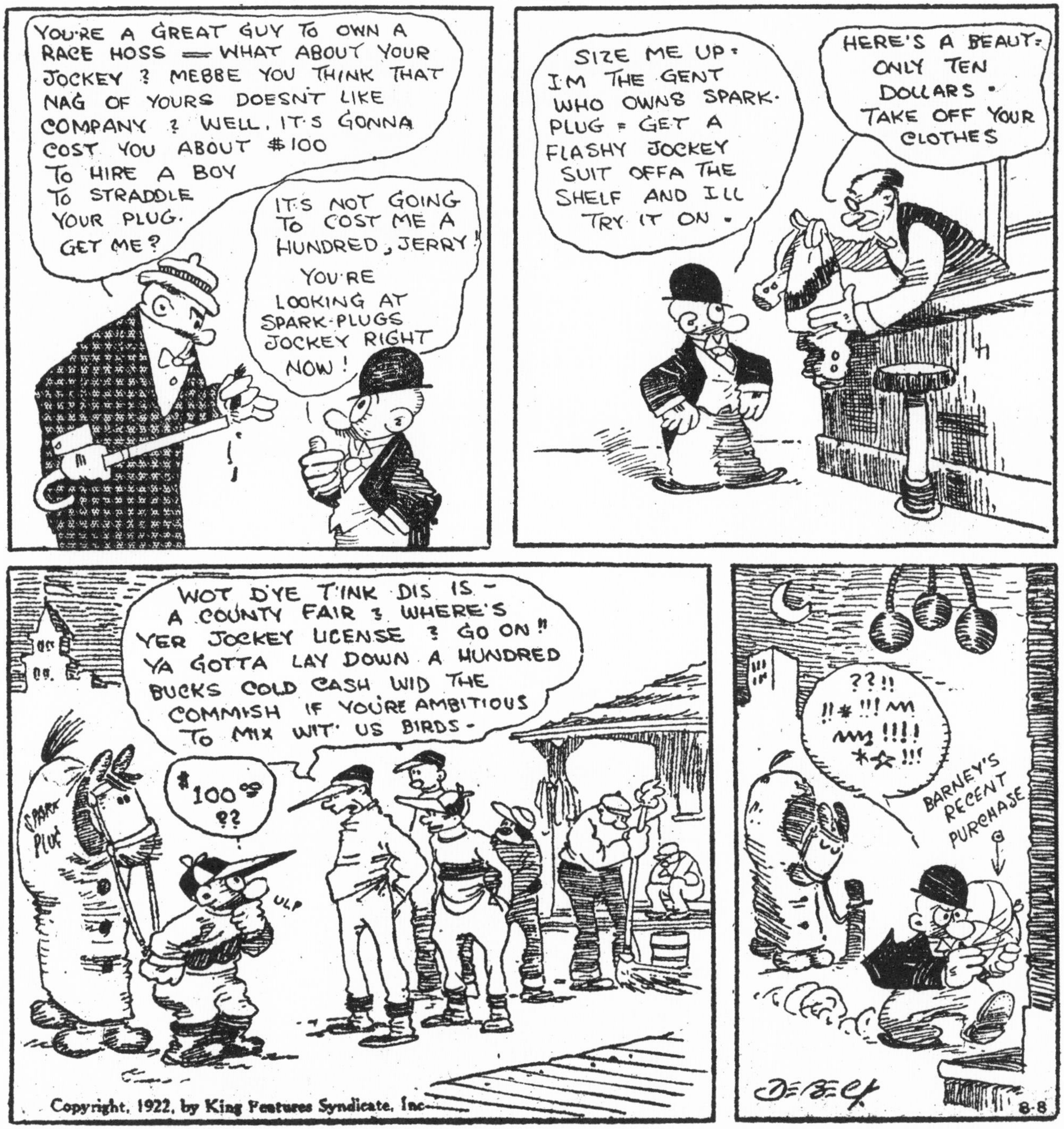

YOU'RE A GREAT GUY TO OWN A RACE HOSS — WHAT ABOUT YOUR JOCKEY ? MEBBE YOU THINK THAT NAG OF YOURS DOESN'T LIKE COMPANY ? WELL, IT'S GONNA COST YOU ABOUT $100 TO HIRE A BOY TO STRADDLE YOUR PLUG. GET ME?
IT'S NOT GOING TO COST ME A HUNDRED, JERRY! YOU'RE LOOKING AT SPARK-PLUGS JOCKEY RIGHT NOW!
SIZE ME UP: I'M THE GENT WHO OWNS SPARK-PLUG = GET A FLASHY JOCKEY SUIT OFFA THE SHELF AND I'LL TRY IT ON.
HERE'S A BEAUT: ONLY TEN DOLLARS. TAKE OFF YOUR CLOTHES
WOT D'YE T'INK DIS IS - A COUNTY FAIR ? WHERE'S YER JOCKEY LICENSE ? GO ON!! YA GOTTA LAY DOWN A HUNDRED BUCKS COLD CASH WID THE COMMISH IF YOU'RE AMBITIOUS TO MIX WIT' US BIRDS -
$100.00 ??
ULP
SPARK PLUG
Copyright, 1922, by King Features Syndicate, Inc
??!!
BARNEY'S RECENT PURCHASE
DeBECK
8-8

Barney Springs a New Idea

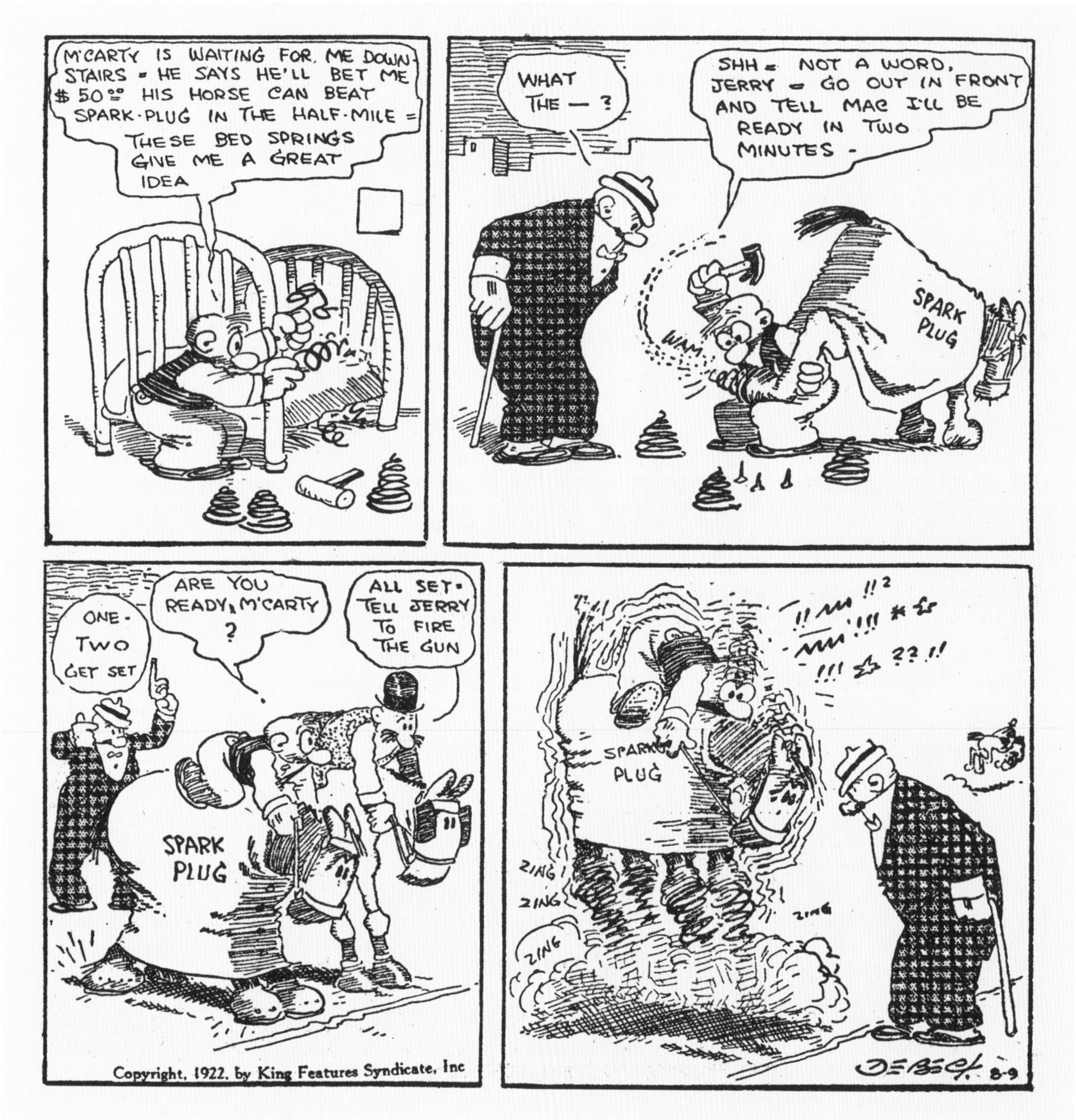

M'CARTY IS WAITING FOR ME DOWN-STAIRS - HE SAYS HE'LL BET ME $50.00 HIS HORSE CAN BEAT SPARK-PLUG IN THE HALF-MILE - THESE BED SPRINGS GIVE ME A GREAT IDEA
WHAT THE — ?
SHH - NOT A WORD, JERRY - GO OUT IN FRONT AND TELL MAC I'LL BE READY IN TWO MINUTES -
WAM
SPARK PLUG
ONE - TWO GET SET
ARE YOU READY, M'CARTY ?
ALL SET - TELL JERRY TO FIRE THE GUN
SPARK PLUG
Copyright, 1922, by King Features Syndicate, Inc
SPARK PLUG
ZING
ZING
ZING
ZING
DEBECK 8-9

What Barney Meant to Say Was "One in a Melon"

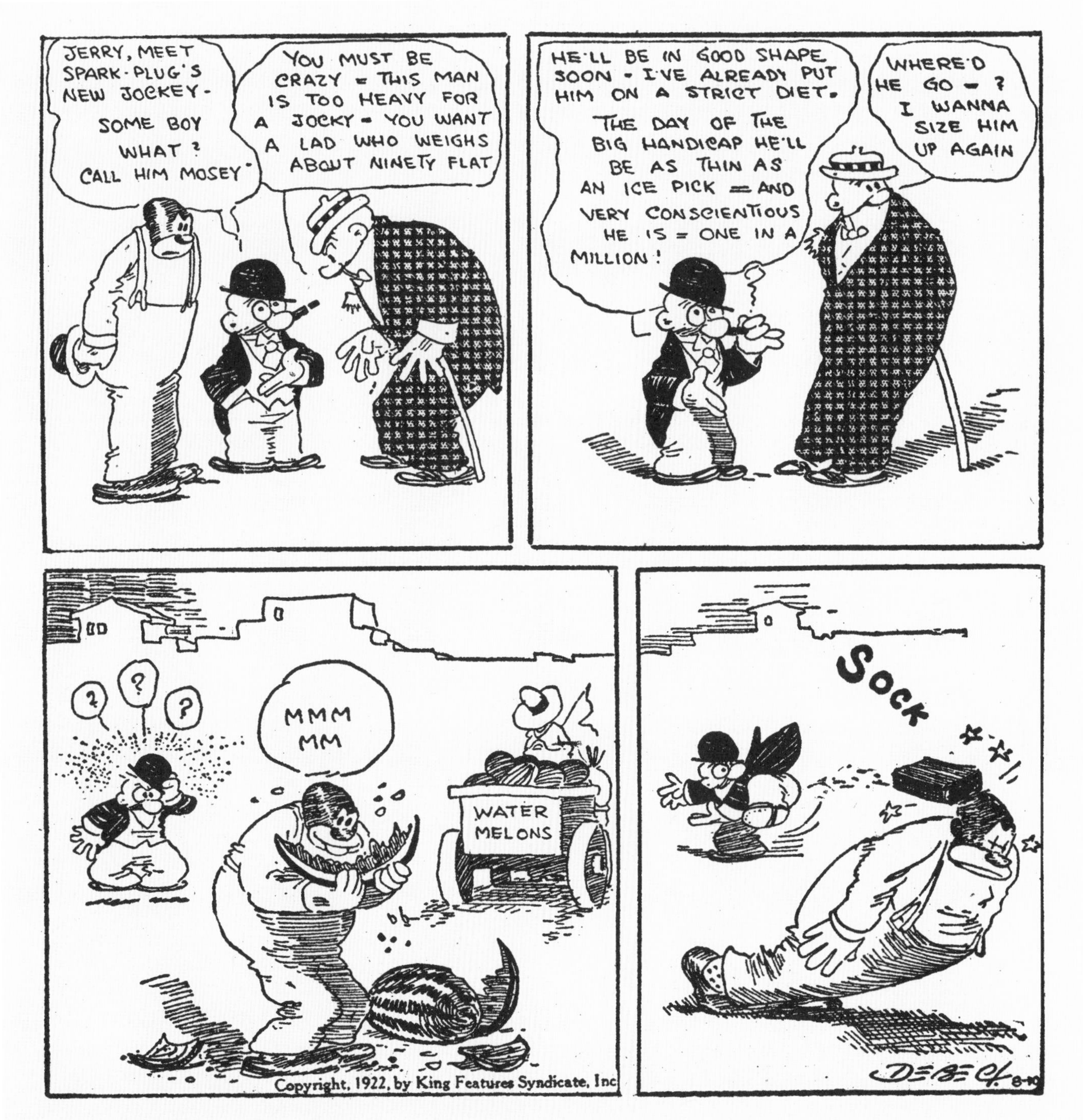
JERRY, MEET SPARK-PLUG'S NEW JOCKEY - SOME BOY WHAT? CALL HIM MOSEY
YOU MUST BE CRAZY = THIS MAN IS TOO HEAVY FOR A JOCKY - YOU WANT A LAD WHO WEIGHS ABOUT NINETY FLAT
HE'LL BE IN GOOD SHAPE SOON - I'VE ALREADY PUT HIM ON A STRICT DIET. THE DAY OF THE BIG HANDICAP HE'LL BE AS THIN AS AN ICE PICK = AND VERY CONSCIENTIOUS HE IS = ONE IN A MILLION!
WHERE'D HE GO - ? I WANNA SIZE HIM UP AGAIN
?
?
?
MMM MM
WATER MELONS
Copyright, 1922, by King Features Syndicate, Inc
SOCK
DEBECK 8-10

That "Pepski" Is the Real Dopeski

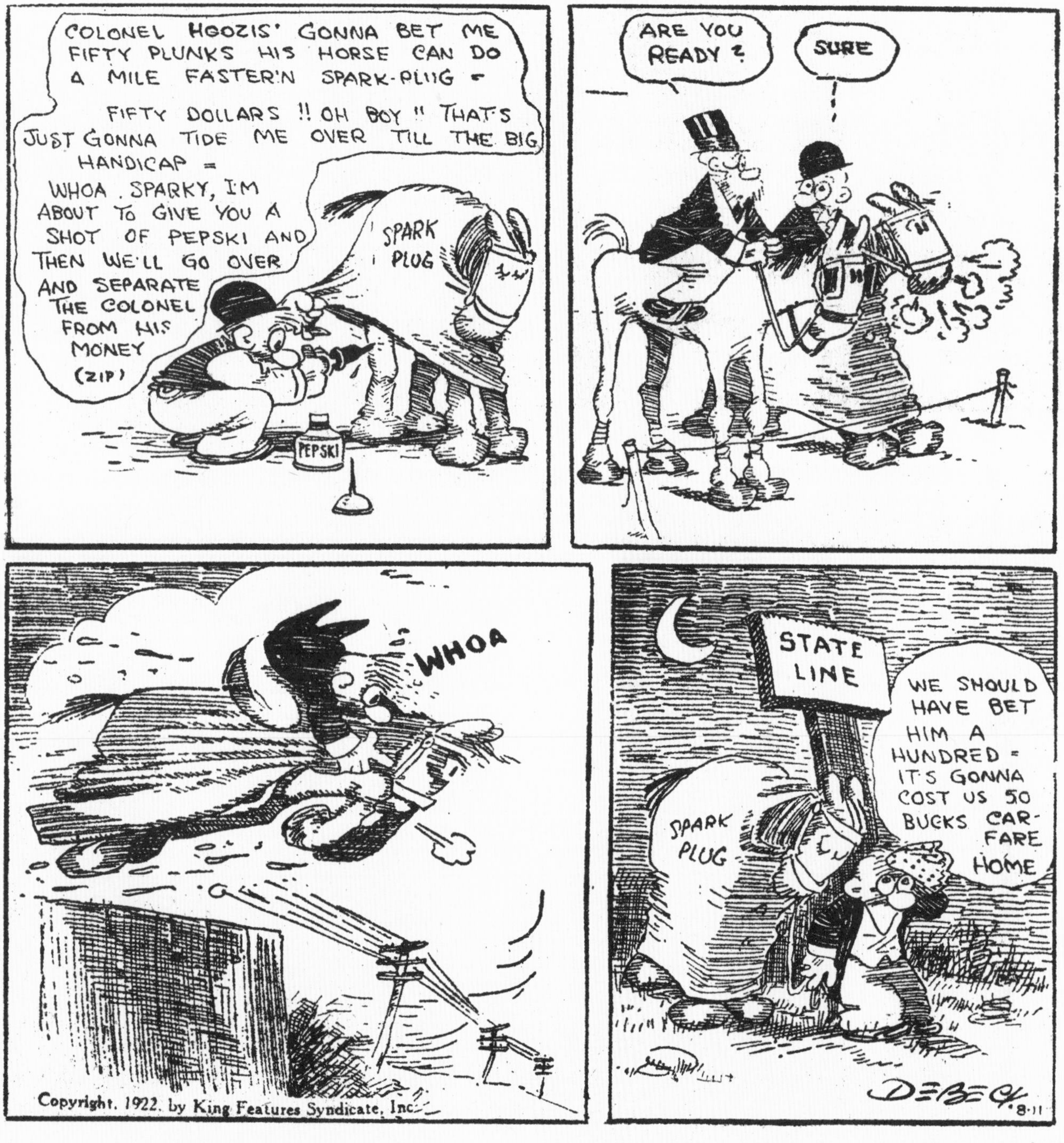
COLONEL HOOZIS' GONNA BET ME FIFTY PLUNKS HIS HORSE CAN DO A MILE FASTER'N SPARK-PLUG =
FIFTY DOLLARS !! OH BOY !! THAT'S JUST GONNA TIDE ME OVER TILL THE BIG HANDICAP =
WHOA, SPARKY, I'M ABOUT TO GIVE YOU A SHOT OF PEPSKI AND THEN WE'LL GO OVER AND SEPARATE THE COLONEL FROM HIS MONEY
(ZIP)
SPARK PLUG
PEPSKI
ARE YOU READY ?
SURE
WHOA
STATE LINE
WE SHOULD HAVE BET HIM A HUNDRED = IT'S GONNA COST US 50 BUCKS CAR-FARE HOME
SPARK PLUG
DEBECK 8-11
Copyright, 1922, by King Features Syndicate, Inc.

Barney's Looking for a Trainer With Real Experience

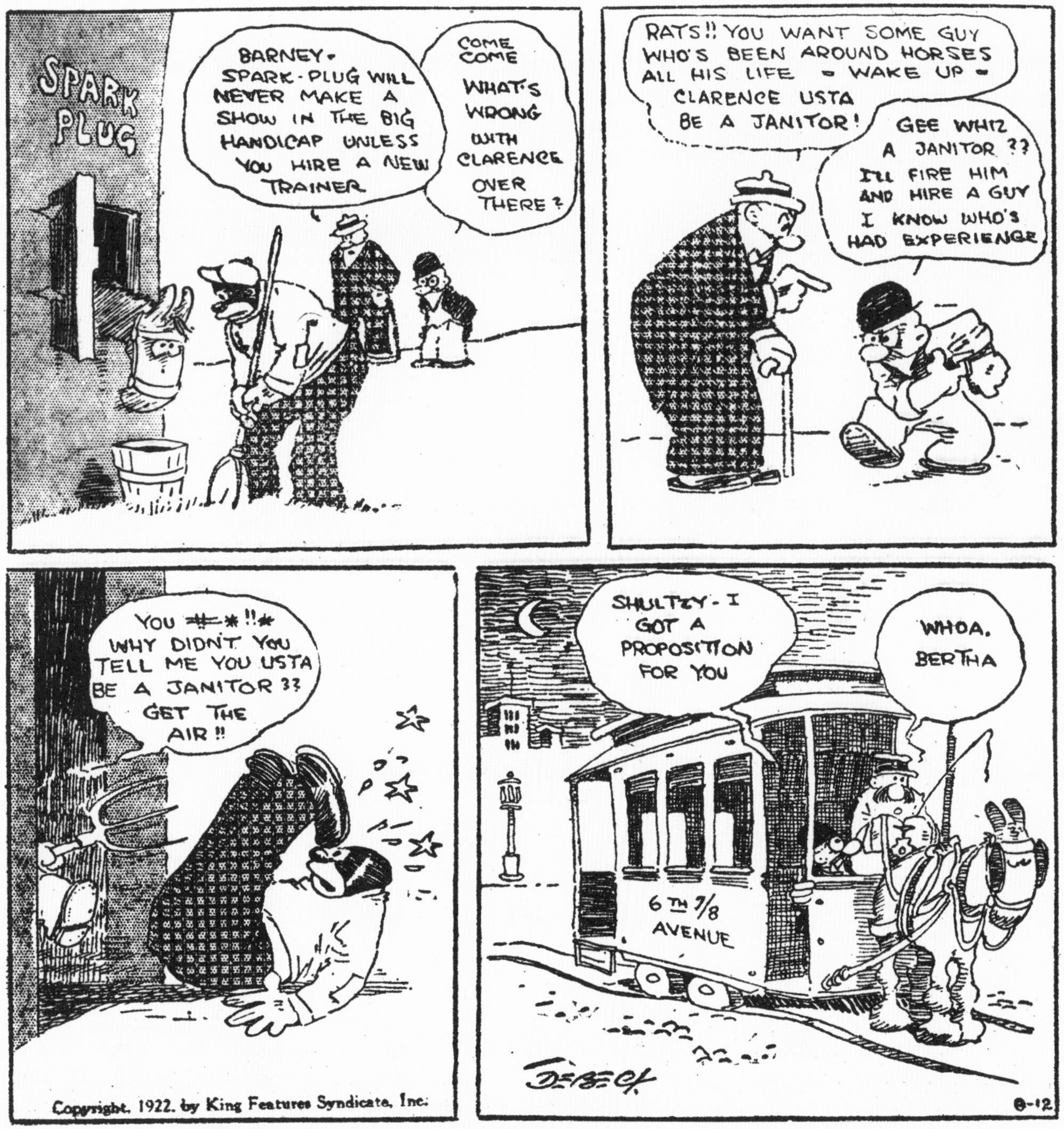
SPARK PLUG
BARNEY- SPARK-PLUG WILL NEVER MAKE A SHOW IN THE BIG HANDICAP UNLESS YOU HIRE A NEW TRAINER
COME COME WHAT'S WRONG WITH CLARENCE OVER THERE?
RATS!! YOU WANT SOME GUY WHO'S BEEN AROUND HORSES ALL HIS LIFE - WAKE UP - CLARENCE USTA BE A JANITOR!
GEE WHIZ A JANITOR ?? I'LL FIRE HIM AND HIRE A GUY I KNOW WHO'S HAD EXPERIENCE
YOU #=*!!* WHY DIDN'T YOU TELL ME YOU USTA BE A JANITOR ?? GET THE AIR!!
SHULTZY - I GOT A PROPOSITION FOR YOU
WHOA, BERTHA
6TH 7/8 AVENUE
DEBECK
8-12
Copyright, 1922, by King Features Syndicate, Inc.

If Spark Plug Can't Run Maybe He Can Swim

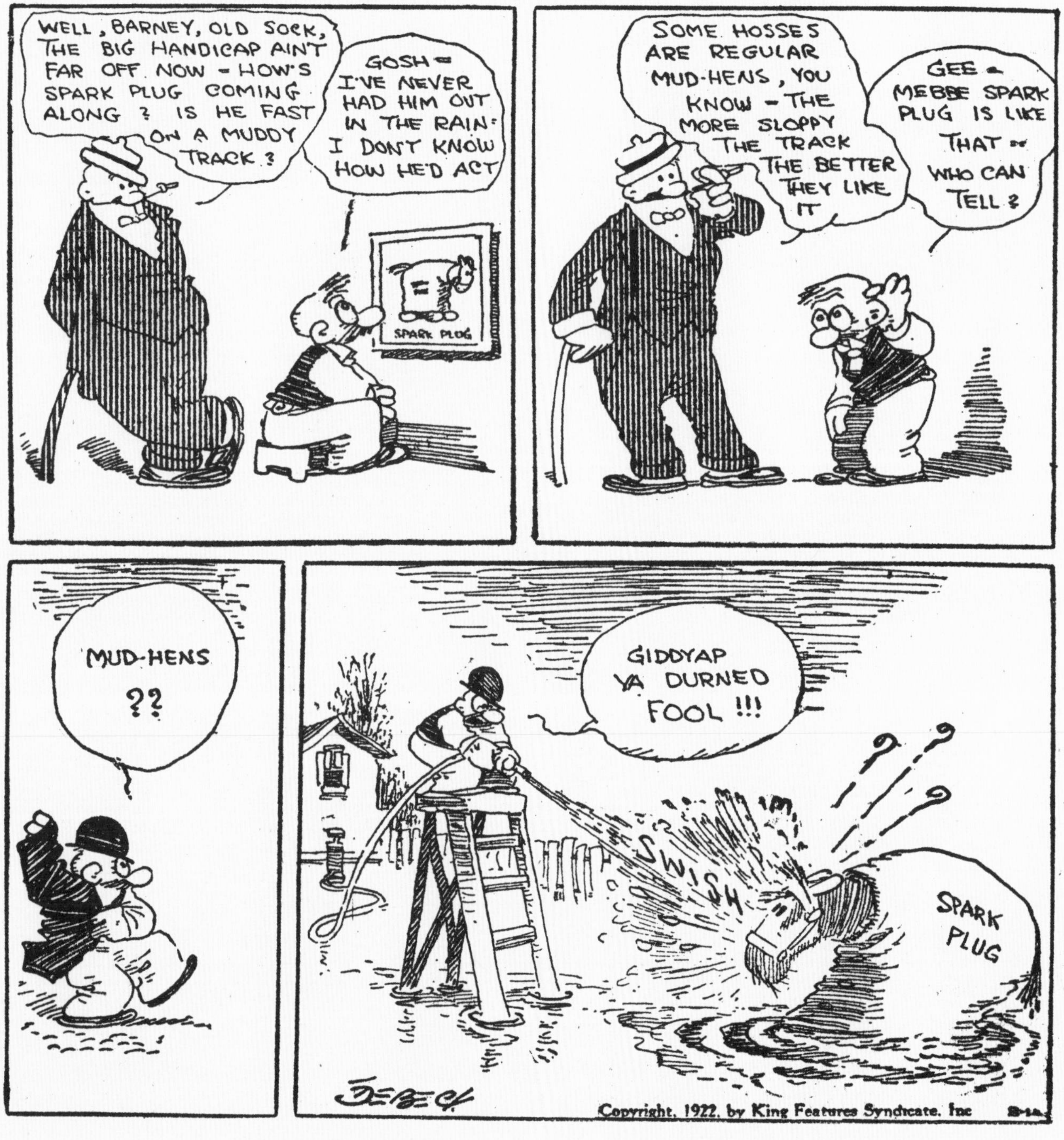
WELL, BARNEY, OLD SOCK, THE BIG HANDICAP AIN'T FAR OFF NOW - HOW'S SPARK PLUG COMING ALONG ? IS HE FAST ON A MUDDY TRACK ?
GOSH - I'VE NEVER HAD HIM OUT IN THE RAIN: I DON'T KNOW HOW HE'D ACT
SPARK PLUG
SOME HOSSES ARE REGULAR MUD-HENS, YOU KNOW - THE MORE SLOPPY THE TRACK THE BETTER THEY LIKE IT
GEE - MEBBE SPARK PLUG IS LIKE THAT - WHO CAN TELL ?
MUD-HENS ??
GIDDYAP YA DURNED FOOL !!!
SWISH
SPARK PLUG
Copyright, 1922, by King Features Syndicate, Inc

The Future Looks Rosy to Barney

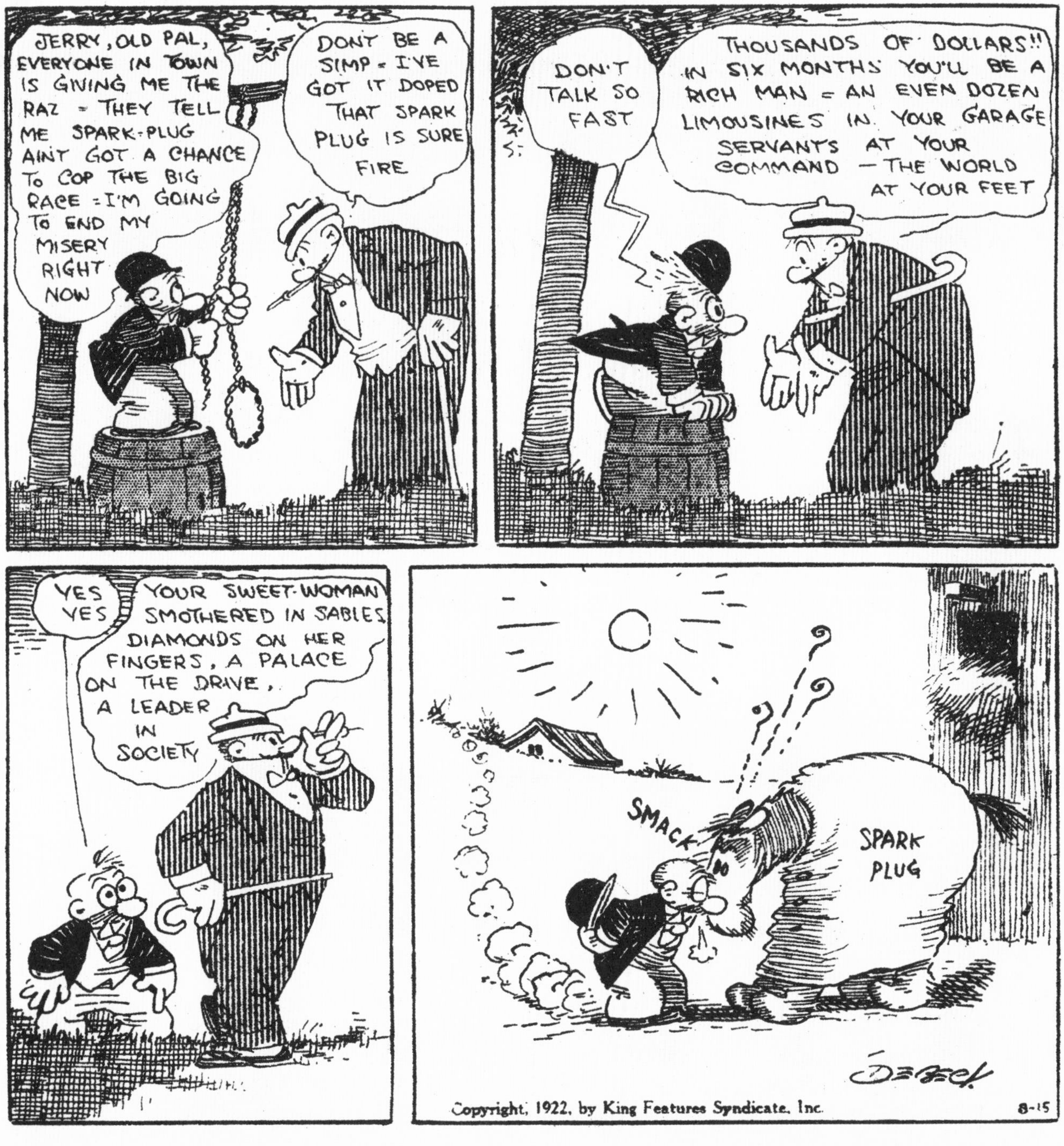
JERRY, OLD PAL, EVERYONE IN TOWN IS GIVING ME THE RAZ = THEY TELL ME SPARK-PLUG AINT GOT A CHANCE TO COP THE BIG RACE = I'M GOING TO END MY MISERY RIGHT NOW
DONT BE A SIMP = I'VE GOT IT DOPED THAT SPARK PLUG IS SURE FIRE
DON'T TALK SO FAST
THOUSANDS OF DOLLARS!! IN SIX MONTHS YOU'LL BE A RICH MAN = AN EVEN DOZEN LIMOUSINES IN YOUR GARAGE SERVANTS AT YOUR COMMAND — THE WORLD AT YOUR FEET
YES YES
YOUR SWEET-WOMAN SMOTHERED IN SABLES DIAMONDS ON HER FINGERS, A PALACE ON THE DRIVE, A LEADER IN SOCIETY
SMACK
SPARK PLUG
DE BECK
Copyright, 1922, by King Features Syndicate, Inc.
8-15

Barney's Nervous, Oh, So Nervous!

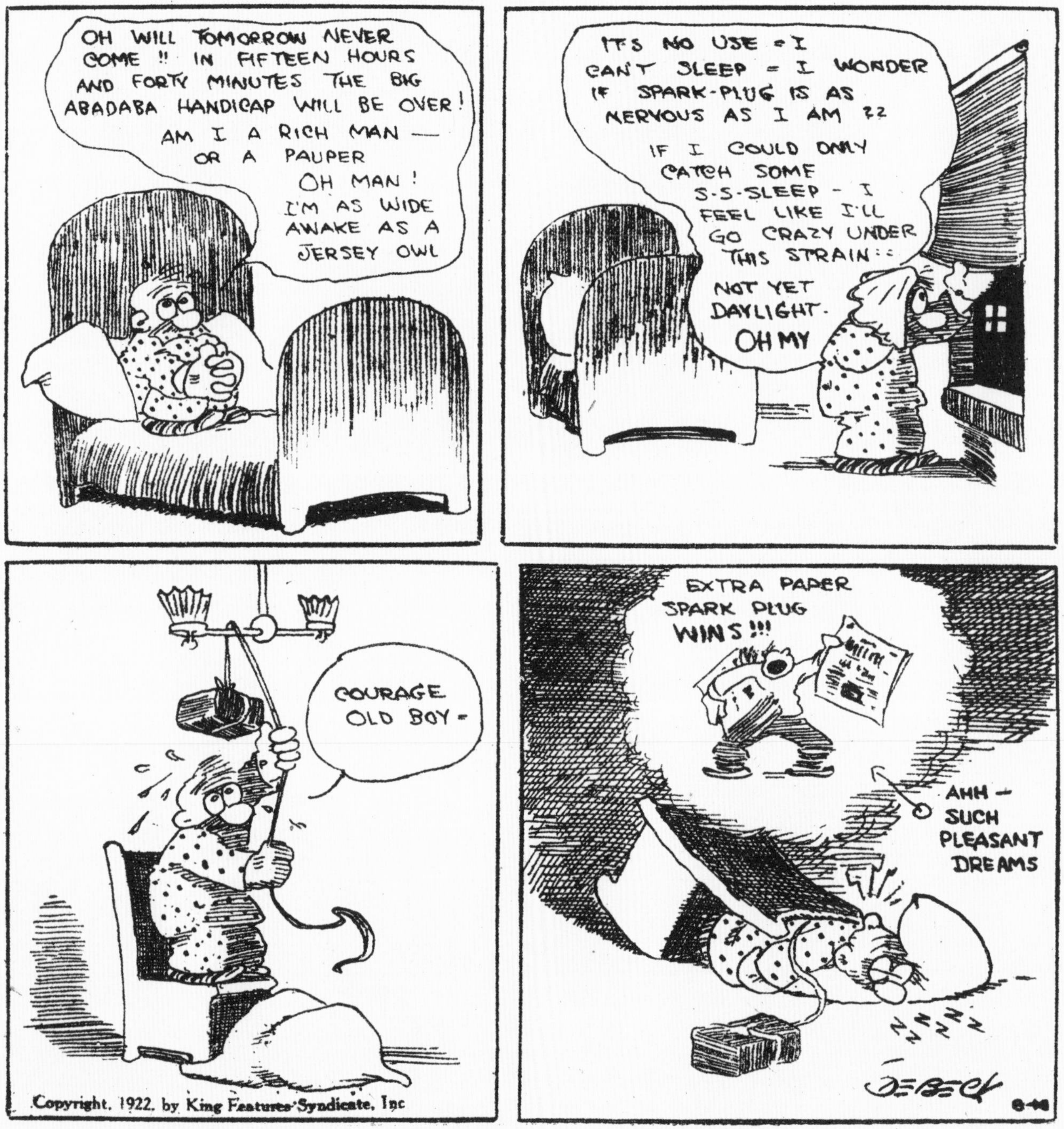

OH WILL TOMORROW NEVER COME !! IN FIFTEEN HOURS AND FORTY MINUTES THE BIG ABADABA HANDICAP WILL BE OVER!
AM I A RICH MAN — OR A PAUPER
OH MAN! I'M AS WIDE AWAKE AS A JERSEY OWL
ITS NO USE = I CAN'T SLEEP = I WONDER IF SPARK-PLUG IS AS NERVOUS AS I AM ??
IF I COULD ONLY CATCH SOME S-S-SLEEP - I FEEL LIKE I'LL GO CRAZY UNDER THIS STRAIN ::
NOT YET DAYLIGHT. OH MY
COURAGE OLD BOY -
EXTRA PAPER SPARK PLUG WINS!!!
AHH - SUCH PLEASANT DREAMS
Z Z Z Z Z
DE BECK
Copyright, 1922, by King Features Syndicate, Inc

Barney Prepared for the Worst

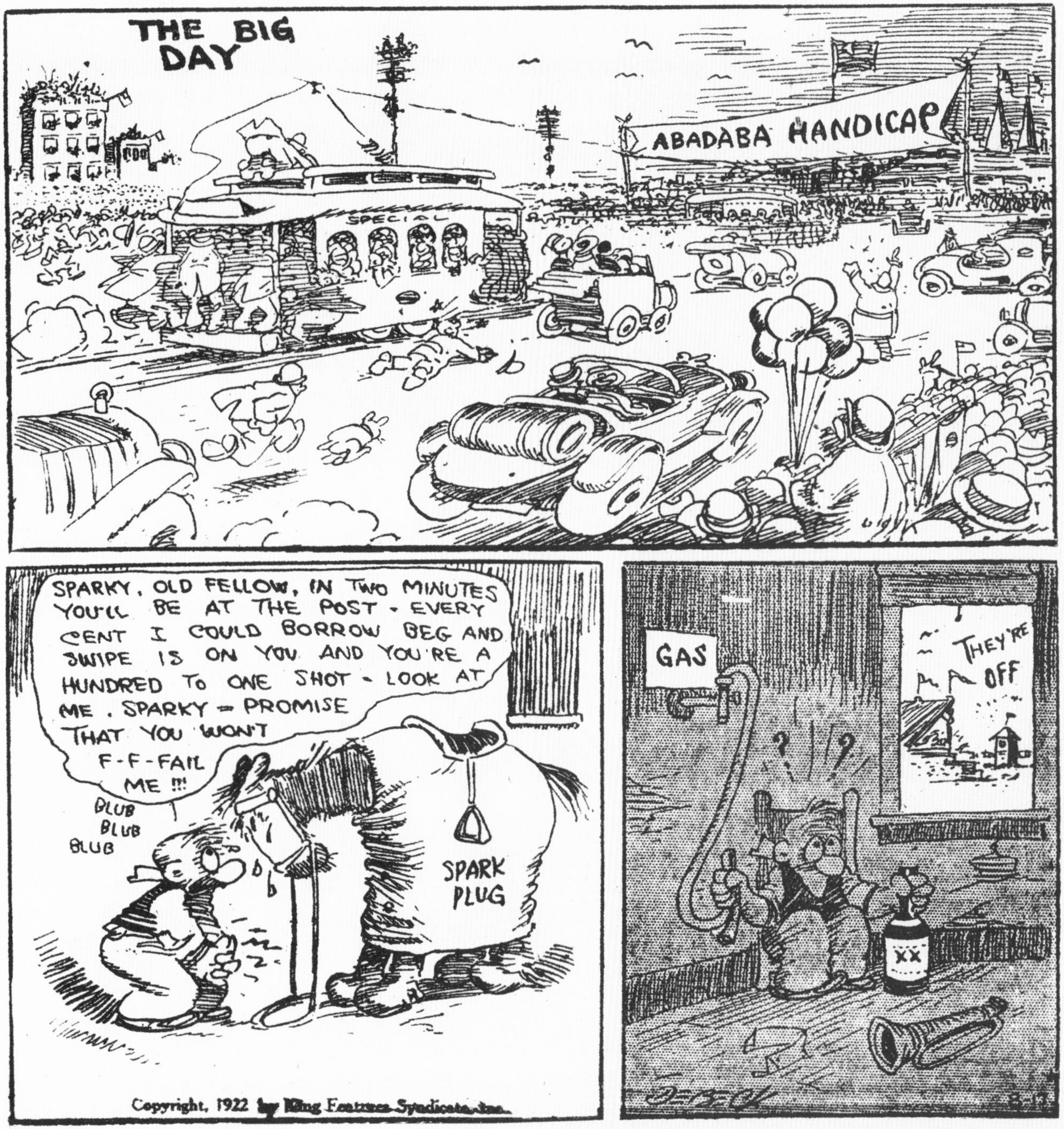
THE BIG DAY
SPECIAL
ABADABA HANDICAP
SPARKY, OLD FELLOW, IN TWO MINUTES YOU'LL BE AT THE POST - EVERY CENT I COULD BORROW BEG AND SWIPE IS ON YOU AND YOU'RE A HUNDRED TO ONE SHOT - LOOK AT ME. SPARKY - PROMISE THAT YOU WON'T F-F-FAIL ME !!!
BLUB BLUB BLUB
SPARK PLUG
Copyright, 1922 by King Features Syndicate, Inc.
GAS
THEY'RE OFF
XX

The Shock is Too Much For Barney

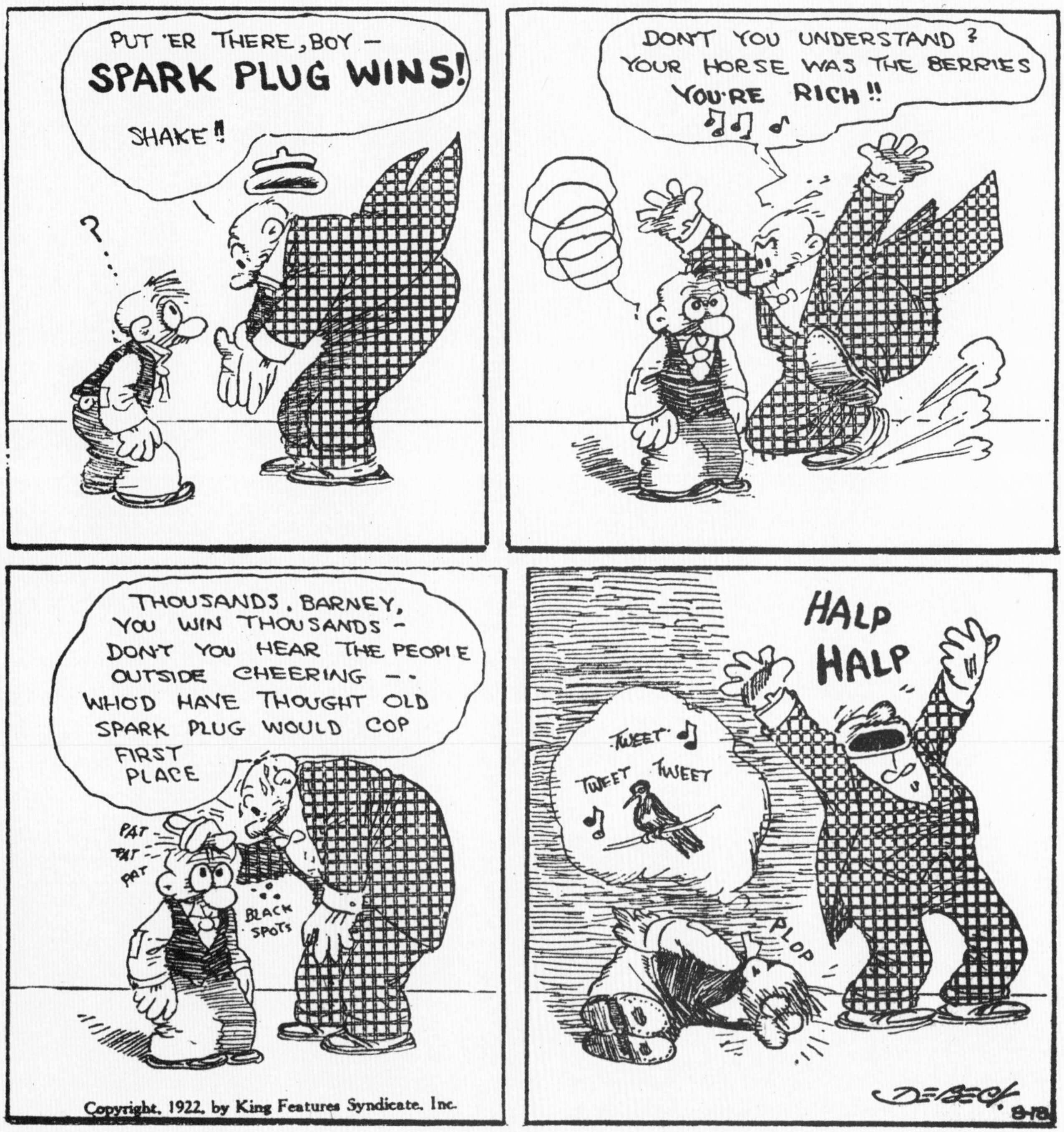
PUT 'ER THERE, BOY - SPARK PLUG WINS! SHAKE!!
?
DON'T YOU UNDERSTAND? YOUR HORSE WAS THE BERRIES YOU'RE RICH!!
THOUSANDS, BARNEY, YOU WIN THOUSANDS - DON'T YOU HEAR THE PEOPLE OUTSIDE CHEERING -- WHO'D HAVE THOUGHT OLD SPARK PLUG WOULD COP FIRST PLACE
PAT PAT PAT
BLACK SPOTS
HALP HALP
TWEET TWEET TWEET
PLOP
Copyright, 1922, by King Features Syndicate, Inc.
DE BECK

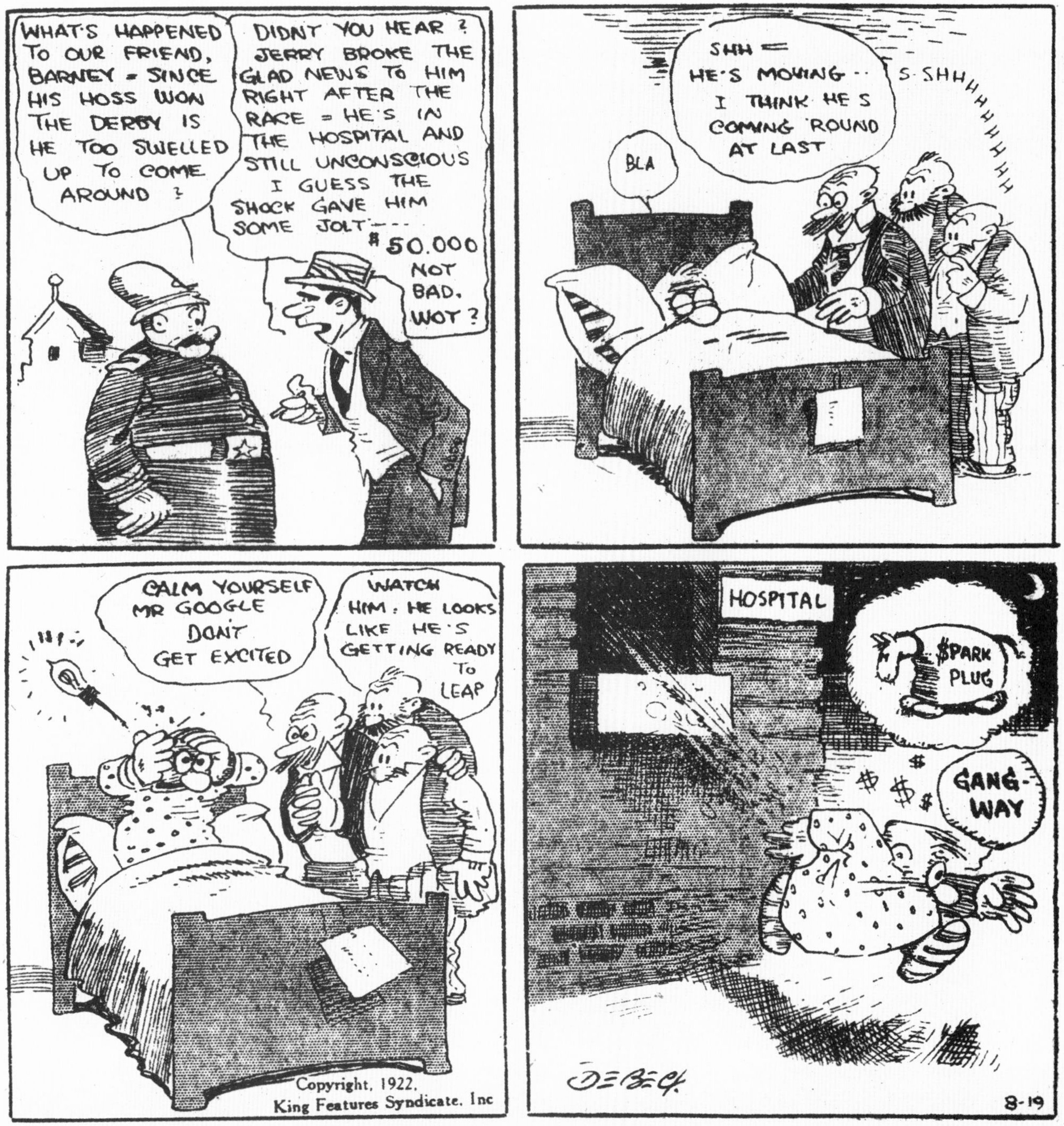
WHAT'S HAPPENED TO OUR FRIEND, BARNEY = SINCE HIS HOSS WON THE DERBY IS HE TOO SWELLED UP TO COME AROUND ?
DIDN'T YOU HEAR ? JERRY BROKE THE GLAD NEWS TO HIM RIGHT AFTER THE RACE = HE'S IN THE HOSPITAL AND STILL UNCONSCIOUS I GUESS THE SHOCK GAVE HIM SOME JOLT---
$50.000 NOT BAD. WOT ?
SHH = HE'S MOVING -- I THINK HE'S COMING ROUND AT LAST
BLA
S-SHHHHHHHHHH
CALM YOURSELF MR GOOGLE DON'T GET EXCITED
WATCH HIM: HE LOOKS LIKE HE'S GETTING READY TO LEAP
HOSPITAL
$PARK PLUG
GANG-WAY
DEBECK
8-19
Copyright, 1922, King Features Syndicate, Inc

Barney Would "Stake" Spark Plug to the Best There Is

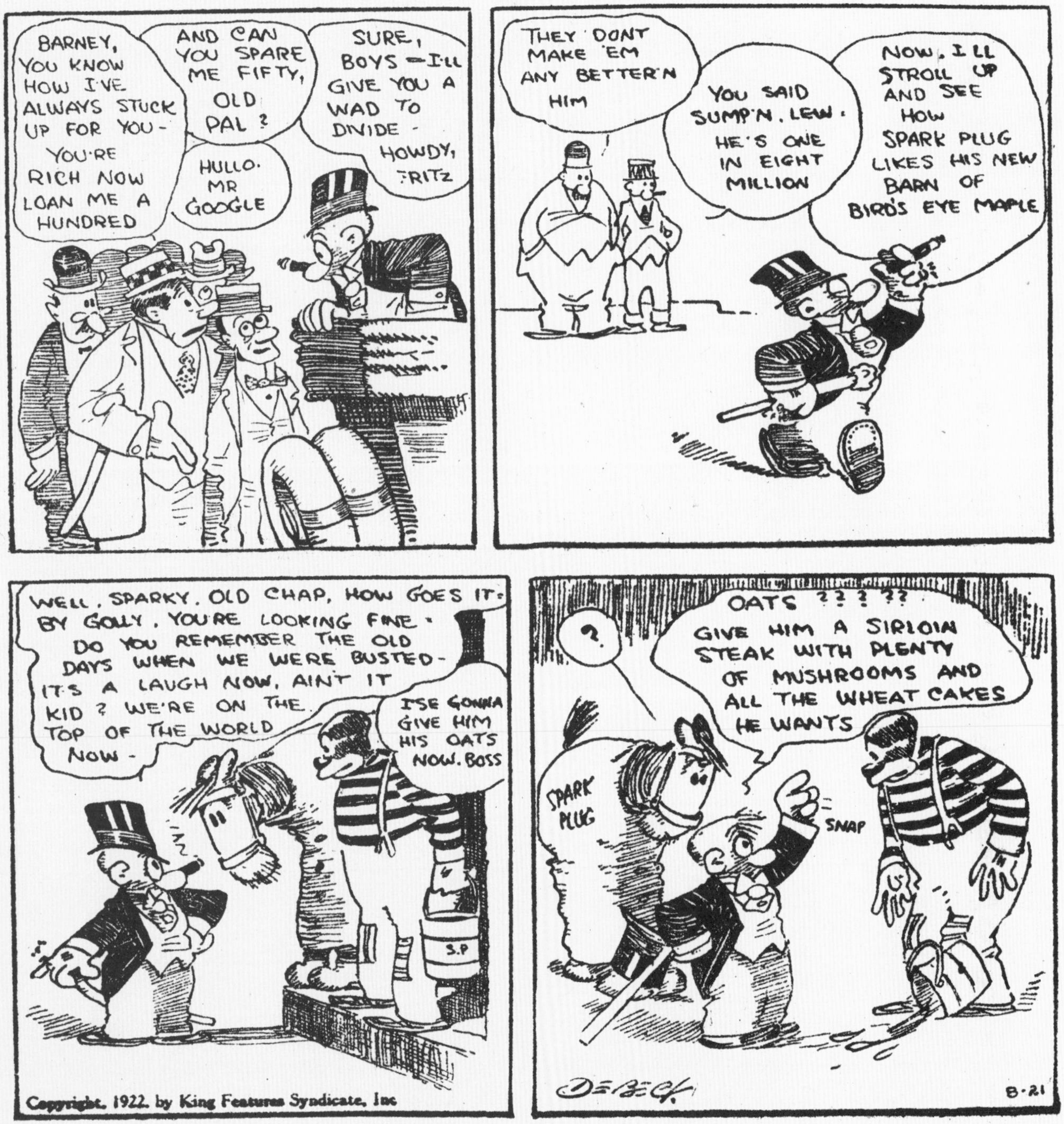
BARNEY, YOU KNOW HOW I'VE ALWAYS STUCK UP FOR YOU - YOU'RE RICH NOW LOAN ME A HUNDRED
AND CAN YOU SPARE ME FIFTY, OLD PAL ?
HULLO. MR GOOGLE
SURE, BOYS - I'LL GIVE YOU A WAD TO DIVIDE - HOWDY, FRITZ
THEY DONT MAKE 'EM ANY BETTER'N HIM
YOU SAID SUMP'N, LEW. HE'S ONE IN EIGHT MILLION
NOW, I'LL STROLL UP AND SEE HOW SPARK PLUG LIKES HIS NEW BARN OF BIRD'S EYE MAPLE
WELL, SPARKY, OLD CHAP, HOW GOES IT - BY GOLLY, YOU'RE LOOKING FINE - DO YOU REMEMBER THE OLD DAYS WHEN WE WERE BUSTED - IT'S A LAUGH NOW, AIN'T IT KID ? WE'RE ON THE TOP OF THE WORLD NOW -
I'SE GONNA GIVE HIM HIS OATS NOW. BOSS
S.P
Copyright, 1922, by King Features Syndicate, Inc
?
OATS ??? ?? GIVE HIM A SIRLOIN STEAK WITH PLENTY OF MUSHROOMS AND ALL THE WHEAT CAKES HE WANTS
SPARK PLUG
SNAP
DE BECK
8-21

Barney's Money Gets Him Something He Doesn't Want

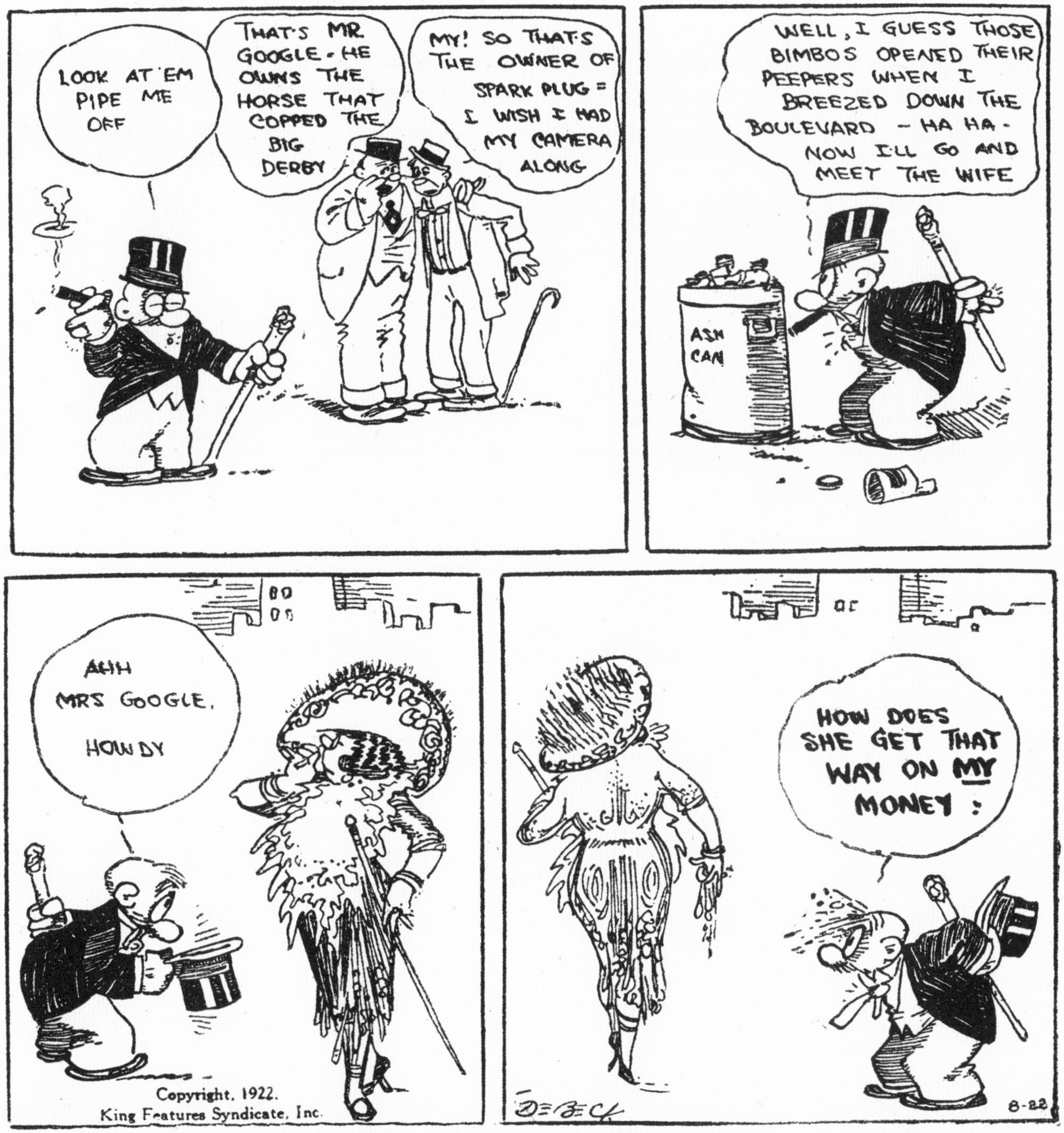
LOOK AT 'EM PIPE ME OFF
THAT'S MR. GOOGLE - HE OWNS THE HORSE THAT COPPED THE BIG DERBY
MY! SO THAT'S THE OWNER OF SPARK PLUG = I WISH I HAD MY CAMERA ALONG
WELL, I GUESS THOSE BIMBOS OPENED THEIR PEEPERS WHEN I BREEZED DOWN THE BOULEVARD - HA HA - NOW I'LL GO AND MEET THE WIFE
ASH CAN
AHH MRS GOOGLE. HOWDY
HOW DOES SHE GET THAT WAY ON MY MONEY :
Copyright, 1922. King Features Syndicate, Inc.
DE BECK
8-22

Four-Leaf Clovers Mean Nothing to Spark Plug

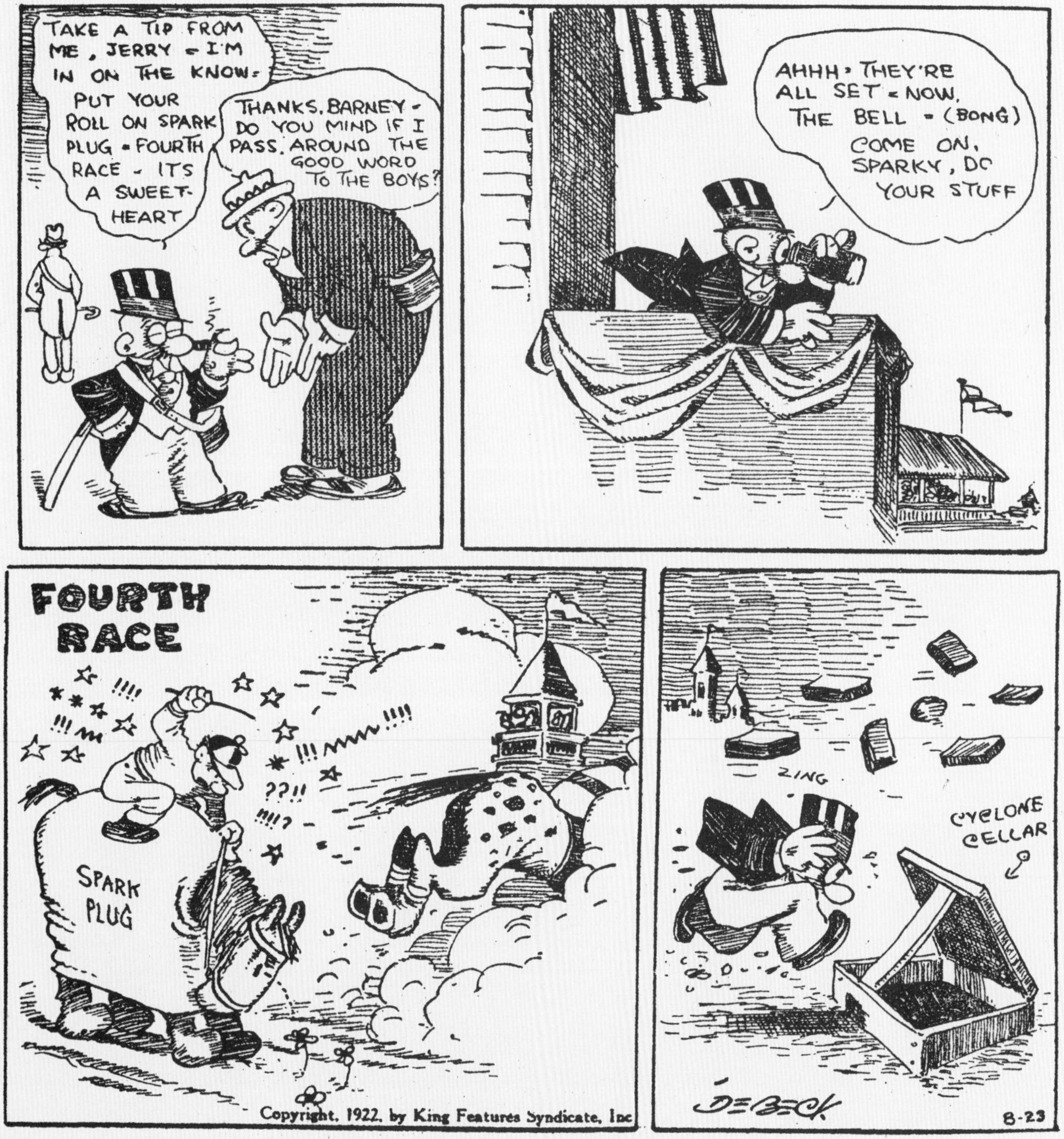
TAKE A TIP FROM ME, JERRY - I'M IN ON THE KNOW - PUT YOUR ROLL ON SPARK PLUG - FOURTH RACE - ITS A SWEET-HEART
THANKS, BARNEY - DO YOU MIND IF I PASS AROUND THE GOOD WORD TO THE BOYS?
AHHH - THEY'RE ALL SET - NOW, THE BELL - (BONG) COME ON, SPARKY, DO YOUR STUFF
FOURTH RACE
SPARK PLUG
!!!! !!! MM !!! MMM !!!! ??!! !!!?
ZING
CYCLONE CELLAR
DE BECK
Copyright, 1922, by King Features Syndicate, Inc
8-23

Barney Has No Kick Coming, But Gets One Just the Same

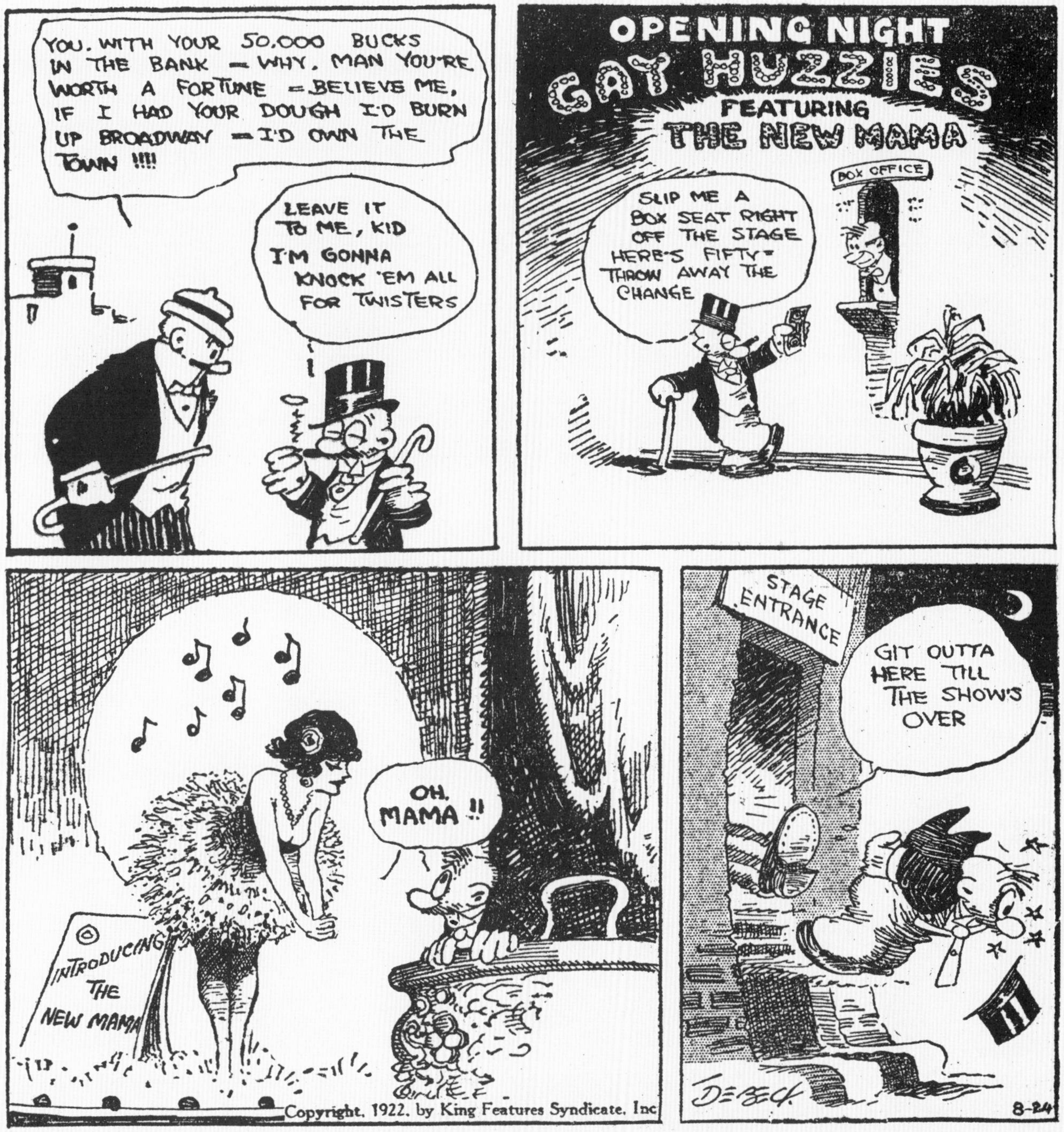
YOU, WITH YOUR 50,000 BUCKS IN THE BANK — WHY, MAN YOU'RE WORTH A FORTUNE — BELIEVE ME, IF I HAD YOUR DOUGH I'D BURN UP BROADWAY — I'D OWN THE TOWN !!!!
LEAVE IT TO ME, KID I'M GONNA KNOCK 'EM ALL FOR TWISTERS
OPENING NIGHT
GAY HUZZIES
FEATURING
THE NEW MAMA
BOX OFFICE
SLIP ME A BOX SEAT RIGHT OFF THE STAGE HERE'S FIFTY — THROW AWAY THE CHANGE
INTRODUCING THE NEW MAMA
OH, MAMA !!
Copyright, 1922, by King Features Syndicate, Inc
STAGE ENTRANCE
GIT OUTTA HERE TILL THE SHOW'S OVER
DEBECK
8-24

Barney Has a Rival, It Seems

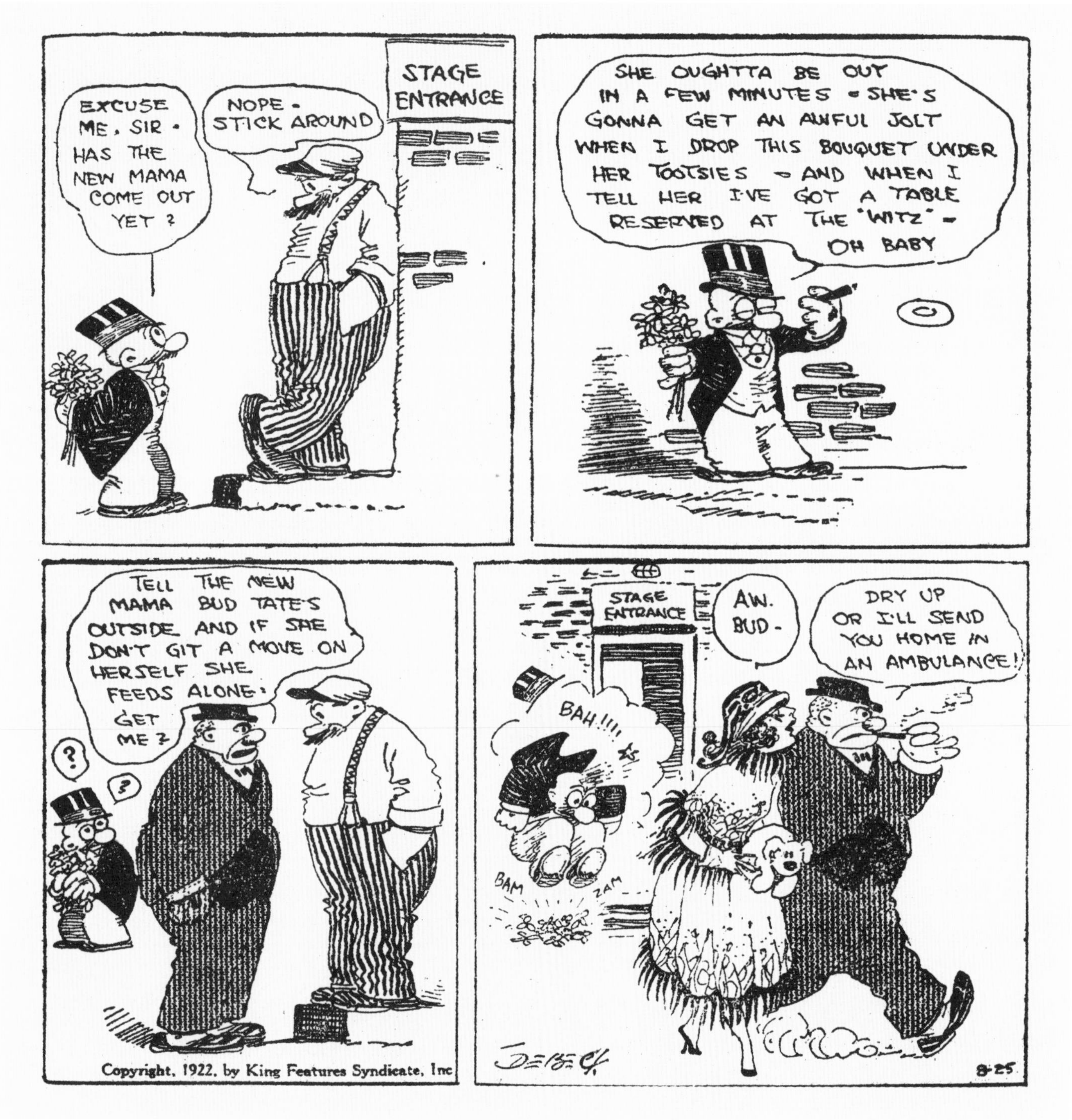
EXCUSE ME, SIR - HAS THE NEW MAMA COME OUT YET ?
NOPE - STICK AROUND
STAGE ENTRANCE
SHE OUGHTTA BE OUT IN A FEW MINUTES - SHE'S GONNA GET AN AWFUL JOLT WHEN I DROP THIS BOUQUET UNDER HER TOOTSIES - AND WHEN I TELL HER I'VE GOT A TABLE RESERVED AT THE "WITZ" - OH BABY
TELL THE NEW MAMA BUD TATE'S OUTSIDE AND IF SHE DON'T GIT A MOVE ON HERSELF SHE FEEDS ALONE - GET ME ?
Copyright, 1922, by King Features Syndicate, Inc
STAGE ENTRANCE
AW. BUD -
DRY UP OR I'LL SEND YOU HOME IN AN AMBULANCE!
BAH!!!!
BAM
ZAM
8-25

Barney Just Can't Make His Heart Behave

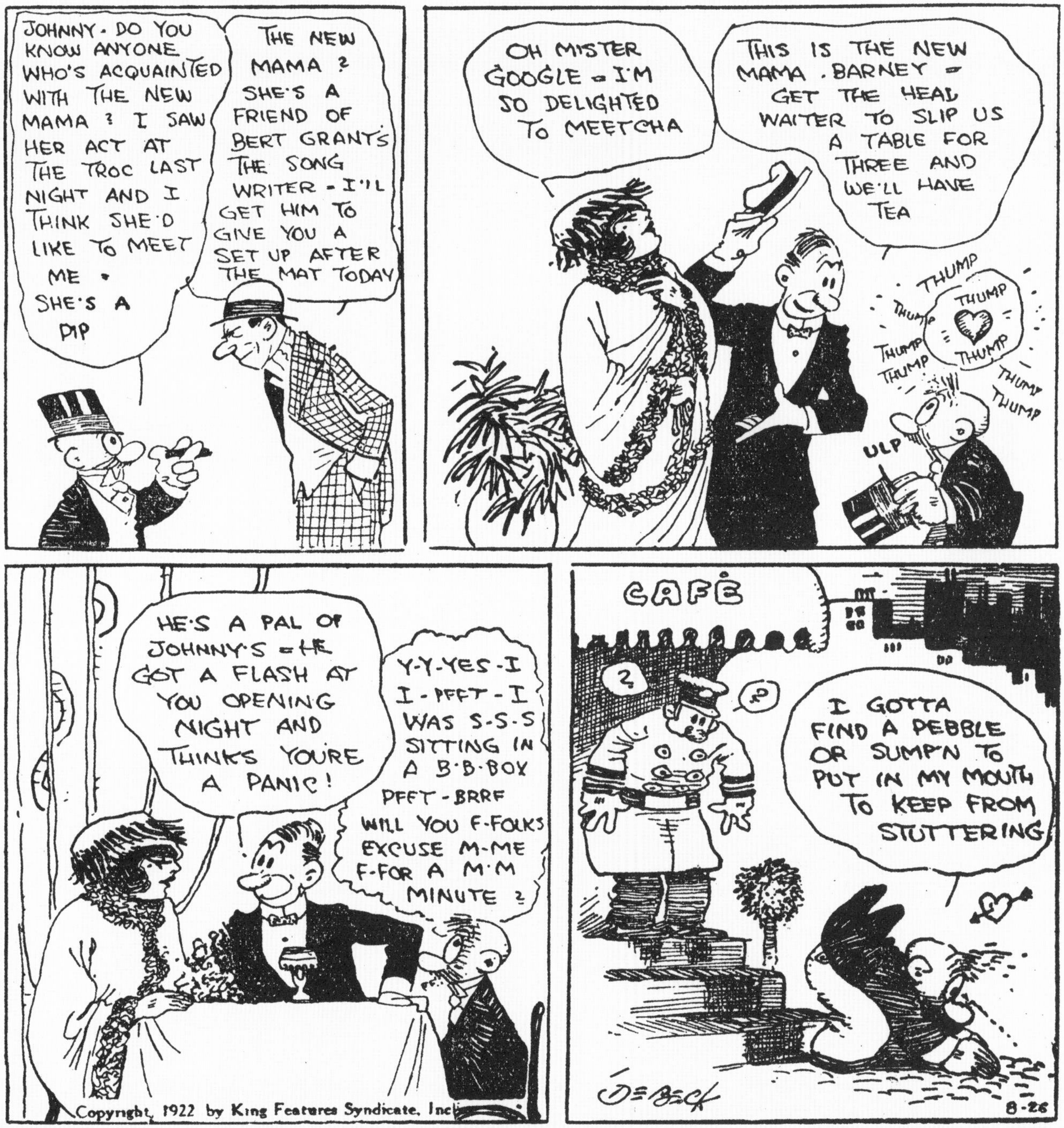
JOHNNY - DO YOU KNOW ANYONE WHO'S ACQUAINTED WITH THE NEW MAMA? I SAW HER ACT AT THE TROC LAST NIGHT AND I THINK SHE'D LIKE TO MEET ME - SHE'S A DIP
THE NEW MAMA? SHE'S A FRIEND OF BERT GRANT'S THE SONG WRITER - I'LL GET HIM TO GIVE YOU A SET UP AFTER THE MAT TODAY
OH MISTER GOOGLE - I'M SO DELIGHTED TO MEETCHA
THIS IS THE NEW MAMA - BARNEY - GET THE HEAD WAITER TO SLIP US A TABLE FOR THREE AND WE'LL HAVE TEA
THUMP THUMP THUMP THUMP THUMP THUMP THUMP THUMP THUMP
ULP
HE'S A PAL OF JOHNNY'S - HE GOT A FLASH AT YOU OPENING NIGHT AND THINKS YOU'RE A PANIC!
Y-Y-YES-I I-PFFT-I WAS S-S-S SITTING IN A B-B-BOX PFFT-BRRF WILL YOU F-FOLKS EXCUSE M-ME F-FOR A M-M MINUTE?
CAFÉ
?
?
I GOTTA FIND A PEBBLE OR SUMP'N TO PUT IN MY MOUTH TO KEEP FROM STUTTERING
Copyright, 1922 by King Features Syndicate, Inc.
DE BECK
8-26

Barney Gets the Gate

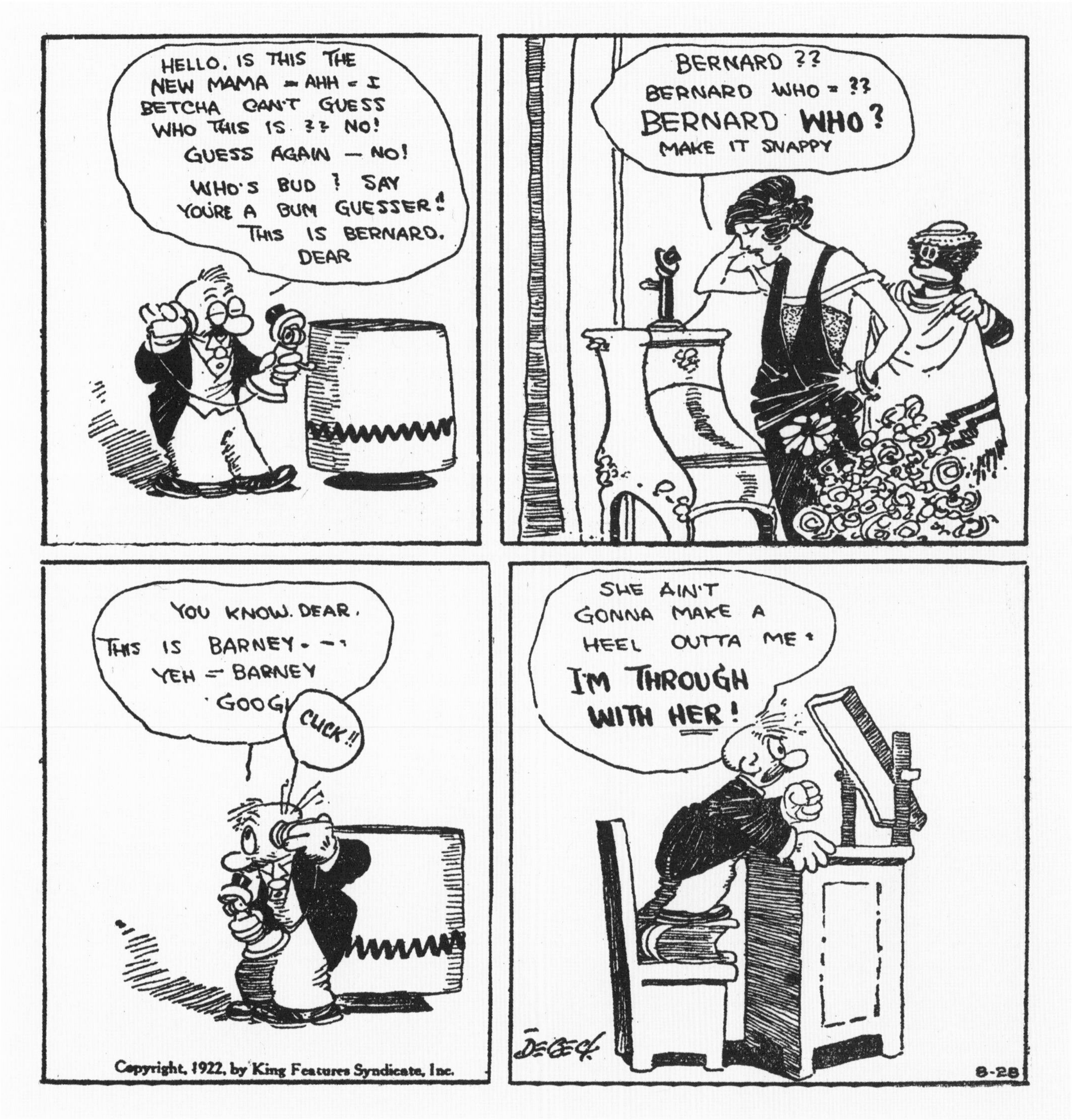
HELLO, IS THIS THE NEW MAMA – AHH – I BETCHA CAN'T GUESS WHO THIS IS ?? NO! GUESS AGAIN – NO! WHO'S BUD ? SAY YOU'RE A BUM GUESSER! THIS IS BERNARD, DEAR
BERNARD ?? BERNARD WHO – ?? BERNARD WHO? MAKE IT SNAPPY
YOU KNOW, DEAR, THIS IS BARNEY – – YEH – BARNEY GOOG
CLICK!!
SHE AIN'T GONNA MAKE A HEEL OUTTA ME – I'M THROUGH WITH HER!
DEBECK
Copyright, 1922, by King Features Syndicate, Inc.
8-28

Barney's Sir Walter Raleigh Stuff Fails to Work

WHAT'S ALL THE GOSSIP I HEAR ON BROADWAY ABOUT YOU AND THE NEW MAMA ?
BUNK
SHE'S ABOUT AS POPULAR WITH ME AS AN OLD MAID'S WRINKLES = IN MY YOUNG LIFE SHE MEANS NOTHING -
THAT'S RATHER ODD = ERNIE YOUNG SLIPPED IT TO ME ON THE Q.T THAT SHE WAS STUCK ON YOU = HE SAW YOUR PICTURE IN A LITTLE DIAMOND LOCKET SHE HAD AROUND HER NECK ..
YOU'RE TOO HARD ON HER, BARNEY = WHY DON'T YOU CALL UP THE POOR GAL AND ACCEPT HER APOLOGY FOR THE WAY SHE'S BEEN ACTING.
SHH = HERE SHE COMES NOW = BY GOLLY, IF SHE AINT CAREFUL SHE'LL GET HER FEET WET
? ? ?
Copyright, 1922, by King Features Syndicate, Inc.
DE BECK
8-29

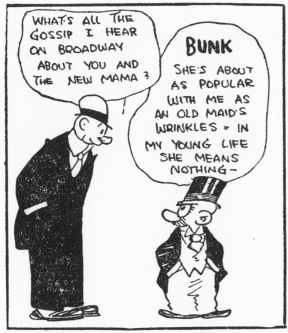

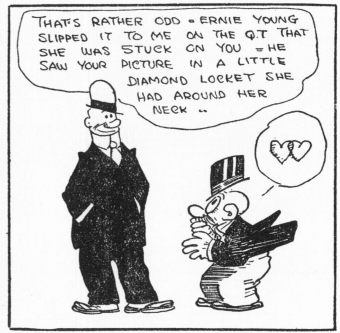

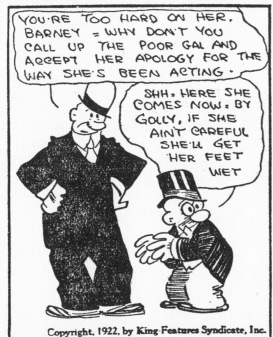

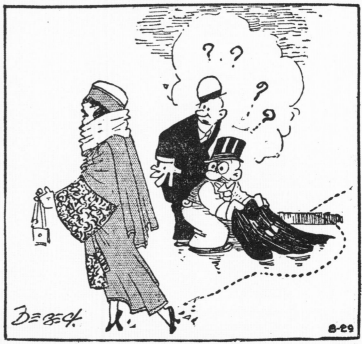

As a Buyer Barney's Busy as a Bee

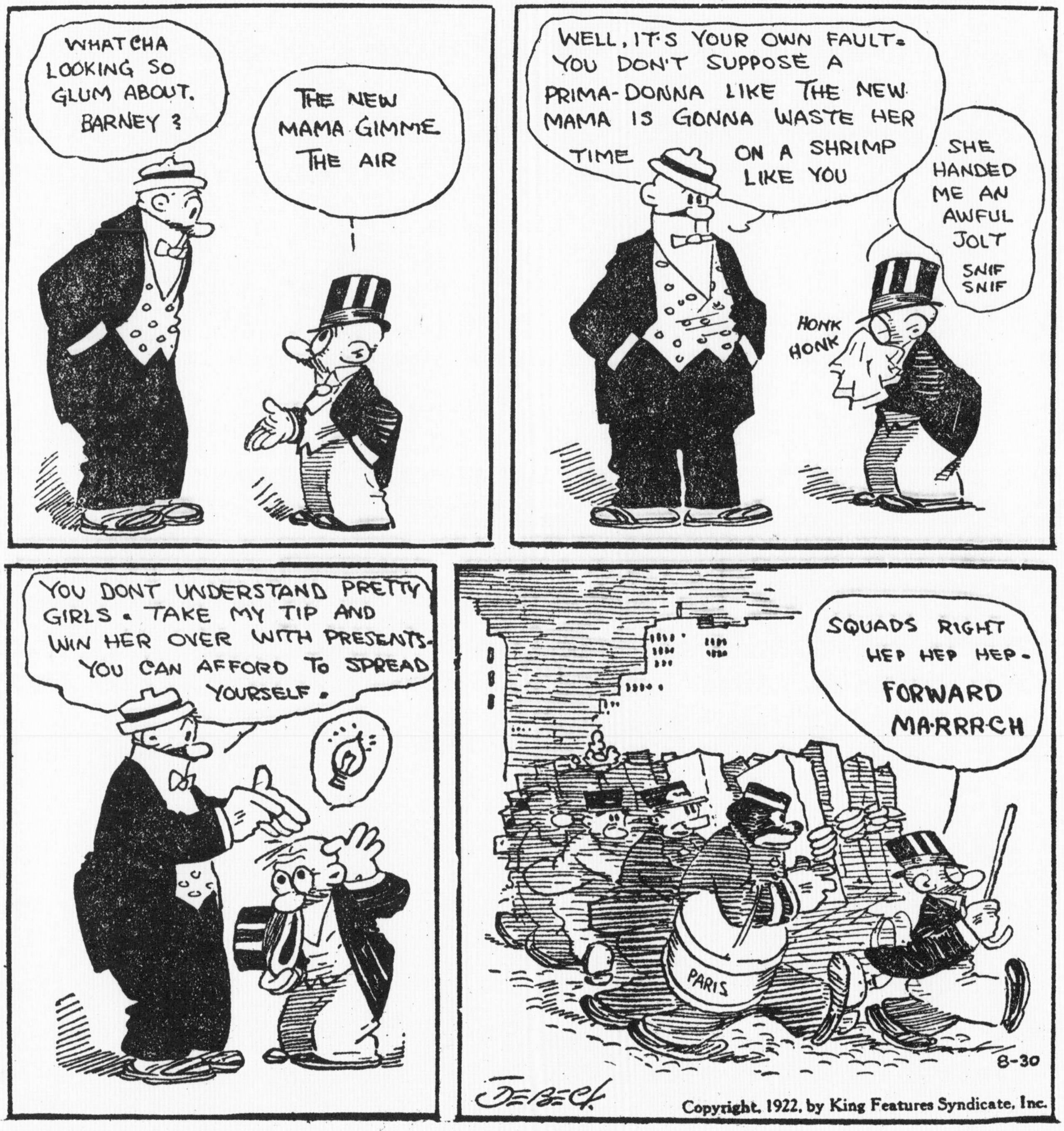
WHATCHA LOOKING SO GLUM ABOUT. BARNEY ?
THE NEW MAMA GIMME THE AIR
WELL, IT'S YOUR OWN FAULT. YOU DON'T SUPPOSE A PRIMA-DONNA LIKE THE NEW MAMA IS GONNA WASTE HER TIME ON A SHRIMP LIKE YOU
SHE HANDED ME AN AWFUL JOLT
SNIF SNIF
HONK HONK
YOU DONT UNDERSTAND PRETTY GIRLS. TAKE MY TIP AND WIN HER OVER WITH PRESENTS- YOU CAN AFFORD TO SPREAD YOURSELF.
SQUADS RIGHT HEP HEP HEP- FORWARD MA-RRR-CH
PARIS
8-30
DeBeck
Copyright, 1922, by King Features Syndicate, Inc.

Barney's "Good Buy" Means Good-bye

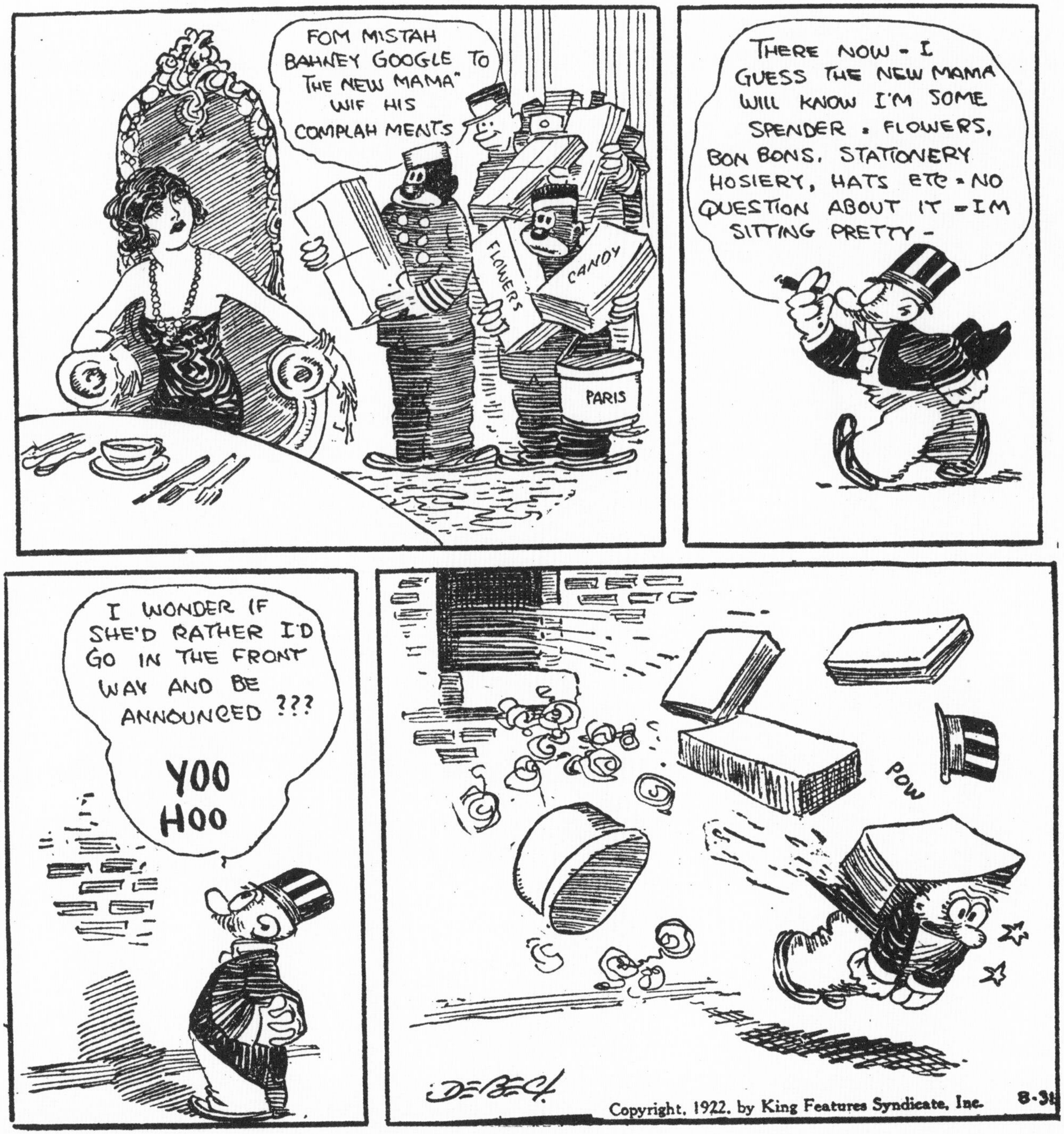
FOM MISTAH BAHNEY GOOGLE TO THE NEW MAMA" WIF HIS COMPLAH MENTS
FLOWERS
CANDY
PARIS
THERE NOW - I GUESS THE NEW MAMA WILL KNOW I'M SOME SPENDER - FLOWERS, BON BONS, STATIONERY HOSIERY, HATS ETC - NO QUESTION ABOUT IT - I'M SITTING PRETTY -
I WONDER IF SHE'D RATHER I'D GO IN THE FRONT WAY AND BE ANNOUNCED ???
YOO HOO
POW
DE BECK
Copyright, 1922, by King Features Syndicate, Inc.
8-31

This Doesn't Make Barney Feel Any Better

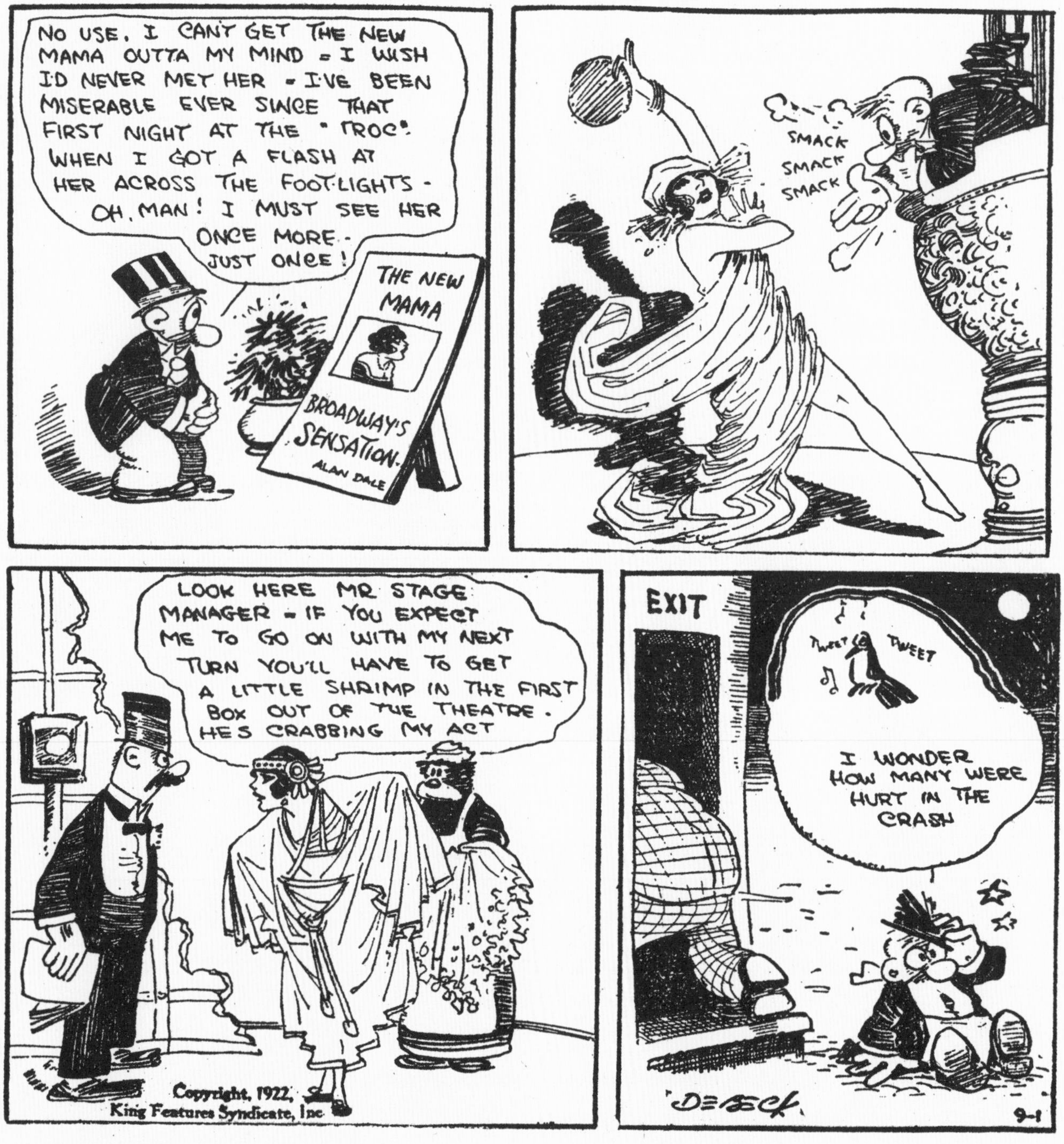

NO USE. I CAN'T GET THE NEW MAMA OUTTA MY MIND - I WISH I'D NEVER MET HER - I'VE BEEN MISERABLE EVER SINCE THAT FIRST NIGHT AT THE "TROC" WHEN I GOT A FLASH AT HER ACROSS THE FOOT-LIGHTS - OH, MAN! I MUST SEE HER ONCE MORE - JUST ONCE!
THE NEW MAMA
BROADWAY'S SENSATION. ALAN DALE
SMACK
SMACK
SMACK
LOOK HERE MR STAGE MANAGER - IF YOU EXPECT ME TO GO ON WITH MY NEXT TURN YOU'LL HAVE TO GET A LITTLE SHRIMP IN THE FIRST BOX OUT OF THE THEATRE. HE'S CRABBING MY ACT
Copyright, 1922, King Features Syndicate, Inc.
EXIT
TWEET
TWEET
I WONDER HOW MANY WERE HURT IN THE CRASH
DEBECK
9-1

And the Truer the Love, the Rougher It Is. Oh, My, Yes!

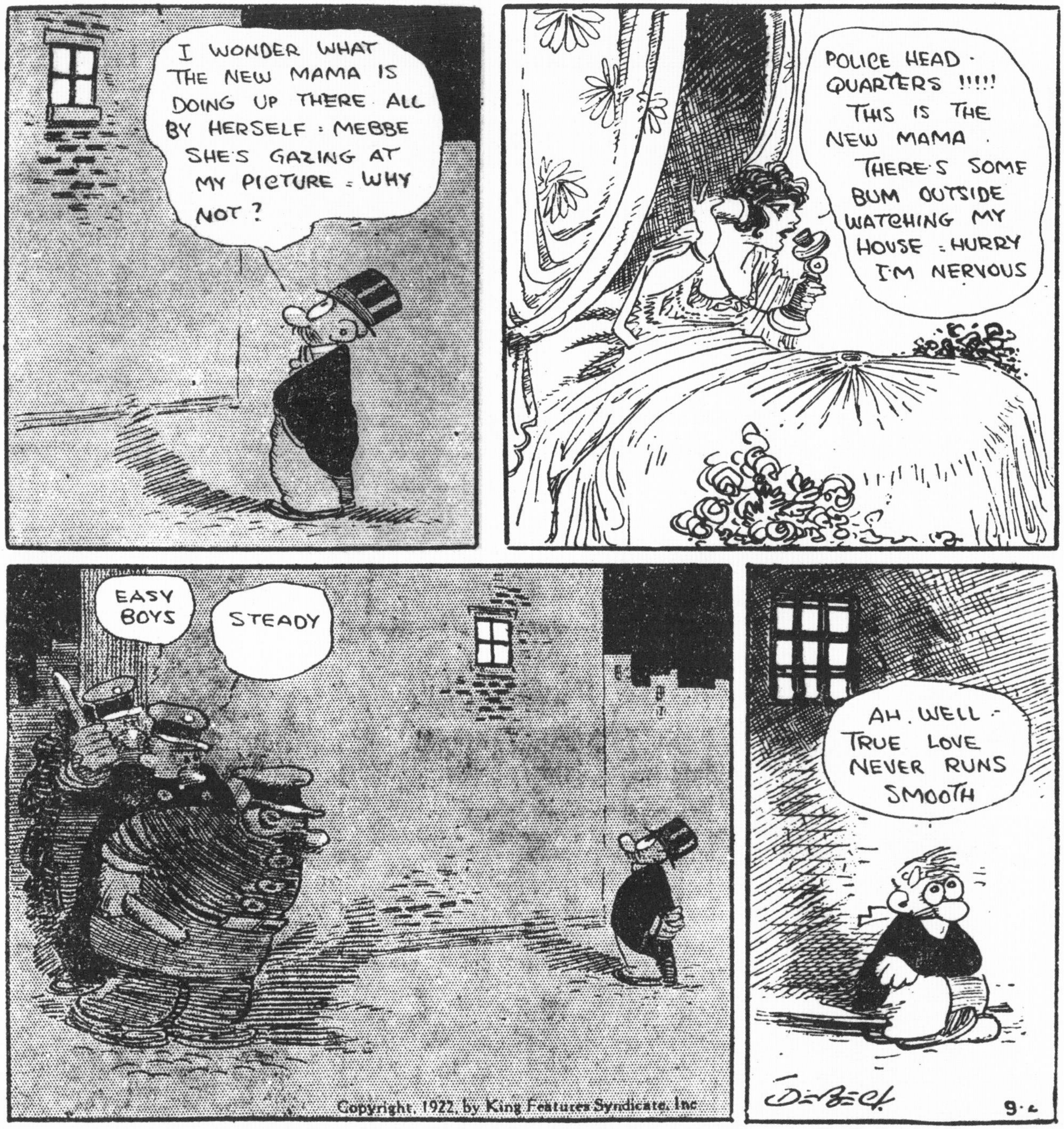
I WONDER WHAT THE NEW MAMA IS DOING UP THERE ALL BY HERSELF - MEBBE SHE'S GAZING AT MY PICTURE - WHY NOT ?
POLICE HEAD-QUARTERS !!!!! THIS IS THE NEW MAMA. THERE'S SOME BUM OUTSIDE WATCHING MY HOUSE - HURRY I'M NERVOUS
EASY BOYS
STEADY
Copyright, 1922, by King Features Syndicate, Inc
AH, WELL - TRUE LOVE NEVER RUNS SMOOTH

Persistency Wins!

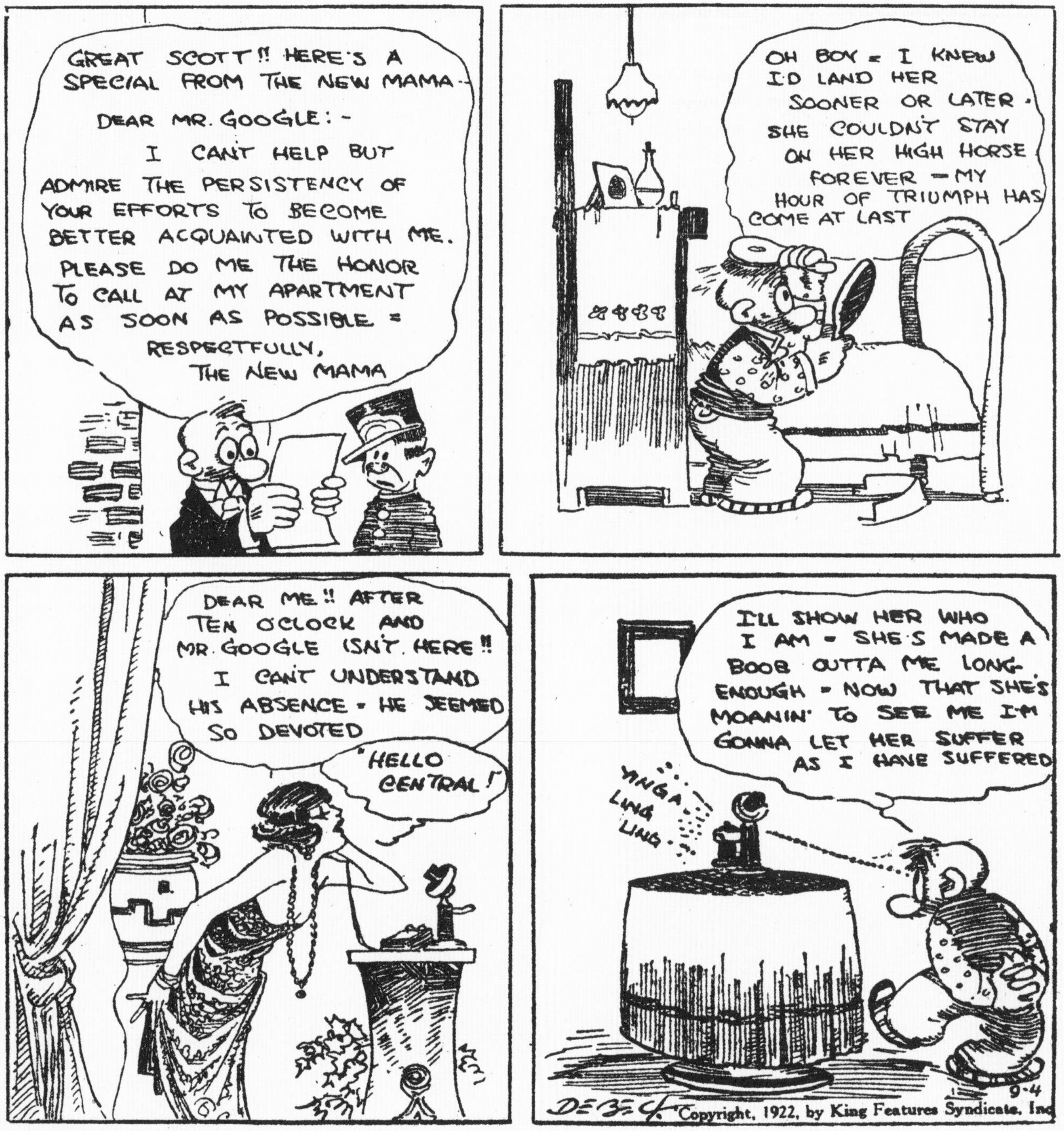

GREAT SCOTT!! HERE'S A SPECIAL FROM THE NEW MAMA - DEAR MR. GOOGLE:- I CAN'T HELP BUT ADMIRE THE PERSISTENCY OF YOUR EFFORTS TO BECOME BETTER ACQUAINTED WITH ME. PLEASE DO ME THE HONOR TO CALL AT MY APARTMENT AS SOON AS POSSIBLE = RESPECTFULLY, THE NEW MAMA
OH BOY = I KNEW I'D LAND HER SOONER OR LATER. SHE COULDN'T STAY ON HER HIGH HORSE FOREVER - MY HOUR OF TRIUMPH HAS COME AT LAST
DEAR ME!! AFTER TEN O'CLOCK AND MR. GOOGLE ISN'T HERE!! I CAN'T UNDERSTAND HIS ABSENCE - HE SEEMED SO DEVOTED
"HELLO CENTRAL!"
I'LL SHOW HER WHO I AM - SHE'S MADE A BOOB OUTTA ME LONG ENOUGH - NOW THAT SHE'S MOANIN' TO SEE ME I'M GONNA LET HER SUFFER AS I HAVE SUFFERED
YINGA LING LING
9-4
DE BECK
Copyright, 1922, by King Features Syndicate, Inc

Isn't Barney the Cold-Hearted Old Cove?

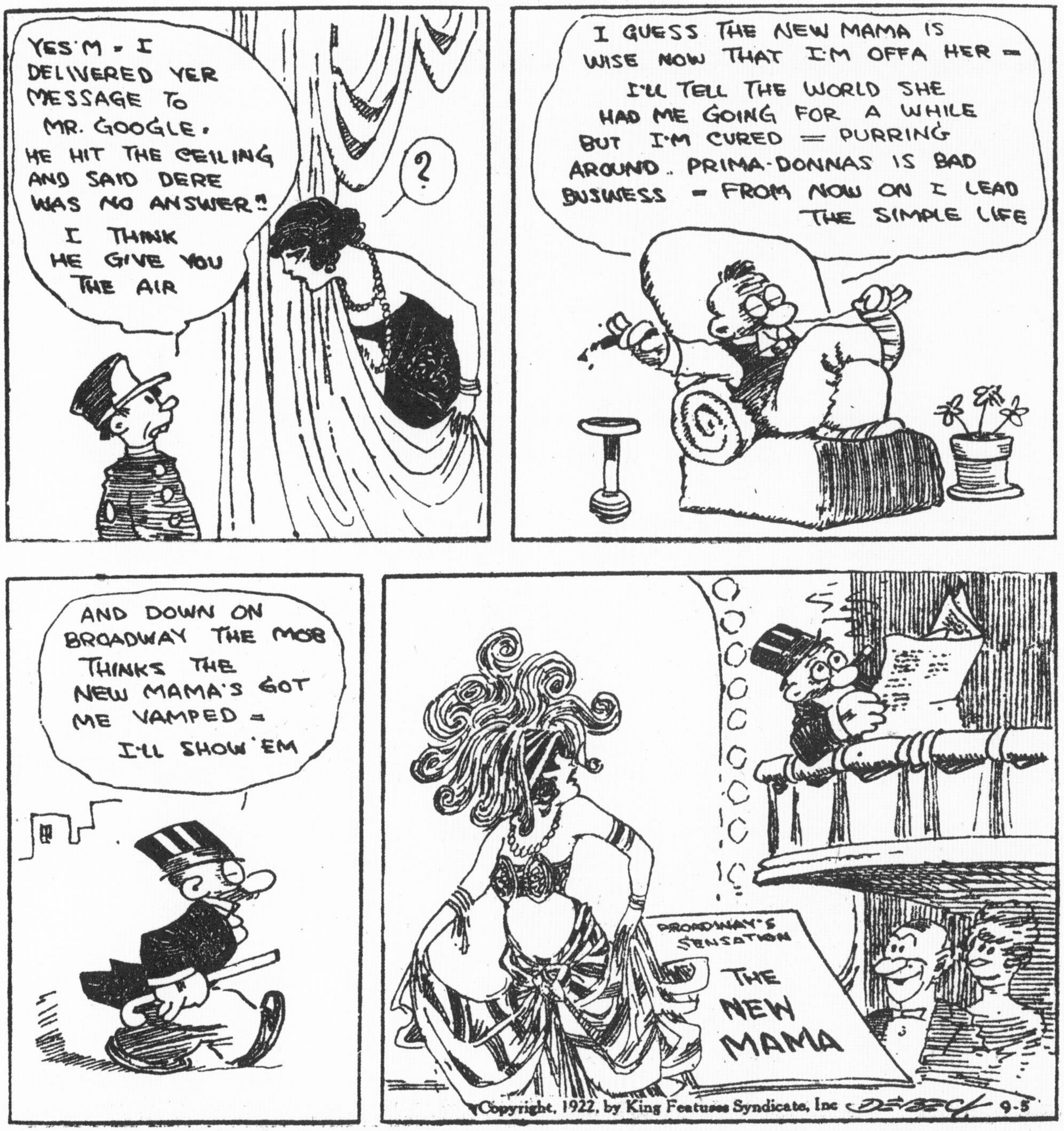
YES'M - I DELIVERED YER MESSAGE TO MR. GOOGLE. HE HIT THE CEILING AND SAID DERE WAS NO ANSWER!! I THINK HE GIVE YOU THE AIR
?
I GUESS THE NEW MAMA IS WISE NOW THAT I'M OFFA HER - I'LL TELL THE WORLD SHE HAD ME GOING FOR A WHILE BUT I'M CURED = PURRING AROUND PRIMA-DONNAS IS BAD BUSINESS - FROM NOW ON I LEAD THE SIMPLE LIFE
AND DOWN ON BROADWAY THE MOB THINKS THE NEW MAMA'S GOT ME VAMPED = I'LL SHOW 'EM
BROADWAY'S SENSATION
THE NEW MAMA
Copyright, 1922, by King Features Syndicate, Inc
9-5

Blondes May Be Barney's Type, but Oh, You Brunette!

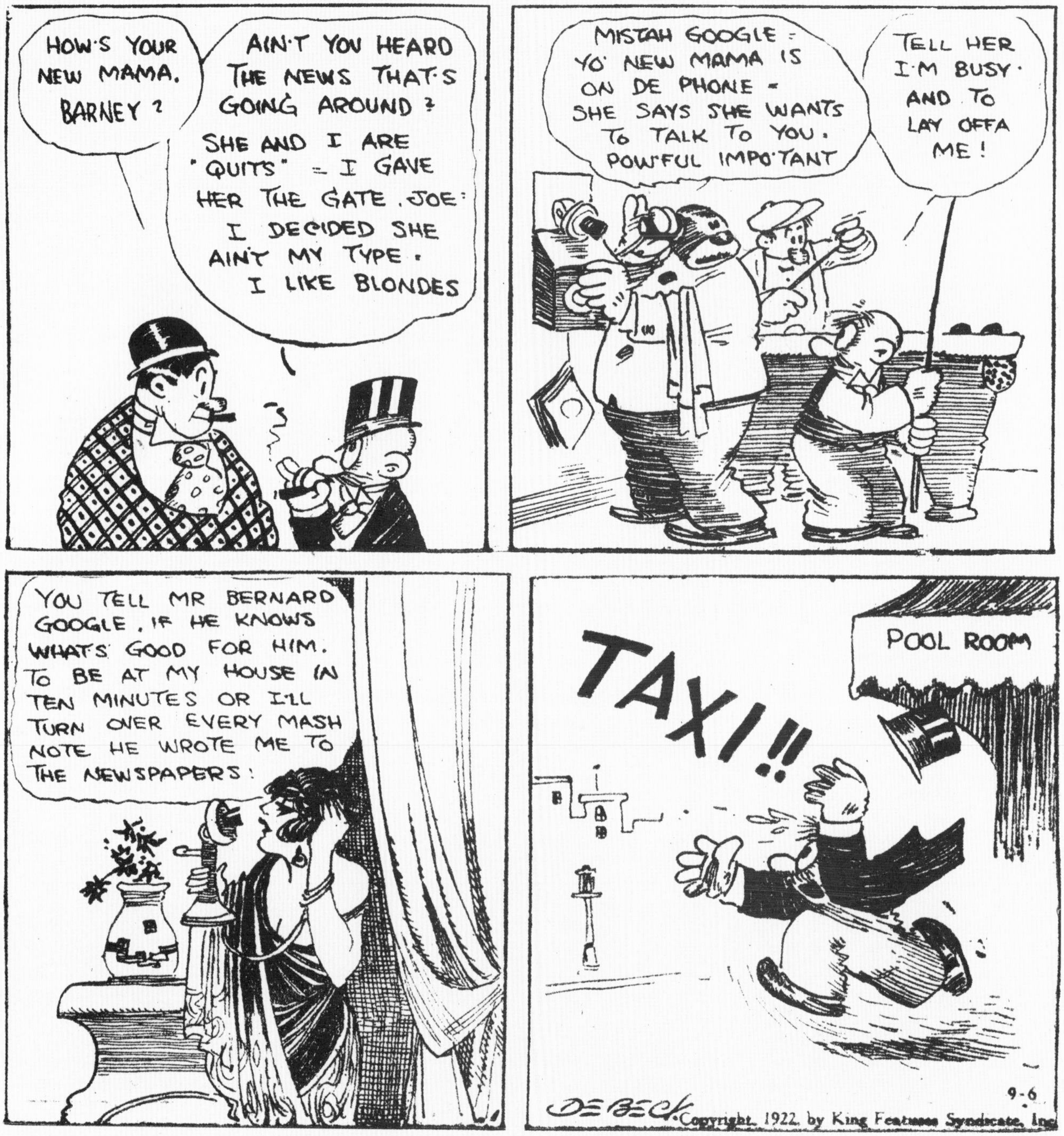
HOW'S YOUR NEW MAMA, BARNEY ?
AIN'T YOU HEARD THE NEWS THAT'S GOING AROUND ?
SHE AND I ARE "QUITS" — I GAVE HER THE GATE, JOE: I DECIDED SHE AIN'T MY TYPE. I LIKE BLONDES
MISTAH GOOGLE — YO' NEW MAMA IS ON DE PHONE — SHE SAYS SHE WANTS TO TALK TO YOU. POW'FUL IMPO'TANT
TELL HER I'M BUSY AND TO LAY OFFA ME!
YOU TELL MR BERNARD GOOGLE, IF HE KNOWS WHAT'S GOOD FOR HIM, TO BE AT MY HOUSE IN TEN MINUTES OR I'LL TURN OVER EVERY MASH NOTE HE WROTE ME TO THE NEWSPAPERS!
POOL ROOM
TAXI!!
9-6
DE BECK
Copyright, 1922, by King Features Syndicate, Inc.

Barney a Blue-Beard? Well, Listen to This

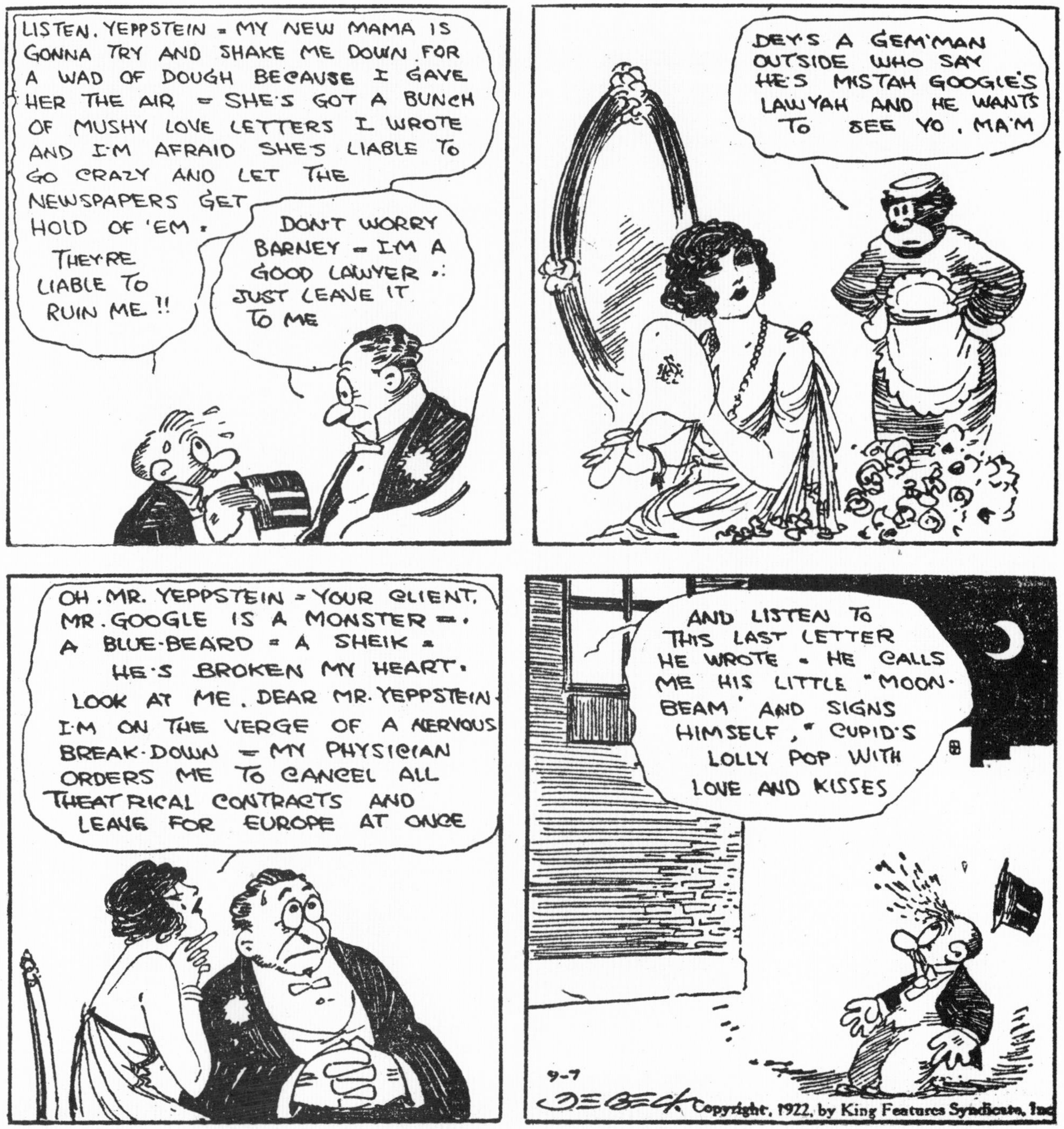

LISTEN, YEPPSTEIN = MY NEW MAMA IS GONNA TRY AND SHAKE ME DOWN FOR A WAD OF DOUGH BECAUSE I GAVE HER THE AIR = SHE'S GOT A BUNCH OF MUSHY LOVE LETTERS I WROTE AND I'M AFRAID SHE'S LIABLE TO GO CRAZY AND LET THE NEWSPAPERS GET HOLD OF 'EM.
THEY'RE LIABLE TO RUIN ME !!
DON'T WORRY BARNEY = I'M A GOOD LAWYER: JUST LEAVE IT TO ME
DEY'S A GEM'MAN OUTSIDE WHO SAY HE'S MISTAH GOOGLE'S LAWYAH AND HE WANTS TO SEE YO, MA'M
OH, MR. YEPPSTEIN = YOUR CLIENT, MR. GOOGLE IS A MONSTER =. A BLUE-BEARD = A SHEIK = HE'S BROKEN MY HEART. LOOK AT ME, DEAR MR. YEPPSTEIN. I'M ON THE VERGE OF A NERVOUS BREAK-DOWN = MY PHYSICIAN ORDERS ME TO CANCEL ALL THEATRICAL CONTRACTS AND LEAVE FOR EUROPE AT ONCE
AND LISTEN TO THIS LAST LETTER HE WROTE - HE CALLS ME HIS LITTLE "MOON-BEAM" AND SIGNS HIMSELF, "CUPID'S LOLLY POP WITH LOVE AND KISSES
9-7
DE BECK
Copyright, 1922, by King Features Syndicate, Inc

Well, It's No Flowery Path Barney's Traveling Now

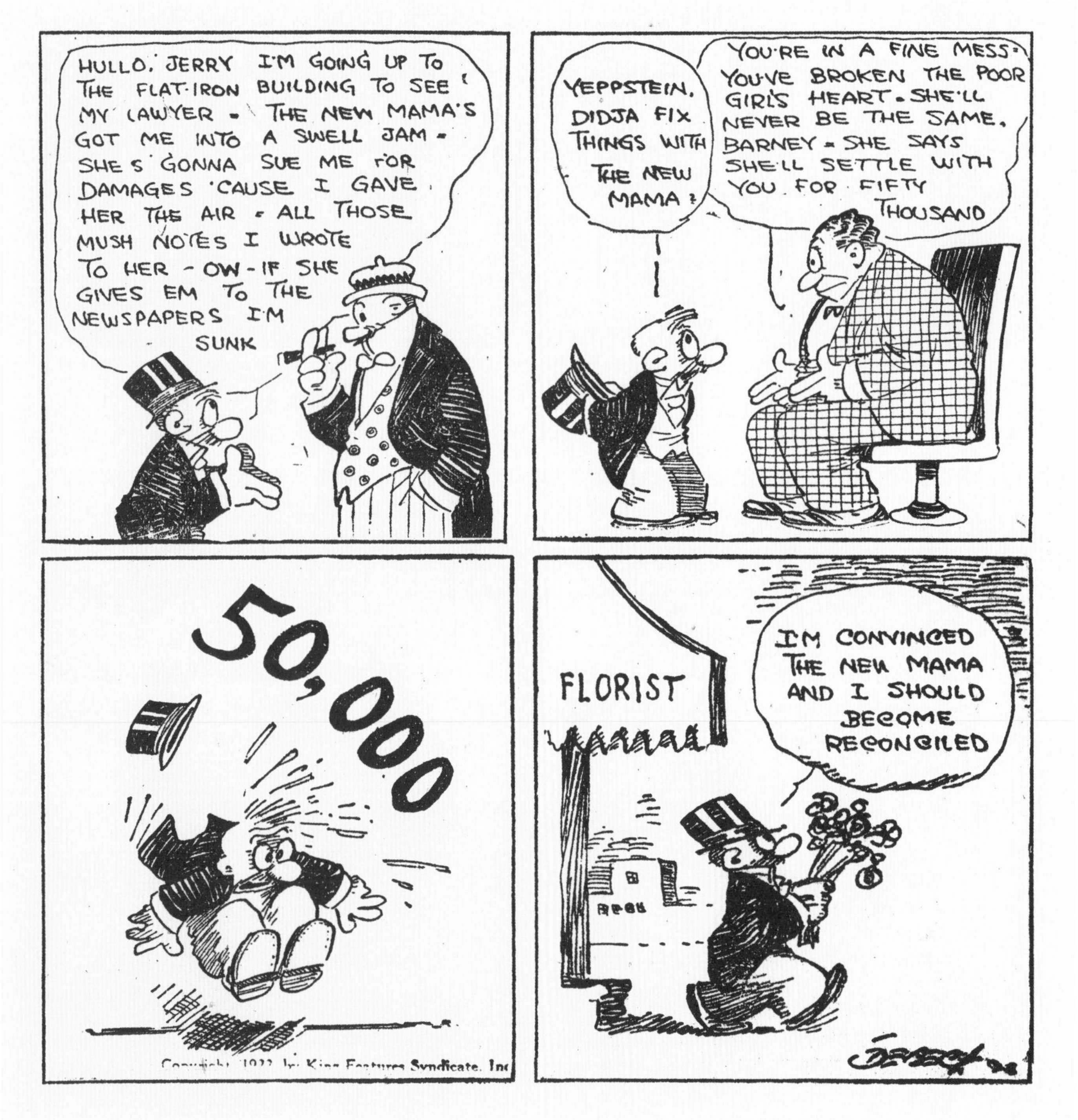
HULLO, JERRY I'M GOING UP TO THE FLAT-IRON BUILDING TO SEE MY LAWYER - THE NEW MAMA'S GOT ME INTO A SWELL JAM - SHE'S GONNA SUE ME FOR DAMAGES 'CAUSE I GAVE HER THE AIR - ALL THOSE MUSH NOTES I WROTE TO HER - OW - IF SHE GIVES EM TO THE NEWSPAPERS I'M SUNK
YEPPSTEIN, DIDJA FIX THINGS WITH THE NEW MAMA?
YOU'RE IN A FINE MESS - YOU'VE BROKEN THE POOR GIRL'S HEART - SHE'LL NEVER BE THE SAME, BARNEY - SHE SAYS SHE'LL SETTLE WITH YOU FOR FIFTY THOUSAND
50,000
FLORIST
I'M CONVINCED THE NEW MAMA AND I SHOULD BECOME RECONCILED
King Features Syndicate, Inc

With $50,000 Bucks at Stake, Can Barney Be Blamed?

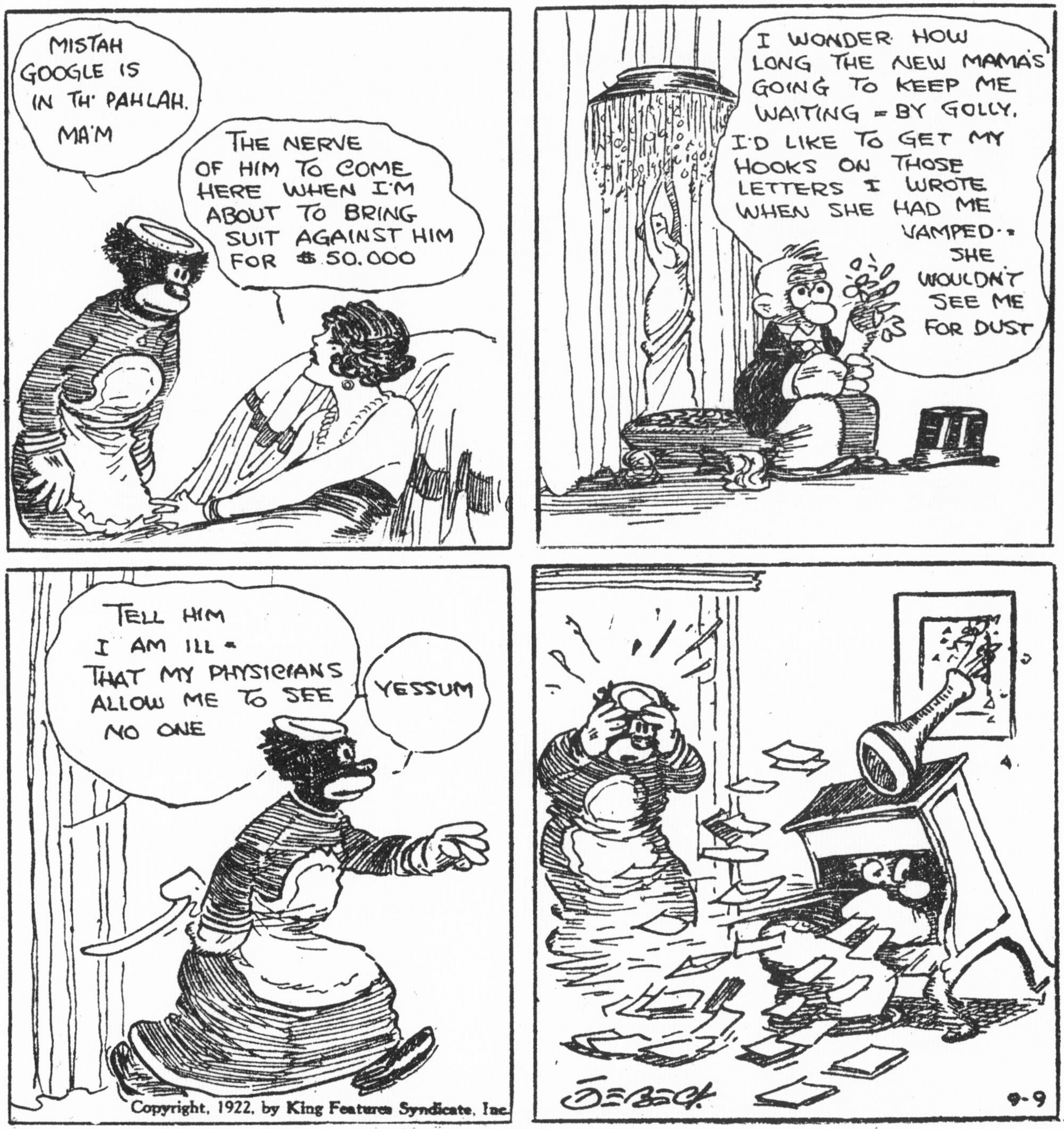
MISTAH GOOGLE IS IN TH' PAHLAH. MA'M
THE NERVE OF HIM TO COME HERE WHEN I'M ABOUT TO BRING SUIT AGAINST HIM FOR $50.000
I WONDER HOW LONG THE NEW MAMA'S GOING TO KEEP ME WAITING – BY GOLLY. I'D LIKE TO GET MY HOOKS ON THOSE LETTERS I WROTE WHEN SHE HAD ME VAMPED – SHE WOULDN'T SEE ME FOR DUST
TELL HIM I AM ILL – THAT MY PHYSICIANS ALLOW ME TO SEE NO ONE
YESSUM
Copyright, 1922, by King Features Syndicate, Inc.
9-9

Barney Learns a Few Facts About Himself

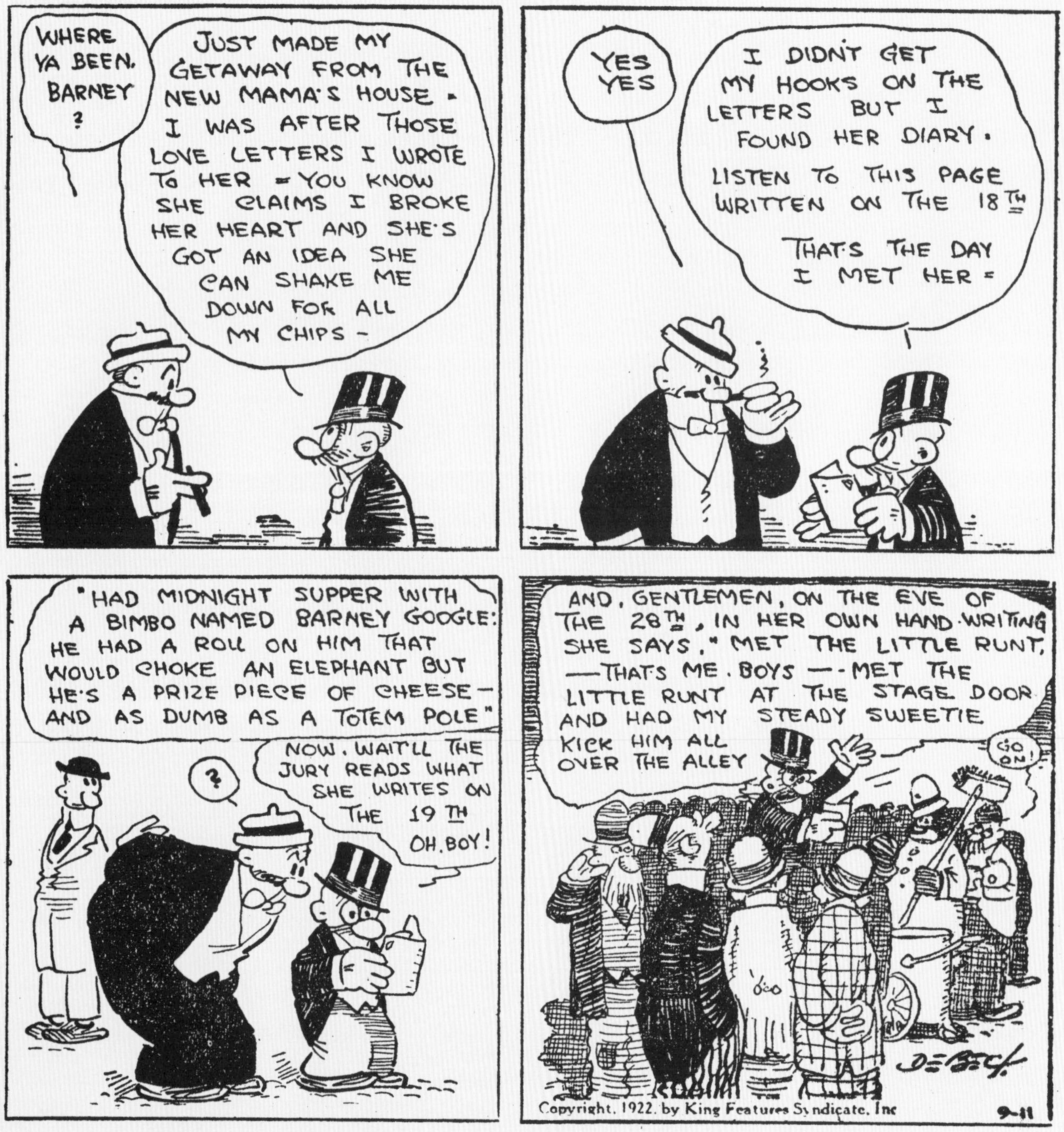
WHERE YA BEEN. BARNEY ?
JUST MADE MY GETAWAY FROM THE NEW MAMA'S HOUSE - I WAS AFTER THOSE LOVE LETTERS I WROTE TO HER - YOU KNOW SHE CLAIMS I BROKE HER HEART AND SHE'S GOT AN IDEA SHE CAN SHAKE ME DOWN FOR ALL MY CHIPS -
YES YES
I DIDN'T GET MY HOOKS ON THE LETTERS BUT I FOUND HER DIARY. LISTEN TO THIS PAGE WRITTEN ON THE 18TH
THAT'S THE DAY I MET HER -
"HAD MIDNIGHT SUPPER WITH A BIMBO NAMED BARNEY GOOGLE: HE HAD A ROLL ON HIM THAT WOULD CHOKE AN ELEPHANT BUT HE'S A PRIZE PIECE OF CHEESE - AND AS DUMB AS A TOTEM POLE"
?
NOW. WAIT'LL THE JURY READS WHAT SHE WRITES ON THE 19TH OH, BOY!
AND, GENTLEMEN, ON THE EVE OF THE 28TH, IN HER OWN HAND WRITING SHE SAYS, "MET THE LITTLE RUNT, —THAT'S ME, BOYS — MET THE LITTLE RUNT AT THE STAGE DOOR AND HAD MY STEADY SWEETIE KICK HIM ALL OVER THE ALLEY
GO ON!
DE BECK
Copyright, 1922, by King Features Syndicate, Inc
9-11

It Isn't Going to Be at Barney's Expense

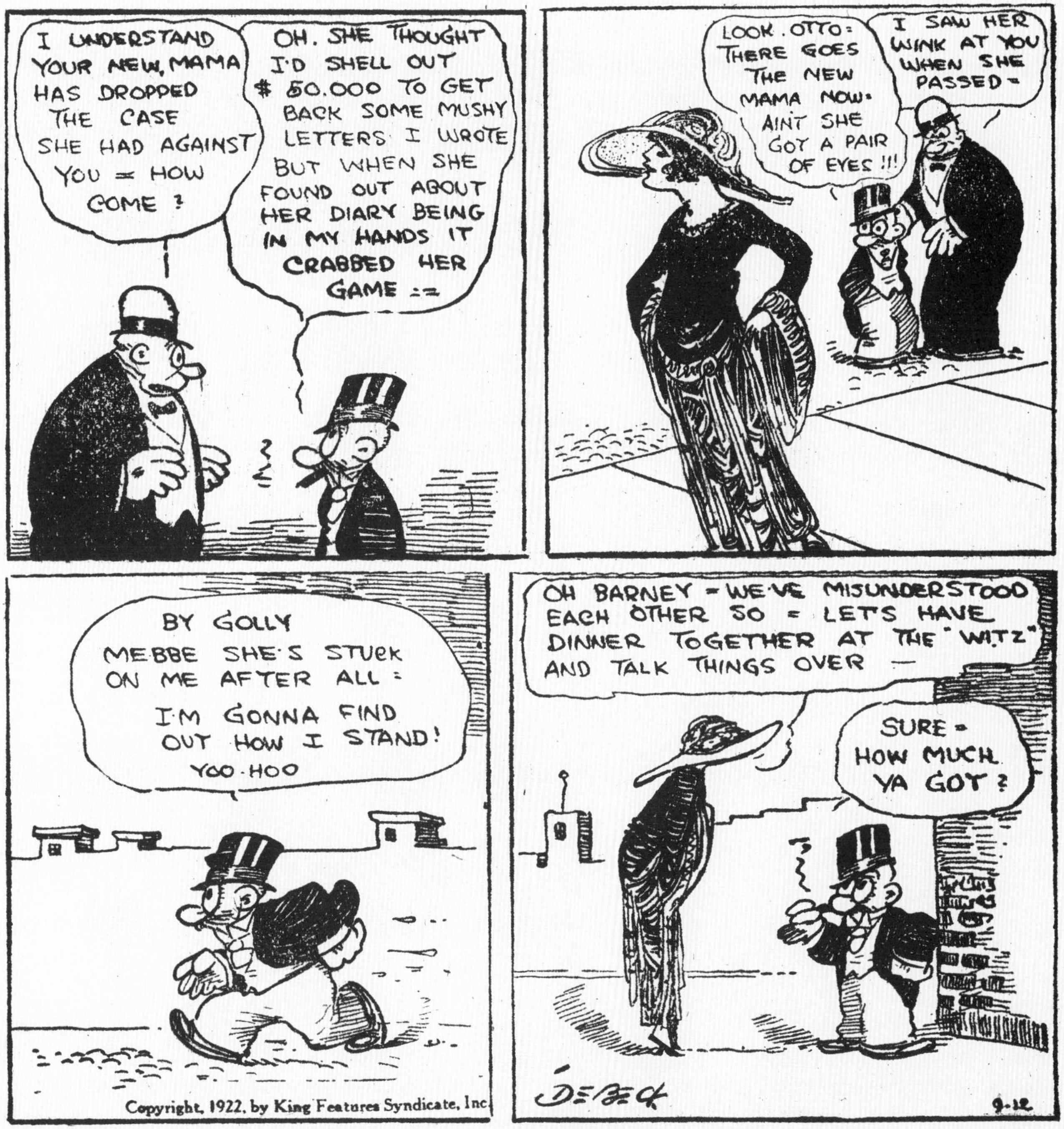

I UNDERSTAND YOUR NEW, MAMA HAS DROPPED THE CASE SHE HAD AGAINST YOU = HOW COME ?
OH. SHE THOUGHT I'D SHELL OUT $ 50.000 TO GET BACK SOME MUSHY LETTERS I WROTE BUT WHEN SHE FOUND OUT ABOUT HER DIARY BEING IN MY HANDS IT CRABBED HER GAME ==
LOOK . OTTO: THERE GOES THE NEW MAMA NOW. AINT SHE GOT A PAIR OF EYES !!!
I SAW HER WINK AT YOU WHEN SHE PASSED =
BY GOLLY MEBBE SHE'S STUCK ON ME AFTER ALL = I'M GONNA FIND OUT HOW I STAND! YOO-HOO
OH BARNEY = WE'VE MISUNDERSTOOD EACH OTHER SO = LET'S HAVE DINNER TOGETHER AT THE "WITZ" AND TALK THINGS OVER —
SURE = HOW MUCH YA GOT ?
Copyright, 1922, by King Features Syndicate, Inc.
DE BECK
9-12

Barney's Some Attraction Himself

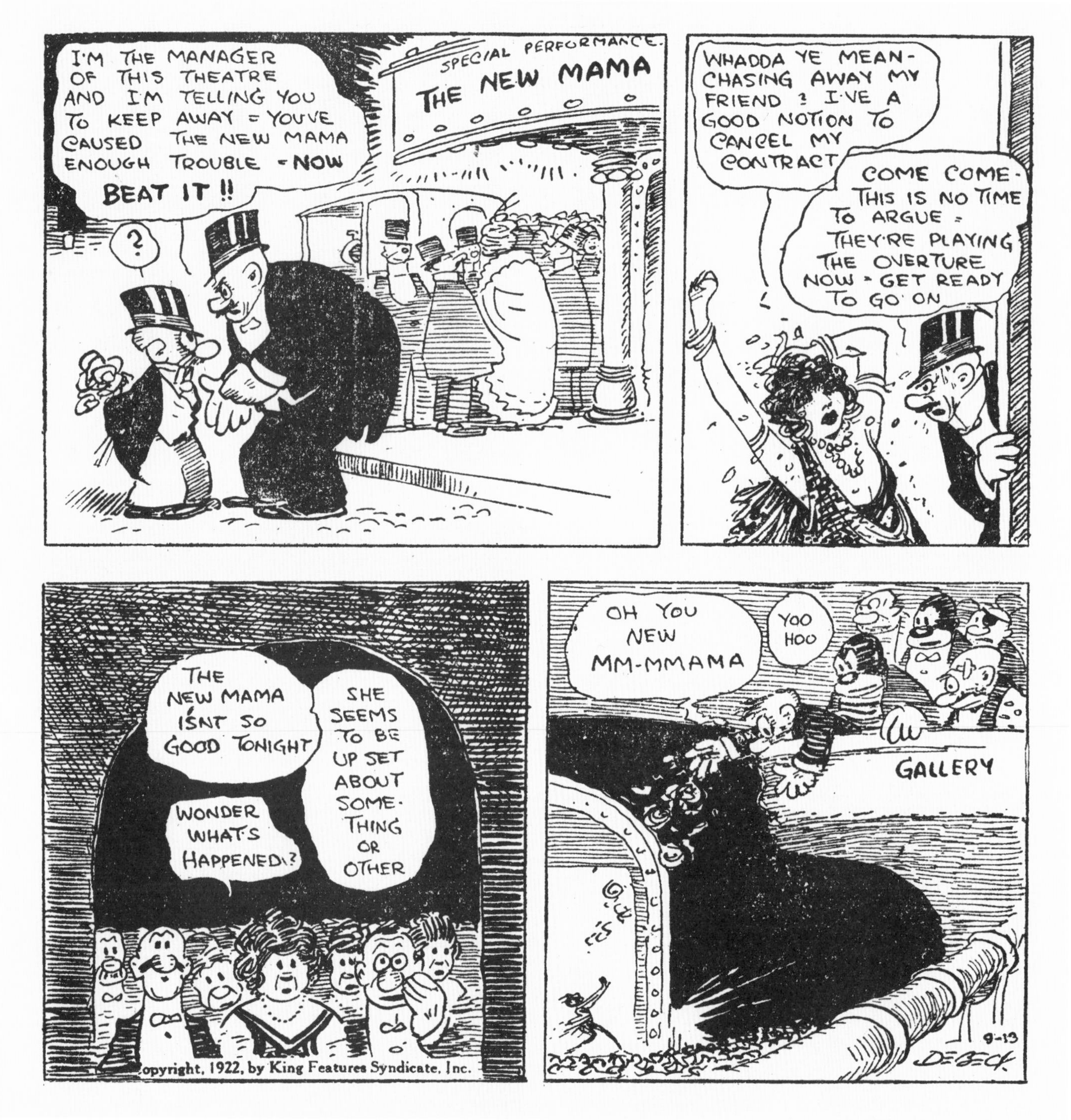
SPECIAL PERFORMANCE
THE NEW MAMA
I'M THE MANAGER OF THIS THEATRE AND I'M TELLING YOU TO KEEP AWAY = YOU'VE CAUSED THE NEW MAMA ENOUGH TROUBLE = NOW BEAT IT !!
?
WHADDA YE MEAN - CHASING AWAY MY FRIEND ? I'VE A GOOD NOTION TO CANCEL MY CONTRACT
COME COME - THIS IS NO TIME TO ARGUE = THEY'RE PLAYING THE OVERTURE NOW = GET READY TO GO ON
THE NEW MAMA ISNT SO GOOD TONIGHT
SHE SEEMS TO BE UP SET ABOUT SOME-THING OR OTHER
WONDER WHAT'S HAPPENED ?
OH YOU NEW MM-MMAMA
YOO HOO
GALLERY
Copyright, 1922, by King Features Syndicate, Inc.
9-13
DE BECK

"Let Her Go," Says Barney

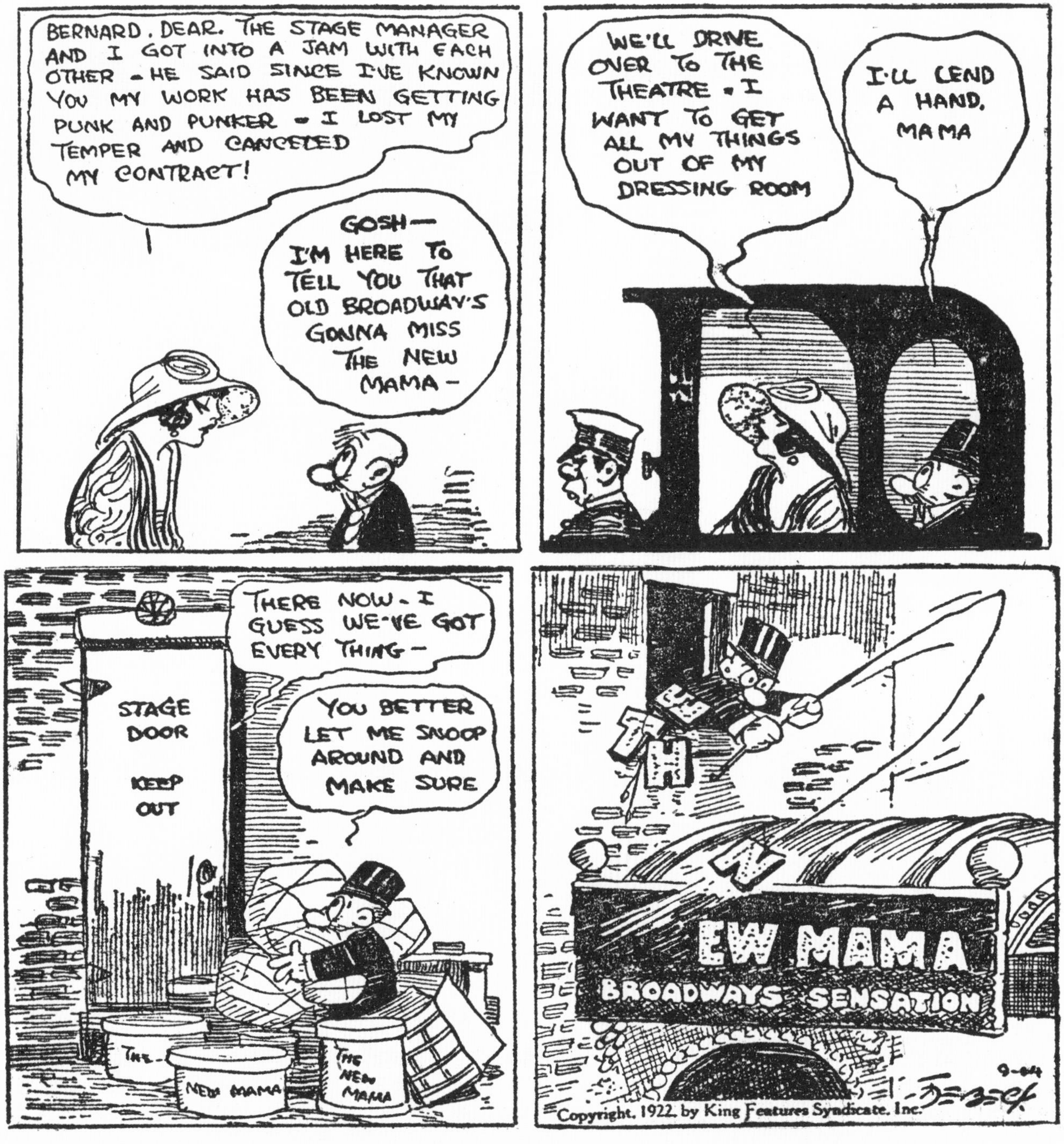
BERNARD. DEAR. THE STAGE MANAGER AND I GOT INTO A JAM WITH EACH OTHER - HE SAID SINCE I'VE KNOWN YOU MY WORK HAS BEEN GETTING PUNK AND PUNKER - I LOST MY TEMPER AND CANCELED MY CONTRACT!
GOSH— I'M HERE TO TELL YOU THAT OLD BROADWAY'S GONNA MISS THE NEW MAMA-
WE'LL DRIVE OVER TO THE THEATRE - I WANT TO GET ALL MY THINGS OUT OF MY DRESSING ROOM
I'LL LEND A HAND. MAMA
THERE NOW - I GUESS WE'VE GOT EVERY THING-
YOU BETTER LET ME SNOOP AROUND AND MAKE SURE
STAGE DOOR
KEEP OUT
THE-
NEW MAMA
THE NEW MAMA
T H
N
EW MAMA
BROADWAYS SENSATION
9-24
Copyright, 1922, by King Features Syndicate, Inc.

When Barney Speaks, He Wants All the Say

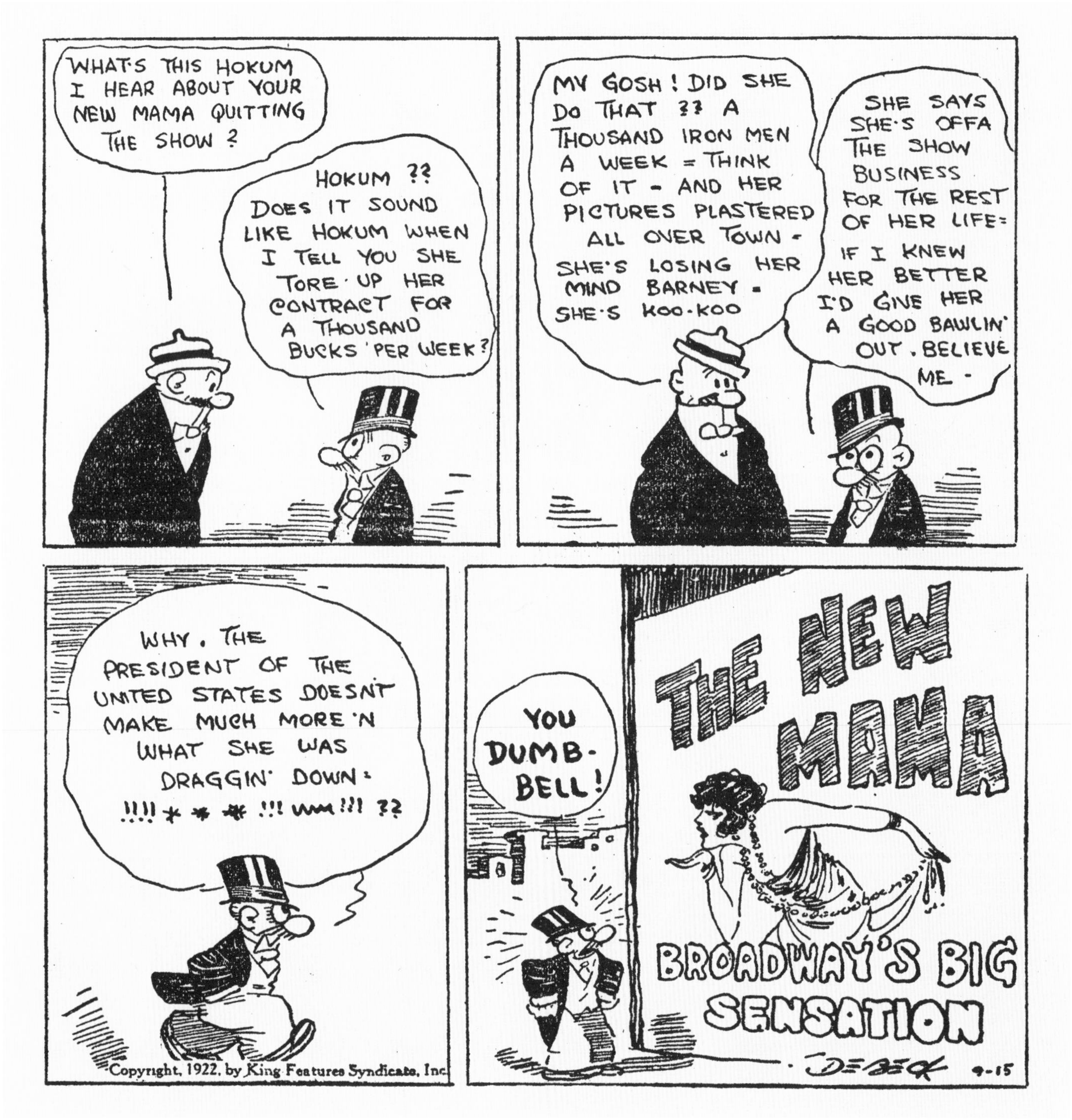
WHAT'S THIS HOKUM I HEAR ABOUT YOUR NEW MAMA QUITTING THE SHOW ?
HOKUM ?? DOES IT SOUND LIKE HOKUM WHEN I TELL YOU SHE TORE UP HER CONTRACT FOR A THOUSAND BUCKS PER WEEK?
MY GOSH ! DID SHE DO THAT ?? A THOUSAND IRON MEN A WEEK = THINK OF IT - AND HER PICTURES PLASTERED ALL OVER TOWN - SHE'S LOSING HER MIND BARNEY - SHE'S KOO-KOO
SHE SAYS SHE'S OFFA THE SHOW BUSINESS FOR THE REST OF HER LIFE= IF I KNEW HER BETTER I'D GIVE HER A GOOD BAWLIN' OUT. BELIEVE ME -
WHY, THE PRESIDENT OF THE UNITED STATES DOESN'T MAKE MUCH MORE'N WHAT SHE WAS DRAGGIN' DOWN = !!!! * * * !!! !!! ??
YOU DUMB-BELL!
THE NEW MAMA
BROADWAY'S BIG SENSATION
DE BECK 9-15
Copyright, 1922, by King Features Syndicate, Inc.

The New Mama Hasn't Lost Out Altogether

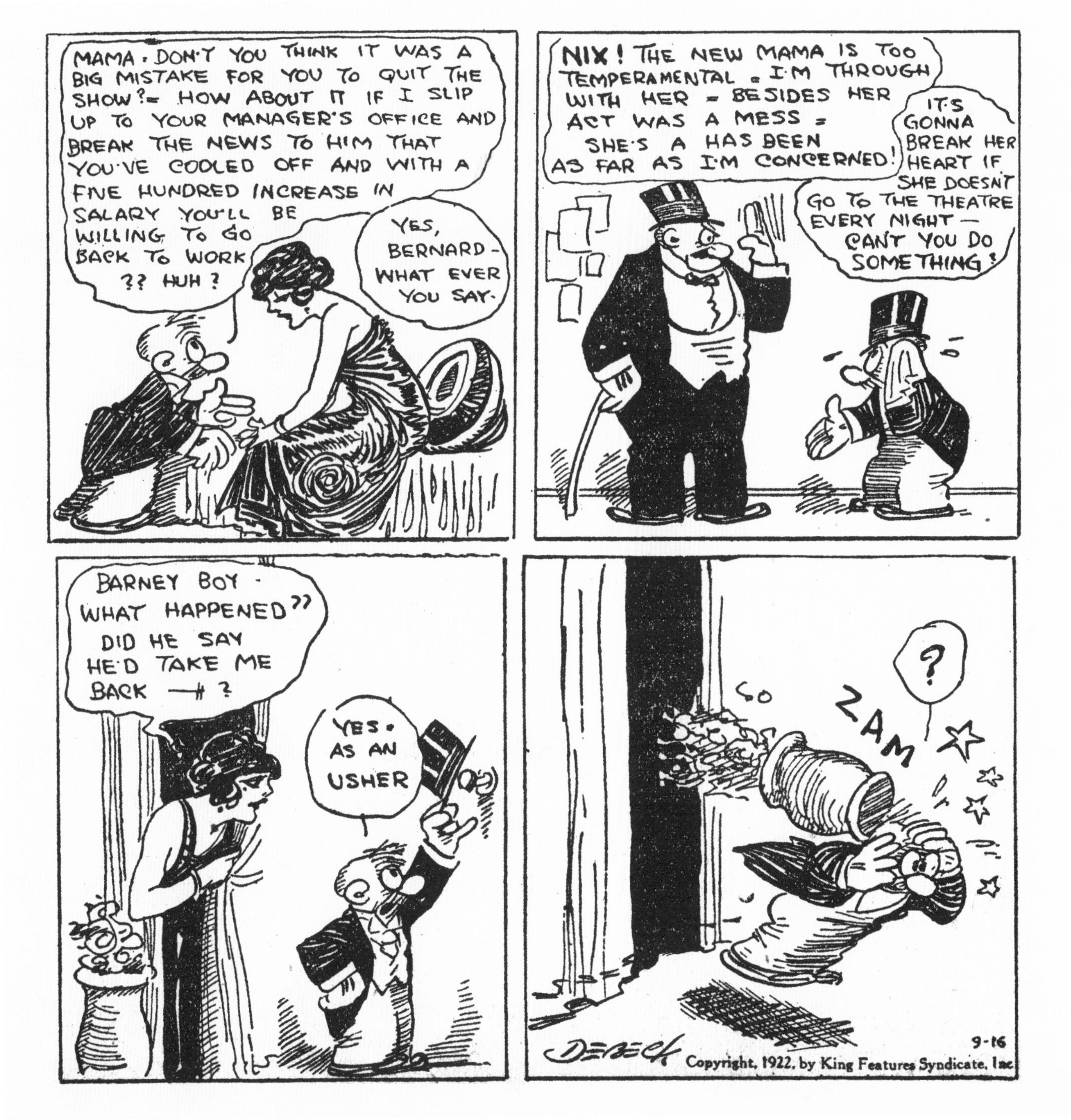
MAMA - DON'T YOU THINK IT WAS A BIG MISTAKE FOR YOU TO QUIT THE SHOW? - HOW ABOUT IT IF I SLIP UP TO YOUR MANAGER'S OFFICE AND BREAK THE NEWS TO HIM THAT YOU'VE COOLED OFF AND WITH A FIVE HUNDRED INCREASE IN SALARY YOU'LL BE WILLING TO GO BACK TO WORK ?? HUH ?
YES, BERNARD - WHAT EVER YOU SAY.
NIX! THE NEW MAMA IS TOO TEMPERAMENTAL - I'M THROUGH WITH HER - BESIDES HER ACT WAS A MESS - SHE'S A HAS BEEN AS FAR AS I'M CONCERNED!
IT'S GONNA BREAK HER HEART IF SHE DOESN'T GO TO THE THEATRE EVERY NIGHT - CAN'T YOU DO SOMETHING?
BARNEY BOY - WHAT HAPPENED?? DID HE SAY HE'D TAKE ME BACK - ?
YES - AS AN USHER
?
ZAM
DEBECK
9-16
Copyright, 1922, by King Features Syndicate, Inc

Barney's Got the Stage Set

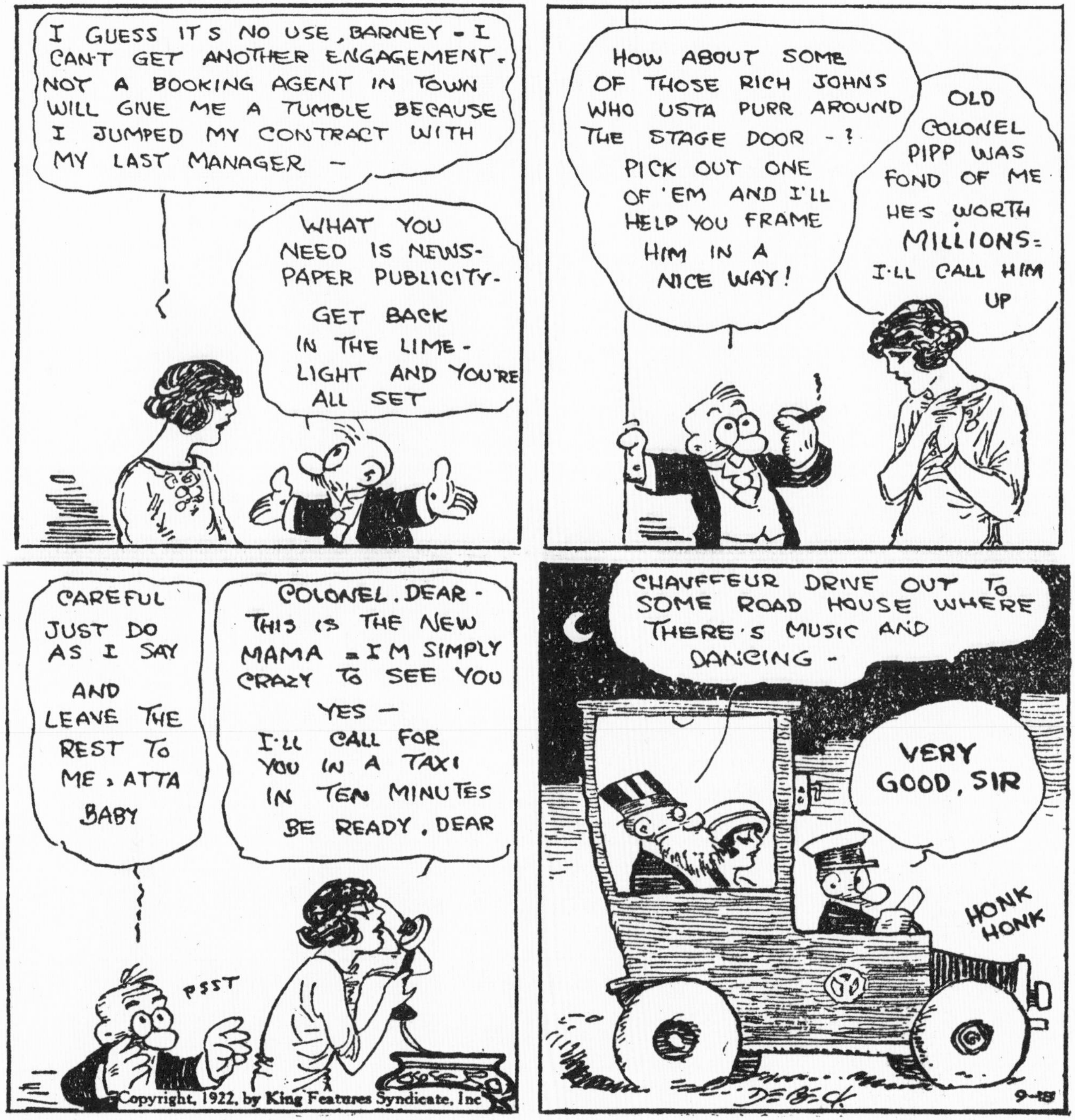

I GUESS IT'S NO USE, BARNEY - I CAN'T GET ANOTHER ENGAGEMENT. NOT A BOOKING AGENT IN TOWN WILL GIVE ME A TUMBLE BECAUSE I JUMPED MY CONTRACT WITH MY LAST MANAGER -
WHAT YOU NEED IS NEWSPAPER PUBLICITY. GET BACK IN THE LIMELIGHT AND YOU'RE ALL SET
HOW ABOUT SOME OF THOSE RICH JOHNS WHO USTA PURR AROUND THE STAGE DOOR -? PICK OUT ONE OF 'EM AND I'LL HELP YOU FRAME HIM IN A NICE WAY!
OLD COLONEL PIPP WAS FOND OF ME. HE'S WORTH MILLIONS = I'LL CALL HIM UP
CAREFUL JUST DO AS I SAY AND LEAVE THE REST TO ME, ATTA BABY
COLONEL, DEAR - THIS IS THE NEW MAMA = I'M SIMPLY CRAZY TO SEE YOU YES - I'LL CALL FOR YOU IN A TAXI IN TEN MINUTES BE READY, DEAR
PSST
Copyright, 1922, by King Features Syndicate, Inc
CHAUFFEUR DRIVE OUT TO SOME ROAD HOUSE WHERE THERE'S MUSIC AND DANCING -
VERY GOOD, SIR
HONK HONK
DE BECK
9-18

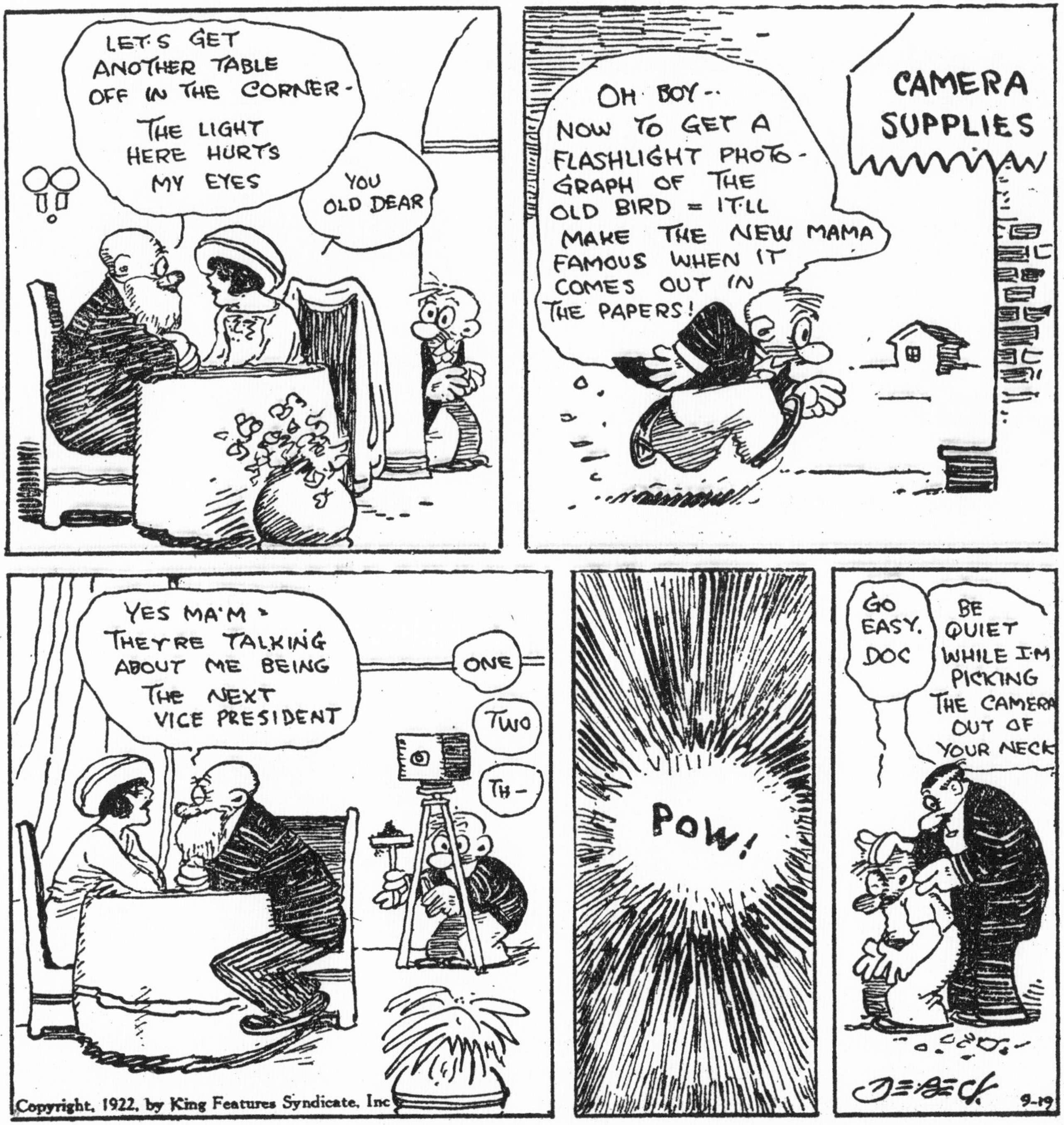
LET'S GET ANOTHER TABLE OFF IN THE CORNER - THE LIGHT HERE HURTS MY EYES
YOU OLD DEAR
OH BOY - NOW TO GET A FLASHLIGHT PHOTOGRAPH OF THE OLD BIRD = IT'LL MAKE THE NEW MAMA FAMOUS WHEN IT COMES OUT IN THE PAPERS!
CAMERA SUPPLIES
YES MA'M - THEY'RE TALKING ABOUT ME BEING THE NEXT VICE PRESIDENT
ONE
TWO
TH -
POW!
GO EASY, DOC
BE QUIET WHILE I'M PICKING THE CAMERA OUT OF YOUR NECK
Copyright, 1922, by King Features Syndicate, Inc
9-19

Barney's In a Pinch

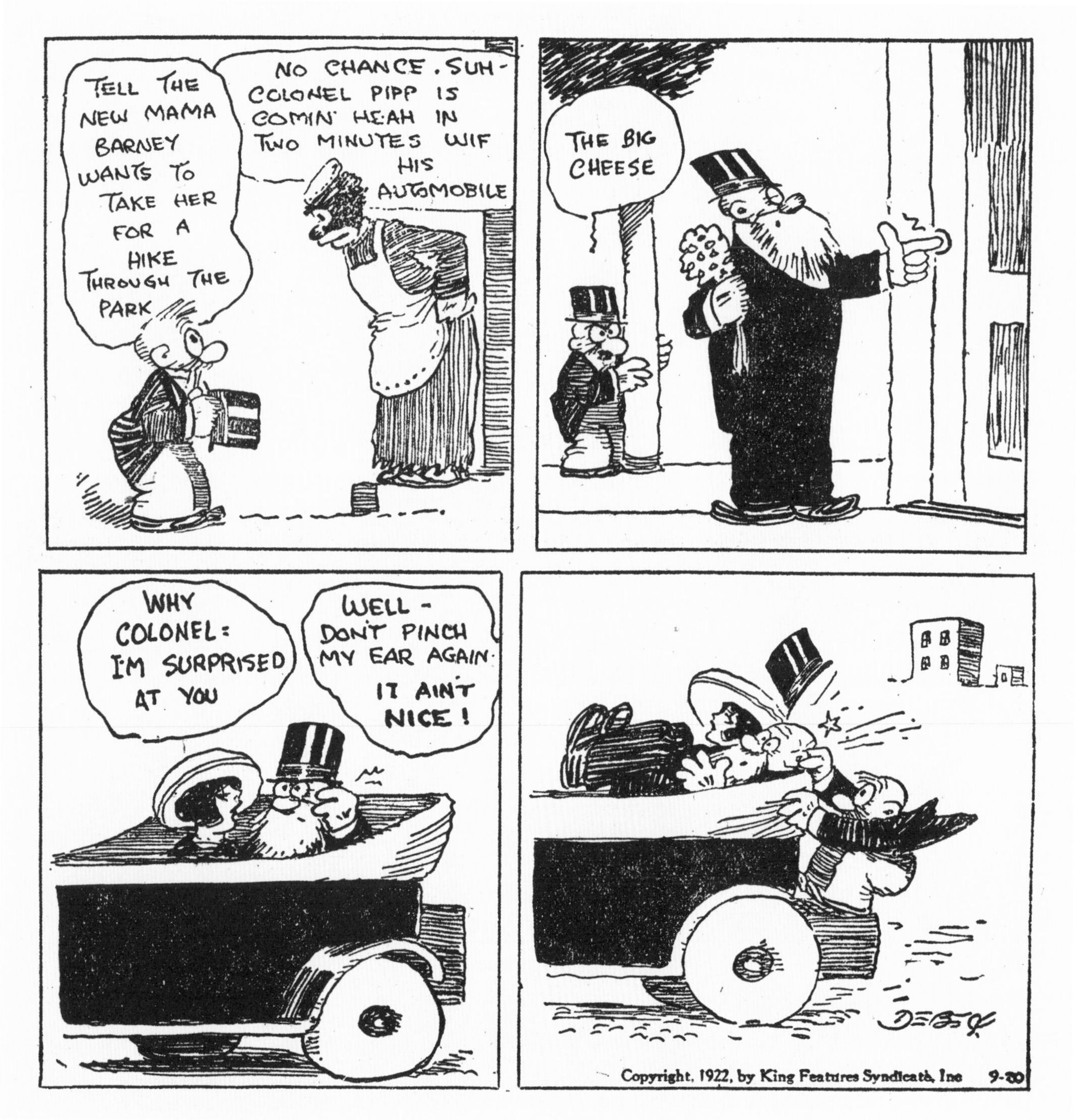

TELL THE NEW MAMA BARNEY WANTS TO TAKE HER FOR A HIKE THROUGH THE PARK
NO CHANCE. SUH - COLONEL PIPP IS COMIN' HEAH IN TWO MINUTES WIF HIS AUTOMOBILE
THE BIG CHEESE
WHY COLONEL: I'M SURPRISED AT YOU
WELL - DON'T PINCH MY EAR AGAIN. IT AIN'T NICE!
Copyright, 1922, by King Features Syndicate, Inc 9-30

Barney Has Some Serious Competition, It Seems

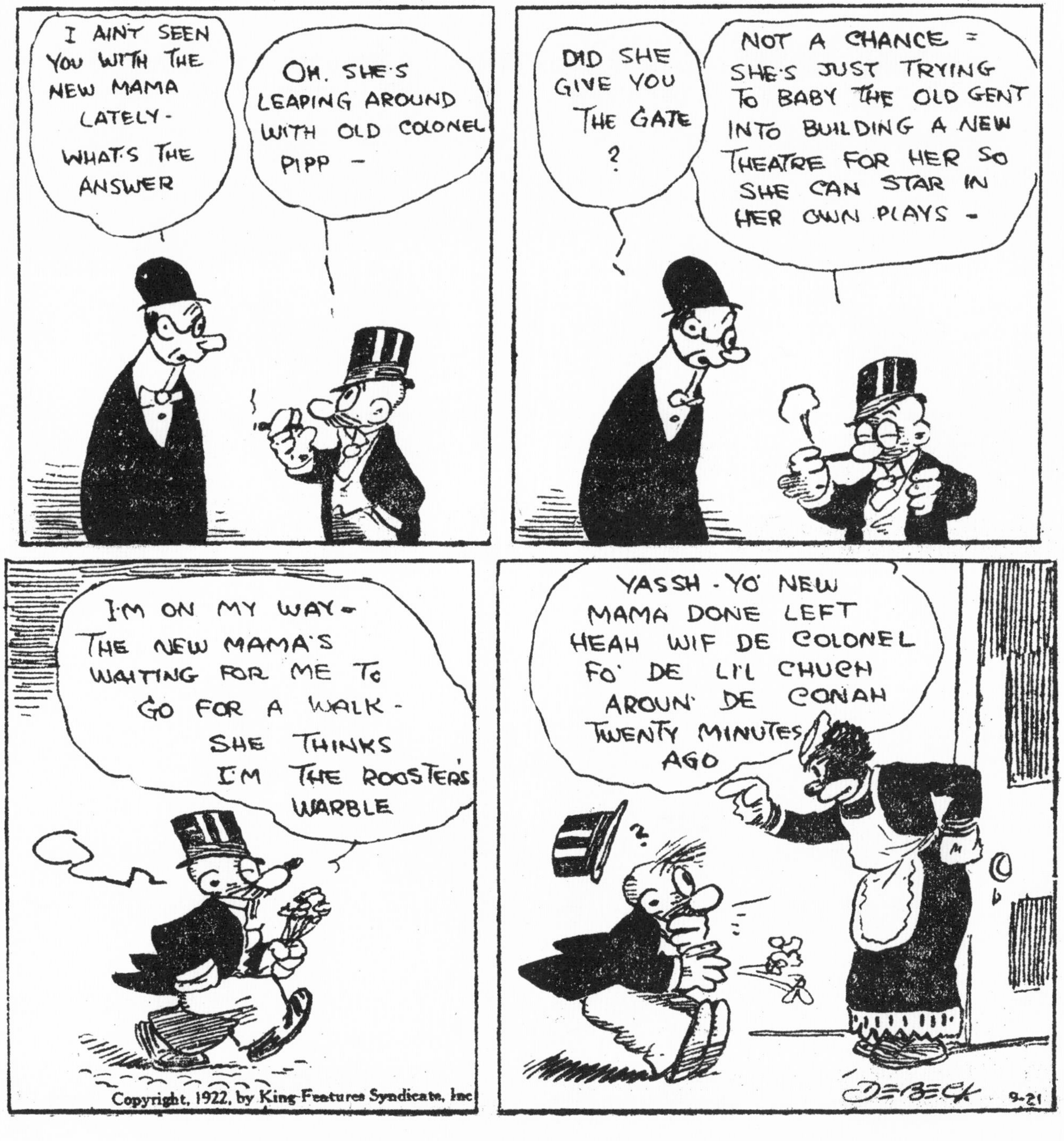
I AIN'T SEEN YOU WITH THE NEW MAMA LATELY - WHAT'S THE ANSWER
OH, SHE'S LEAPING AROUND WITH OLD COLONEL PIPP -
DID SHE GIVE YOU THE GATE ?
NOT A CHANCE = SHE'S JUST TRYING TO BABY THE OLD GENT INTO BUILDING A NEW THEATRE FOR HER SO SHE CAN STAR IN HER OWN PLAYS -
I'M ON MY WAY - THE NEW MAMA'S WAITING FOR ME TO GO FOR A WALK - SHE THINKS I'M THE ROOSTER'S WARBLE
YASSH - YO' NEW MAMA DONE LEFT HEAH WIF DE COLONEL FO' DE LI'L CHUCH AROUN' DE CONAH TWENTY MINUTES AGO
?
Copyright, 1922, by King Features Syndicate, Inc
DEBECK 9-21

Barney Still Has a Chance

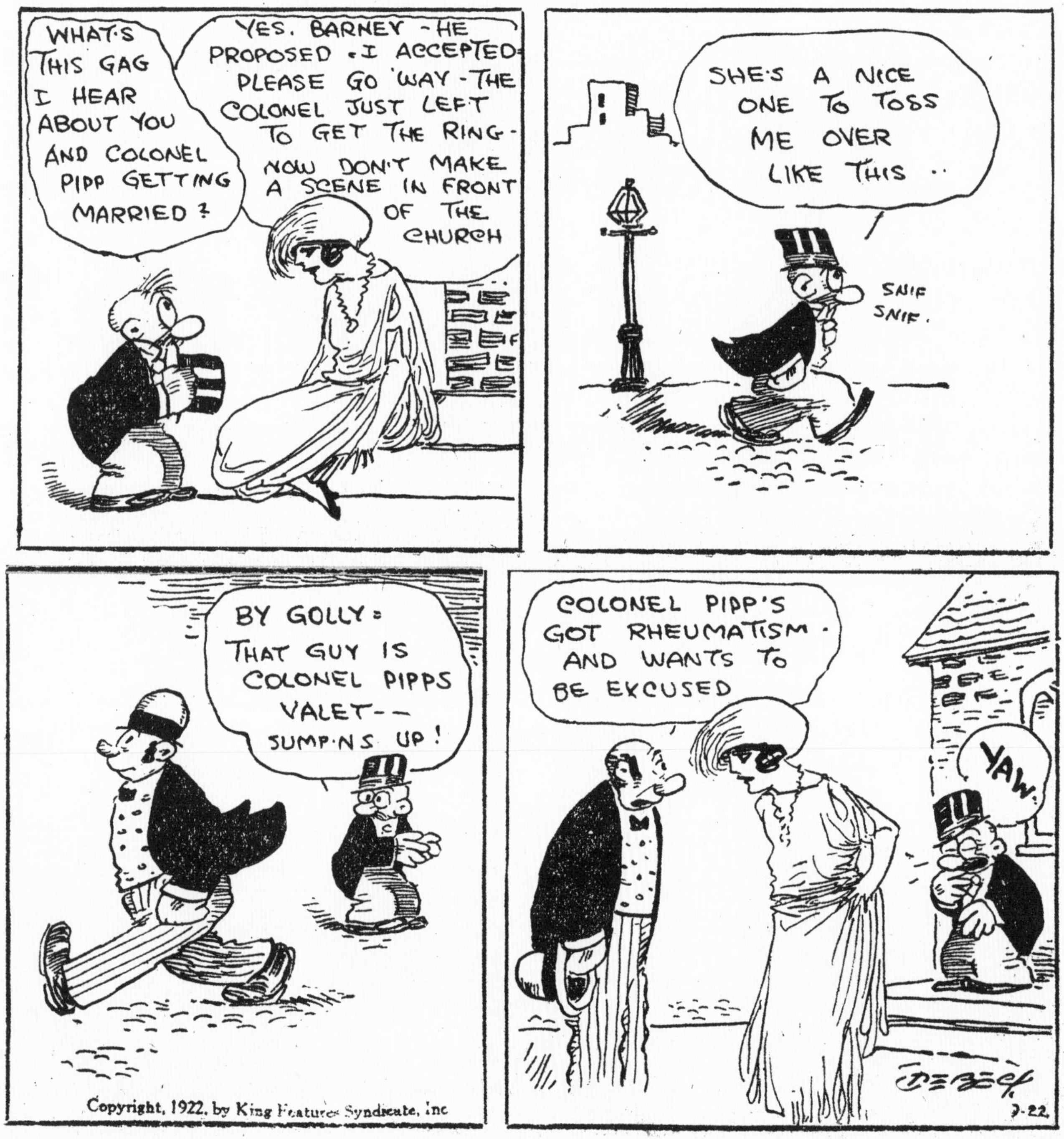
WHAT'S THIS GAG I HEAR ABOUT YOU AND COLONEL PIPP GETTING MARRIED?
YES. BARNEY - HE PROPOSED - I ACCEPTED - PLEASE GO 'WAY - THE COLONEL JUST LEFT TO GET THE RING - NOW DON'T MAKE A SCENE IN FRONT OF THE CHURCH
SHE'S A NICE ONE TO TOSS ME OVER LIKE THIS ..
SNIF SNIF.
BY GOLLY - THAT GUY IS COLONEL PIPPS VALET -- SUMP'N'S UP!
COLONEL PIPP'S GOT RHEUMATISM - AND WANTS TO BE EXCUSED
YAW.
Copyright, 1922, by King Features Syndicate, Inc
DEBECK
7-22.

Barney Also Gets Flattened Out

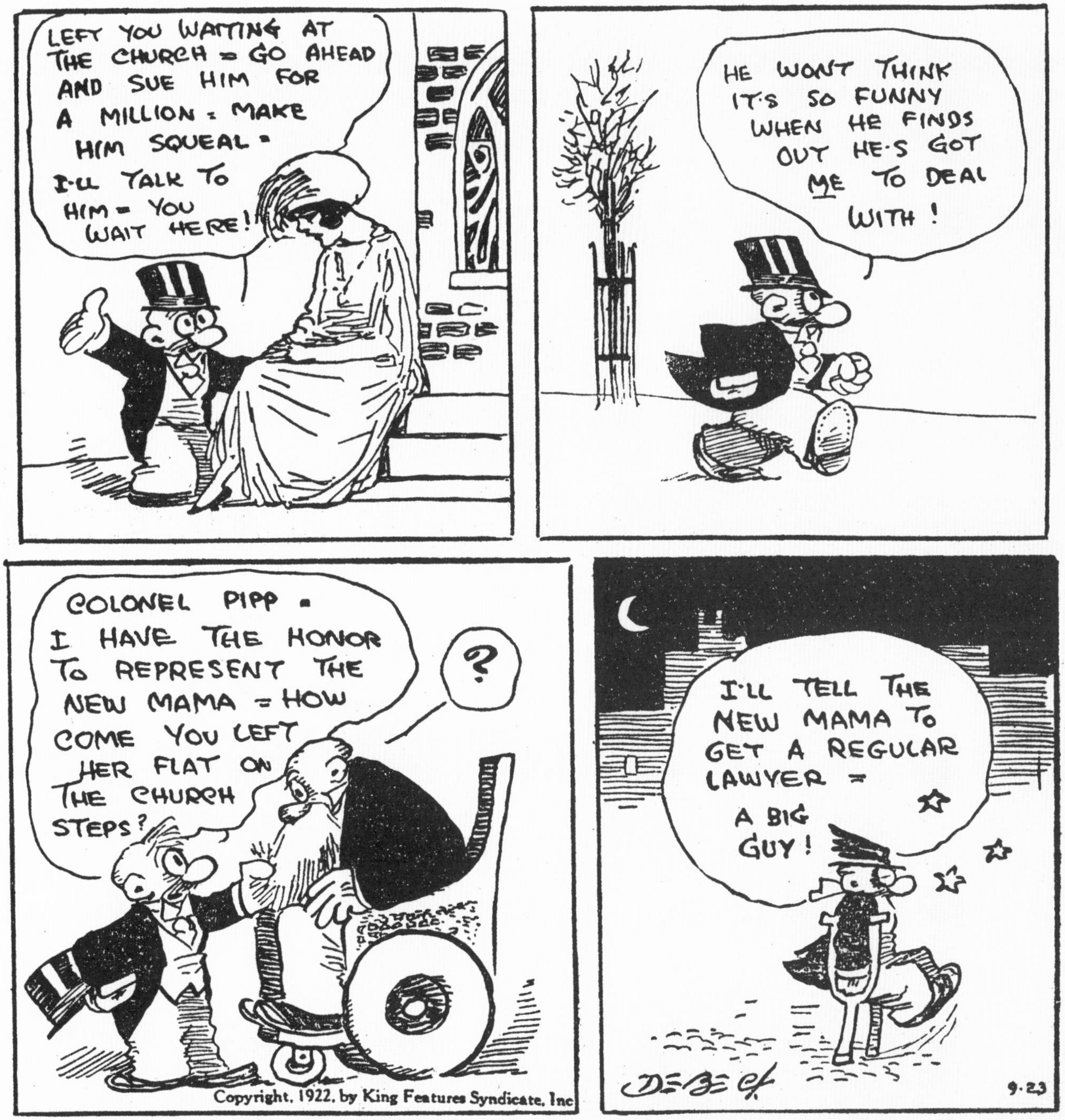
LEFT YOU WAITING AT THE CHURCH = GO AHEAD AND SUE HIM FOR A MILLION = MAKE HIM SQUEAL = I'LL TALK TO HIM = YOU WAIT HERE!
HE WONT THINK IT'S SO FUNNY WHEN HE FINDS OUT HE'S GOT ME TO DEAL WITH!
COLONEL PIPP = I HAVE THE HONOR TO REPRESENT THE NEW MAMA = HOW COME YOU LEFT HER FLAT ON THE CHURCH STEPS?
?
I'LL TELL THE NEW MAMA TO GET A REGULAR LAWYER = A BIG GUY!
Copyright, 1922, by King Features Syndicate, Inc.
DE BECK
9.23

Barney Gets Wise, But a Little Too Late

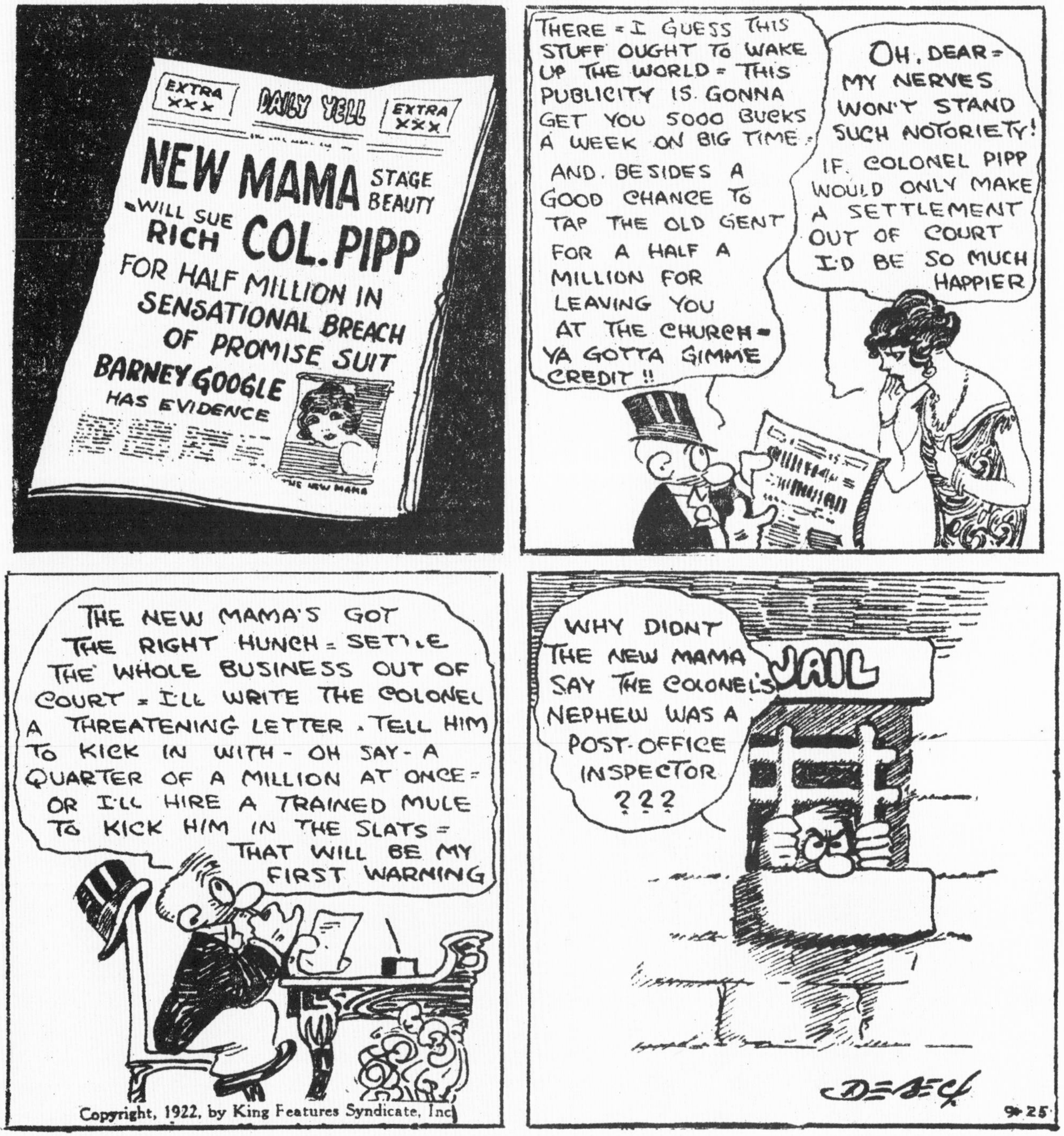
EXTRA XXX
DAILY YELL
EXTRA XXX
NEW MAMA STAGE BEAUTY
WILL SUE RICH COL. PIPP
FOR HALF MILLION IN SENSATIONAL BREACH OF PROMISE SUIT
BARNEY GOOGLE HAS EVIDENCE
THE NEW MAMA
THERE = I GUESS THIS STUFF OUGHT TO WAKE UP THE WORLD = THIS PUBLICITY IS GONNA GET YOU 5000 BUCKS A WEEK ON BIG TIME = AND, BESIDES A GOOD CHANCE TO TAP THE OLD GENT FOR A HALF A MILLION FOR LEAVING YOU AT THE CHURCH = YA GOTTA GIMME CREDIT !!
OH, DEAR = MY NERVES WON'T STAND SUCH NOTORIETY! IF COLONEL PIPP WOULD ONLY MAKE A SETTLEMENT OUT OF COURT I'D BE SO MUCH HAPPIER
THE NEW MAMA'S GOT THE RIGHT HUNCH = SETTLE THE WHOLE BUSINESS OUT OF COURT = I'LL WRITE THE COLONEL A THREATENING LETTER . TELL HIM TO KICK IN WITH - OH SAY - A QUARTER OF A MILLION AT ONCE = OR I'LL HIRE A TRAINED MULE TO KICK HIM IN THE SLATS = THAT WILL BE MY FIRST WARNING
WHY DIDNT THE NEW MAMA SAY THE COLONEL'S NEPHEW WAS A POST-OFFICE INSPECTOR ???
JAIL
DEBECK
9-25

Barney Finds Himself Down and Out

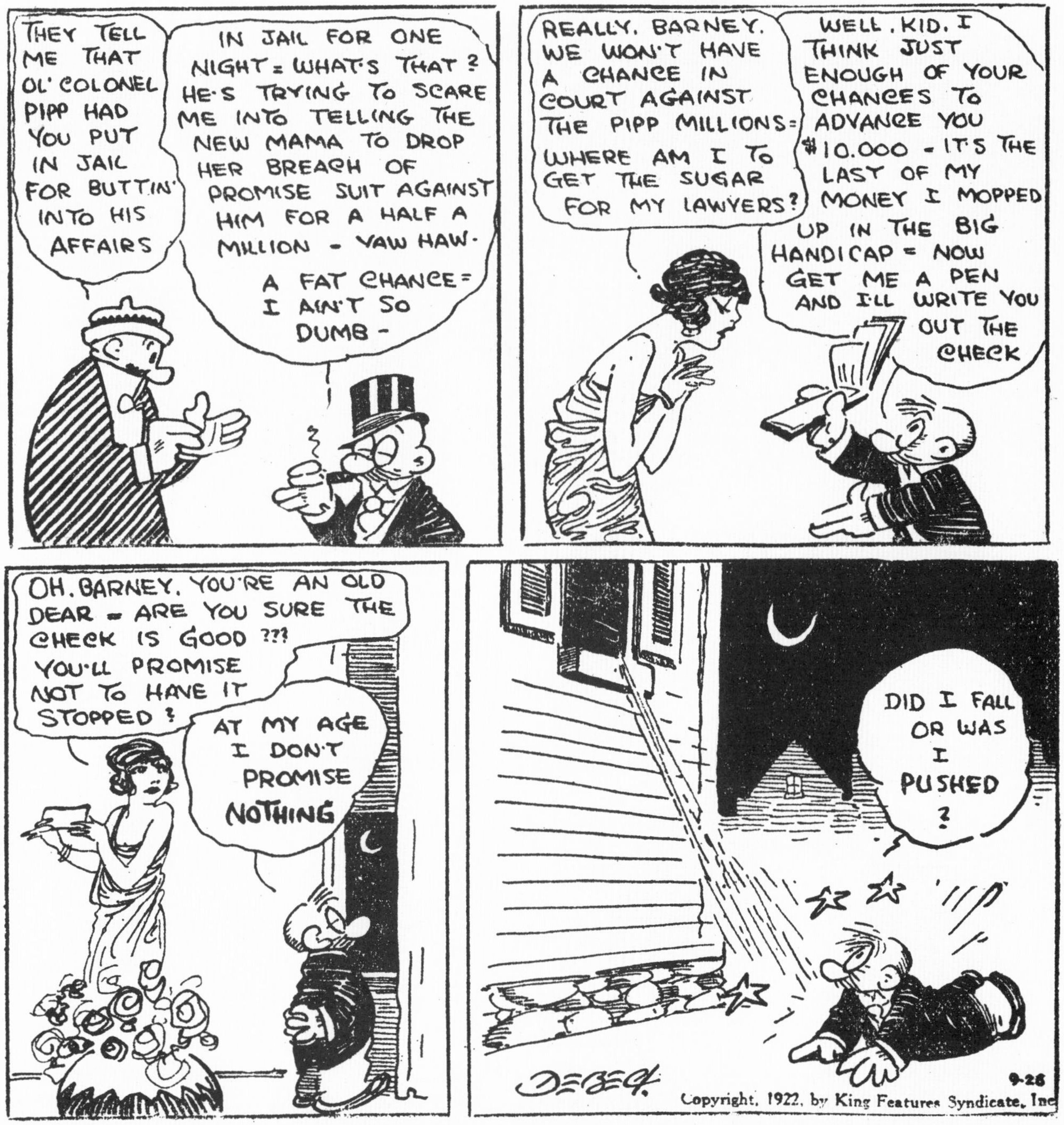
THEY TELL ME THAT OL' COLONEL PIPP HAD YOU PUT IN JAIL FOR BUTTIN' INTO HIS AFFAIRS
IN JAIL FOR ONE NIGHT = WHAT'S THAT? HE'S TRYING TO SCARE ME INTO TELLING THE NEW MAMA TO DROP HER BREACH OF PROMISE SUIT AGAINST HIM FOR A HALF A MILLION - YAW HAW - A FAT CHANCE = I AIN'T SO DUMB -
REALLY, BARNEY, WE WON'T HAVE A CHANCE IN COURT AGAINST THE PIPP MILLIONS = WHERE AM I TO GET THE SUGAR FOR MY LAWYERS?
WELL, KID, I THINK JUST ENOUGH OF YOUR CHANCES TO ADVANCE YOU $10.000 - IT'S THE LAST OF MY MONEY I MOPPED UP IN THE BIG HANDICAP = NOW GET ME A PEN AND I'LL WRITE YOU OUT THE CHECK
OH, BARNEY, YOU'RE AN OLD DEAR - ARE YOU SURE THE CHECK IS GOOD ??? YOU'LL PROMISE NOT TO HAVE IT STOPPED?
AT MY AGE I DON'T PROMISE NOTHING
DID I FALL OR WAS I PUSHED ?
DEBECK
9-28
Copyright, 1922, by King Features Syndicate, Inc

The Colonel Exchanges One Suit for Another

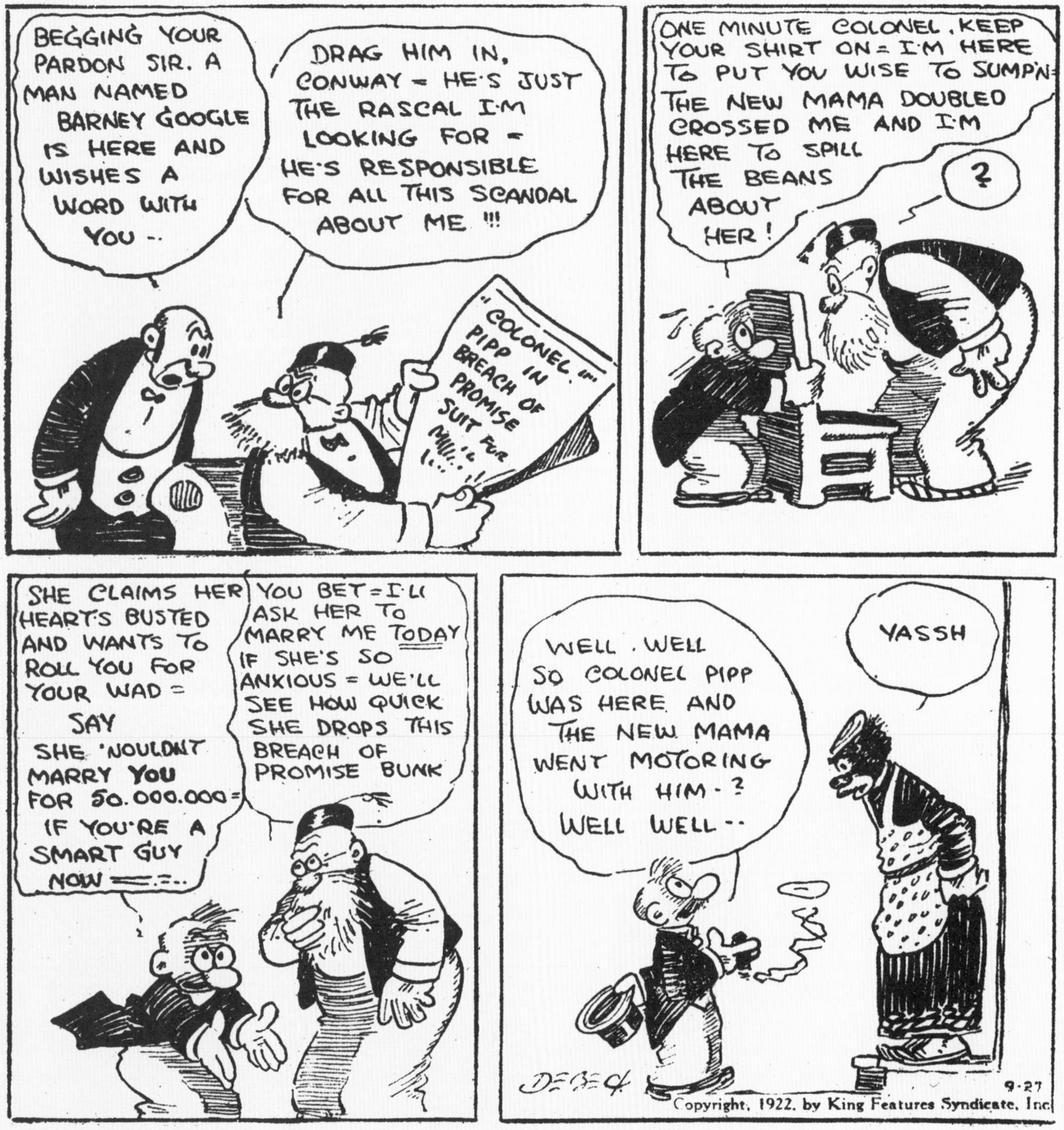
BEGGING YOUR PARDON SIR. A MAN NAMED BARNEY GOOGLE IS HERE AND WISHES A WORD WITH YOU --
DRAG HIM IN, CONWAY = HE'S JUST THE RASCAL I'M LOOKING FOR = HE'S RESPONSIBLE FOR ALL THIS SCANDAL ABOUT ME !!!
"COLONEL PIPP IN BREACH OF PROMISE SUIT FOR
ONE MINUTE COLONEL, KEEP YOUR SHIRT ON = I'M HERE TO PUT YOU WISE TO SUMP'N = THE NEW MAMA DOUBLED CROSSED ME AND I'M HERE TO SPILL THE BEANS ABOUT HER!
?
SHE CLAIMS HER HEART'S BUSTED AND WANTS TO ROLL YOU FOR YOUR WAD = SAY SHE WOULDN'T MARRY YOU FOR 50.000.000 = IF YOU'RE A SMART GUY NOW
YOU BET = I'LL ASK HER TO MARRY ME TODAY IF SHE'S SO ANXIOUS = WE'LL SEE HOW QUICK SHE DROPS THIS BREACH OF PROMISE BUNK
WELL. WELL SO COLONEL PIPP WAS HERE AND THE NEW MAMA WENT MOTORING WITH HIM - ? WELL WELL --
YASSH
DE BECK
9-27
Copyright, 1922, by King Features Syndicate, Inc.

The Colonel Takes the Breach Out of His Promise

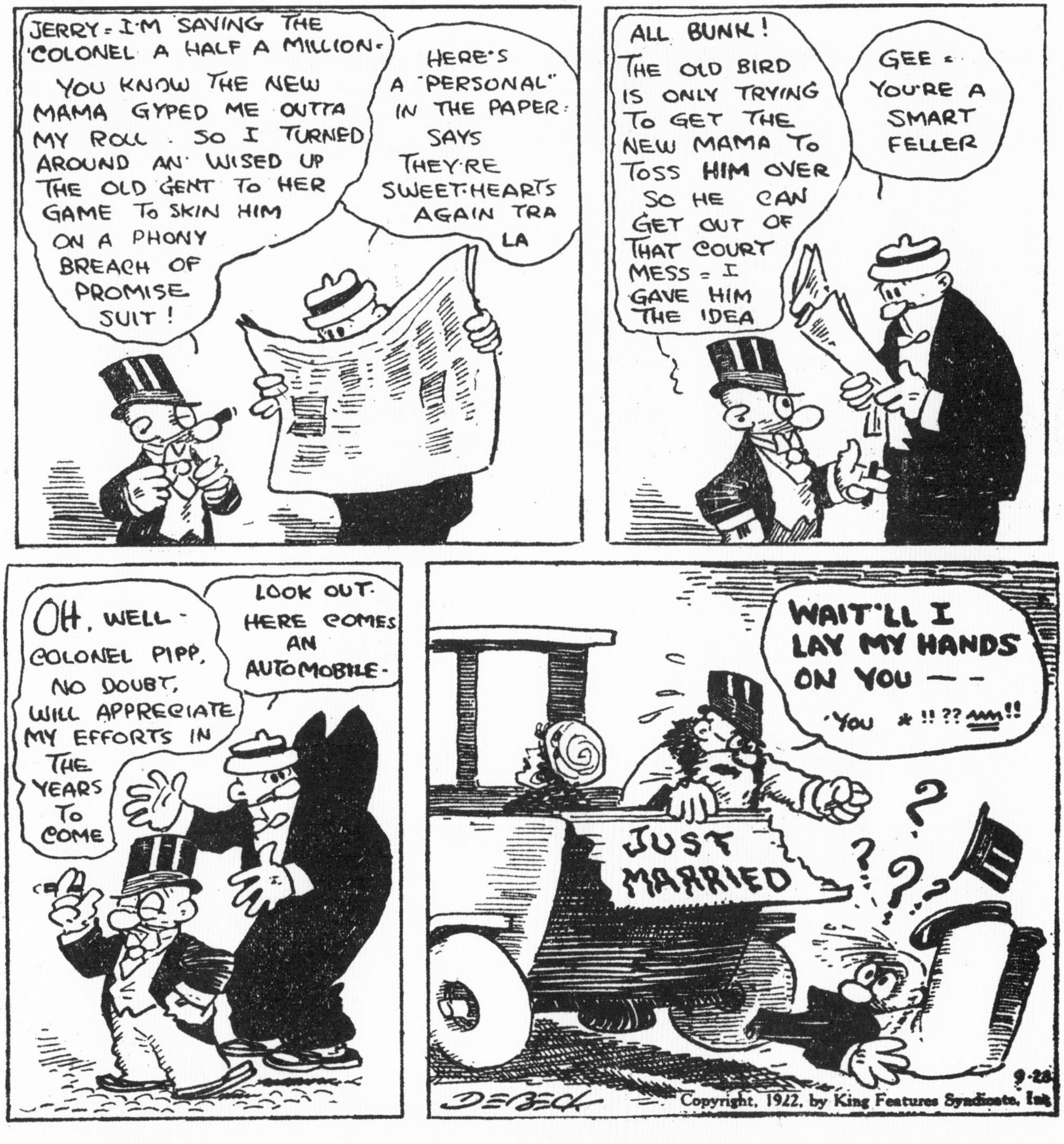
JERRY = I'M SAVING THE 'COLONEL A HALF A MILLION. YOU KNOW THE NEW MAMA GYPED ME OUTTA MY ROLL. SO I TURNED AROUND AN' WISED UP THE OLD GENT TO HER GAME TO SKIN HIM ON A PHONY BREACH OF PROMISE SUIT!
HERE'S A "PERSONAL" IN THE PAPER: SAYS THEY'RE SWEET-HEARTS AGAIN TRA LA
ALL BUNK! THE OLD BIRD IS ONLY TRYING TO GET THE NEW MAMA TO TOSS HIM OVER SO HE CAN GET OUT OF THAT COURT MESS = I GAVE HIM THE IDEA
GEE = YOU'RE A SMART FELLER
OH, WELL - COLONEL PIPP, NO DOUBT, WILL APPRECIATE MY EFFORTS IN THE YEARS TO COME
LOOK OUT. HERE COMES AN AUTOMOBILE.
WAIT'LL I LAY MY HANDS ON YOU -- 'YOU * !! ?? !!
JUST MARRIED
DEBECK
9-28
Copyright, 1922, by King Features Syndicate, Inc.

At Least They Have the Same Opinion About Barney

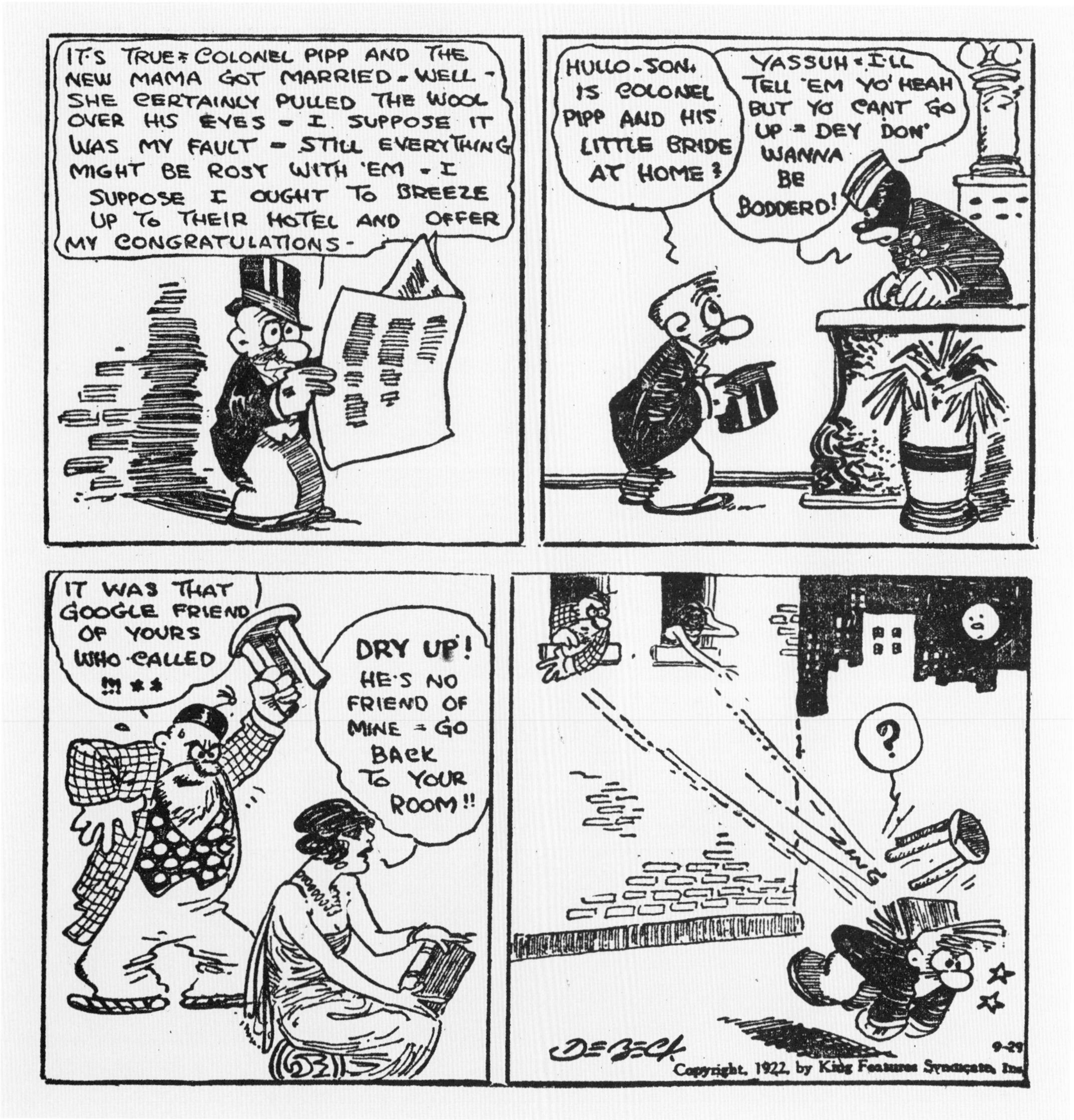
IT'S TRUE = COLONEL PIPP AND THE NEW MAMA GOT MARRIED - WELL - SHE CERTAINLY PULLED THE WOOL OVER HIS EYES = I SUPPOSE IT WAS MY FAULT = STILL EVERYTHING MIGHT BE ROSY WITH 'EM - I SUPPOSE I OUGHT TO BREEZE UP TO THEIR HOTEL AND OFFER MY CONGRATULATIONS -
HULLO - SON. IS COLONEL PIPP AND HIS LITTLE BRIDE AT HOME?
YASSUH = I'LL TELL 'EM YO' HEAH BUT YO CANT GO UP = DEY DON' WANNA BE BODDERD!
IT WAS THAT GOOGLE FRIEND OF YOURS WHO CALLED !!! * *
DRY UP! HE'S NO FRIEND OF MINE = GO BACK TO YOUR ROOM!!
?
9-29
Copyright, 1922, by King Features Syndicate, Inc.

The Colonel Is to Be Congratulated. Oh My, Yes!

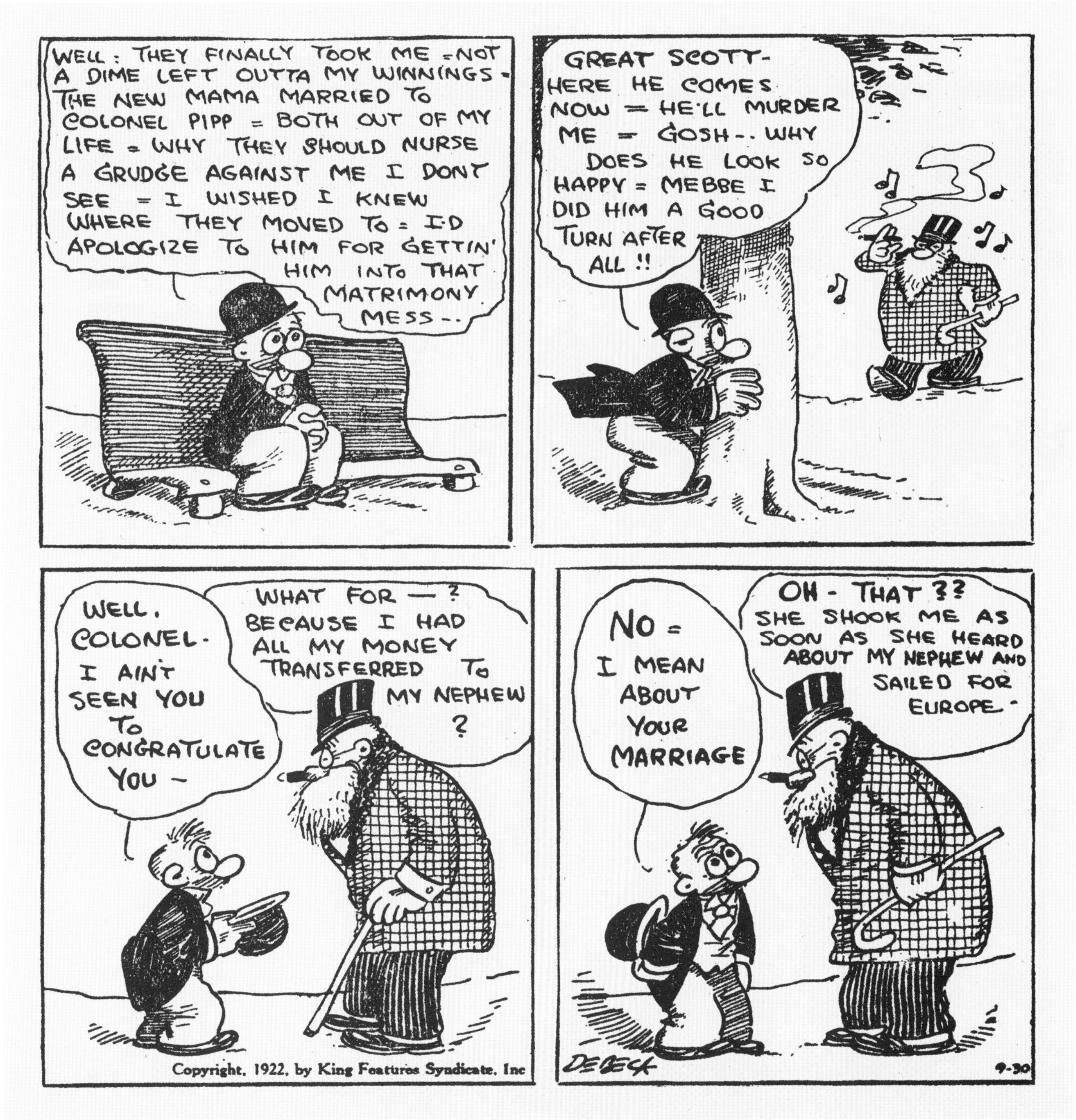

WELL: THEY FINALLY TOOK ME = NOT A DIME LEFT OUTTA MY WINNINGS - THE NEW MAMA MARRIED TO COLONEL PIPP = BOTH OUT OF MY LIFE = WHY THEY SHOULD NURSE A GRUDGE AGAINST ME I DONT SEE = I WISHED I KNEW WHERE THEY MOVED TO = I'D APOLOGIZE TO HIM FOR GETTIN' HIM INTO THAT MATRIMONY MESS --
GREAT SCOTT - HERE HE COMES NOW = HE'LL MURDER ME = GOSH -- WHY DOES HE LOOK SO HAPPY = MEBBE I DID HIM A GOOD TURN AFTER ALL !!
WELL, COLONEL - I AIN'T SEEN YOU TO CONGRATULATE YOU -
WHAT FOR — ? BECAUSE I HAD ALL MY MONEY TRANSFERRED TO MY NEPHEW ?
NO = I MEAN ABOUT YOUR MARRIAGE
OH - THAT ?? SHE SHOOK ME AS SOON AS SHE HEARD ABOUT MY NEPHEW AND SAILED FOR EUROPE -
Copyright, 1922, by King Features Syndicate, Inc
DEBECK
9-30

Barney Hits the Trail. He's Hunting for Spark Plug

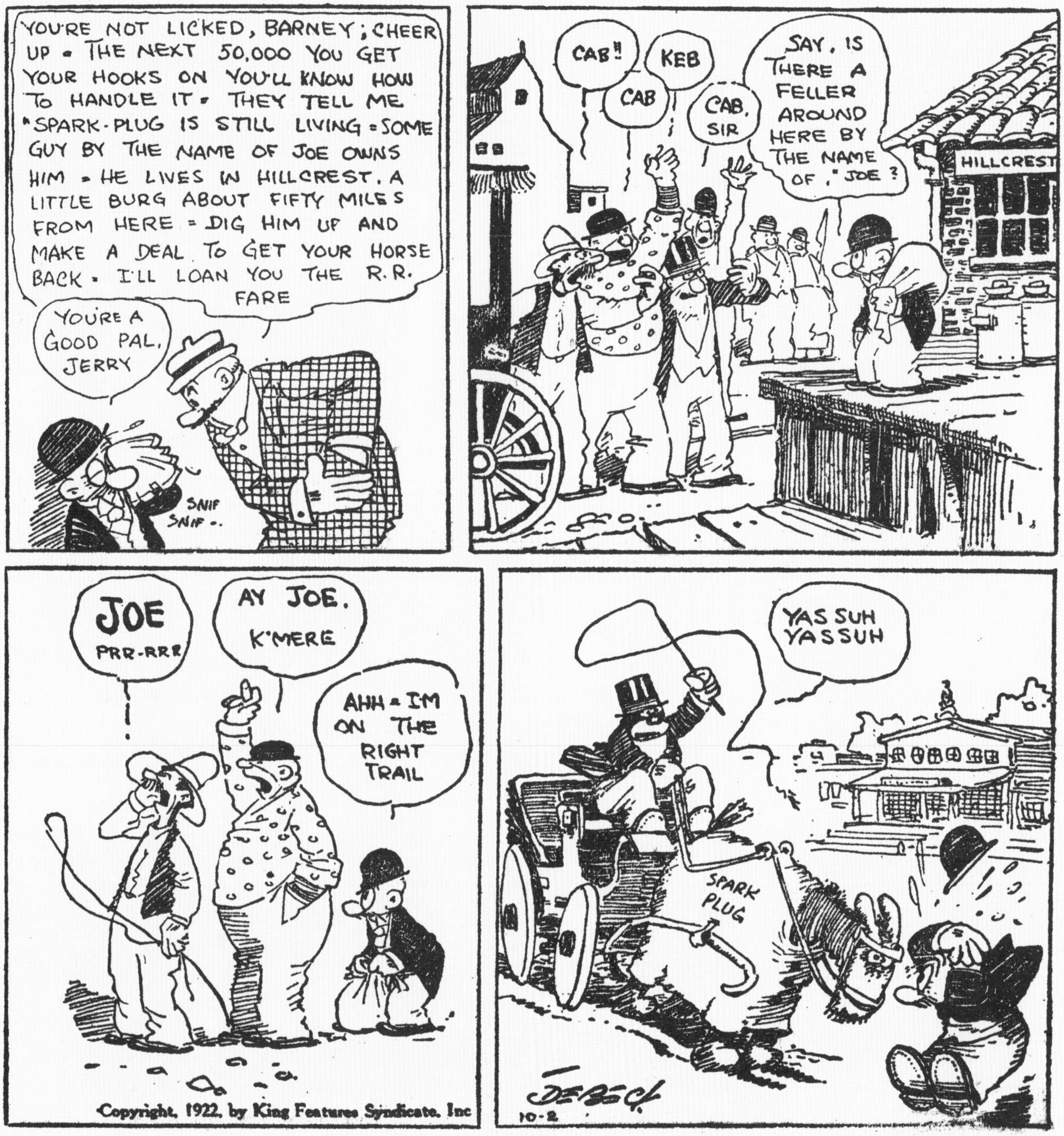
YOU'RE NOT LICKED, BARNEY; CHEER UP - THE NEXT 50,000 YOU GET YOUR HOOKS ON YOU'LL KNOW HOW TO HANDLE IT - THEY TELL ME "SPARK-PLUG IS STILL LIVING - SOME GUY BY THE NAME OF JOE OWNS HIM - HE LIVES IN HILLCREST, A LITTLE BURG ABOUT FIFTY MILES FROM HERE - DIG HIM UP AND MAKE A DEAL TO GET YOUR HORSE BACK - I'LL LOAN YOU THE R.R. FARE
YOU'RE A GOOD PAL, JERRY
SNIF SNIF -.
CAB!!
KEB
CAB
CAB, SIR
SAY, IS THERE A FELLER AROUND HERE BY THE NAME OF, "JOE ?
HILLCREST
JOE PRR-RRR
AY JOE, K'MERE
AHH - I'M ON THE RIGHT TRAIL
Copyright, 1922, by King Features Syndicate, Inc
YAS SUH YASSUH
SPARK PLUG
DEBECK
10-2

It's Just a Question of Raising the Dough

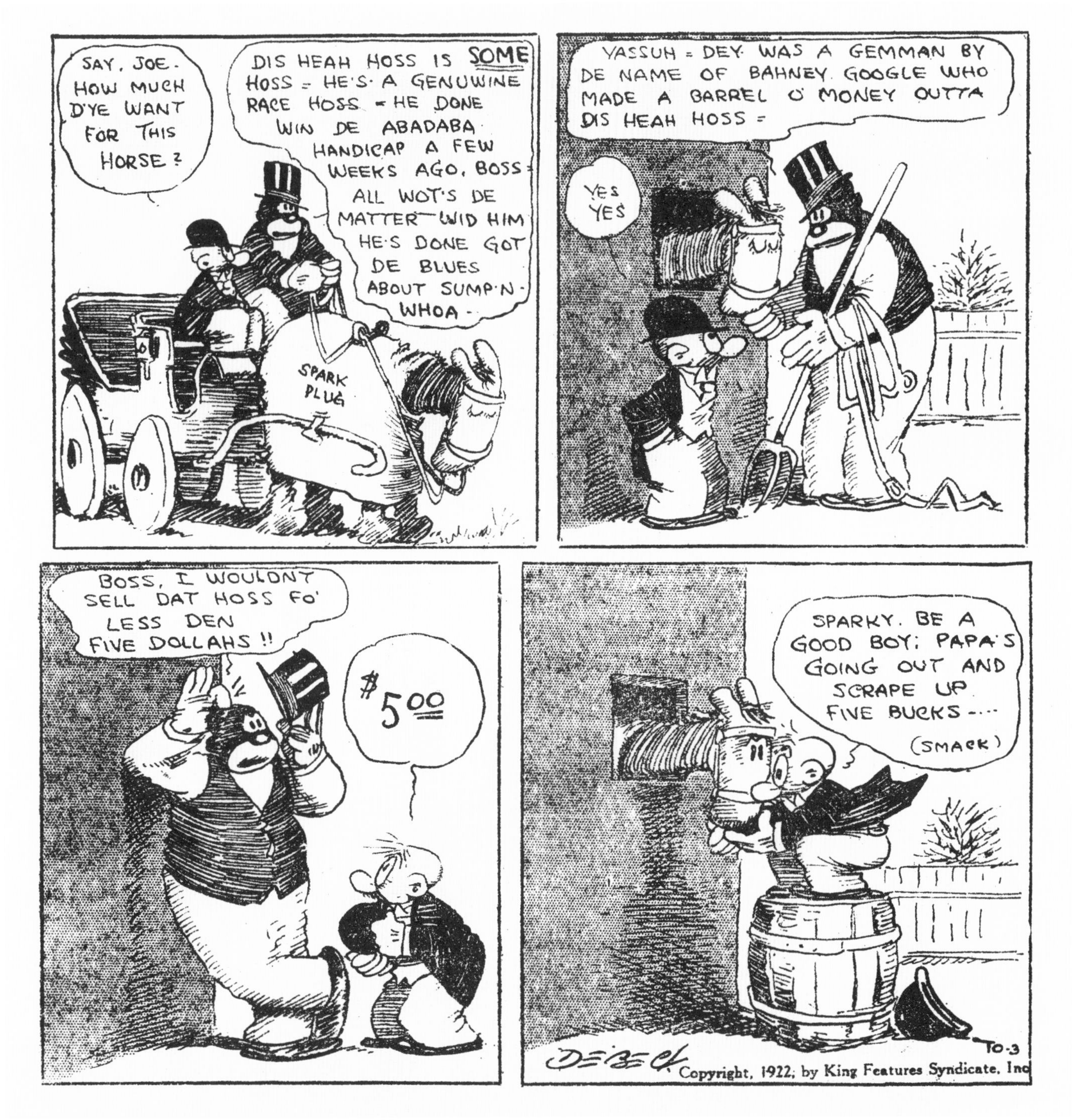

SAY, JOE - HOW MUCH D'YE WANT FOR THIS HORSE ?
DIS HEAH HOSS IS SOME HOSS = HE'S A GENUWINE RACE HOSS - HE DONE WIN DE ABADABA HANDICAP A FEW WEEKS AGO, BOSS = ALL WOT'S DE MATTER WID HIM HE'S DONE GOT DE BLUES ABOUT SUMP'N - WHOA -
SPARK PLUG
YASSUH = DEY WAS A GEMMAN BY DE NAME OF BAHNEY GOOGLE WHO MADE A BARREL O' MONEY OUTTA DIS HEAH HOSS =
YES YES
BOSS, I WOULDNT SELL DAT HOSS FO' LESS DEN FIVE DOLLAHS !!
$5.00
SPARKY. BE A GOOD BOY; PAPA'S GOING OUT AND SCRAPE UP FIVE BUCKS -...
(SMACK)
10-3
DEBECK
Copyright, 1922, by King Features Syndicate, Inc

Barney Ought to Have Made it $50,000

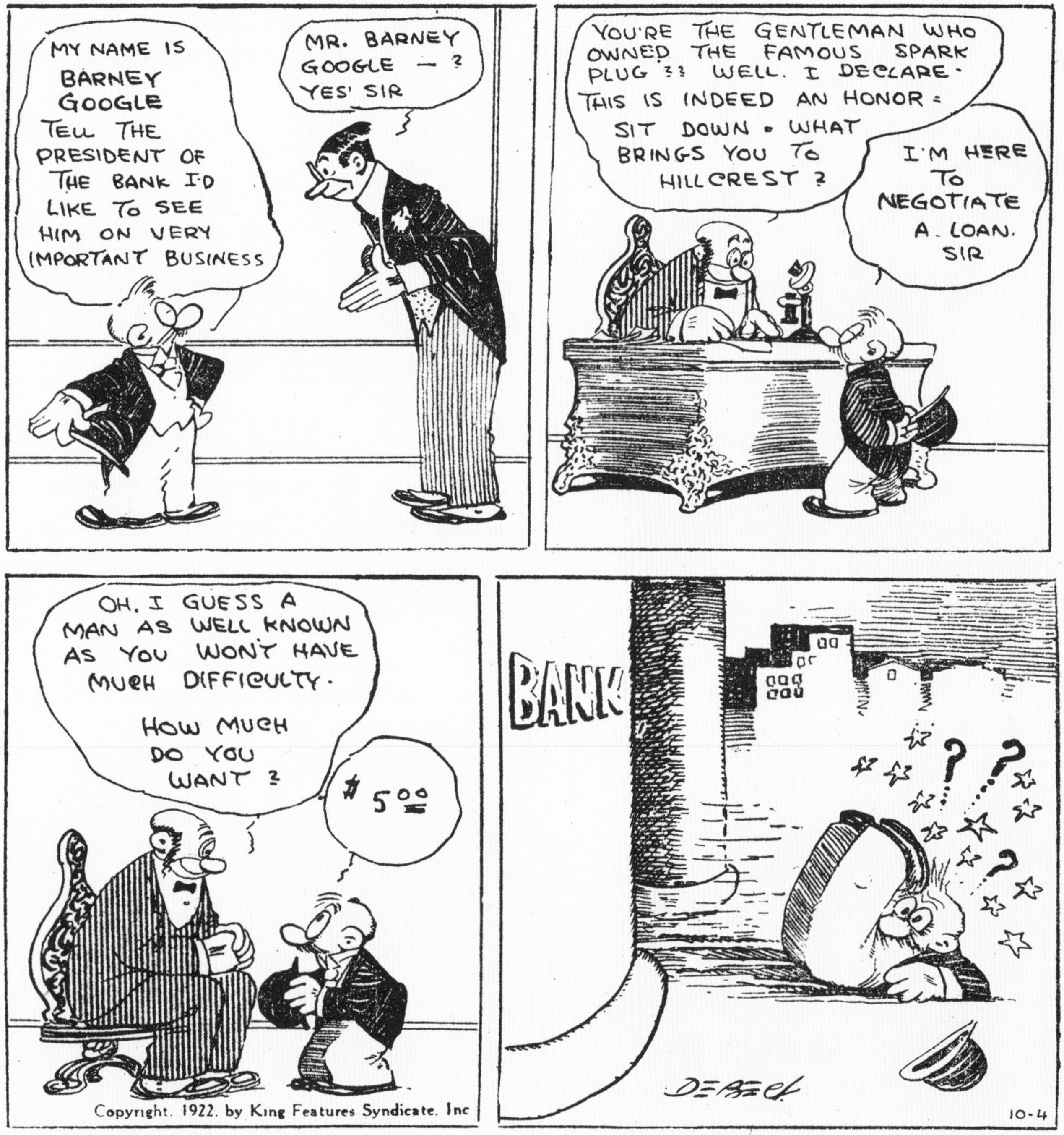

MY NAME IS BARNEY GOOGLE TELL THE PRESIDENT OF THE BANK I'D LIKE TO SEE HIM ON VERY IMPORTANT BUSINESS
MR. BARNEY GOOGLE — ? YES' SIR
YOU'RE THE GENTLEMAN WHO OWNED THE FAMOUS SPARK PLUG ?? WELL. I DECLARE. THIS IS INDEED AN HONOR =
SIT DOWN = WHAT BRINGS YOU TO HILLCREST ?
I'M HERE TO NEGOTIATE A LOAN. SIR
OH. I GUESS A MAN AS WELL KNOWN AS YOU WON'T HAVE MUCH DIFFICULTY.
HOW MUCH DO YOU WANT ?
$5.00
BANK
Copyright. 1922. by King Features Syndicate. Inc
DEBECK
10-4

Barney Raises the Dough and Spark Plug Is His

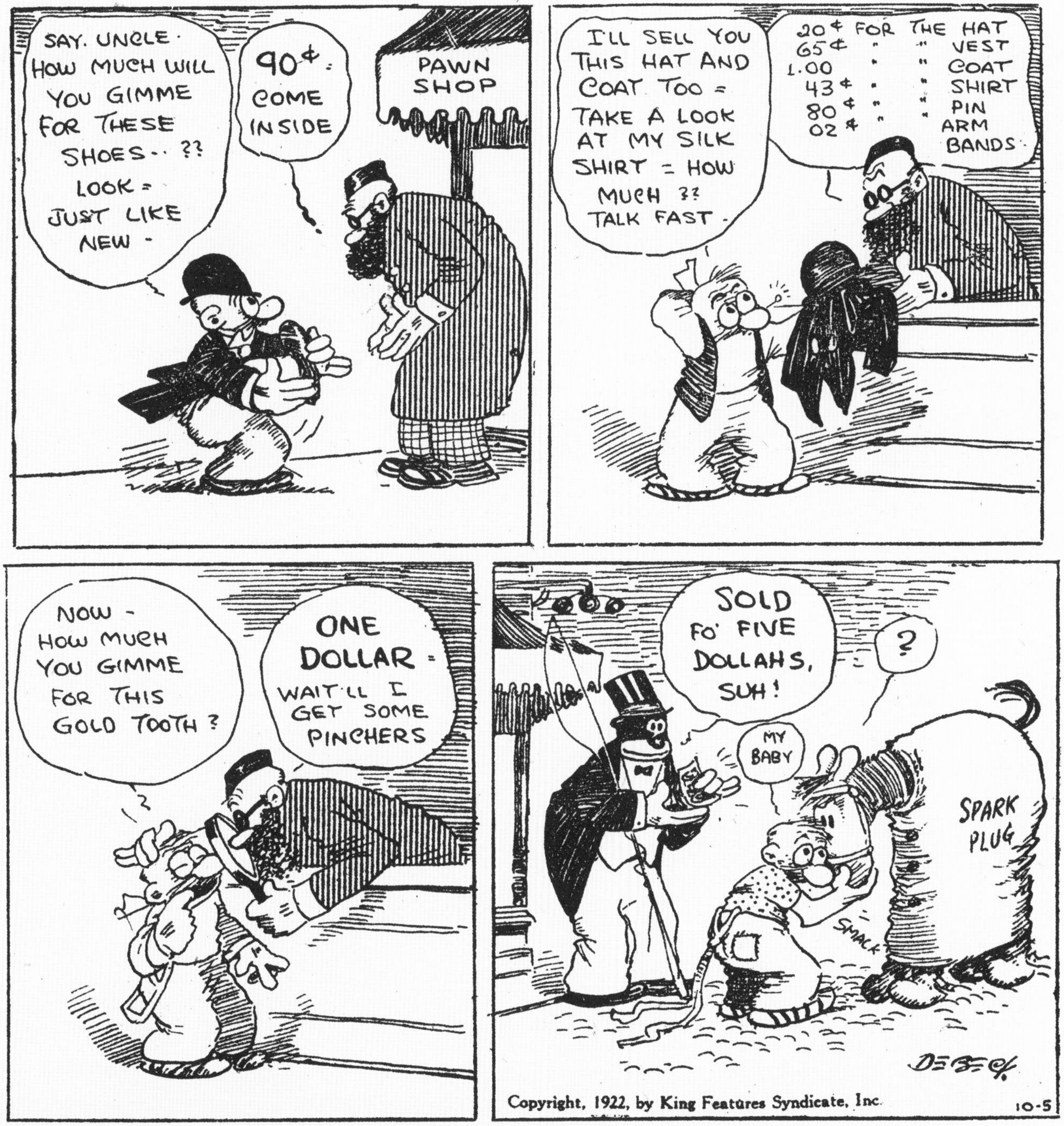
SAY. UNCLE - HOW MUCH WILL YOU GIMME FOR THESE SHOES.. ?? LOOK = JUST LIKE NEW -
90¢ = COME INSIDE
PAWN SHOP
I'LL SELL YOU THIS HAT AND COAT TOO = TAKE A LOOK AT MY SILK SHIRT = HOW MUCH ?? TALK FAST -
20¢ FOR THE HAT
65¢ " " VEST
1.00 " " COAT
43¢ " " SHIRT
80¢ " " PIN
02¢ " " ARM BANDS
NOW - HOW MUCH YOU GIMME FOR THIS GOLD TOOTH ?
ONE DOLLAR = WAIT'LL I GET SOME PINCHERS
SOLD FO' FIVE DOLLAHS, SUH!
?
MY BABY
SMACK
SPARK PLUG
DE BECK
Copyright, 1922, by King Features Syndicate, Inc.
10-5

Barney and Spark Plug Are Now On the Way Home

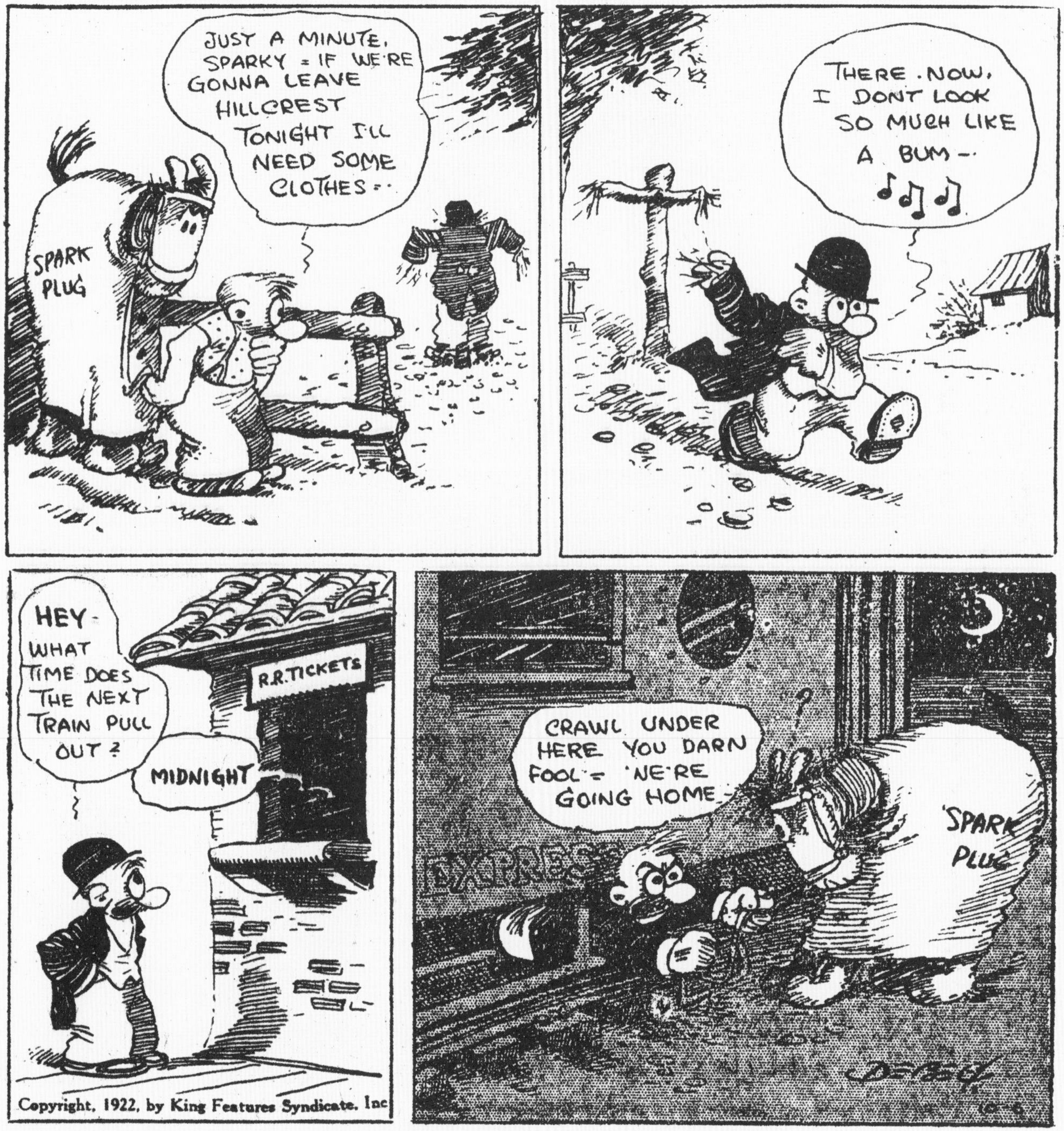
JUST A MINUTE, SPARKY = IF WE'RE GONNA LEAVE HILLCREST TONIGHT I'LL NEED SOME CLOTHES - -
SPARK PLUG
THERE, NOW, I DONT LOOK SO MUCH LIKE A BUM -
HEY - WHAT TIME DOES THE NEXT TRAIN PULL OUT ?
R.R. TICKETS
MIDNIGHT
Copyright, 1922, by King Features Syndicate, Inc
CRAWL UNDER HERE YOU DARN FOOL = WE'RE GOING HOME -
EXPRES
SPARK PLUG
DeBECK

Barney Can't Afford To Take Any Chances With Spark Plug

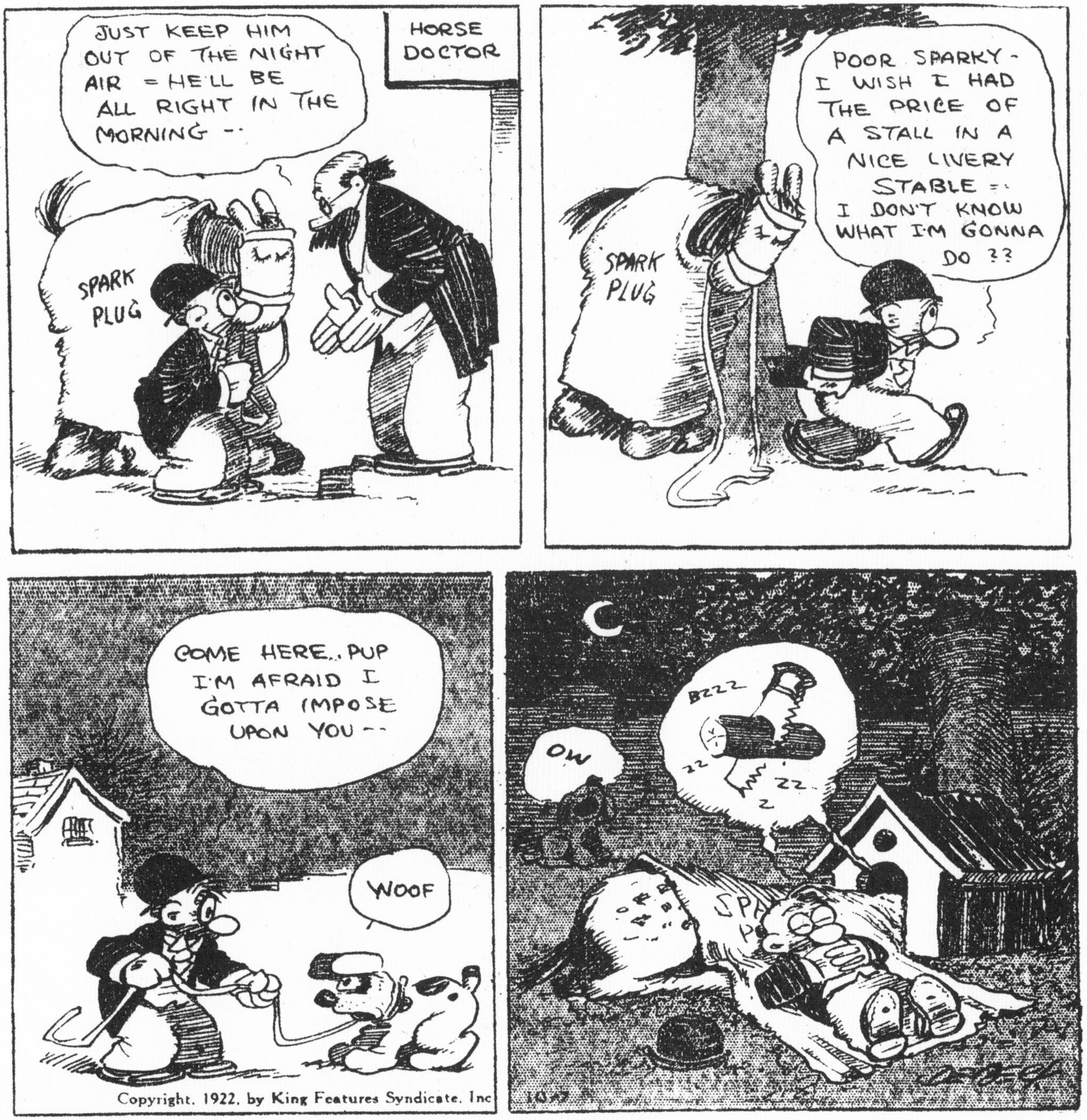
JUST KEEP HIM OUT OF THE NIGHT AIR = HE'LL BE ALL RIGHT IN THE MORNING --
HORSE DOCTOR
SPARK PLUG
POOR SPARKY - I WISH I HAD THE PRICE OF A STALL IN A NICE LIVERY STABLE = I DON'T KNOW WHAT I'M GONNA DO ??
SPARK PLUG
COME HERE.. PUP I'M AFRAID I GOTTA IMPOSE UPON YOU --
WOOF
BZZZ
OW
Copyright, 1922, by King Features Syndicate, Inc

If Spark Plug Doesn't Weaken, Barney Can Eat Again

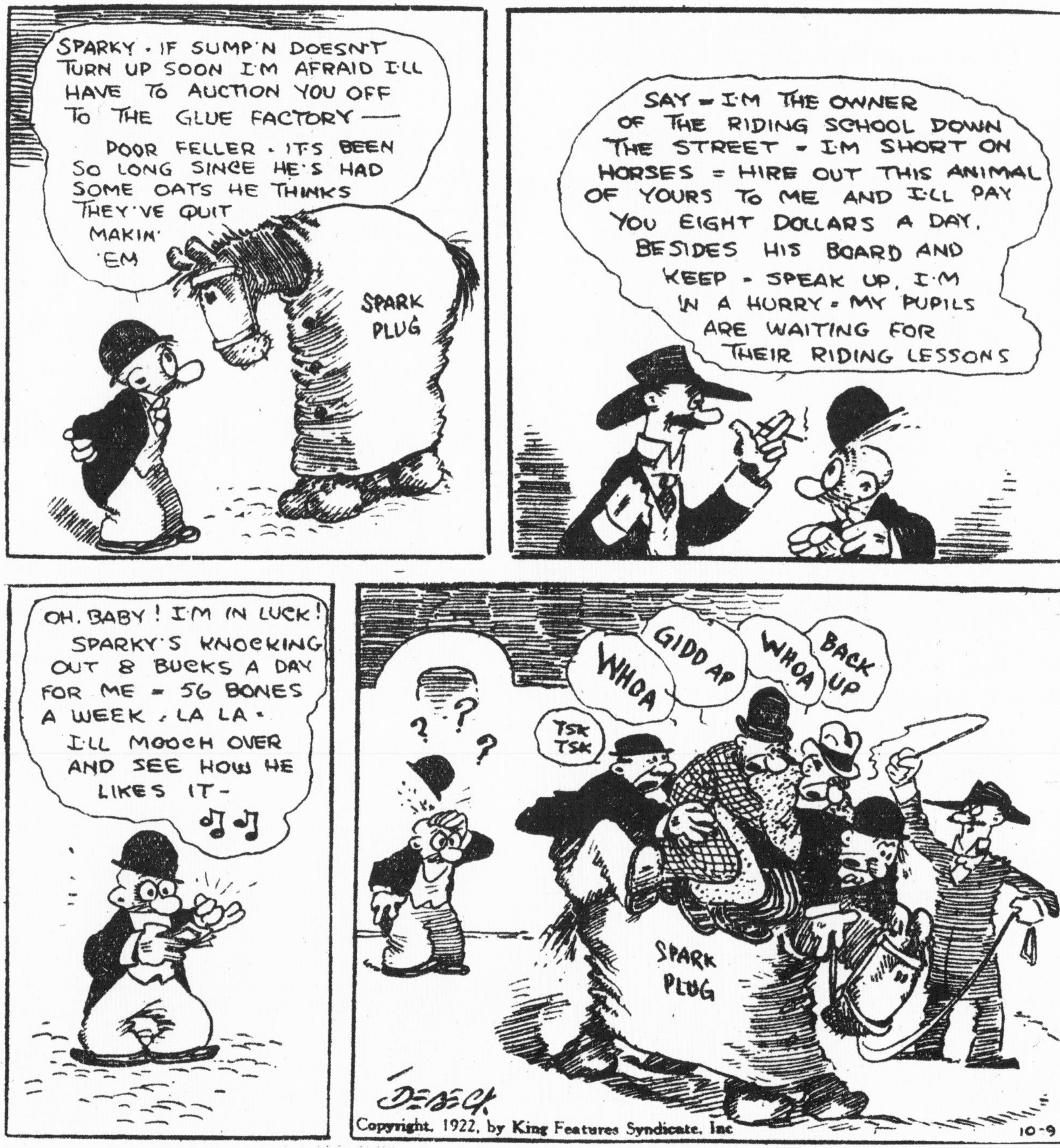
SPARKY - IF SUMP'N DOESN'T TURN UP SOON I'M AFRAID I'LL HAVE TO AUCTION YOU OFF TO THE GLUE FACTORY —
POOR FELLER - IT'S BEEN SO LONG SINCE HE'S HAD SOME OATS HE THINKS THEY'VE QUIT MAKIN' 'EM
SPARK PLUG
SAY - I'M THE OWNER OF THE RIDING SCHOOL DOWN THE STREET - I'M SHORT ON HORSES = HIRE OUT THIS ANIMAL OF YOURS TO ME AND I'LL PAY YOU EIGHT DOLLARS A DAY, BESIDES HIS BOARD AND KEEP - SPEAK UP, I'M IN A HURRY - MY PUPILS ARE WAITING FOR THEIR RIDING LESSONS
OH, BABY! I'M IN LUCK! SPARKY'S KNOCKING OUT 8 BUCKS A DAY FOR ME = 56 BONES A WEEK, LA LA -
I'LL MOOCH OVER AND SEE HOW HE LIKES IT -
WHOA
GIDDAP
WHOA
BACK UP
TSK TSK
? ? ?
SPARK PLUG
DE BECK
Copyright, 1922, by King Features Syndicate, Inc
10-9

Spark Plug Evidently Has a Kick

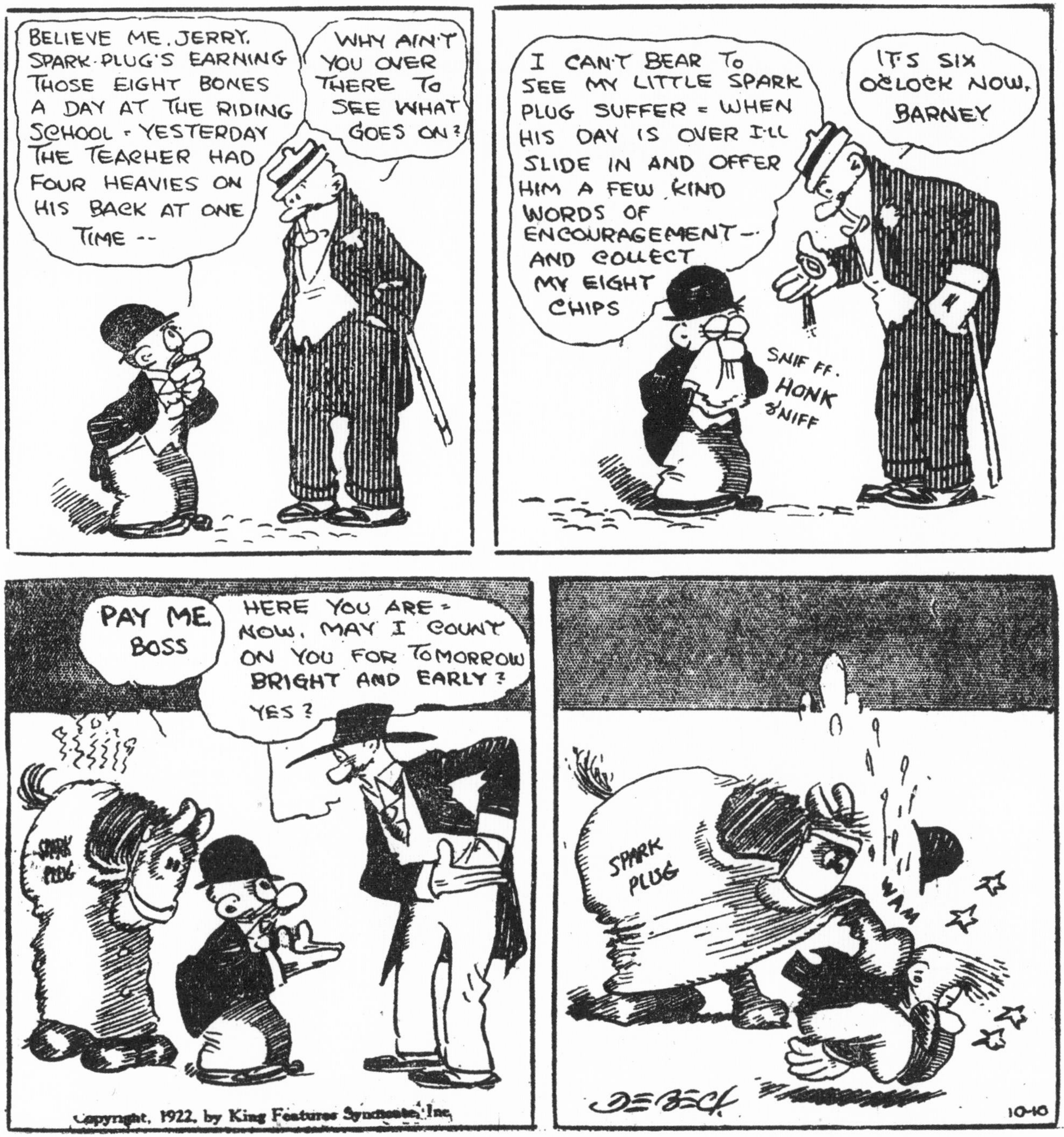

BELIEVE ME, JERRY, SPARK-PLUG'S EARNING THOSE EIGHT BONES A DAY AT THE RIDING SCHOOL = YESTERDAY THE TEACHER HAD FOUR HEAVIES ON HIS BACK AT ONE TIME --
WHY AIN'T YOU OVER THERE TO SEE WHAT GOES ON?
I CAN'T BEAR TO SEE MY LITTLE SPARK PLUG SUFFER = WHEN HIS DAY IS OVER I'LL SLIDE IN AND OFFER HIM A FEW KIND WORDS OF ENCOURAGEMENT -- AND COLLECT MY EIGHT CHIPS
IT'S SIX O'CLOCK NOW, BARNEY
SNIF FF. HONK SNIFF
PAY ME, BOSS
HERE YOU ARE = NOW, MAY I COUNT ON YOU FOR TOMORROW BRIGHT AND EARLY? YES?
SPARK PLUG
SPARK PLUG
WAM
DE BECK
10-10
Copyright, 1922, by King Features Syndicate, Inc.

Well, Well, Evidently Spark Plug's No Rocking Chair

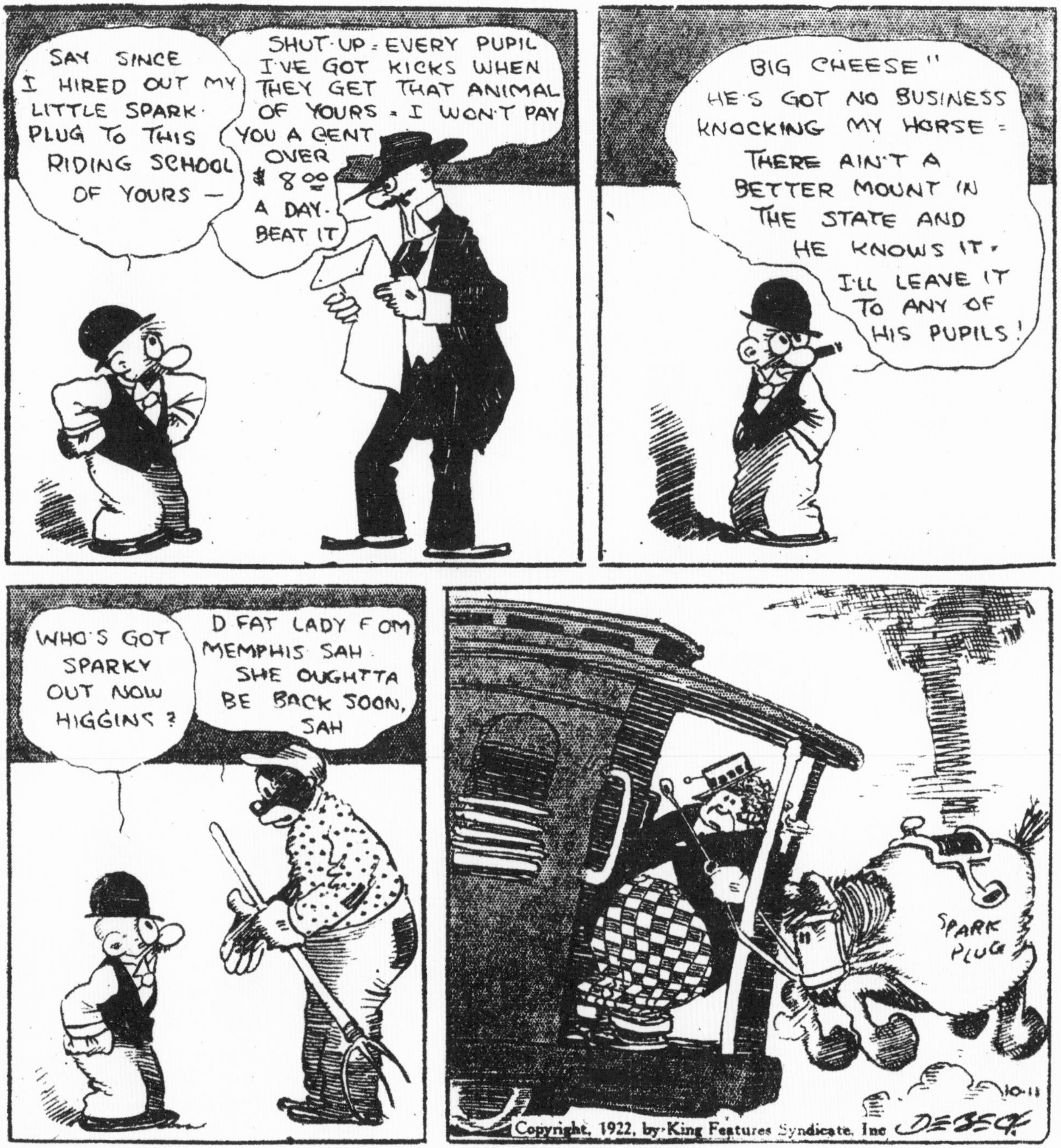

SAY SINCE I HIRED OUT MY LITTLE SPARK-PLUG TO THIS RIDING SCHOOL OF YOURS —
SHUT-UP = EVERY PUPIL I'VE GOT KICKS WHEN THEY GET THAT ANIMAL OF YOURS = I WON'T PAY YOU A CENT OVER $8.00 A DAY. BEAT IT
BIG CHEESE" HE'S GOT NO BUSINESS KNOCKING MY HORSE = THERE AIN'T A BETTER MOUNT IN THE STATE AND HE KNOWS IT. I'LL LEAVE IT TO ANY OF HIS PUPILS!
WHO'S GOT SPARKY OUT NOW HIGGINS ?
D FAT LADY F OM MEMPHIS SAH SHE OUGHTTA BE BACK SOON, SAH
SPARK PLUG
10-11
Copyright, 1922, by King Features Syndicate, Inc
DEBECK

Spark Plug Is Now a Star in the Milky Way

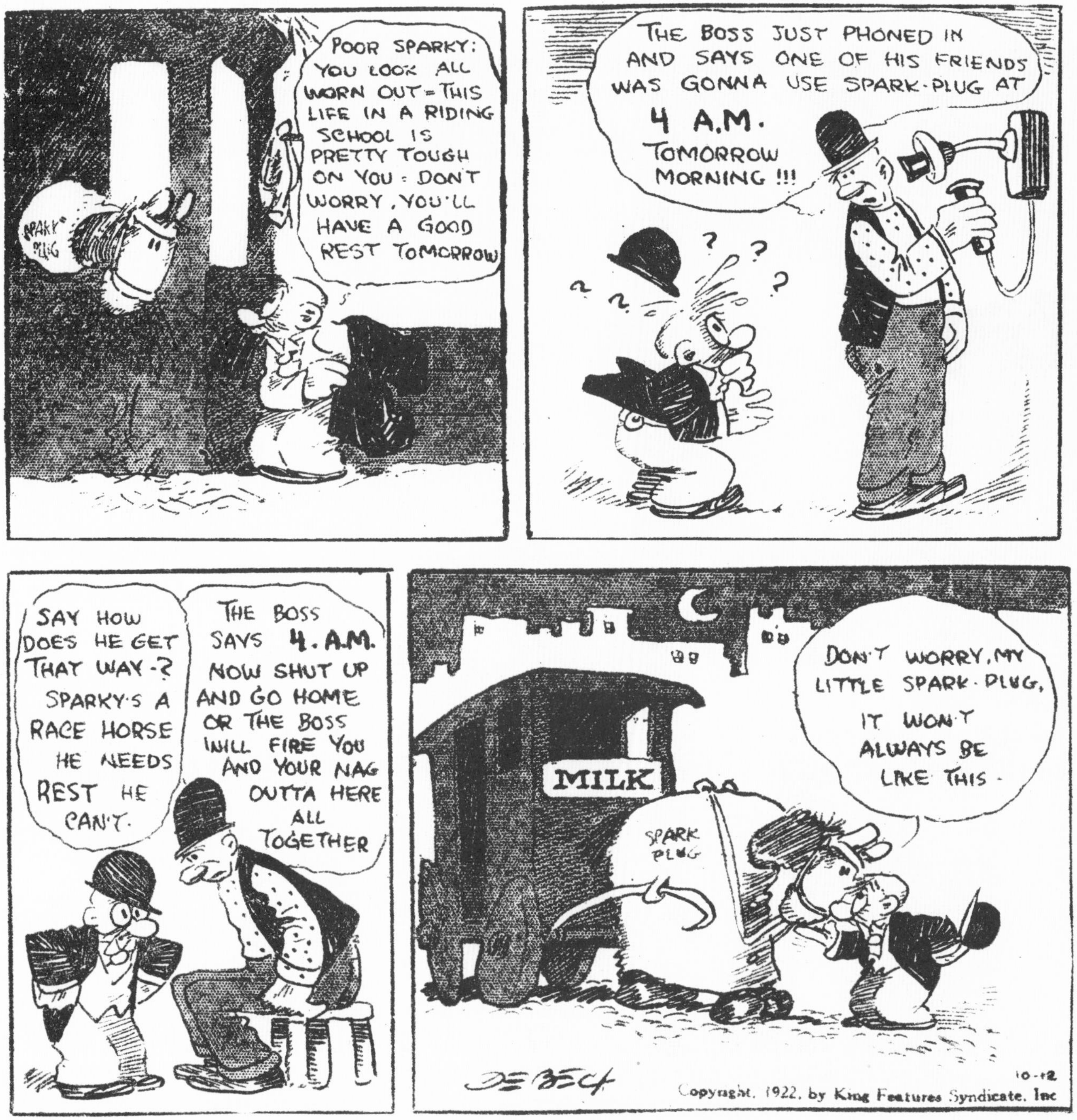

POOR SPARKY: YOU LOOK ALL WORN OUT = THIS LIFE IN A RIDING SCHOOL IS PRETTY TOUGH ON YOU = DON'T WORRY, YOU'LL HAVE A GOOD REST TOMORROW
"SPARKY" PLUG
THE BOSS JUST PHONED IN AND SAYS ONE OF HIS FRIENDS WAS GONNA USE SPARK-PLUG AT 4 A.M. TOMORROW MORNING !!!
SAY HOW DOES HE GET THAT WAY-? SPARKY'S A RACE HORSE HE NEEDS REST HE CAN'T.
THE BOSS SAYS 4. A.M. NOW SHUT UP AND GO HOME OR THE BOSS WILL FIRE YOU AND YOUR NAG OUTTA HERE ALL TOGETHER
MILK
SPARK PLUG
DON'T WORRY, MY LITTLE SPARK-PLUG, IT WON'T ALWAYS BE LIKE THIS -
DE BECK
10-12
Copyright, 1922, by King Features Syndicate, Inc

Barney is Determined to Make a Cleaning Somehow

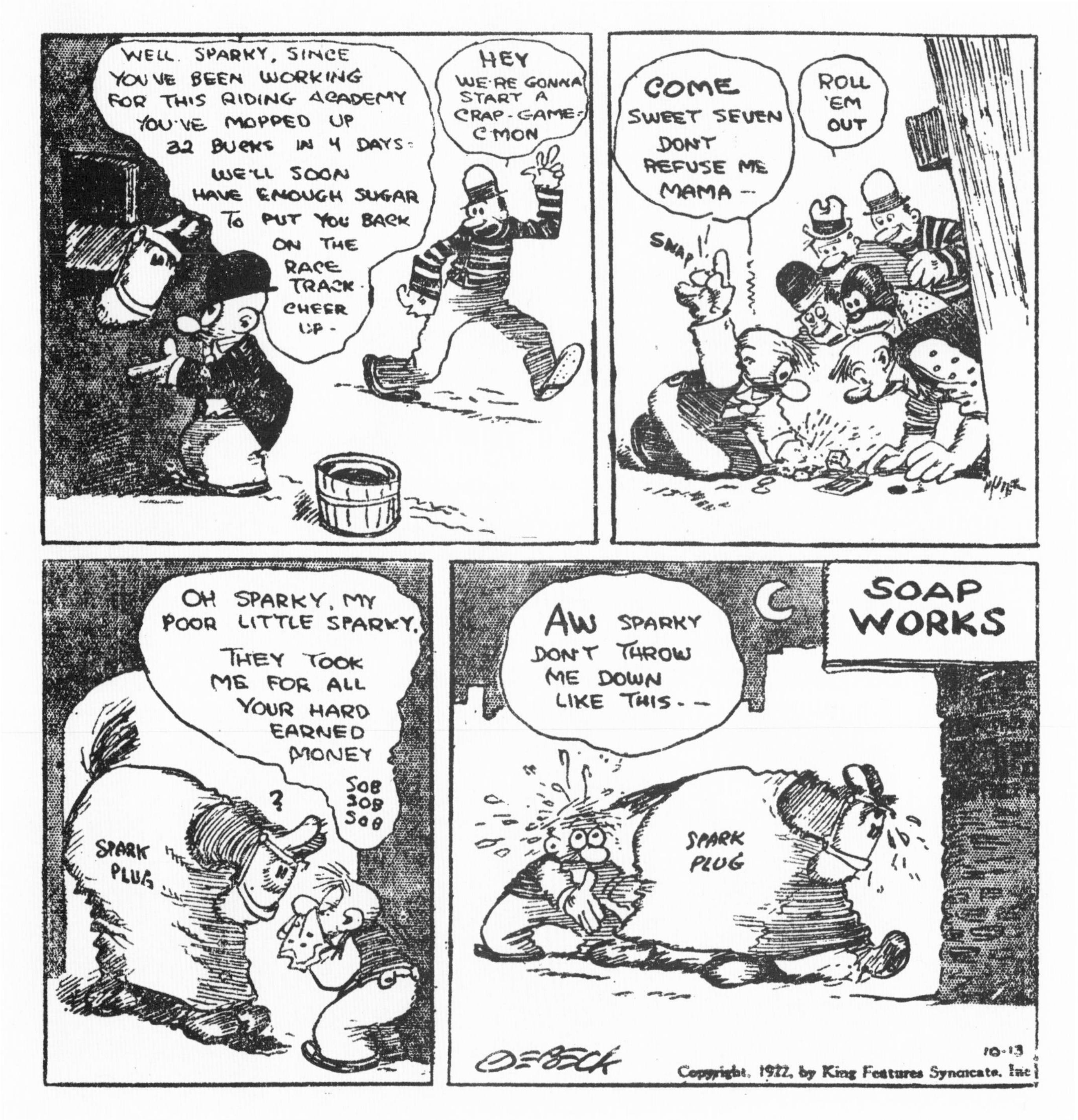
WELL SPARKY, SINCE YOU'VE BEEN WORKING FOR THIS RIDING ACADEMY YOU'VE MOPPED UP 32 BUCKS IN 4 DAYS- WE'LL SOON HAVE ENOUGH SUGAR TO PUT YOU BACK ON THE RACE TRACK- CHEER UP-
HEY WE'RE GONNA START A CRAP-GAME- C'MON
COME SWEET SEVEN DON'T REFUSE ME MAMA-
ROLL 'EM OUT
SNAP
OH SPARKY, MY POOR LITTLE SPARKY. THEY TOOK ME FOR ALL YOUR HARD EARNED MONEY
SOB SOB SOB
?
SPARK PLUG
SOAP WORKS
AW SPARKY DON'T THROW ME DOWN LIKE THIS.-
SPARK PLUG
10-13
Copyright, 1922, by King Features Syndicate, Inc.

But Barney Recovers in Time to Eat

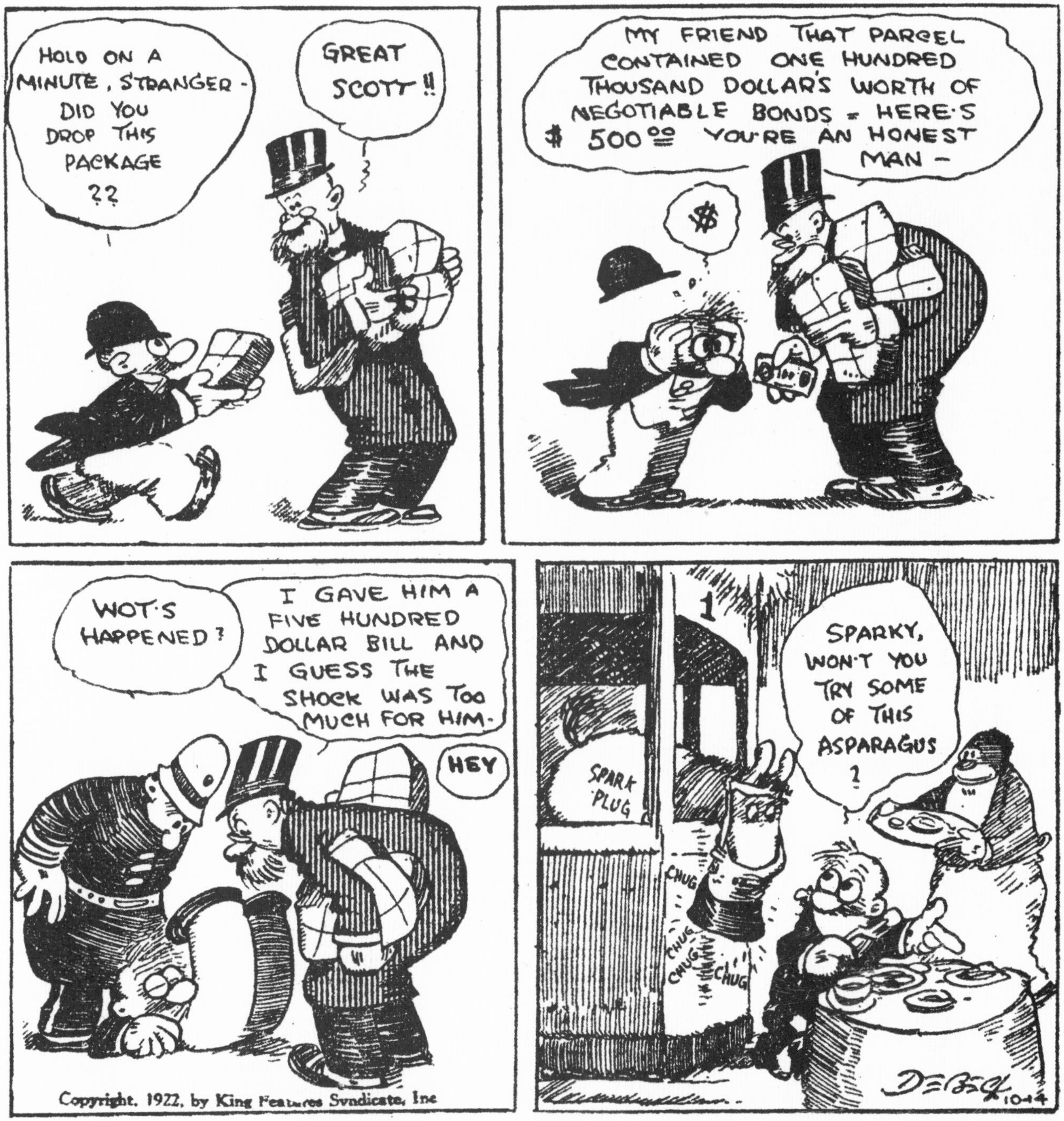
HOLD ON A MINUTE, STRANGER - DID YOU DROP THIS PACKAGE ??
GREAT SCOTT !!
MY FRIEND THAT PARCEL CONTAINED ONE HUNDRED THOUSAND DOLLAR'S WORTH OF NEGOTIABLE BONDS = HERE'S $ 500.00 YOU'RE AN HONEST MAN -
$
WOT'S HAPPENED ?
I GAVE HIM A FIVE HUNDRED DOLLAR BILL AND I GUESS THE SHOCK WAS TOO MUCH FOR HIM.
HEY
1
SPARK PLUG
CHUG
CHUG
CHUG
CHUG
SPARKY, WON'T YOU TRY SOME OF THIS ASPARAGUS ?
DEBECK 10-14
Copyright, 1922, by King Features Syndicate, Inc

A Conspiracy Against the Sugar Cane Sweepstakes

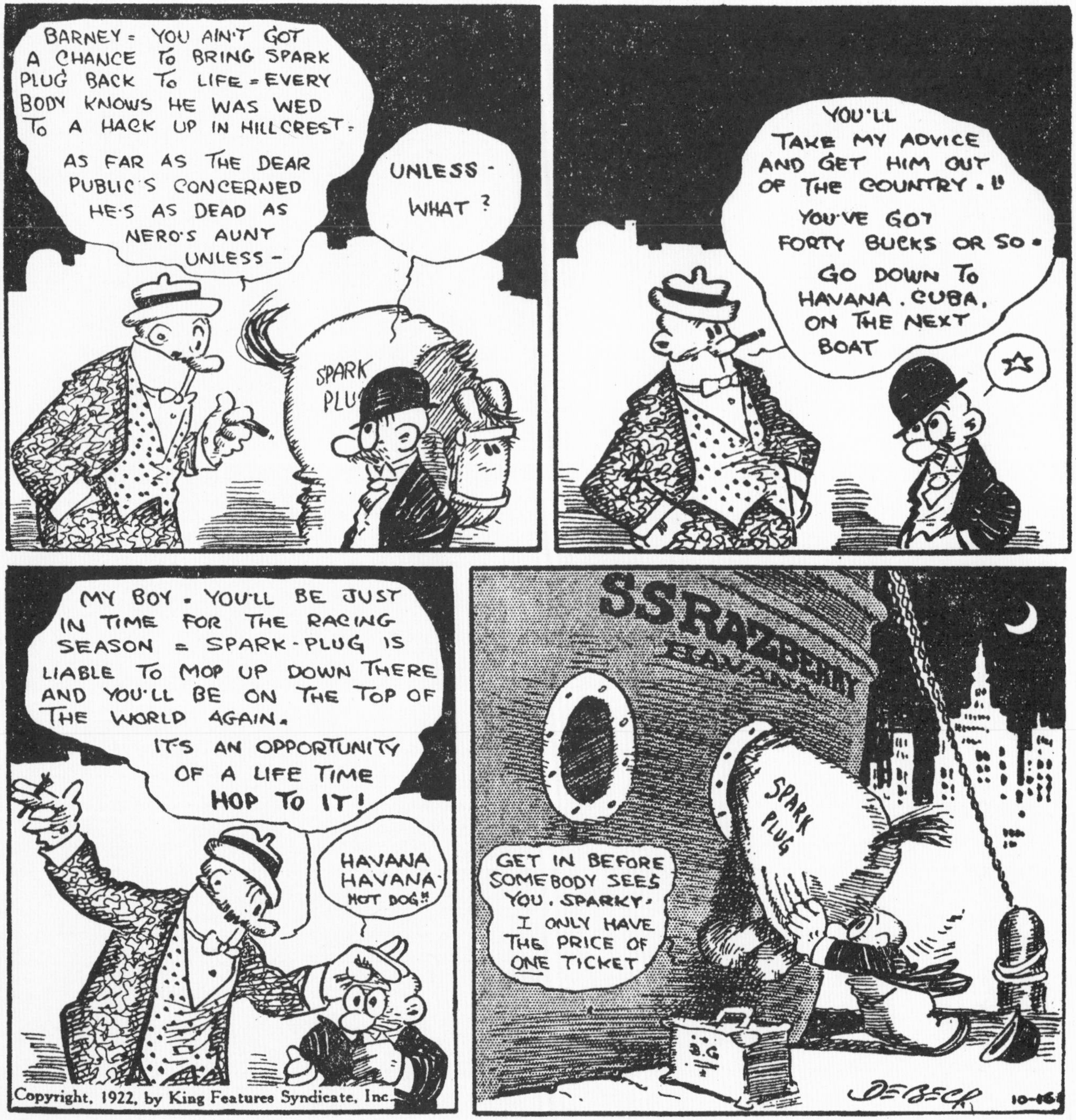
BARNEY = YOU AIN'T GOT A CHANCE TO BRING SPARK PLUG BACK TO LIFE = EVERY BODY KNOWS HE WAS WED TO A HACK UP IN HILLCREST =
AS FAR AS THE DEAR PUBLIC'S CONCERNED HE'S AS DEAD AS NERO'S AUNT UNLESS -
UNLESS - WHAT ?
SPARK PLUG
YOU'LL TAKE MY ADVICE AND GET HIM OUT OF THE COUNTRY . !!
YOU'VE GOT FORTY BUCKS OR SO .
GO DOWN TO HAVANA . CUBA, ON THE NEXT BOAT
MY BOY . YOU'LL BE JUST IN TIME FOR THE RACING SEASON = SPARK-PLUG IS LIABLE TO MOP UP DOWN THERE AND YOU'LL BE ON THE TOP OF THE WORLD AGAIN.
IT'S AN OPPORTUNITY OF A LIFE TIME
HOP TO IT!
HAVANA HAVANA HOT DOG!!
SS RAZBERRY
HAVANA
SPARK PLUG
GET IN BEFORE SOMEBODY SEES YOU . SPARKY .
I ONLY HAVE THE PRICE OF ONE TICKET
B.G
Copyright, 1922, by King Features Syndicate, Inc.
DE BECK
10-16

Rocked in a Cradle On the Deep!

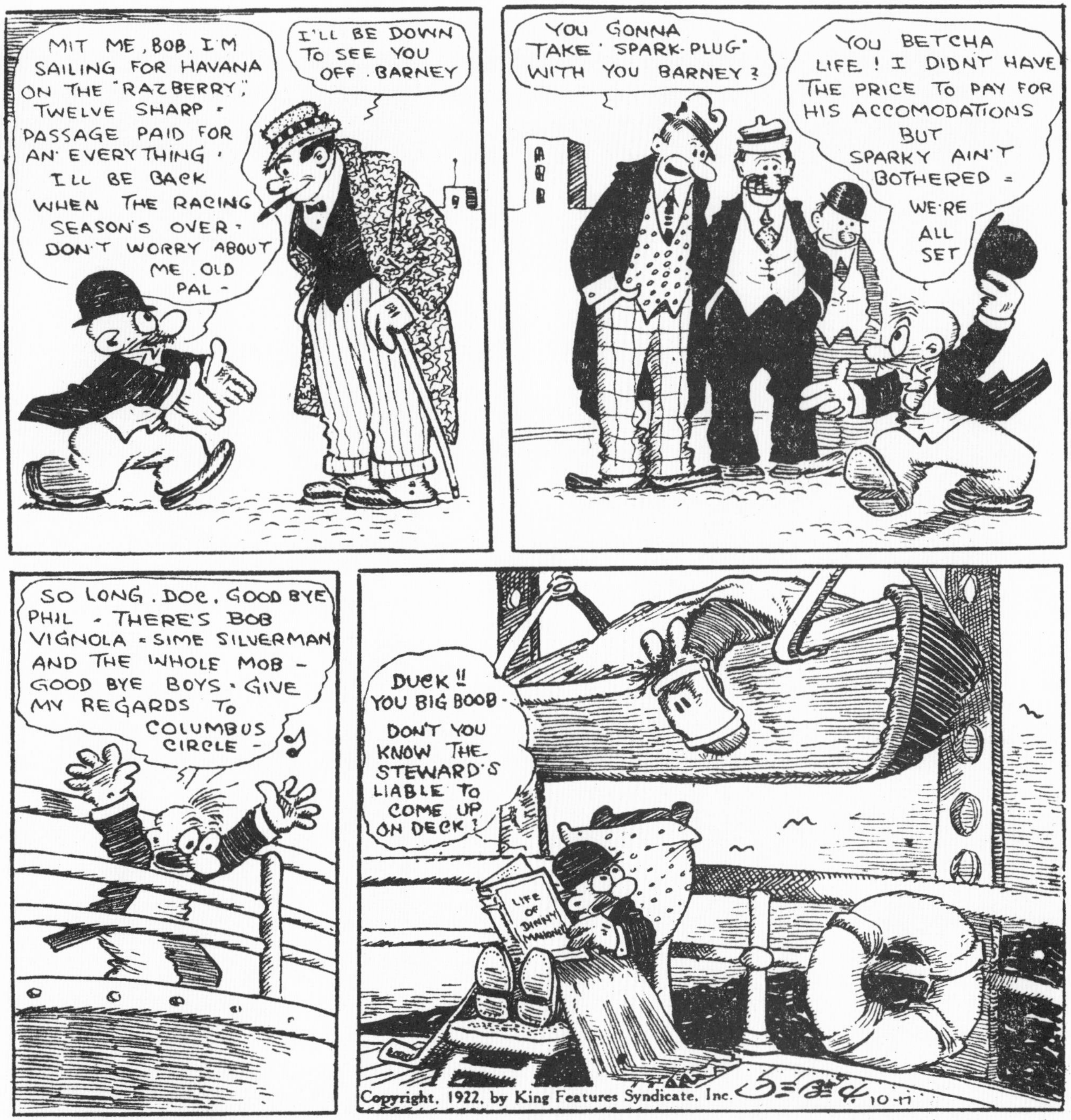
MIT ME, BOB. I'M SAILING FOR HAVANA ON THE "RAZBERRY," TWELVE SHARP = PASSAGE PAID FOR AN' EVERYTHING · I'LL BE BACK WHEN THE RACING SEASON'S OVER = DON'T WORRY ABOUT ME. OLD PAL -
I'LL BE DOWN TO SEE YOU OFF. BARNEY
YOU GONNA TAKE "SPARK-PLUG" WITH YOU BARNEY?
YOU BETCHA LIFE! I DIDN'T HAVE THE PRICE TO PAY FOR HIS ACCOMODATIONS BUT SPARKY AIN'T BOTHERED = WE'RE ALL SET
SO LONG. DOC. GOOD BYE PHIL - THERE'S BOB VIGNOLA = SIME SILVERMAN AND THE WHOLE MOB - GOOD BYE BOYS · GIVE MY REGARDS TO COLUMBUS CIRCLE -
DUCK!! YOU BIG BOOB - DON'T YOU KNOW THE STEWARD'S LIABLE TO COME UP ON DECK?
LIFE OF JIMMY MAHONEY
Copyright, 1922, by King Features Syndicate, Inc.
10-17

Some Mixture! Black and White and a Horse's Neck

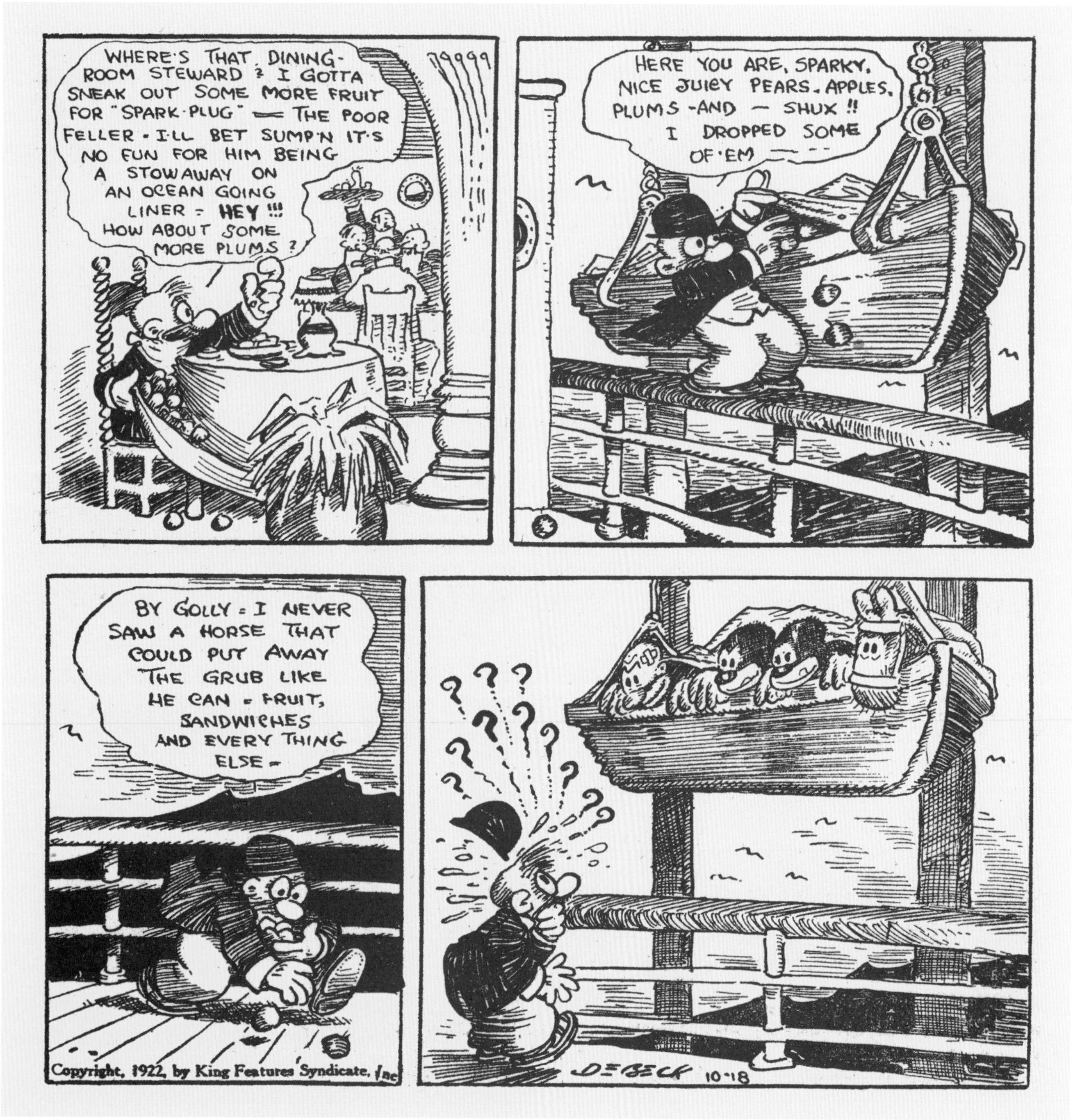

WHERE'S THAT DINING-ROOM STEWARD ? I GOTTA SNEAK OUT SOME MORE FRUIT FOR "SPARK-PLUG" — THE POOR FELLER - I'LL BET SUMP'N IT'S NO FUN FOR HIM BEING A STOWAWAY ON AN OCEAN GOING LINER - HEY !!! HOW ABOUT SOME MORE PLUMS ?
HERE YOU ARE, SPARKY. NICE JUICY PEARS - APPLES, PLUMS - AND — SHUX !! I DROPPED SOME OF 'EM — — —
BY GOLLY - I NEVER SAW A HORSE THAT COULD PUT AWAY THE GRUB LIKE HE CAN - FRUIT, SANDWICHES AND EVERY THING ELSE -
Copyright, 1922, by King Features Syndicate, Inc
DE BECK 10-18

Testing the Stability of the Upper Berth

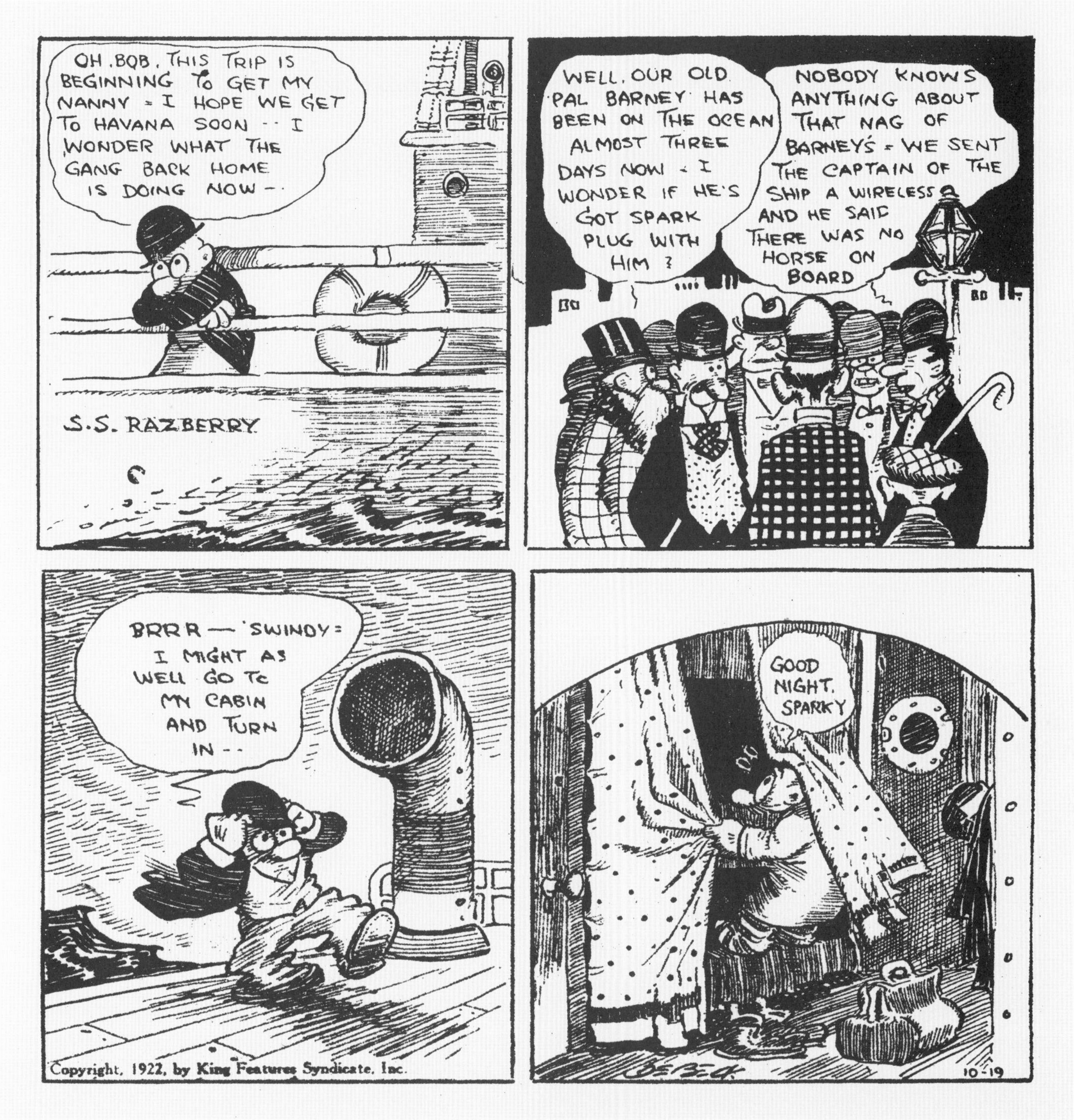
OH, BOB, THIS TRIP IS BEGINNING TO GET MY NANNY = I HOPE WE GET TO HAVANA SOON -- I WONDER WHAT THE GANG BACK HOME IS DOING NOW --
S.S. RAZBERRY
WELL, OUR OLD PAL BARNEY HAS BEEN ON THE OCEAN ALMOST THREE DAYS NOW - I WONDER IF HE'S GOT SPARK PLUG WITH HIM ?
NOBODY KNOWS ANYTHING ABOUT THAT NAG OF BARNEY'S = WE SENT THE CAPTAIN OF THE SHIP A WIRELESS AND HE SAID THERE WAS NO HORSE ON BOARD
BRRR — SWINDY = I MIGHT AS WELL GO TO MY CABIN AND TURN IN --
GOOD NIGHT, SPARKY
Copyright, 1922, by King Features Syndicate, Inc.
10-19

Why Barney Got So Much Attention

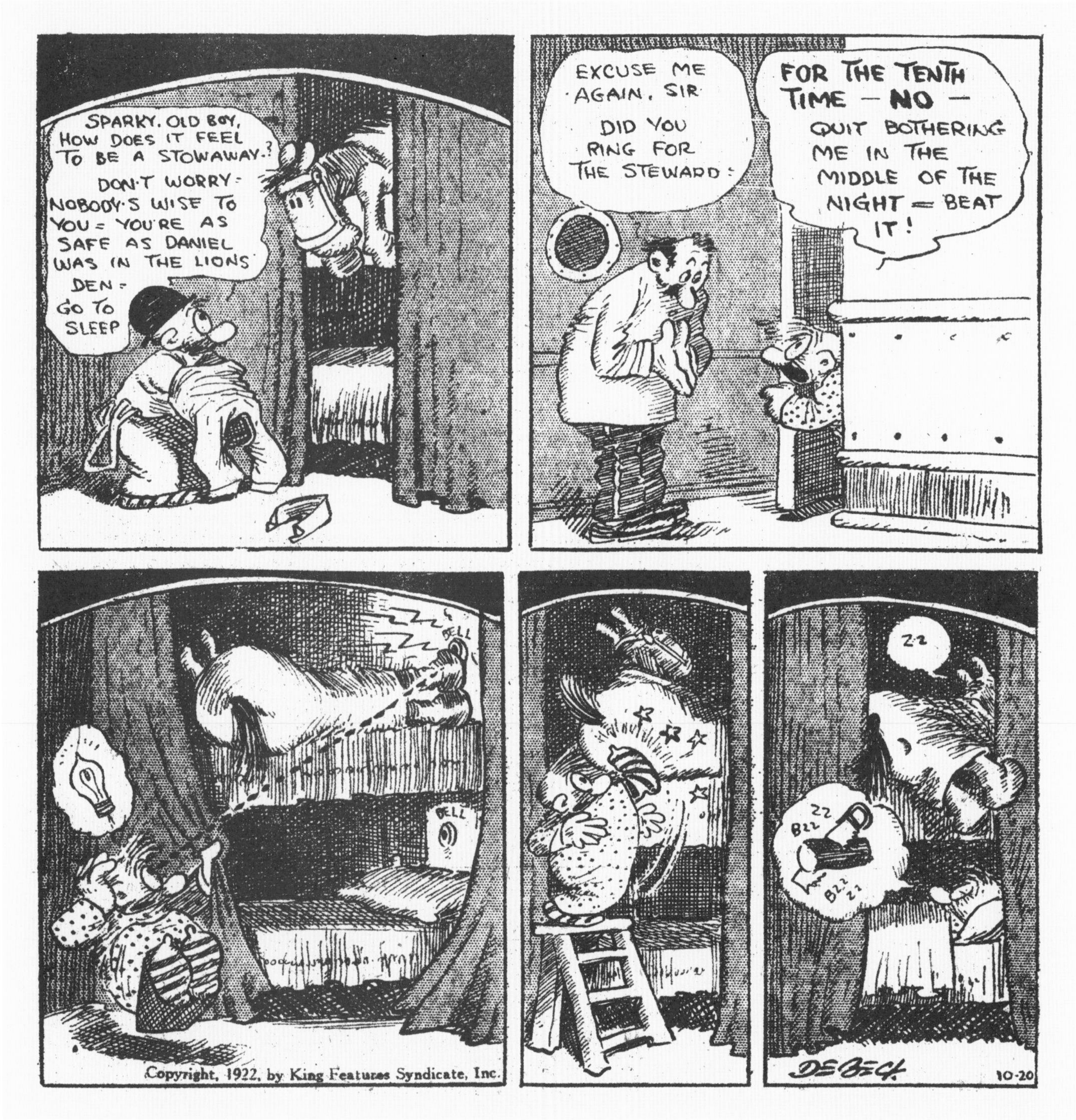
SPARKY, OLD BOY, HOW DOES IT FEEL TO BE A STOWAWAY.?
DON'T WORRY - NOBODY'S WISE TO YOU = YOU'RE AS SAFE AS DANIEL WAS IN THE LIONS' DEN -
GO TO SLEEP
EXCUSE ME AGAIN, SIR
DID YOU RING FOR THE STEWARD:
FOR THE TENTH TIME - NO - QUIT BOTHERING ME IN THE MIDDLE OF THE NIGHT = BEAT IT!
BELL
BELL
Z-Z
BZZ
BZZ
Copyright, 1922, by King Features Syndicate, Inc.
DE BECK
10-20

"The Poet's Eye, in a Fine Frenzy Rolling"

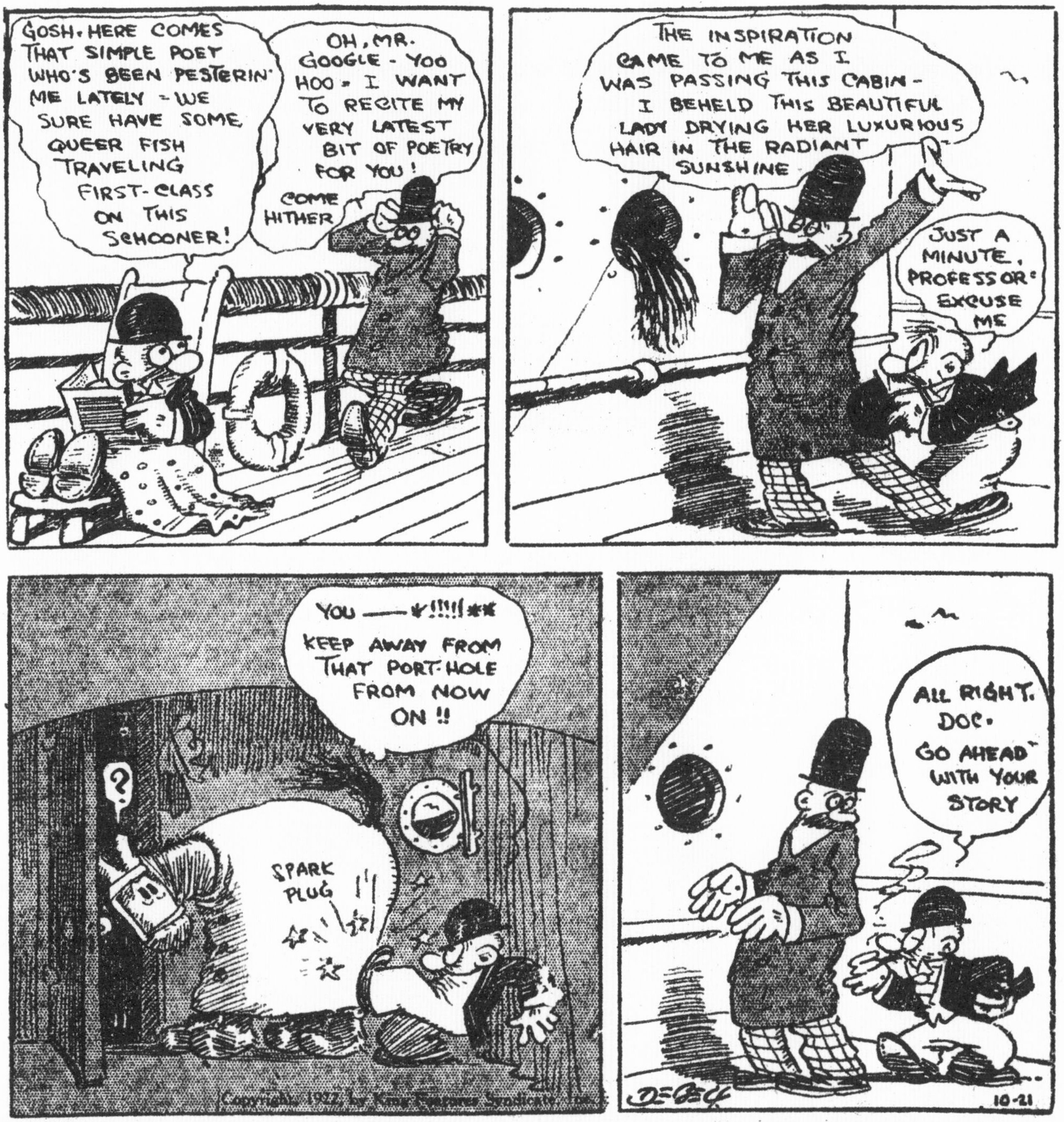

GOSH. HERE COMES THAT SIMPLE POET WHO'S BEEN PESTERIN' ME LATELY - WE SURE HAVE SOME QUEER FISH TRAVELING FIRST-CLASS ON THIS SCHOONER!
OH, MR. GOOGLE - YOO HOO - I WANT TO RECITE MY VERY LATEST BIT OF POETRY FOR YOU!
COME HITHER
THE INSPIRATION CAME TO ME AS I WAS PASSING THIS CABIN - I BEHELD THIS BEAUTIFUL LADY DRYING HER LUXURIOUS HAIR IN THE RADIANT SUNSHINE
JUST A MINUTE, PROFESSOR - EXCUSE ME
YOU —— *!!!!**
KEEP AWAY FROM THAT PORT-HOLE FROM NOW ON !!
?
SPARK PLUG
Copyright 1922 by King Features Syndicate, Inc.
ALL RIGHT. DOC - GO AHEAD WITH YOUR STORY
DE BECK
10-21

Towing a Total Loss of One Horse Power

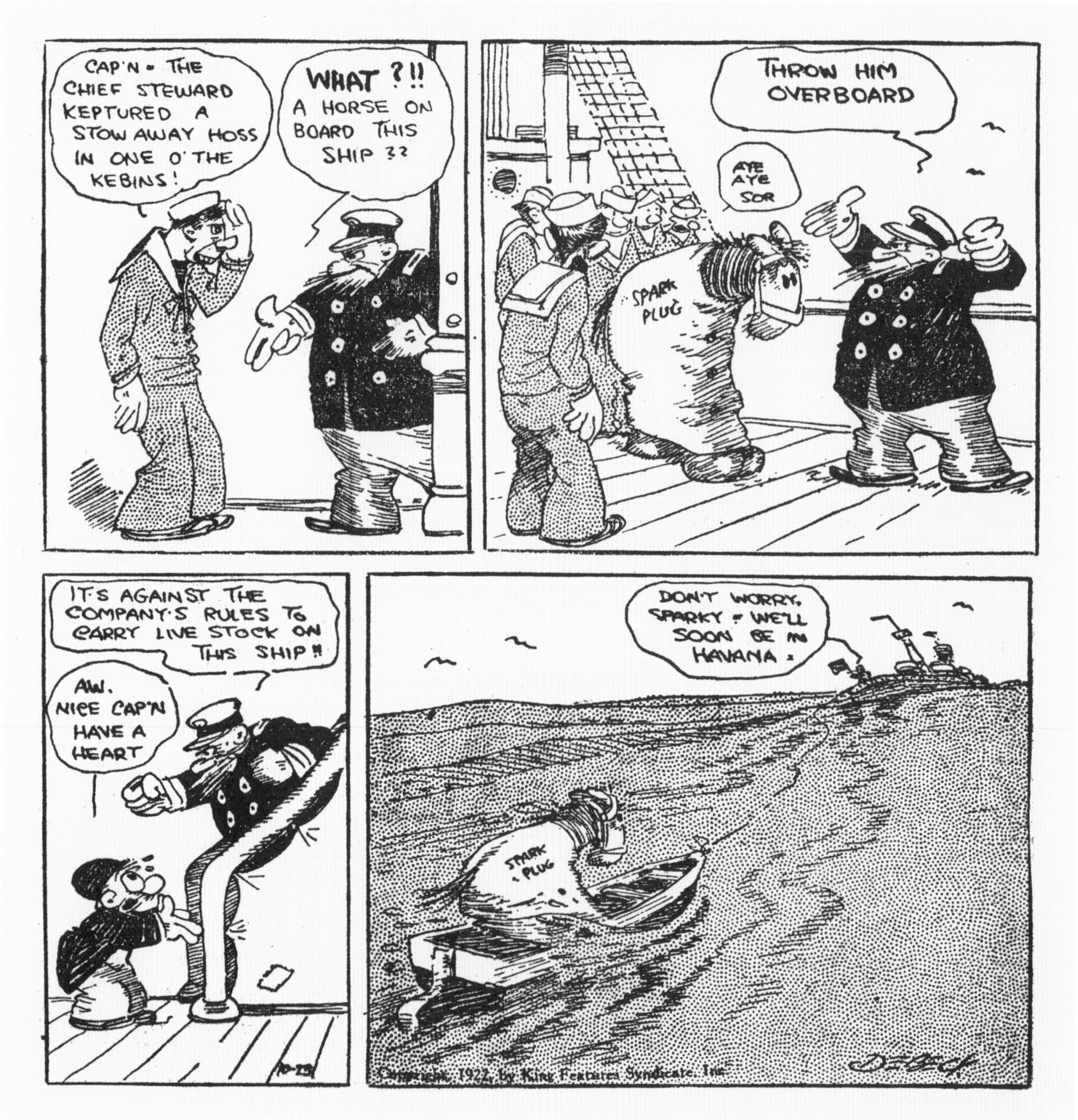
CAP'N - THE CHIEF STEWARD KEPTURED A STOW AWAY HOSS IN ONE O' THE KEBINS!
WHAT ?!! A HORSE ON BOARD THIS SHIP ??
THROW HIM OVERBOARD
AYE AYE SOR
SPARK PLUG
IT'S AGAINST THE COMPANY'S RULES TO CARRY LIVE STOCK ON THIS SHIP!!
AW. NICE CAP'N HAVE A HEART
DON'T WORRY, SPARKY - WE'LL SOON BE IN HAVANA.
SPARK PLUG
Copyright, 1922, by King Features Syndicate, Inc.

Set Adrift Without a Trace

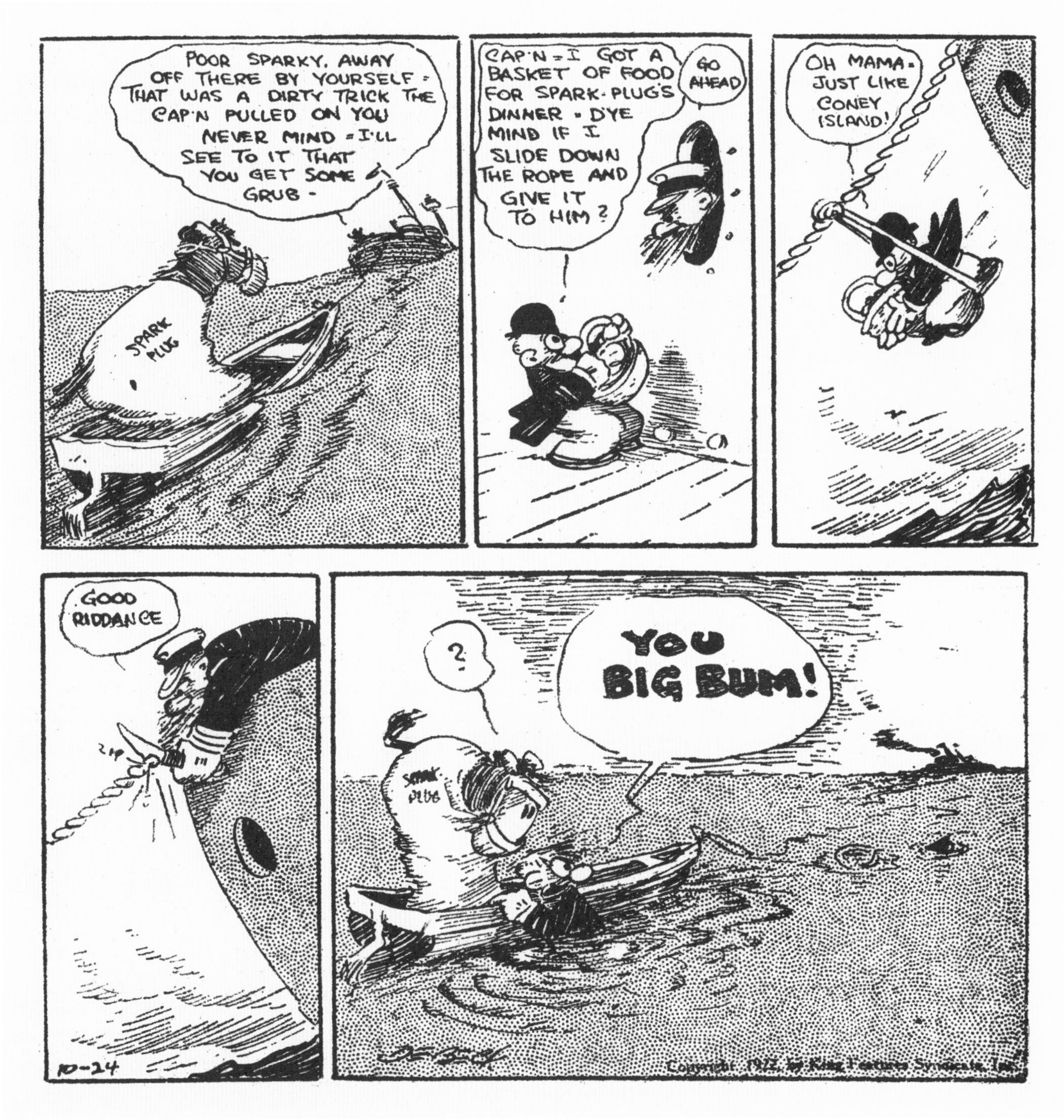

POOR SPARKY, AWAY OFF THERE BY YOURSELF - THAT WAS A DIRTY TRICK THE CAP'N PULLED ON YOU
NEVER MIND - I'LL SEE TO IT THAT YOU GET SOME GRUB -
SPARK PLUG
CAP'N - I GOT A BASKET OF FOOD FOR SPARK-PLUG'S DINNER - D'YE MIND IF I SLIDE DOWN THE ROPE AND GIVE IT TO HIM?
GO AHEAD
OH MAMA - JUST LIKE CONEY ISLAND!
GOOD RIDDANCE
ZIP
10-24
?
YOU BIG BUM!
SPARK PLUG
Copyright 1922, by King Features Syndicate, Inc.

"Not Guilty! The Captain Was Justified!"

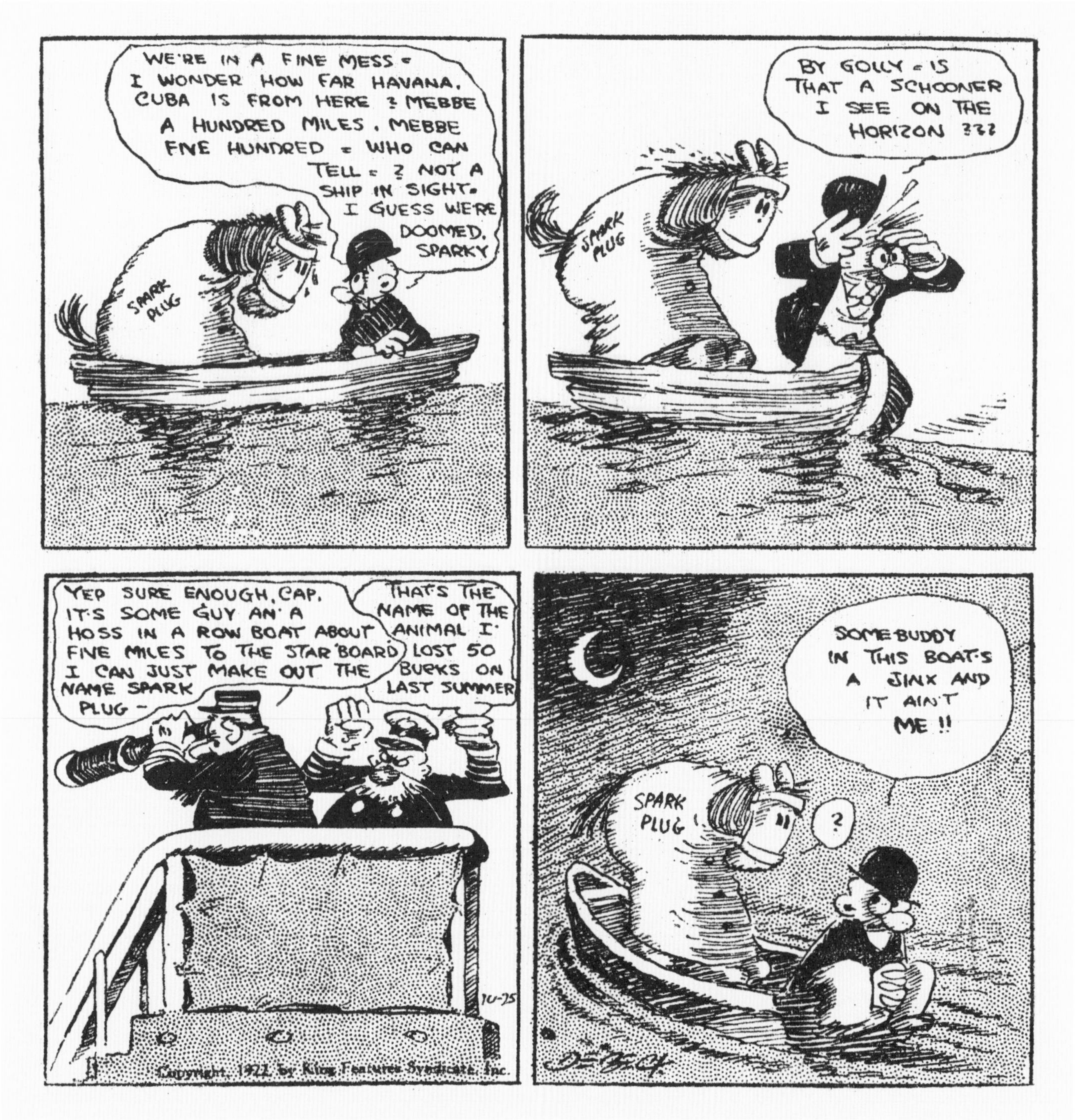
WE'RE IN A FINE MESS = I WONDER HOW FAR HAVANA, CUBA IS FROM HERE ? MEBBE A HUNDRED MILES, MEBBE FIVE HUNDRED = WHO CAN TELL = ? NOT A SHIP IN SIGHT. I GUESS WE'RE DOOMED, SPARKY
SPARK PLUG
BY GOLLY = IS THAT A SCHOONER I SEE ON THE HORIZON ???
SPARK PLUG
YEP SURE ENOUGH, CAP, IT'S SOME GUY AN' A HOSS IN A ROW BOAT ABOUT FIVE MILES TO THE STAR'BOARD I CAN JUST MAKE OUT THE NAME SPARK PLUG -
THAT'S THE NAME OF THE ANIMAL I LOST 50 BUCKS ON LAST SUMMER
Copyright, 1922, by King Features Syndicate, Inc.
SOME BUDDY IN THIS BOAT'S A JINX AND IT AIN'T ME !!
SPARK PLUG
?

If Spark Plug Isn't a Mudhen He's at Least a Kingfisher!

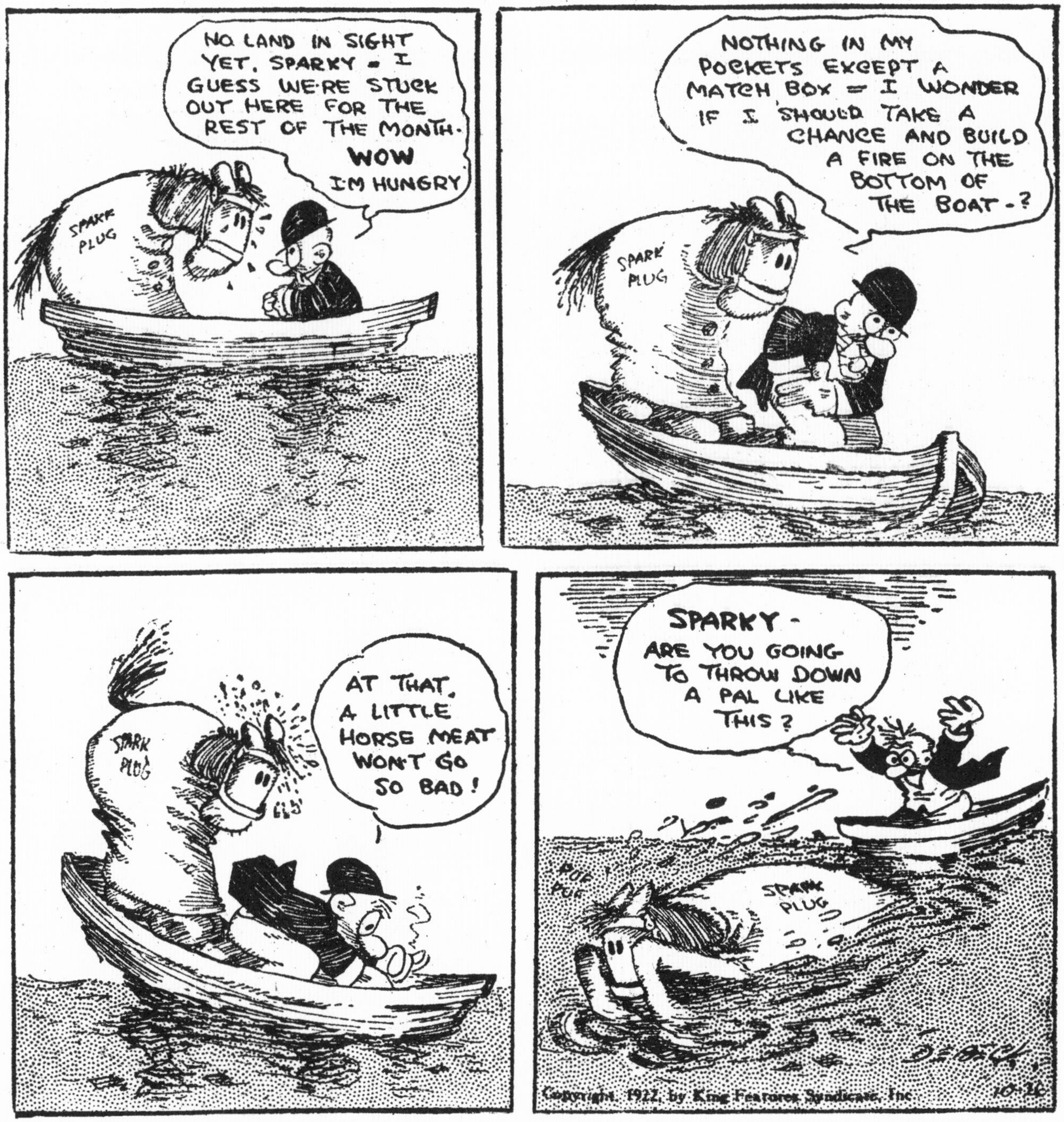
NO LAND IN SIGHT YET, SPARKY = I GUESS WE'RE STUCK OUT HERE FOR THE REST OF THE MONTH.
WOW
I'M HUNGRY
SPARK PLUG
NOTHING IN MY POCKETS EXCEPT A MATCH BOX = I WONDER IF I SHOULD TAKE A CHANCE AND BUILD A FIRE ON THE BOTTOM OF THE BOAT-?
SPARK PLUG
SPARK PLUG
AT THAT, A LITTLE HORSE MEAT WON'T GO SO BAD!
SPARKY - ARE YOU GOING TO THROW DOWN A PAL LIKE THIS?
PUF PUF
SPARK PLUG
Copyright, 1922, by King Features Syndicate, Inc.

Sparky Prefers a Cold Duck to a Hot Steak

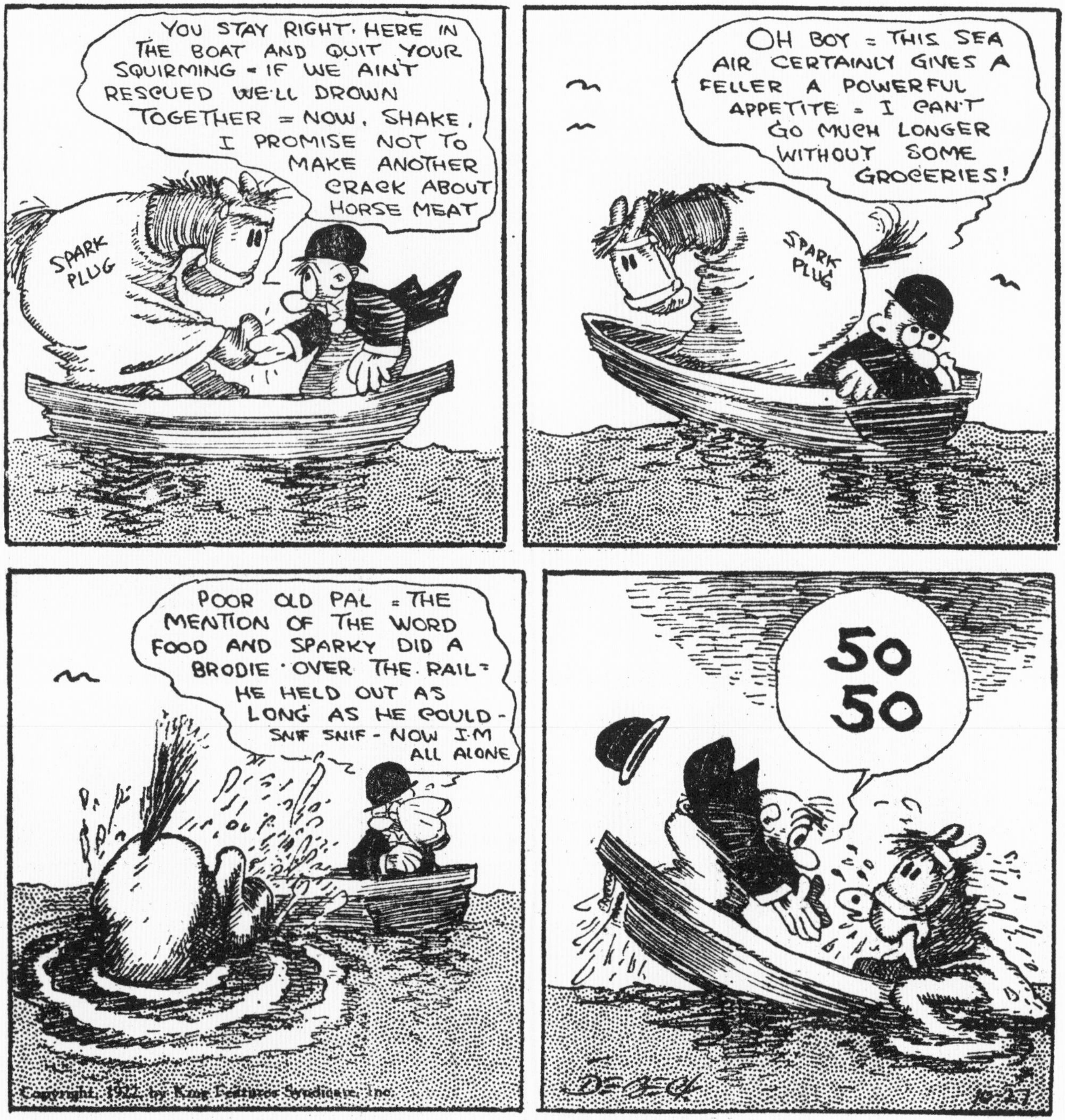

YOU STAY RIGHT HERE IN THE BOAT AND QUIT YOUR SQUIRMING - IF WE AIN'T RESCUED WE'LL DROWN TOGETHER = NOW, SHAKE, I PROMISE NOT TO MAKE ANOTHER CRACK ABOUT HORSE MEAT
SPARK PLUG
OH BOY = THIS SEA AIR CERTAINLY GIVES A FELLER A POWERFUL APPETITE = I CAN'T GO MUCH LONGER WITHOUT SOME GROCERIES!
SPARK PLUG
POOR OLD PAL = THE MENTION OF THE WORD FOOD AND SPARKY DID A BRODIE OVER THE RAIL = HE HELD OUT AS LONG AS HE COULD - SNIF SNIF - NOW I'M ALL ALONE
50 50
Copyright, 1922, by King Features Syndicate, Inc.

Barney Appeases Hunger With an Havana "Filler"

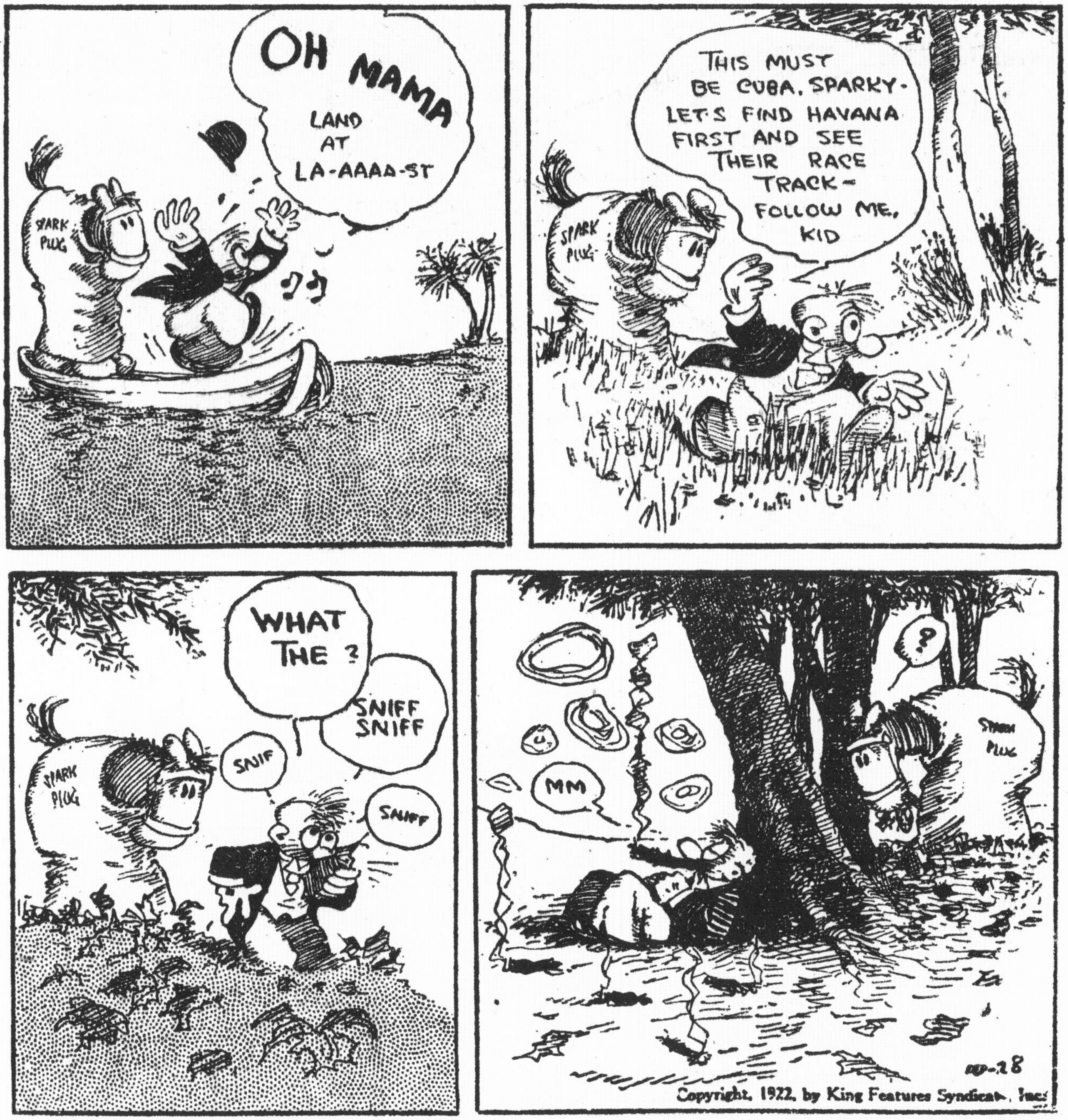
OH MAMA
LAND AT LA-AAAA-ST
SPARK PLUG
THIS MUST BE CUBA, SPARKY- LET'S FIND HAVANA FIRST AND SEE THEIR RACE TRACK- FOLLOW ME, KID
SPARK PLUG
WHAT THE ?
SNIFF SNIFF
SNIF
SNIFF
SPARK PLUG
?
MM
SPARK PLUG
Copyright, 1922, by King Features Syndicate, Inc.

Hunger Knows No Conscience

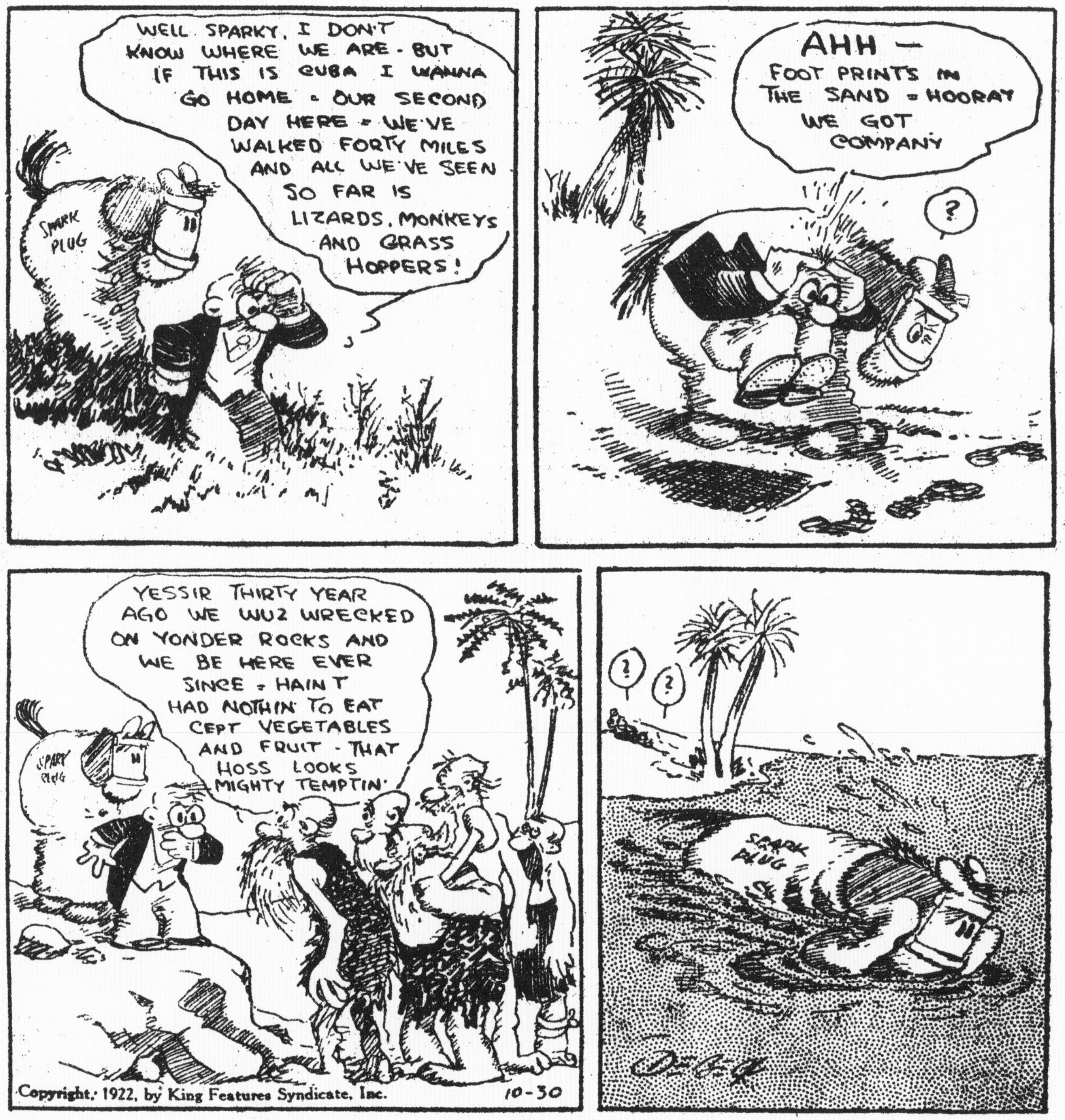
WELL SPARKY, I DON'T KNOW WHERE WE ARE - BUT IF THIS IS CUBA I WANNA GO HOME = OUR SECOND DAY HERE = WE'VE WALKED FORTY MILES AND ALL WE'VE SEEN SO FAR IS LIZARDS, MONKEYS AND GRASS HOPPERS!
SPARK PLUG
AHH - FOOT PRINTS IN THE SAND = HOORAY WE GOT COMPANY
?
YESSIR THIRTY YEAR AGO WE WUZ WRECKED ON YONDER ROCKS AND WE BE HERE EVER SINCE = HAIN'T HAD NOTHIN' TO EAT CEPT VEGETABLES AND FRUIT - THAT HOSS LOOKS MIGHTY TEMPTIN'
SPARK PLUG
?
?
SPARK PLUG
Copyright, 1922, by King Features Syndicate, Inc.
10-30

A Stake Won! A Steak Lost!

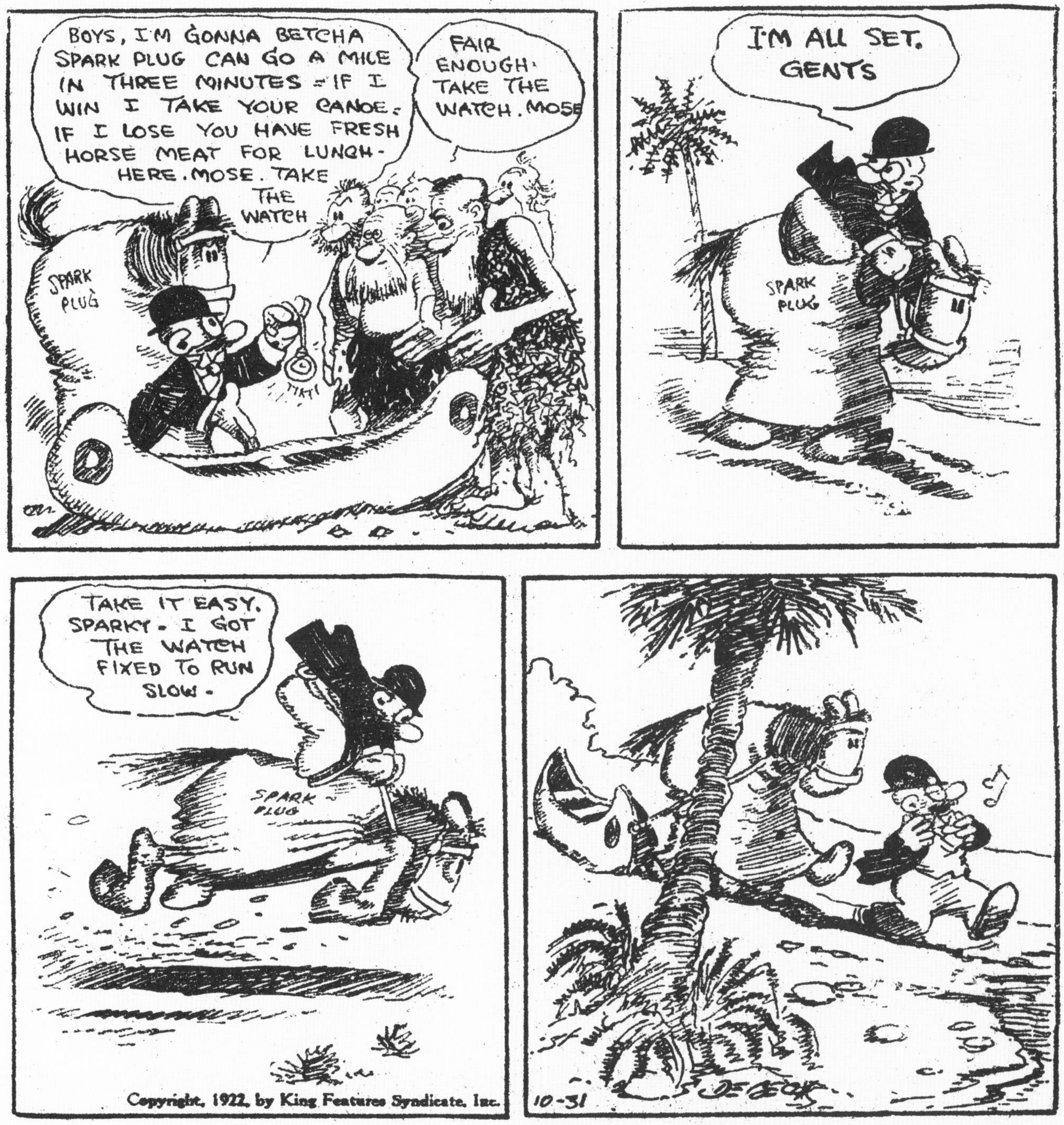
BOYS, I'M GONNA BETCHA SPARK PLUG CAN GO A MILE IN THREE MINUTES - IF I WIN I TAKE YOUR CANOE. IF I LOSE YOU HAVE FRESH HORSE MEAT FOR LUNCH - HERE. MOSE. TAKE THE WATCH
FAIR ENOUGH. TAKE THE WATCH. MOSE
SPARK PLUG
I'M ALL SET. GENTS
SPARK PLUG
TAKE IT EASY, SPARKY - I GOT THE WATCH FIXED TO RUN SLOW -
SPARK - PLUG
Copyright, 1922, by King Features Syndicate, Inc.
10-31
DE BECK

Sparky Goes Over On His Own Tip!

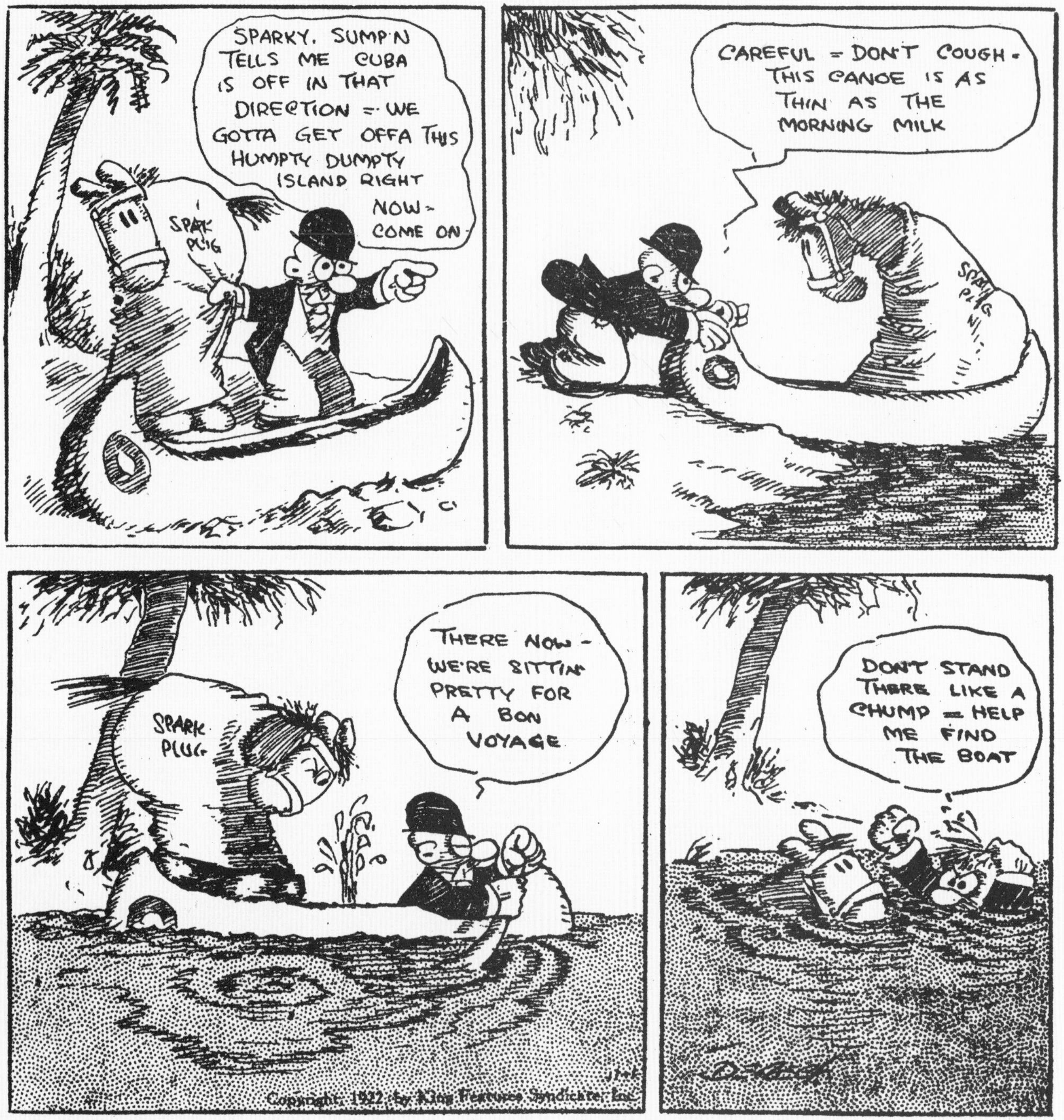
SPARKY. SUMP'N TELLS ME CUBA IS OFF IN THAT DIRECTION = WE GOTTA GET OFFA THIS HUMPTY DUMPTY ISLAND RIGHT NOW - COME ON
SPARK PLUG
CAREFUL = DON'T COUGH - THIS CANOE IS AS THIN AS THE MORNING MILK
SPARK PLUG
THERE NOW - WE'RE SITTIN' PRETTY FOR A BON VOYAGE
SPARK PLUG
DON'T STAND THERE LIKE A CHUMP = HELP ME FIND THE BOAT
Copyright 1922 by King Features Syndicate, Inc.

Sparky'll Win His Next Race—If It Rains!

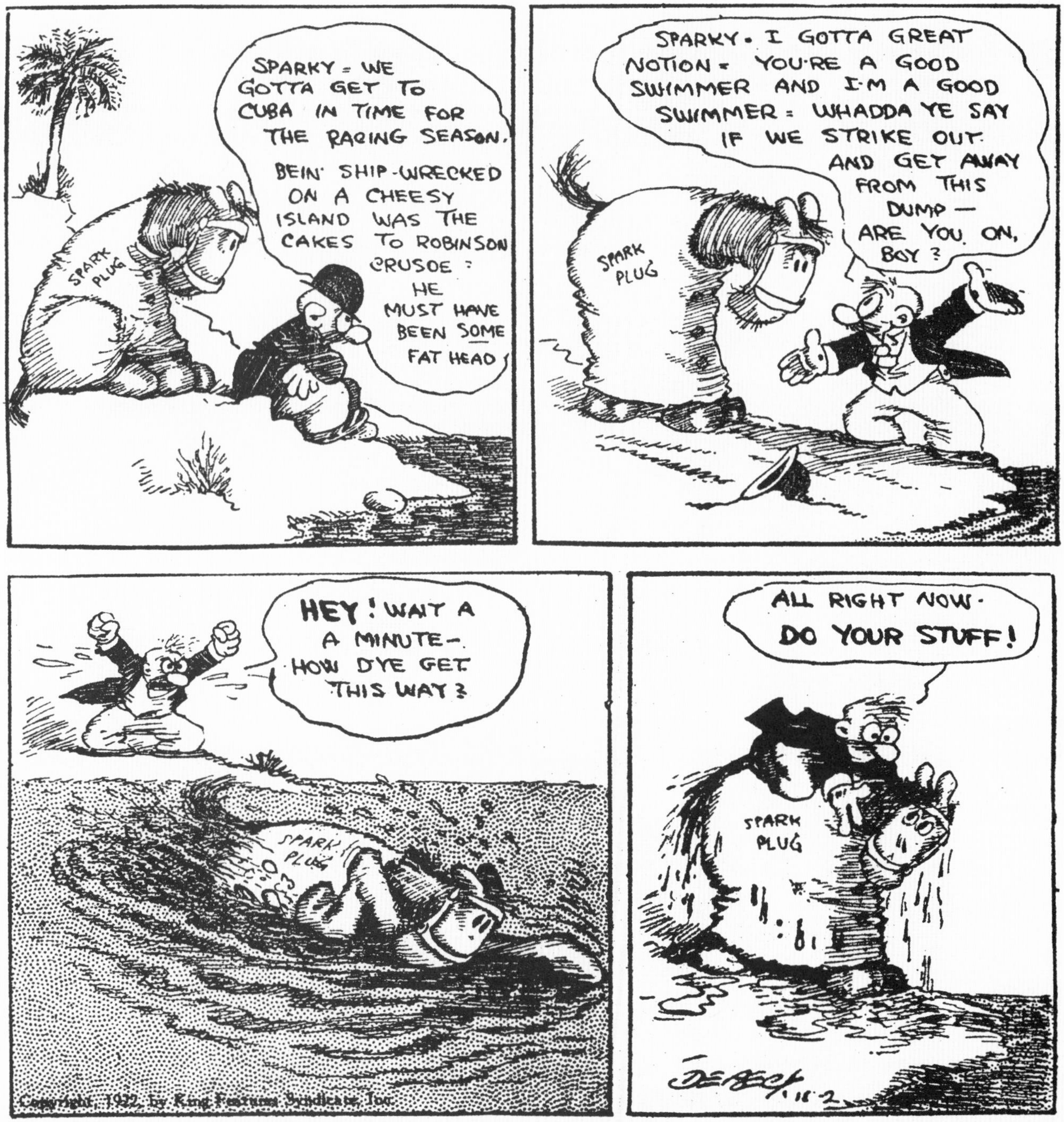
SPARKY = WE GOTTA GET TO CUBA IN TIME FOR THE RACING SEASON.
BEIN' SHIP-WRECKED ON A CHEESY ISLAND WAS THE CAKES TO ROBINSON CRUSOE = HE MUST HAVE BEEN SOME FAT HEAD
SPARK PLUG
SPARKY • I GOTTA GREAT NOTION = YOU'RE A GOOD SWIMMER AND I'M A GOOD SWIMMER = WHADDA YE SAY IF WE STRIKE OUT AND GET AWAY FROM THIS DUMP — ARE YOU ON, BOY ?
SPARK PLUG
HEY! WAIT A A MINUTE— HOW D'YE GET THIS WAY ?
SPARK PLUG
ALL RIGHT NOW - DO YOUR STUFF!
SPARK PLUG
DEBECK

Sparky Won't Be "Smoked Beef" Yet a While!

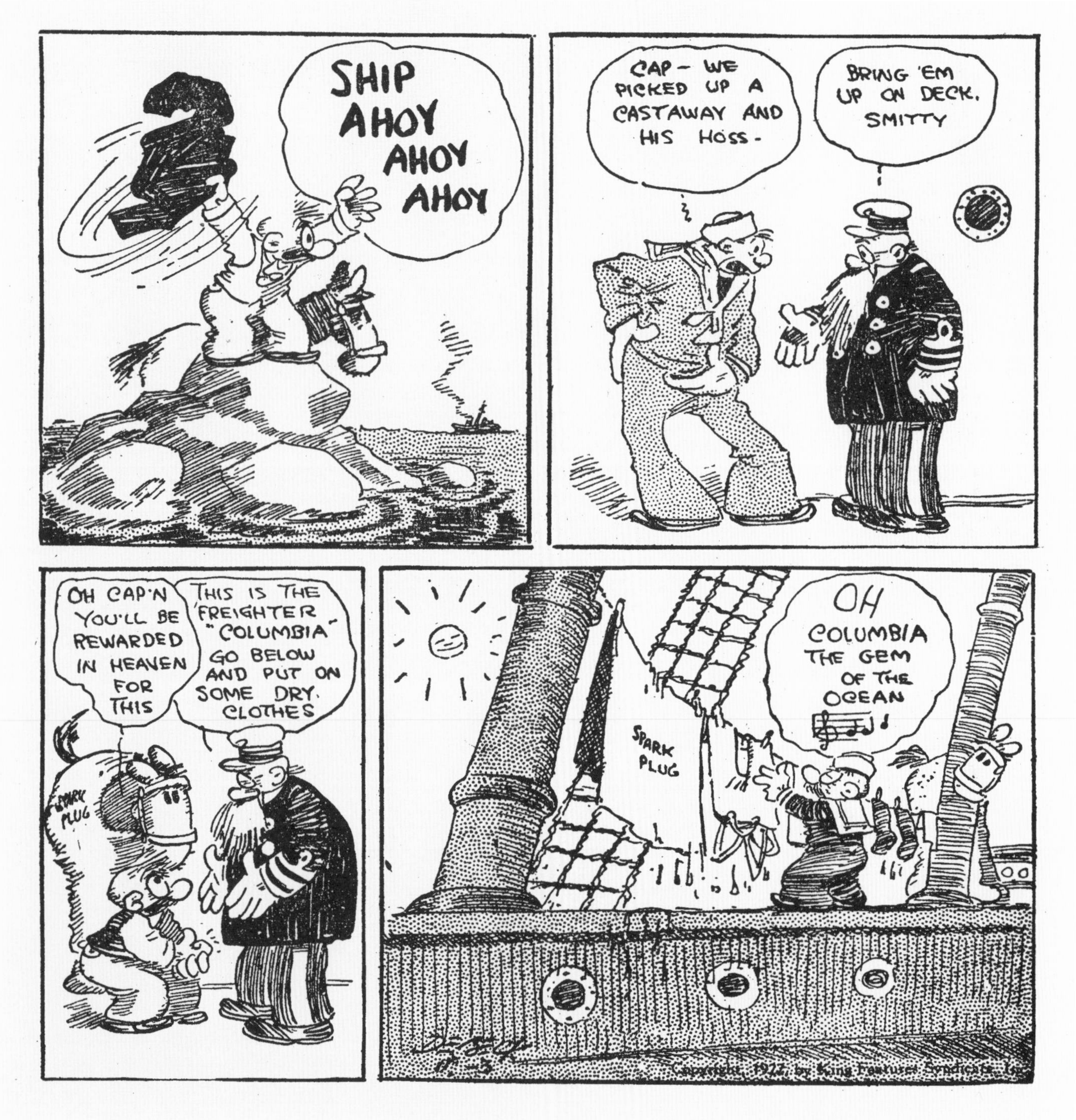
SHIP AHOY AHOY AHOY AHOY
CAP - WE PICKED UP A CASTAWAY AND HIS HOSS -
BRING 'EM UP ON DECK. SMITTY
OH CAP'N YOU'LL BE REWARDED IN HEAVEN FOR THIS
THIS IS THE FREIGHTER "COLUMBIA" GO BELOW AND PUT ON SOME DRY CLOTHES
SPARK PLUG
OH COLUMBIA THE GEM OF THE OCEAN
SPARK PLUG
Copyright, 1922, by King Features Syndicate, Inc.

There's Nothing Wrong With Sparky's Sea Legs!

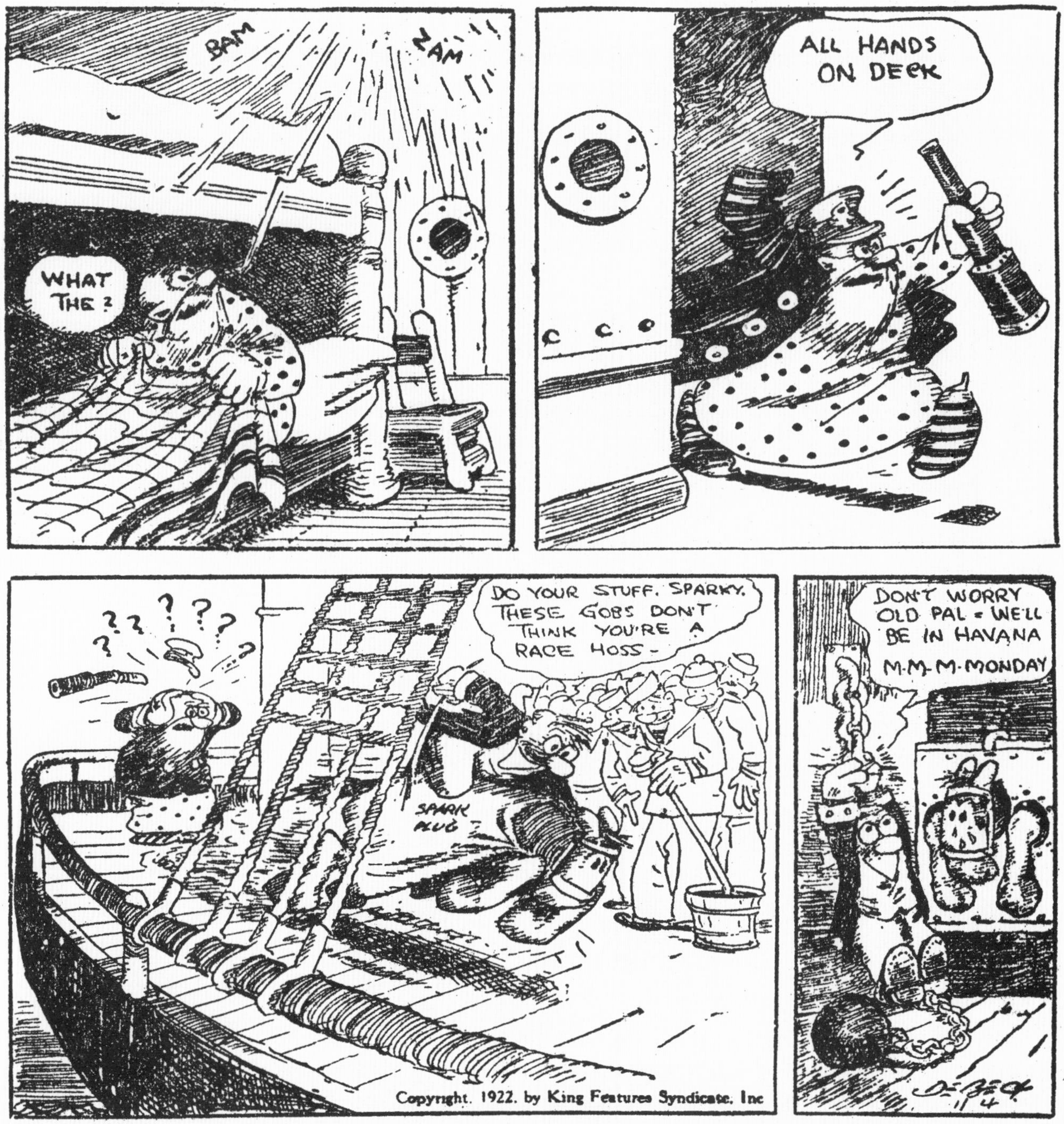
BAM
ZAM
WHAT THE?
ALL HANDS ON DECK
DO YOUR STUFF, SPARKY. THESE GOBS DON'T THINK YOU'RE A RACE HOSS -
SPARK PLUG
DON'T WORRY OLD PAL - WE'LL BE IN HAVANA
M-M-M-MONDAY
Copyright. 1922. by King Features Syndicate. Inc
DE BECK 11-4

And Barney's "Lot" Would Be a Sad One

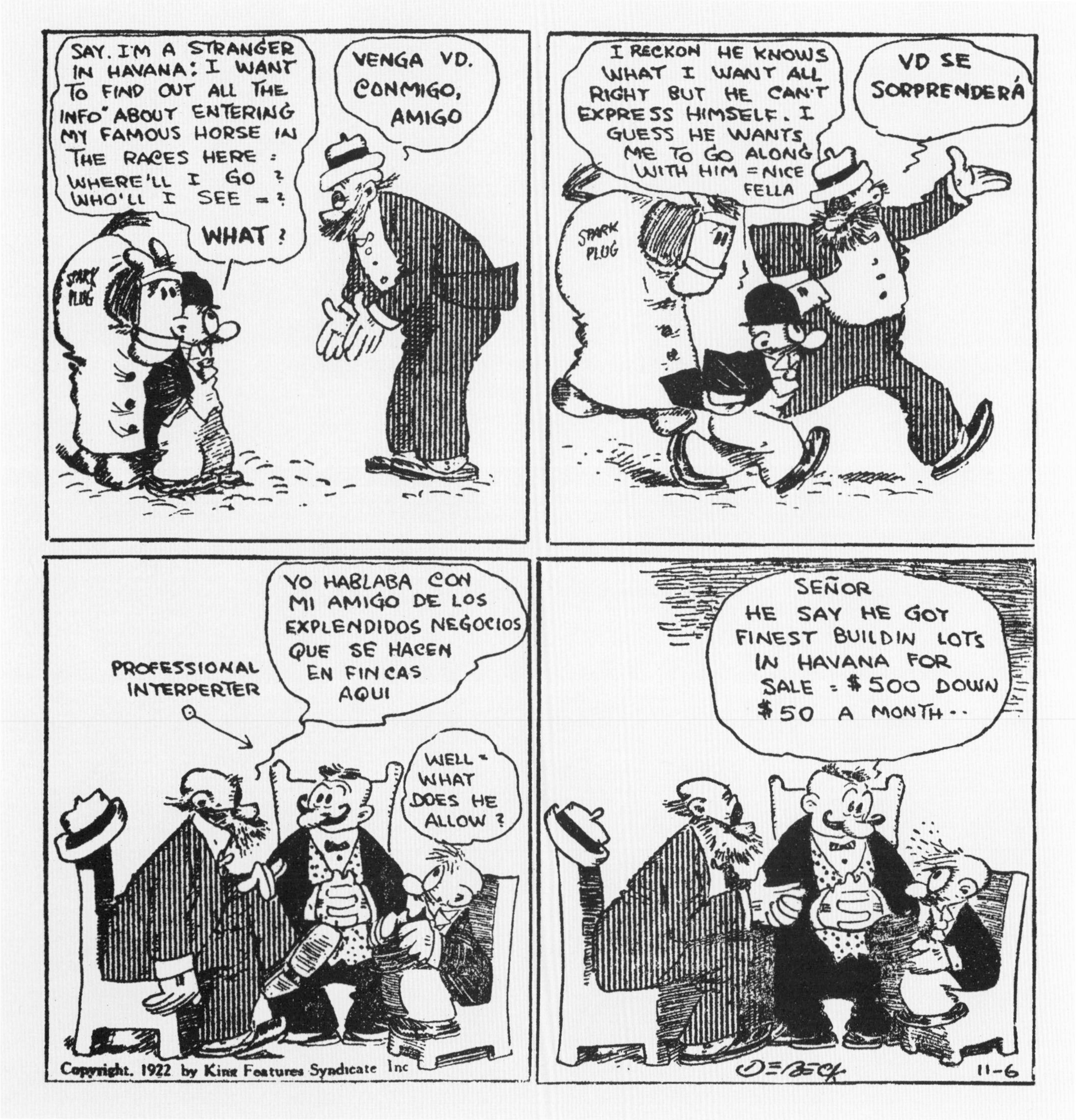
SAY. I'M A STRANGER IN HAVANA: I WANT TO FIND OUT ALL THE INFO' ABOUT ENTERING MY FAMOUS HORSE IN THE RACES HERE: WHERE'LL I GO? WHO'LL I SEE =?
VENGA VD. CONMIGO, AMIGO
WHAT?
SPARK PLUG
I RECKON HE KNOWS WHAT I WANT ALL RIGHT BUT HE CAN'T EXPRESS HIMSELF. I GUESS HE WANTS ME TO GO ALONG WITH HIM = NICE FELLA
VD SE SORPRENDERÁ
SPARK PLUG
YO HABLABA CON MI AMIGO DE LOS EXPLENDIDOS NEGOCIOS QUE SE HACEN EN FINCAS AQUI
PROFESSIONAL INTERPERTER
WELL - WHAT DOES HE ALLOW?
SEÑOR HE SAY HE GOT FINEST BUILDIN LOTS IN HAVANA FOR SALE = $500 DOWN $50 A MONTH..
Copyright. 1922 by King Features Syndicate Inc
DEBECK
11-6

It May Be Best That Barney Doesn't Know for How Long He's In

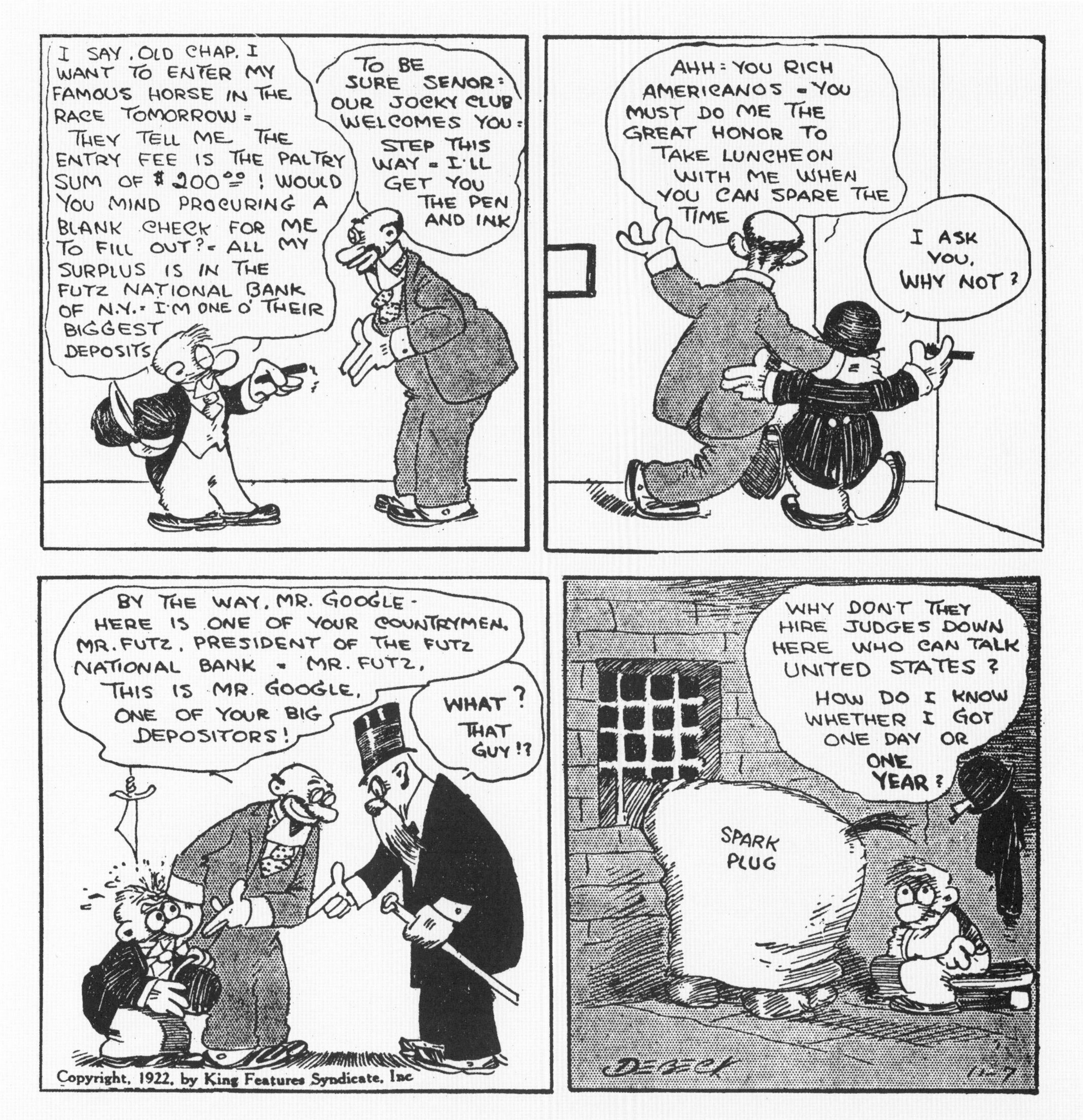

I SAY, OLD CHAP, I WANT TO ENTER MY FAMOUS HORSE IN THE RACE TOMORROW = THEY TELL ME THE ENTRY FEE IS THE PALTRY SUM OF $200.00 ! WOULD YOU MIND PROCURING A BLANK CHECK FOR ME TO FILL OUT? = ALL MY SURPLUS IS IN THE FUTZ NATIONAL BANK OF N.Y. = I'M ONE O' THEIR BIGGEST DEPOSITS
TO BE SURE SENOR: OUR JOCKY CLUB WELCOMES YOU: STEP THIS WAY = I'LL GET YOU THE PEN AND INK
AHH: YOU RICH AMERICANOS = YOU MUST DO ME THE GREAT HONOR TO TAKE LUNCHEON WITH ME WHEN YOU CAN SPARE THE TIME
I ASK YOU, WHY NOT?
BY THE WAY, MR. GOOGLE - HERE IS ONE OF YOUR COUNTRYMEN, MR. FUTZ, PRESIDENT OF THE FUTZ NATIONAL BANK - MR. FUTZ, THIS IS MR. GOOGLE, ONE OF YOUR BIG DEPOSITORS!
WHAT? THAT GUY!?
Copyright, 1922, by King Features Syndicate, Inc
WHY DON'T THEY HIRE JUDGES DOWN HERE WHO CAN TALK UNITED STATES? HOW DO I KNOW WHETHER I GOT ONE DAY OR ONE YEAR?
SPARK PLUG
DE BECK
12-7

Sparky Was in Such a Playful Mood

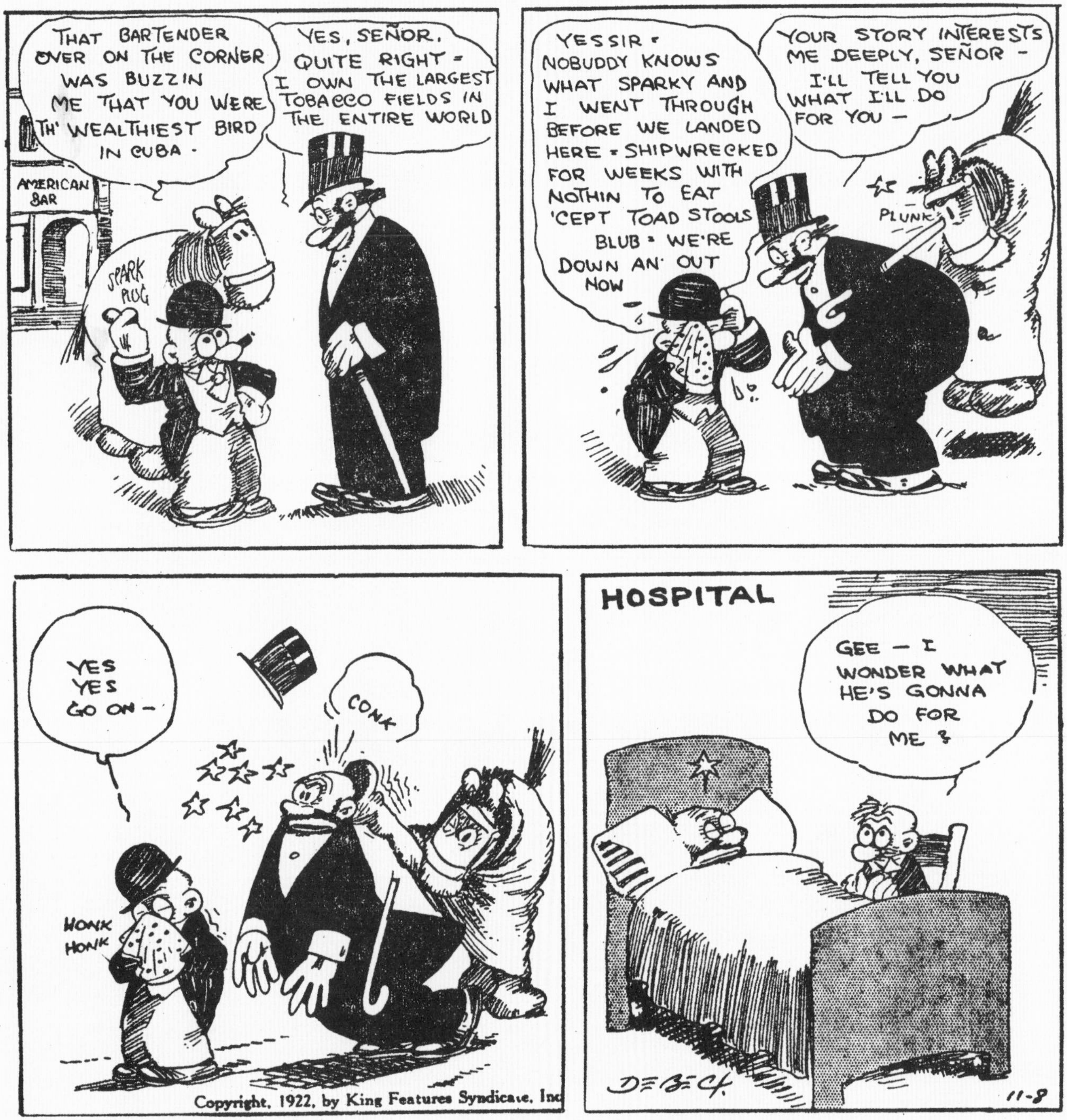
THAT BARTENDER OVER ON THE CORNER WAS BUZZIN ME THAT YOU WERE TH' WEALTHIEST BIRD IN CUBA -
YES, SEÑOR. QUITE RIGHT = I OWN THE LARGEST TOBACCO FIELDS IN THE ENTIRE WORLD
AMERICAN BAR
SPARK PLUG
YESSIR = NOBUDDY KNOWS WHAT SPARKY AND I WENT THROUGH BEFORE WE LANDED HERE = SHIPWRECKED FOR WEEKS WITH NOTHIN TO EAT 'CEPT TOAD STOOLS BLUB = WE'RE DOWN AN' OUT NOW
YOUR STORY INTERESTS ME DEEPLY, SEÑOR - I'LL TELL YOU WHAT I'LL DO FOR YOU -
PLUNK
YES YES GO ON -
CONK
HONK HONK
HOSPITAL
GEE - I WONDER WHAT HE'S GONNA DO FOR ME ?
DE BECK
11-8

Barney Finds Out What's Coming and Goes

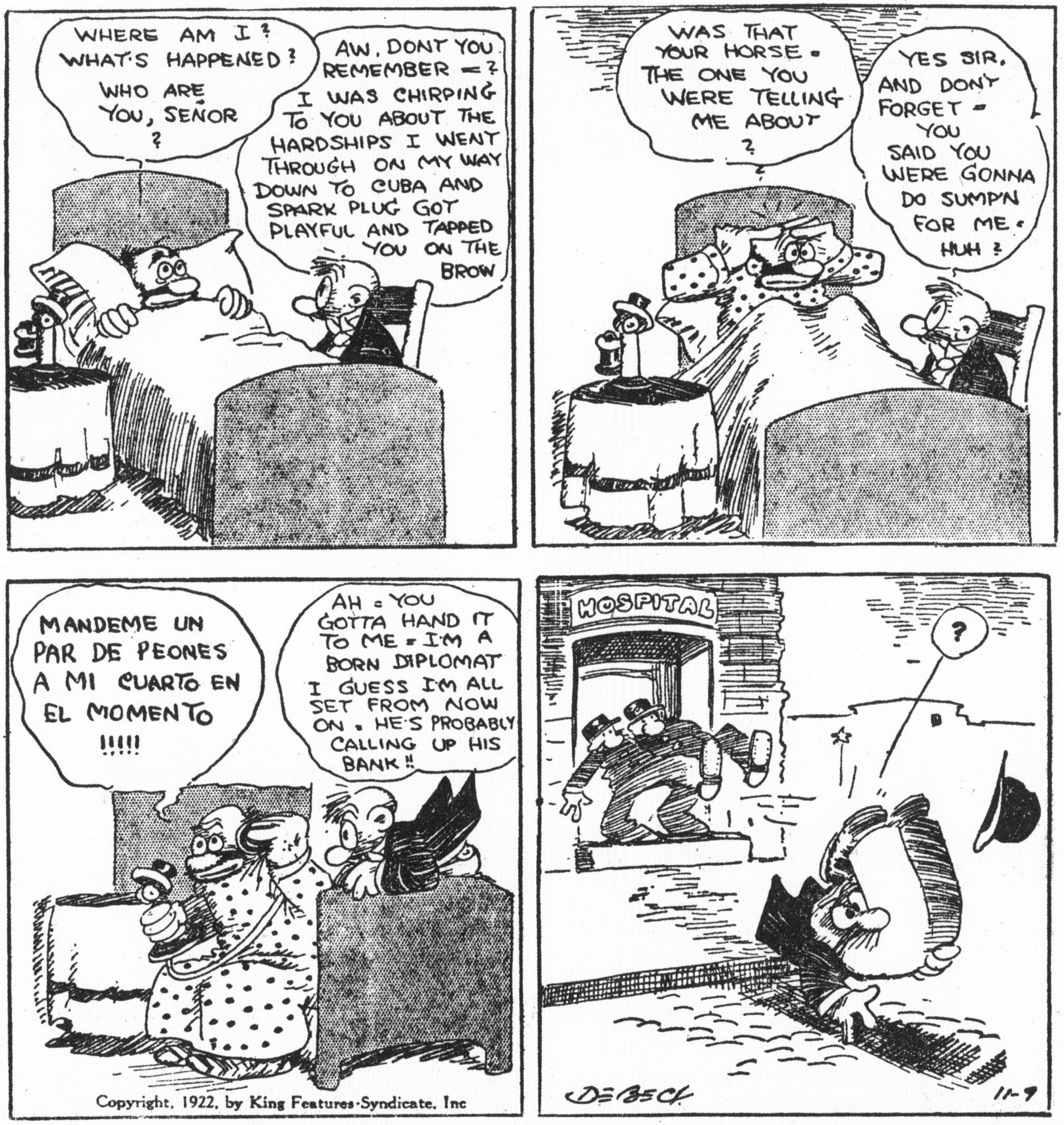
WHERE AM I? WHAT'S HAPPENED? WHO ARE YOU, SEÑOR?
AW, DONT YOU REMEMBER -? I WAS CHIRPING TO YOU ABOUT THE HARDSHIPS I WENT THROUGH ON MY WAY DOWN TO CUBA AND SPARK PLUG GOT PLAYFUL AND TAPPED YOU ON THE BROW
WAS THAT YOUR HORSE - THE ONE YOU WERE TELLING ME ABOUT?
YES SIR, AND DON'T FORGET - YOU SAID YOU WERE GONNA DO SUMP'N FOR ME - HUH?
MANDEME UN PAR DE PEONES A MI CUARTO EN EL MOMENTO !!!!!
AH - YOU GOTTA HAND IT TO ME - I'M A BORN DIPLOMAT I GUESS I'M ALL SET FROM NOW ON - HE'S PROBABLY CALLING UP HIS BANK!!
HOSPITAL
?
Copyright, 1922, by King Features Syndicate, Inc
DE BECK
11-9

No Explanations Were Needed

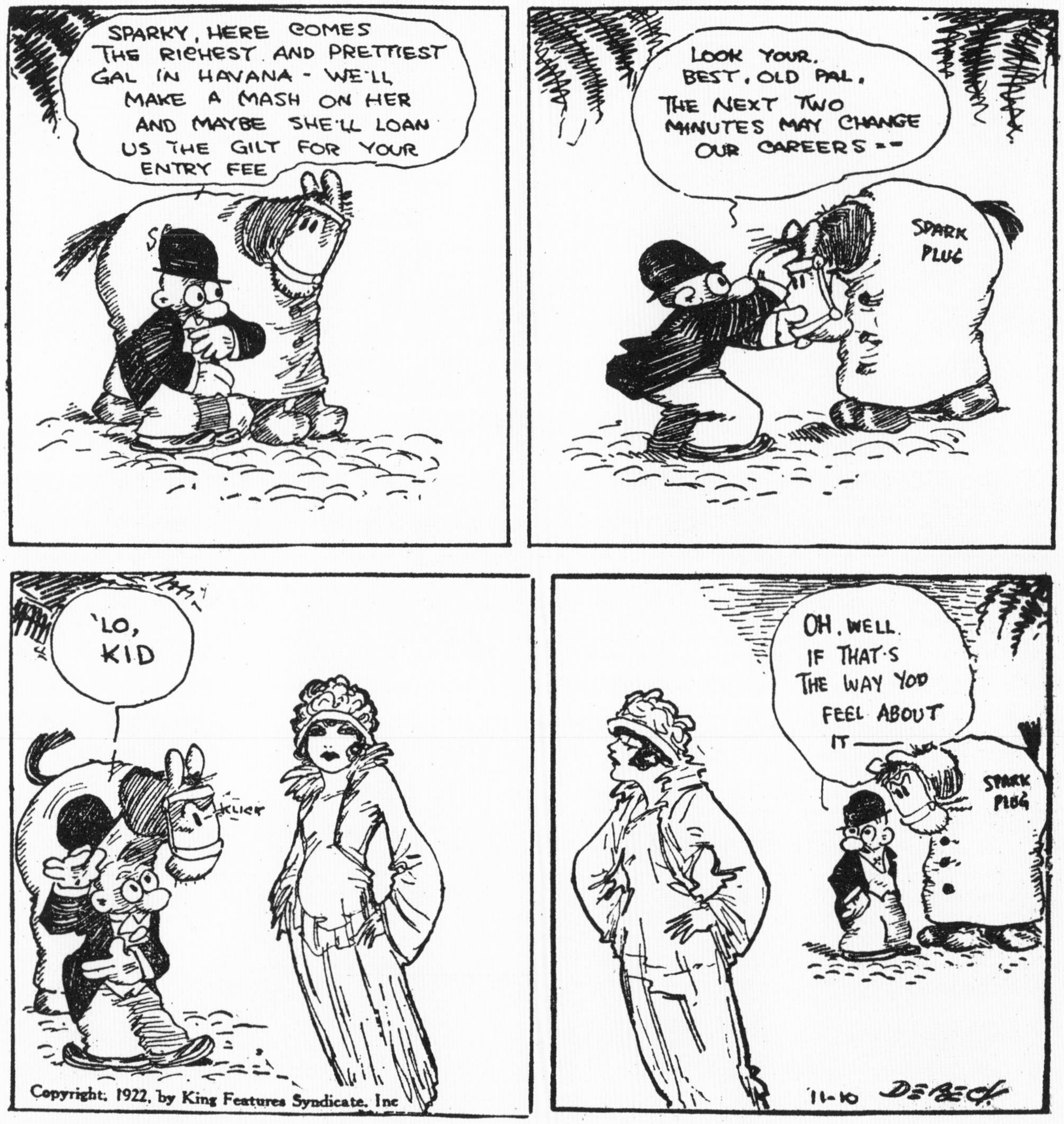
SPARKY, HERE COMES THE RICHEST AND PRETTIEST GAL IN HAVANA - WE'LL MAKE A MASH ON HER AND MAYBE SHE'LL LOAN US THE GILT FOR YOUR ENTRY FEE
LOOK YOUR. BEST, OLD PAL. THE NEXT TWO MINUTES MAY CHANGE OUR CAREERS --
SPARK PLUG
'LO, KID
KLICK
OH, WELL. IF THAT'S THE WAY YOU FEEL ABOUT IT —
SPARK PLUG
Copyright, 1922, by King Features Syndicate, Inc
11-10 DEBECK

Now Barney Wishes He Hadn't Found Out

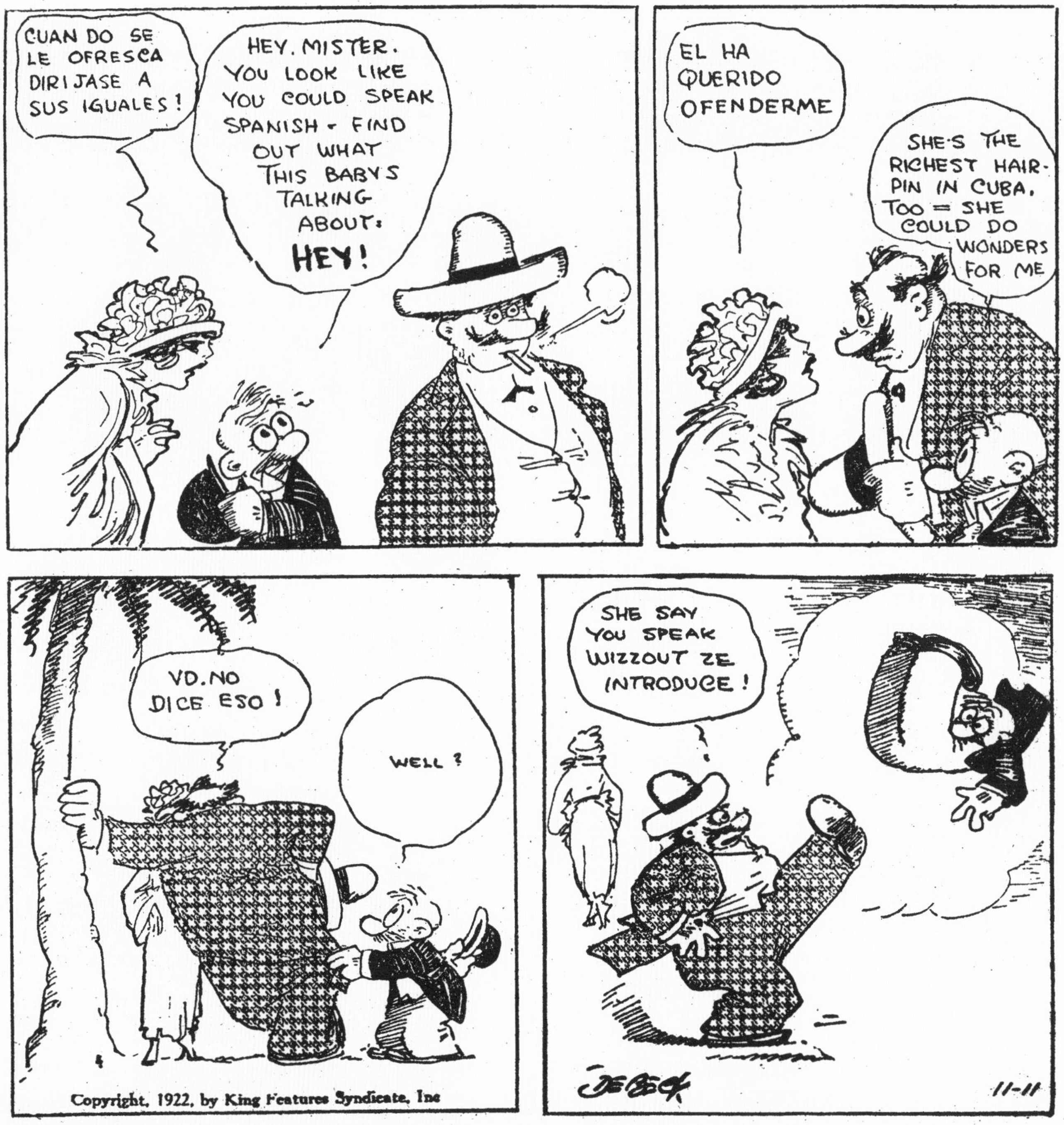
CUAN DO SE LE OFRESCA DIRIJASE A SUS IGUALES!
HEY, MISTER. YOU LOOK LIKE YOU COULD SPEAK SPANISH - FIND OUT WHAT THIS BABY'S TALKING ABOUT: HEY!
EL HA QUERIDO OFENDERME
SHE'S THE RICHEST HAIR-PIN IN CUBA, TOO = SHE COULD DO WONDERS FOR ME
VD. NO DICE ESO!
WELL?
SHE SAY YOU SPEAK WIZZOUT ZE INTRODUCE!
DE BECK
11-11

Sparky's Shade Is as Good as a Sheltering Palm

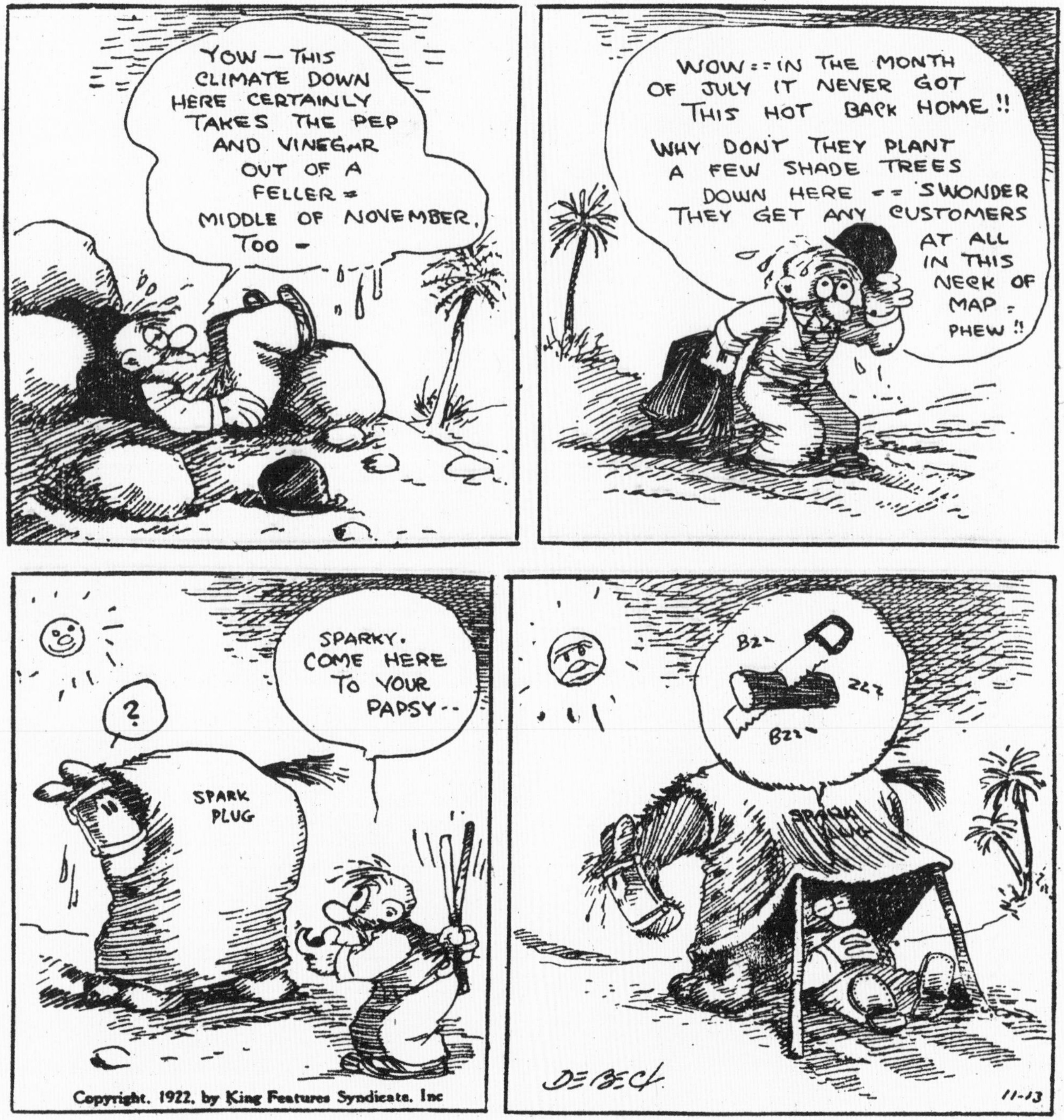
YOW — THIS CLIMATE DOWN HERE CERTAINLY TAKES THE PEP AND VINEGAR OUT OF A FELLER = MIDDLE OF NOVEMBER, TOO -
WOW :: IN THE MONTH OF JULY IT NEVER GOT THIS HOT BACK HOME !! WHY DON'T THEY PLANT A FEW SHADE TREES DOWN HERE -- SWONDER THEY GET ANY CUSTOMERS AT ALL IN THIS NECK OF MAP = PHEW !!
?
SPARK PLUG
SPARKY. COME HERE TO YOUR PAPSY --
BZZ
ZZZ
BZZ
DE BECK
Copyright, 1922, by King Features Syndicate, Inc
11-13

It's a Sad, Sad "Tale"

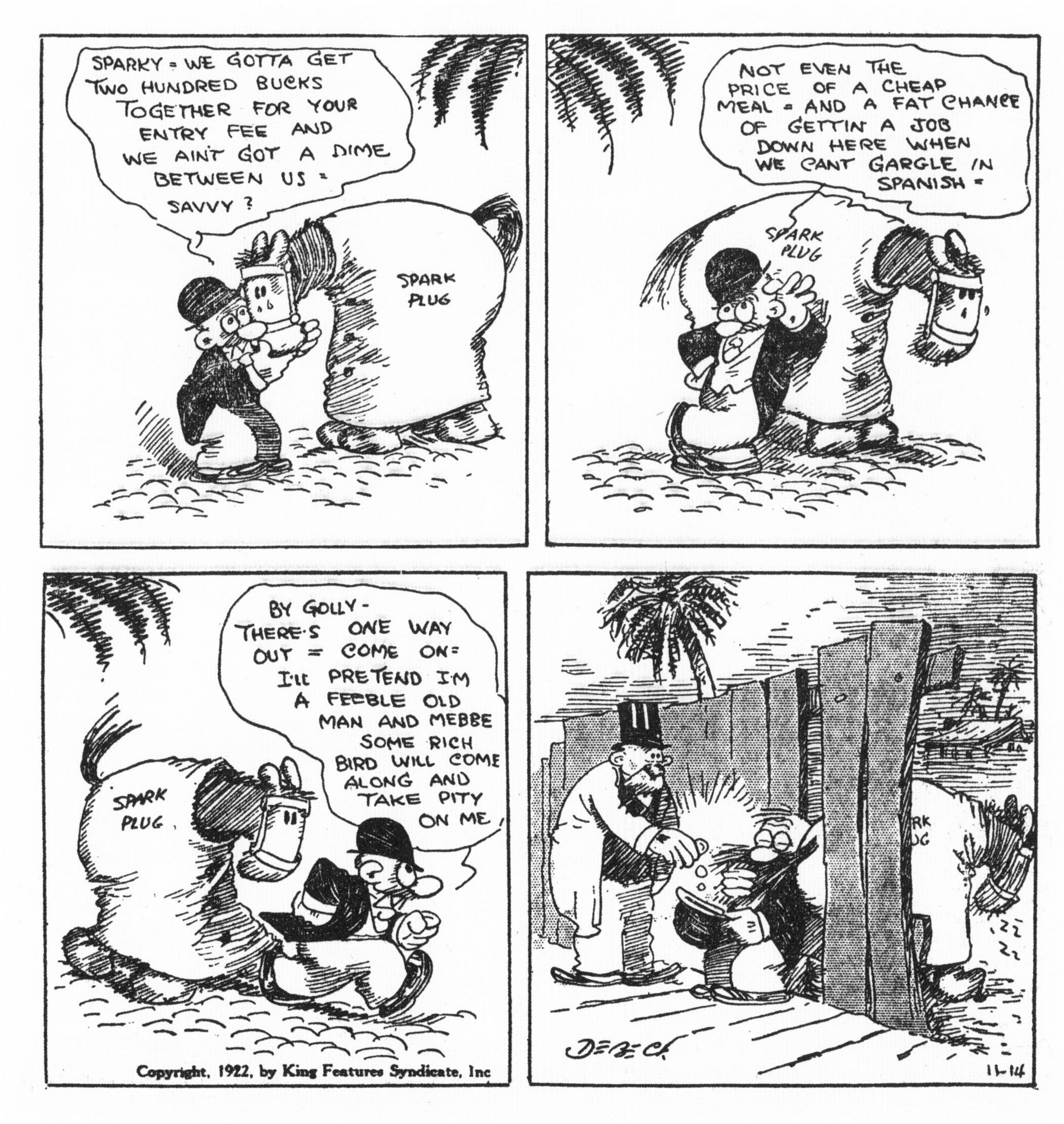
SPARKY = WE GOTTA GET TWO HUNDRED BUCKS TOGETHER FOR YOUR ENTRY FEE AND WE AIN'T GOT A DIME BETWEEN US = SAVVY ?
SPARK PLUG
NOT EVEN THE PRICE OF A CHEAP MEAL = AND A FAT CHANCE OF GETTIN' A JOB DOWN HERE WHEN WE CANT GARGLE IN SPANISH =
SPARK PLUG
BY GOLLY - THERE'S ONE WAY OUT = COME ON = I'LL PRETEND I'M A FEEBLE OLD MAN AND MEBBE SOME RICH BIRD WILL COME ALONG AND TAKE PITY ON ME
SPARK PLUG
Copyright, 1922, by King Features Syndicate, Inc
RK
UG
DEBECK
11-14

Well, Anyhow, Sparky Can See the Others Run

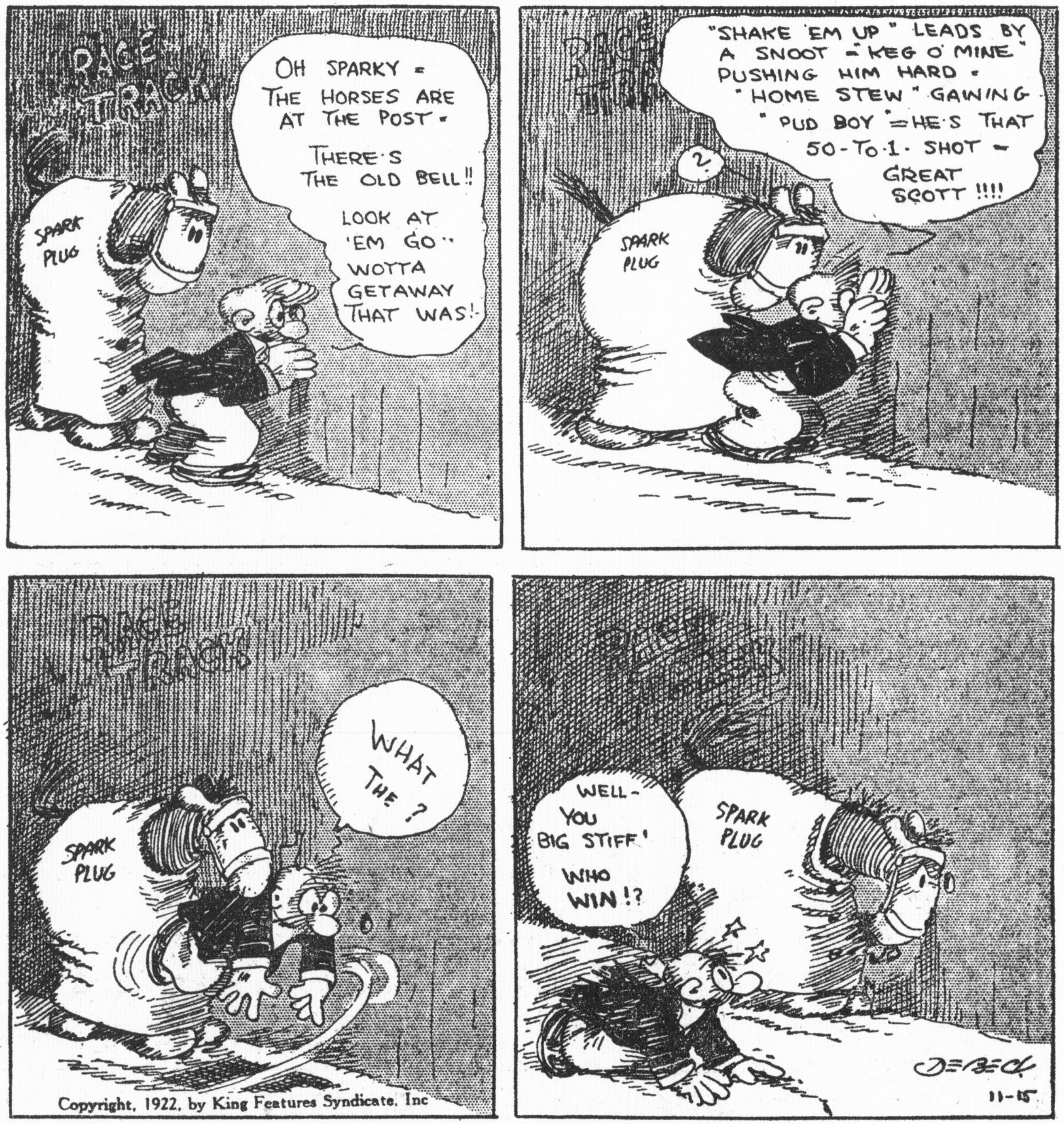
RACE TRACK
SPARK PLUG
OH SPARKY - THE HORSES ARE AT THE POST - THERE'S THE OLD BELL!! LOOK AT 'EM GO.. WOTTA GETAWAY THAT WAS!
"SHAKE 'EM UP" LEADS BY A SNOOT - "KEG O' MINE" PUSHING HIM HARD - "HOME STEW" GAINING - "PUD BOY" - HE'S THAT 50-TO-1- SHOT - GREAT SCOTT !!!!
WHAT THE ?
WELL - YOU BIG STIFF! WHO WIN!?
DE BECK
11-15

Spark Plug Isn't Going Hungry if Barney Can Help It

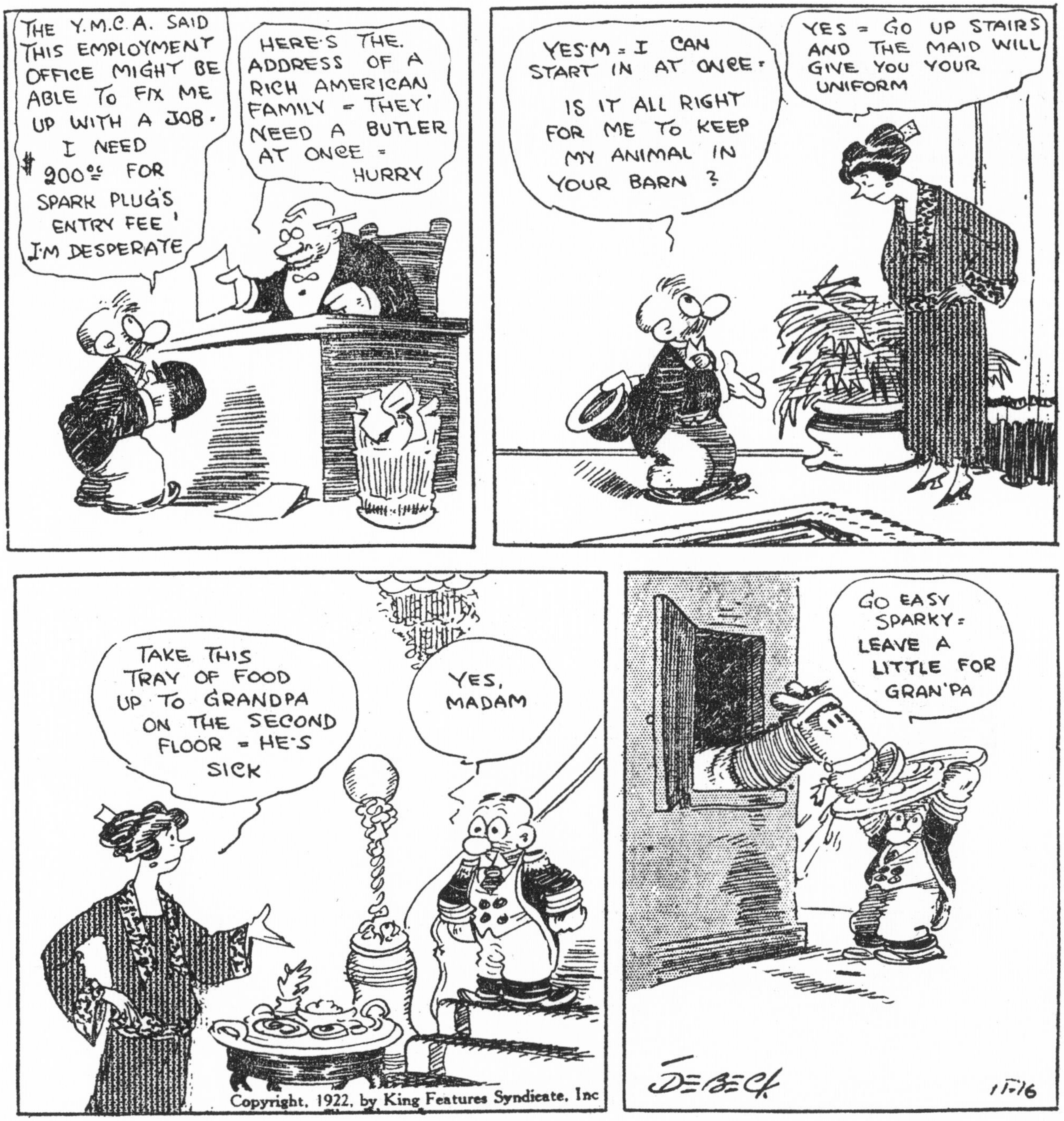
THE Y.M.C.A. SAID THIS EMPLOYMENT OFFICE MIGHT BE ABLE TO FIX ME UP WITH A JOB. I NEED $200.00 FOR SPARK PLUG'S ENTRY FEE I'M DESPERATE
HERE'S THE ADDRESS OF A RICH AMERICAN FAMILY - THEY NEED A BUTLER AT ONCE - HURRY
YES'M - I CAN START IN AT ONCE - IS IT ALL RIGHT FOR ME TO KEEP MY ANIMAL IN YOUR BARN ?
YES - GO UP STAIRS AND THE MAID WILL GIVE YOU YOUR UNIFORM
TAKE THIS TRAY OF FOOD UP TO GRANDPA ON THE SECOND FLOOR - HE'S SICK
YES, MADAM
GO EASY SPARKY - LEAVE A LITTLE FOR GRAN'PA
DE BECK
11-16
Copyright, 1922, by King Features Syndicate, Inc

Barney Ought to Get a Job With the Weather Bureau

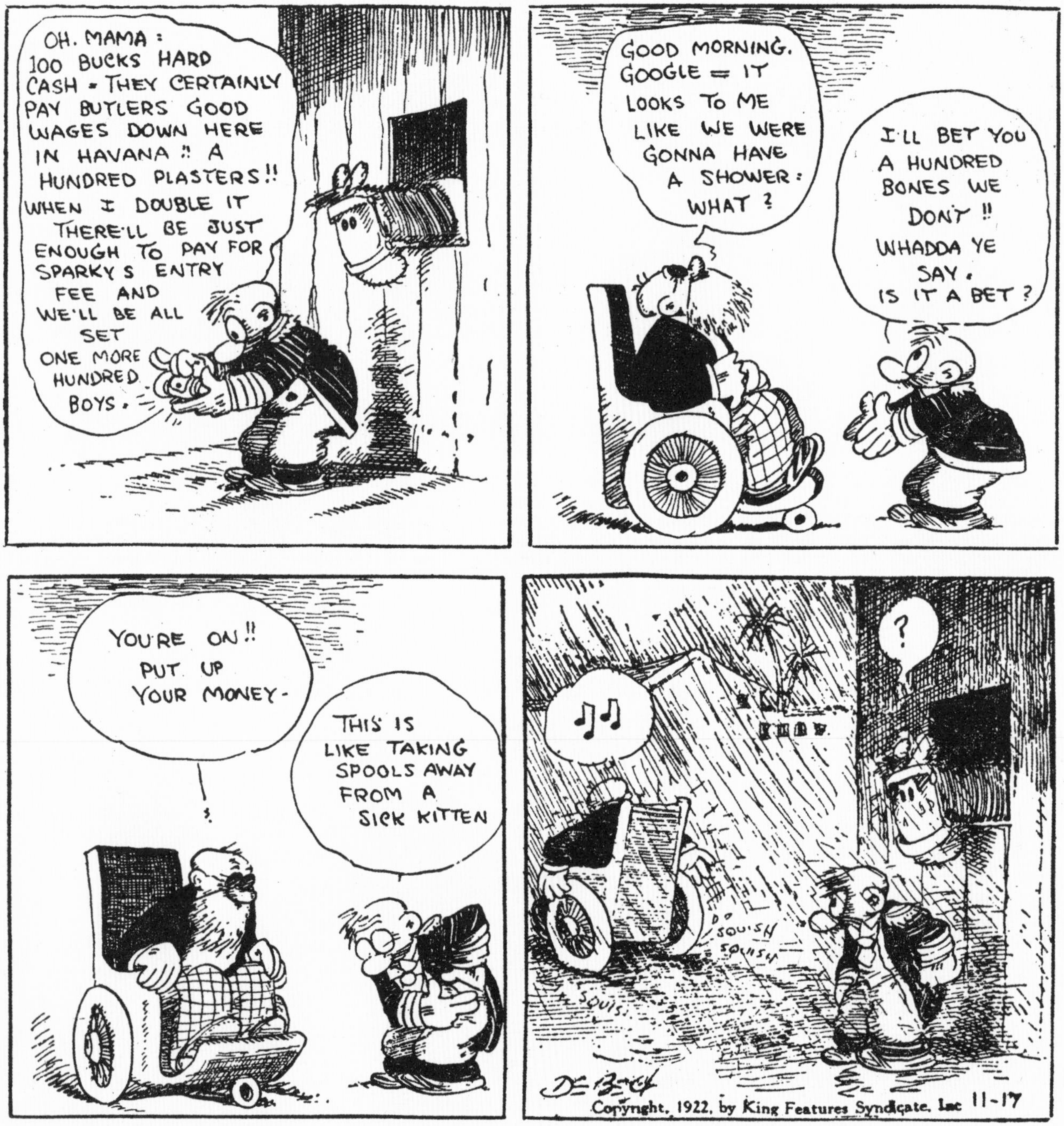
OH. MAMA: 100 BUCKS HARD CASH - THEY CERTAINLY PAY BUTLERS GOOD WAGES DOWN HERE IN HAVANA !! A HUNDRED PLASTERS!! WHEN I DOUBLE IT THERE'LL BE JUST ENOUGH TO PAY FOR SPARKY'S ENTRY FEE AND WE'LL BE ALL SET ONE MORE HUNDRED BOYS.
GOOD MORNING. GOOGLE = IT LOOKS TO ME LIKE WE WERE GONNA HAVE A SHOWER: WHAT?
I'LL BET YOU A HUNDRED BONES WE DON'T !! WHADDA YE SAY. IS IT A BET?
YOU'RE ON!! PUT UP YOUR MONEY-
THIS IS LIKE TAKING SPOOLS AWAY FROM A SICK KITTEN
?
DO
SQUISH
SQUISH
SQUIS
DE BECK
Copyright, 1922, by King Features Syndicate, Inc 11-17

Spark Plug Is Some Soup Fiend

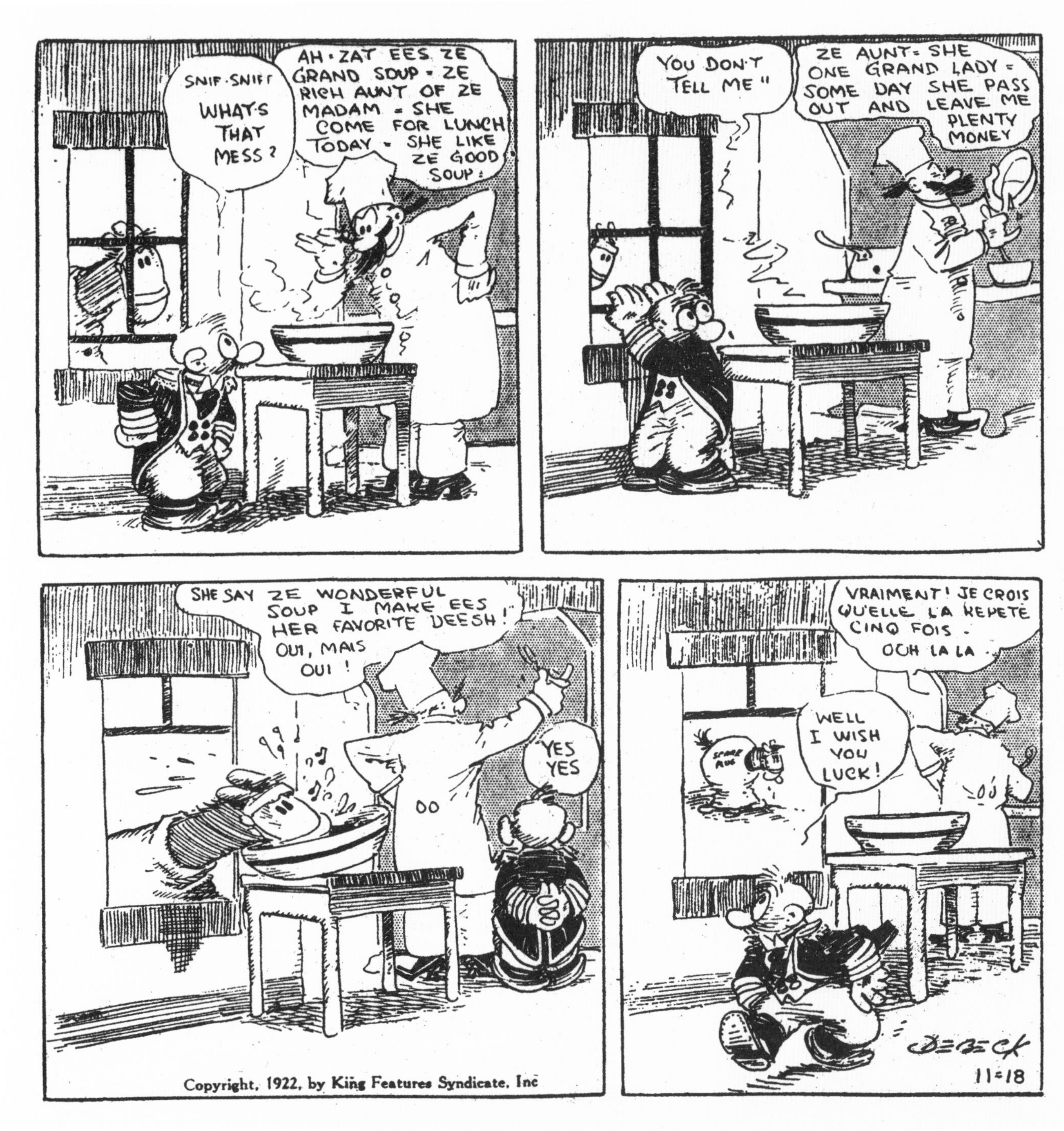

SNIF-SNIFF
WHAT'S THAT MESS?
AH - ZAT EES ZE GRAND SOUP - ZE RICH AUNT OF ZE MADAM - SHE COME FOR LUNCH TODAY - SHE LIKE ZE GOOD SOUP!
YOU DON'T TELL ME"
ZE AUNT - SHE ONE GRAND LADY - SOME DAY SHE PASS OUT AND LEAVE ME PLENTY MONEY
SHE SAY ZE WONDERFUL SOUP I MAKE EES HER FAVORITE DEESH! OUI, MAIS OUI!
YES YES
VRAIMENT! JE CROIS QU'ELLE LA REPETE CINQ FOIS - OOH LA LA
WELL I WISH YOU LUCK!
Copyright, 1922, by King Features Syndicate, Inc
DEBECK
11-18

Spark Plug Needs an Invalid's Chair

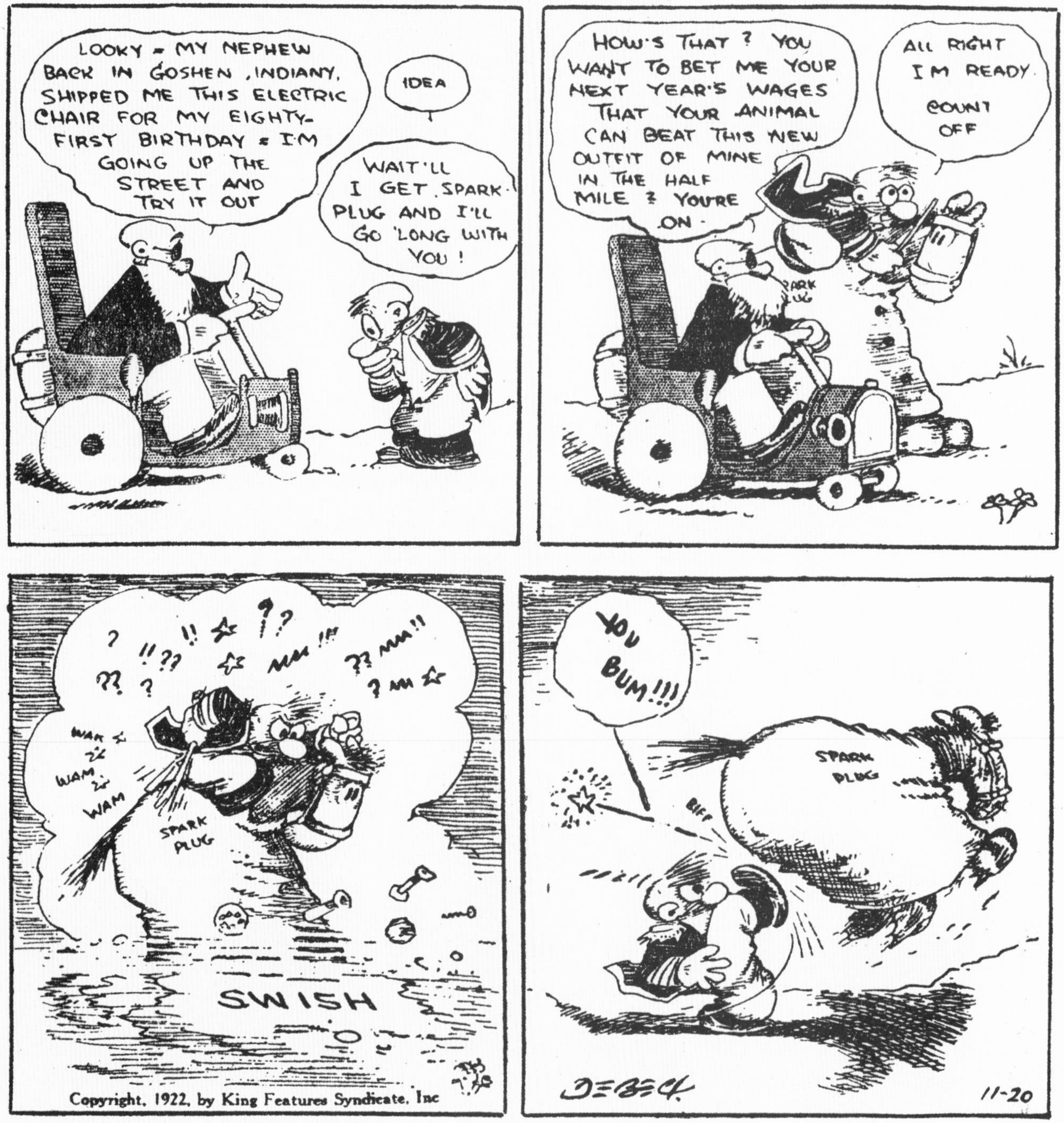
LOOKY - MY NEPHEW BACK IN GOSHEN, INDIANY, SHIPPED ME THIS ELECTRIC CHAIR FOR MY EIGHTY-FIRST BIRTHDAY = I'M GOING UP THE STREET AND TRY IT OUT
IDEA
WAIT'LL I GET SPARK PLUG AND I'LL GO 'LONG WITH YOU!
HOW'S THAT? YOU WANT TO BET ME YOUR NEXT YEAR'S WAGES THAT YOUR ANIMAL CAN BEAT THIS NEW OUTFIT OF MINE IN THE HALF MILE? YOU'RE ON.
ALL RIGHT I'M READY. COUNT OFF
SPARK PLUG
? !! ?? !! ☆ ?? ?? ? ☆ MM !!! ?? MM !! ? MM ☆
WAM ☆ WAM WAM
SPARK PLUG
SWISH
Copyright, 1922, by King Features Syndicate, Inc
YOU BUM!!!
SPARK PLUG
BIFF
DEBECK
11-20

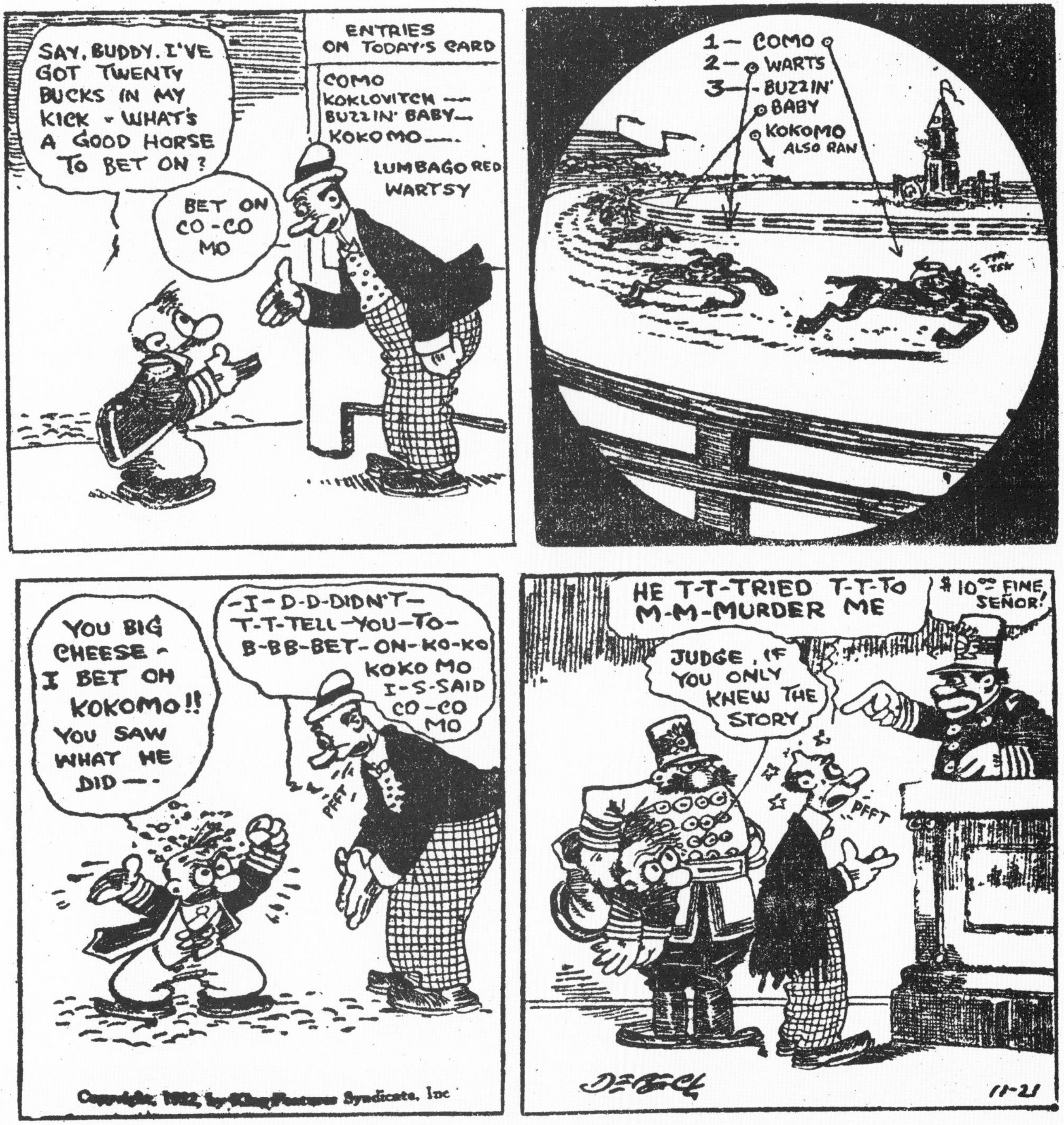
SAY, BUDDY. I'VE GOT TWENTY BUCKS IN MY KICK - WHAT'S A GOOD HORSE TO BET ON?
ENTRIES ON TODAY'S CARD
COMO
KOKLOVITCH —
BUZZIN' BABY —
KOKOMO —
LUMBAGO RED
WARTSY
BET ON CO-CO MO
1— COMO
2— WARTS
3— BUZZIN' BABY
KOKOMO ALSO RAN
YOU BIG CHEESE - I BET ON KOKOMO!! YOU SAW WHAT HE DID —
-I-D-D-DIDN'T-T-T-TELL-YOU-TO-B-BB-BET-ON-KO-KO KOKO MO I-S-SAID CO-CO MO
PFFT
Copyright, 1922, by King Features Syndicate, Inc
HE T-T-TRIED T-T-TO M-M-MURDER ME
$10.00 FINE, SEÑOR!
JUDGE, IF YOU ONLY KNEW THE STORY
PFFT
11-21

And Sparky Believed It!

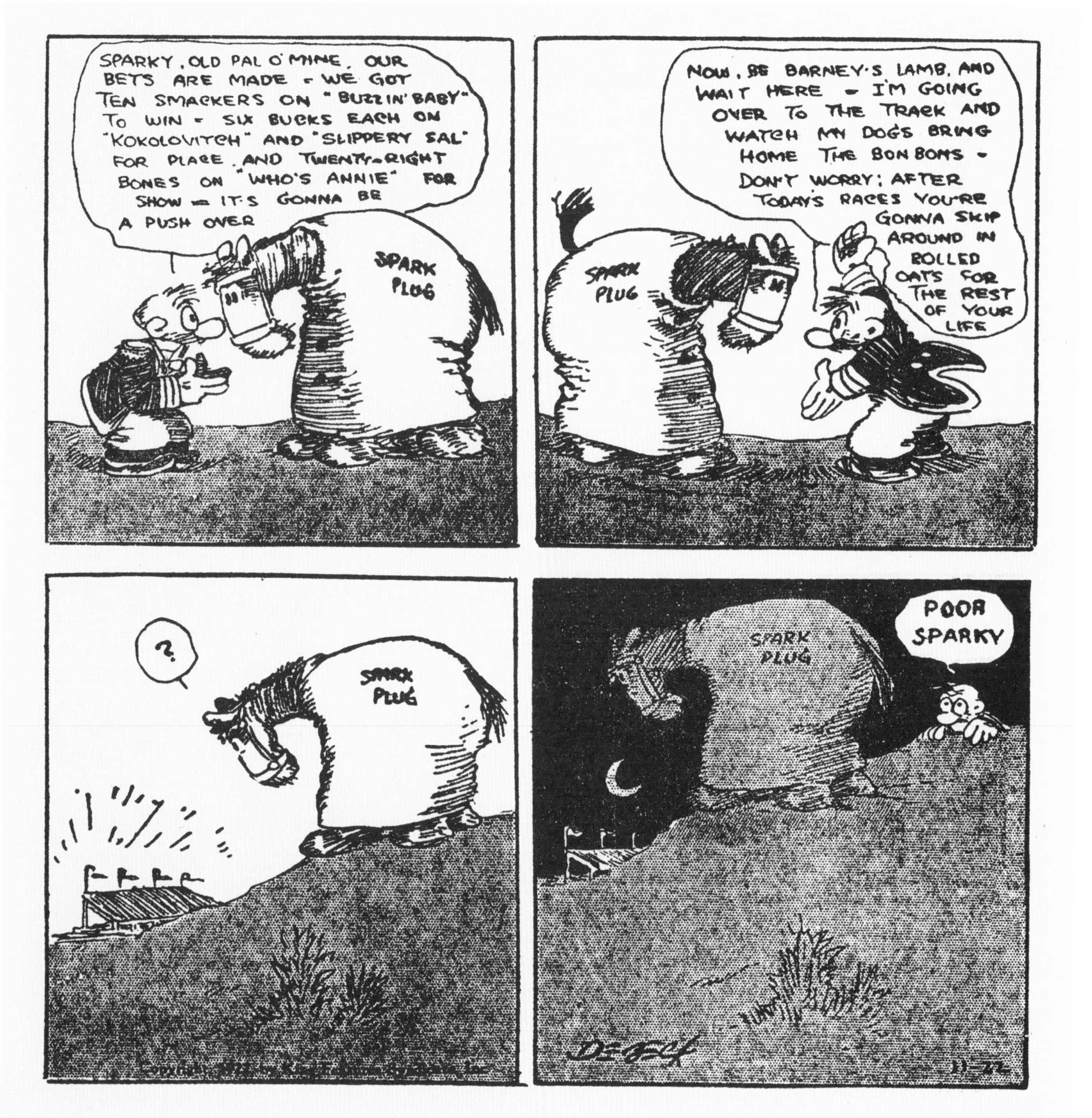
SPARKY, OLD PAL O' MINE, OUR BETS ARE MADE - WE GOT TEN SMACKERS ON "BUZZIN' BABY" TO WIN - SIX BUCKS EACH ON "KOKOLOVITCH" AND "SLIPPERY SAL" FOR PLACE AND TWENTY-EIGHT BONES ON "WHO'S ANNIE" FOR SHOW - IT'S GONNA BE A PUSH OVER
SPARK PLUG
NOW, BE BARNEY'S LAMB, AND WAIT HERE - I'M GOING OVER TO THE TRACK AND WATCH MY DOGS BRING HOME THE BON BONS - DON'T WORRY: AFTER TODAY'S RACES YOU'RE GONNA SKIP AROUND IN ROLLED OATS FOR THE REST OF YOUR LIFE
SPARK PLUG
?
SPARK PLUG
SPARK PLUG
POOR SPARKY
11-22

Barney Gets Out of a Hole

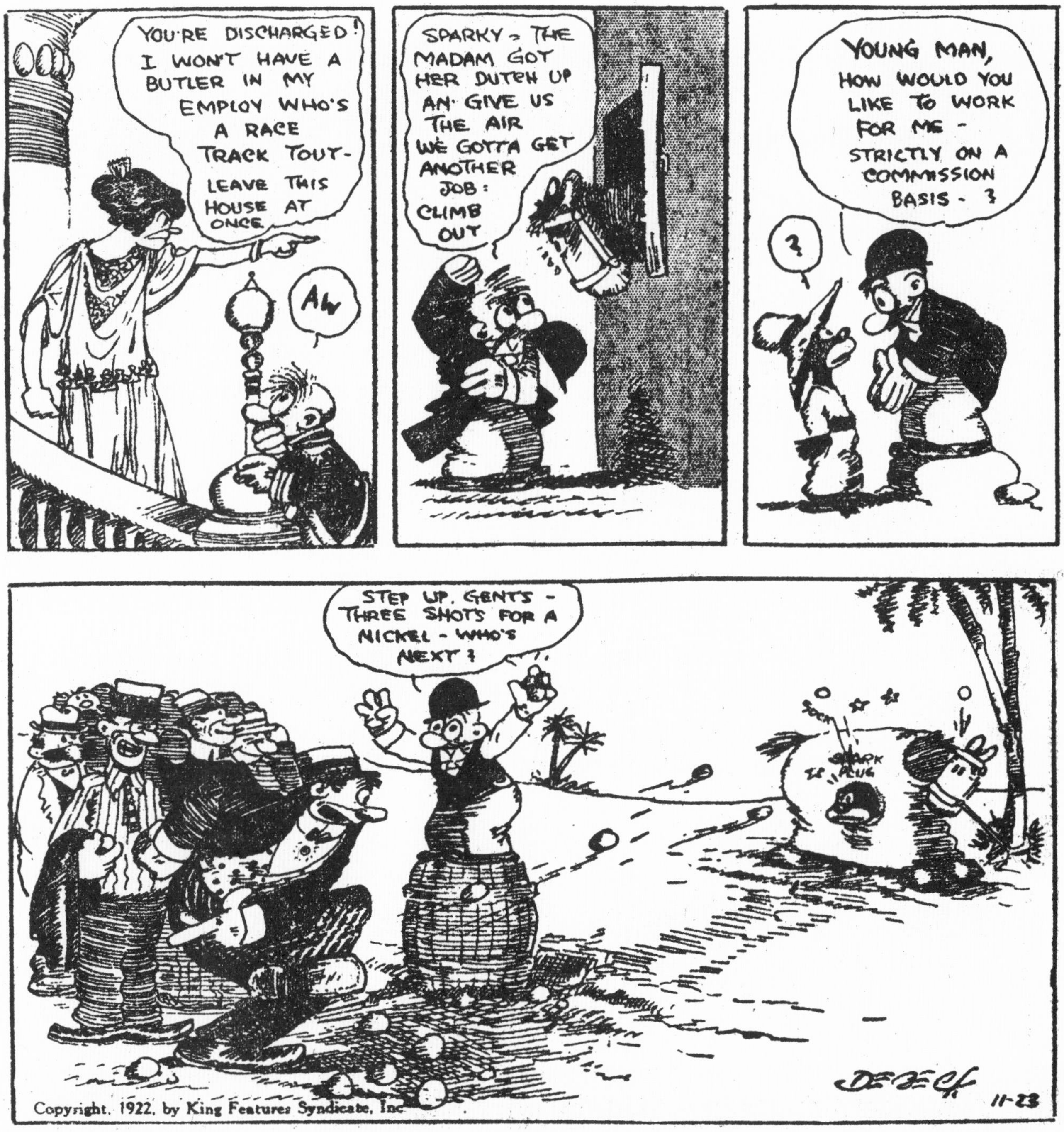

YOU'RE DISCHARGED! I WON'T HAVE A BUTLER IN MY EMPLOY WHO'S A RACE TRACK TOUT- LEAVE THIS HOUSE AT ONCE
AW
SPARKY - THE MADAM GOT HER DUTCH UP AN' GIVE US THE AIR WE GOTTA GET ANOTHER JOB: CLIMB OUT
YOUNG MAN, HOW WOULD YOU LIKE TO WORK FOR ME - STRICTLY ON A COMMISSION BASIS - ?
?
STEP UP, GENTS - THREE SHOTS FOR A NICKEL - WHO'S NEXT ?
SPARK PLUG
DE BECK
11-23
Copyright, 1922, by King Features Syndicate, Inc.

Sparky's Getting All Set for the Big Day Tomorrow

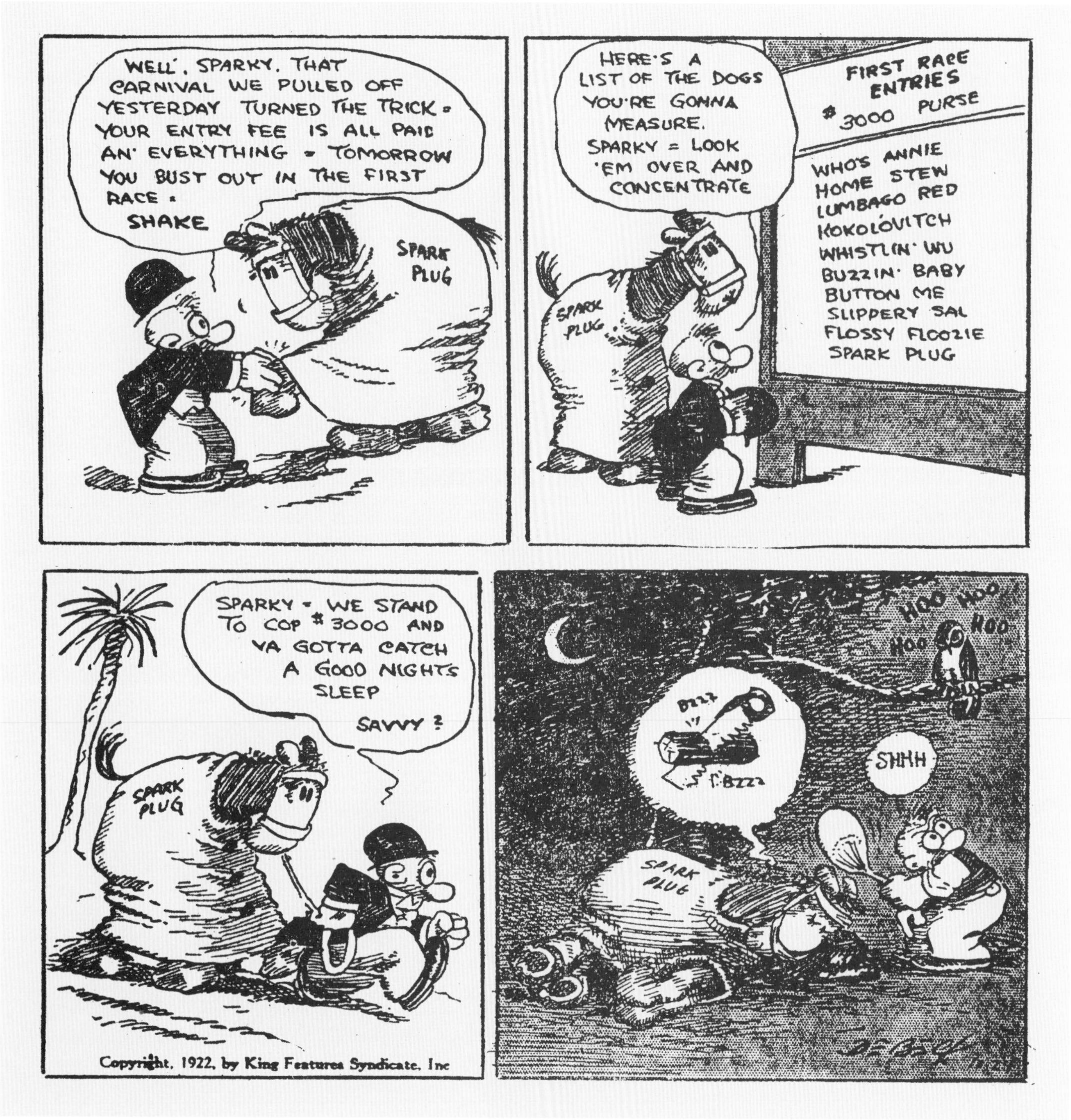

WELL', SPARKY, THAT CARNIVAL WE PULLED OFF YESTERDAY TURNED THE TRICK - YOUR ENTRY FEE IS ALL PAID AN' EVERYTHING - TOMORROW YOU BUST OUT IN THE FIRST RACE - SHAKE
SPARK PLUG
HERE'S A LIST OF THE DOGS YOU'RE GONNA MEASURE. SPARKY - LOOK 'EM OVER AND CONCENTRATE
FIRST RACE ENTRIES
$3000 PURSE
WHO'S ANNIE
HOME STEW
LUMBAGO RED
KOKOLOVITCH
WHISTLIN' WU
BUZZIN' BABY
BUTTON ME
SLIPPERY SAL
FLOSSY FLOOZIE
SPARK PLUG
SPARK PLUG
SPARKY - WE STAND TO COP $3000 AND YA GOTTA CATCH A GOOD NIGHTS SLEEP
SAVVY ?
SPARK PLUG
HOO HOO HOO HOO
BZZZ
BZZZ
SHHH
SPARK PLUG

Copyright, 1922, by King Features Syndicate, Inc

Does Spark Plug Win? Oh, Look at This!

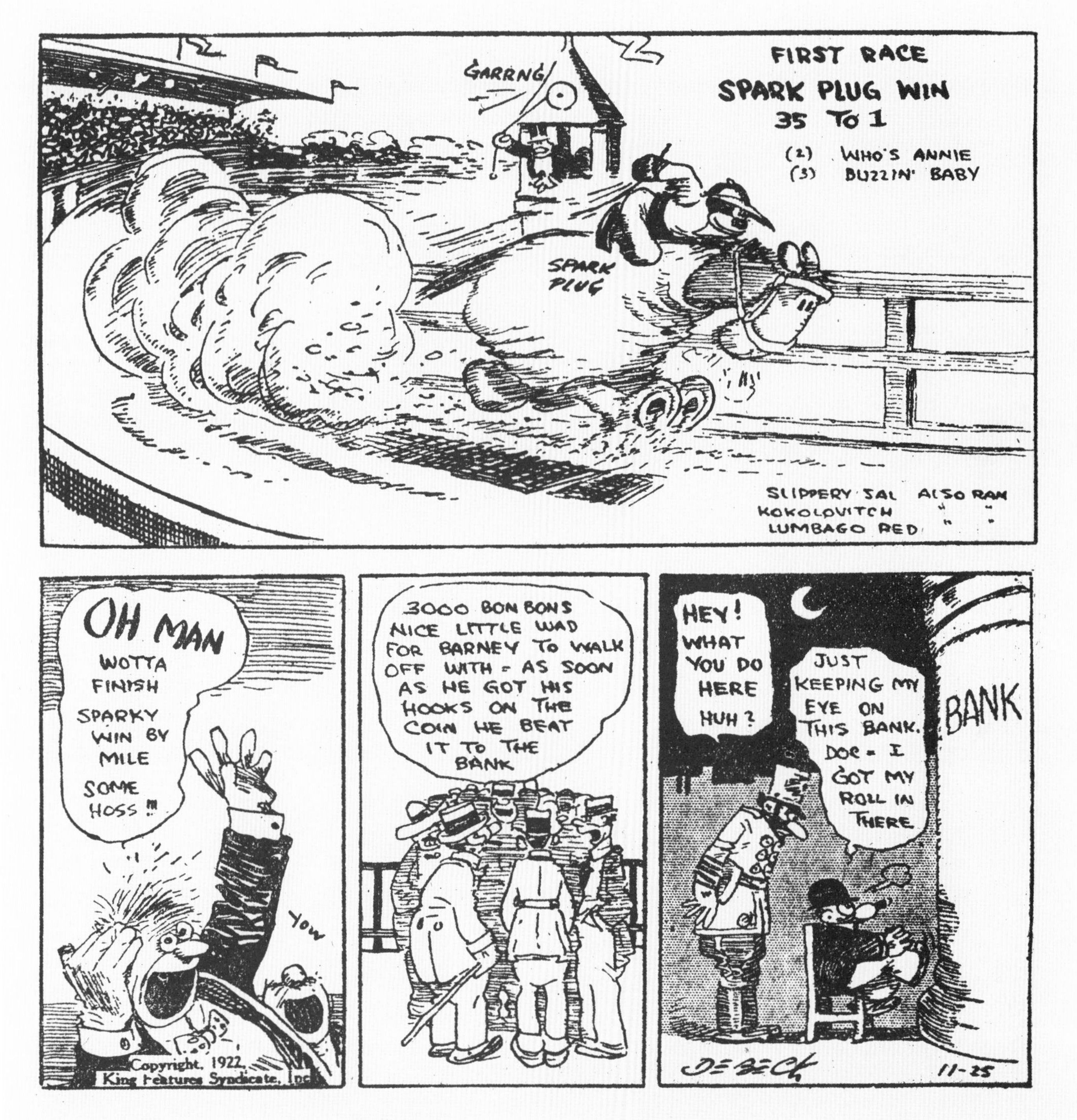
GARRNG
FIRST RACE
SPARK PLUG WIN
35 TO 1
(2) WHO'S ANNIE
(3) BUZZIN' BABY
SPARK PLUG
SLIPPERY SAL ALSO RAN
KOKOLOVITCH " "
LUMBAGO RED " "
OH MAN WOTTA FINISH SPARKY WIN BY MILE SOME HOSS !!!
YOW
Copyright, 1922, King Features Syndicate, Inc.
3000 BON BONS NICE LITTLE WAD FOR BARNEY TO WALK OFF WITH - AS SOON AS HE GOT HIS HOOKS ON THE COIN HE BEAT IT TO THE BANK
HEY! WHAT YOU DO HERE HUH?
JUST KEEPING MY EYE ON THIS BANK. DOC - I GOT MY ROLL IN THERE
BANK
DE BECK
11-25

A Panama Is Just So Much Fodder to Sparky

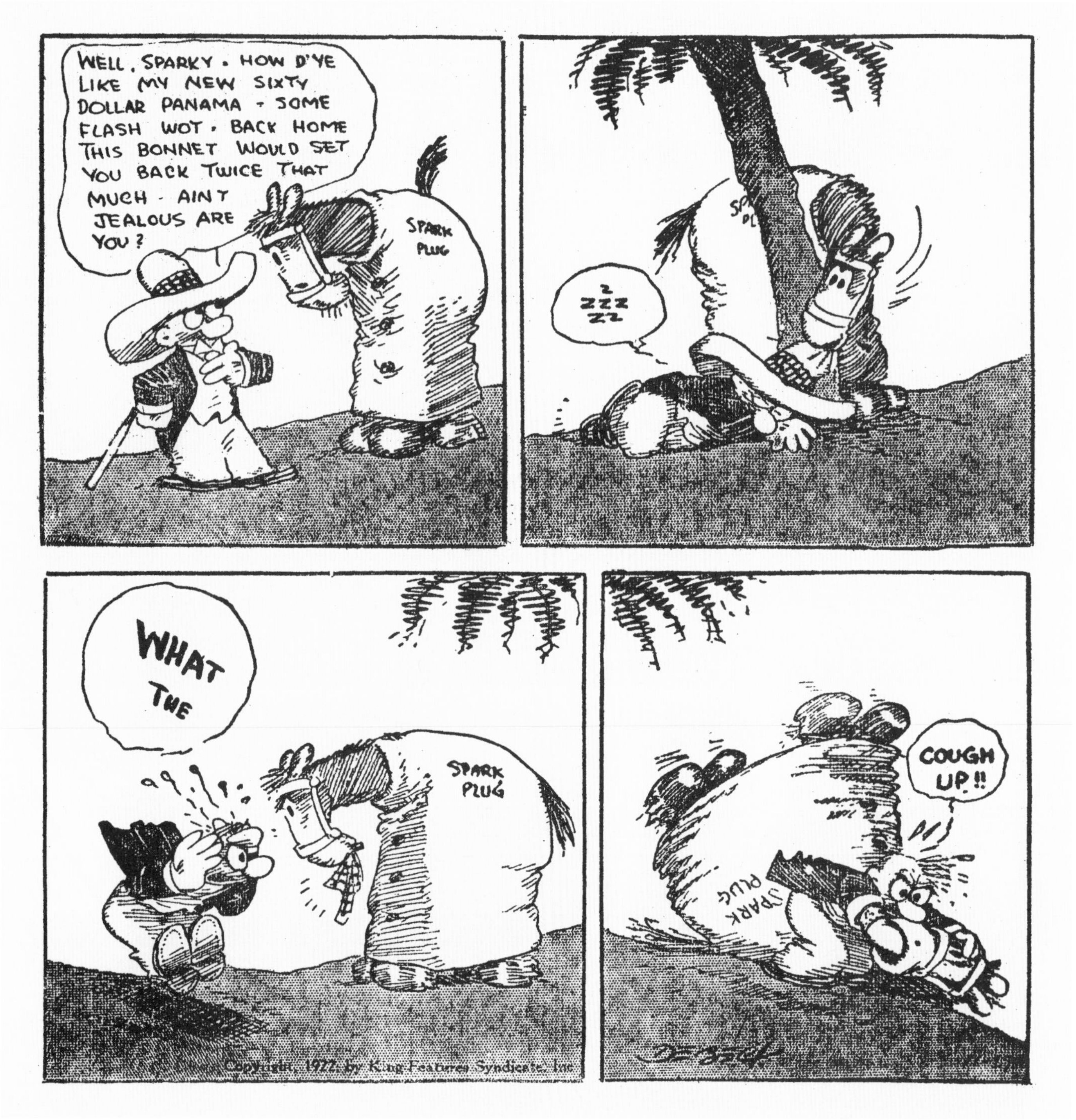
WELL, SPARKY - HOW D'YE LIKE MY NEW SIXTY DOLLAR PANAMA - SOME FLASH WOT - BACK HOME THIS BONNET WOULD SET YOU BACK TWICE THAT MUCH - AINT JEALOUS ARE YOU?
SPARK PLUG
Z ZZZ ZZ
WHAT THE
SPARK PLUG
COUGH UP!!
SPARK PLUG
Copyright, 1922, by King Features Syndicate, Inc.
DEBECK

Sparky Wins, But Congratulations Are Not in Order

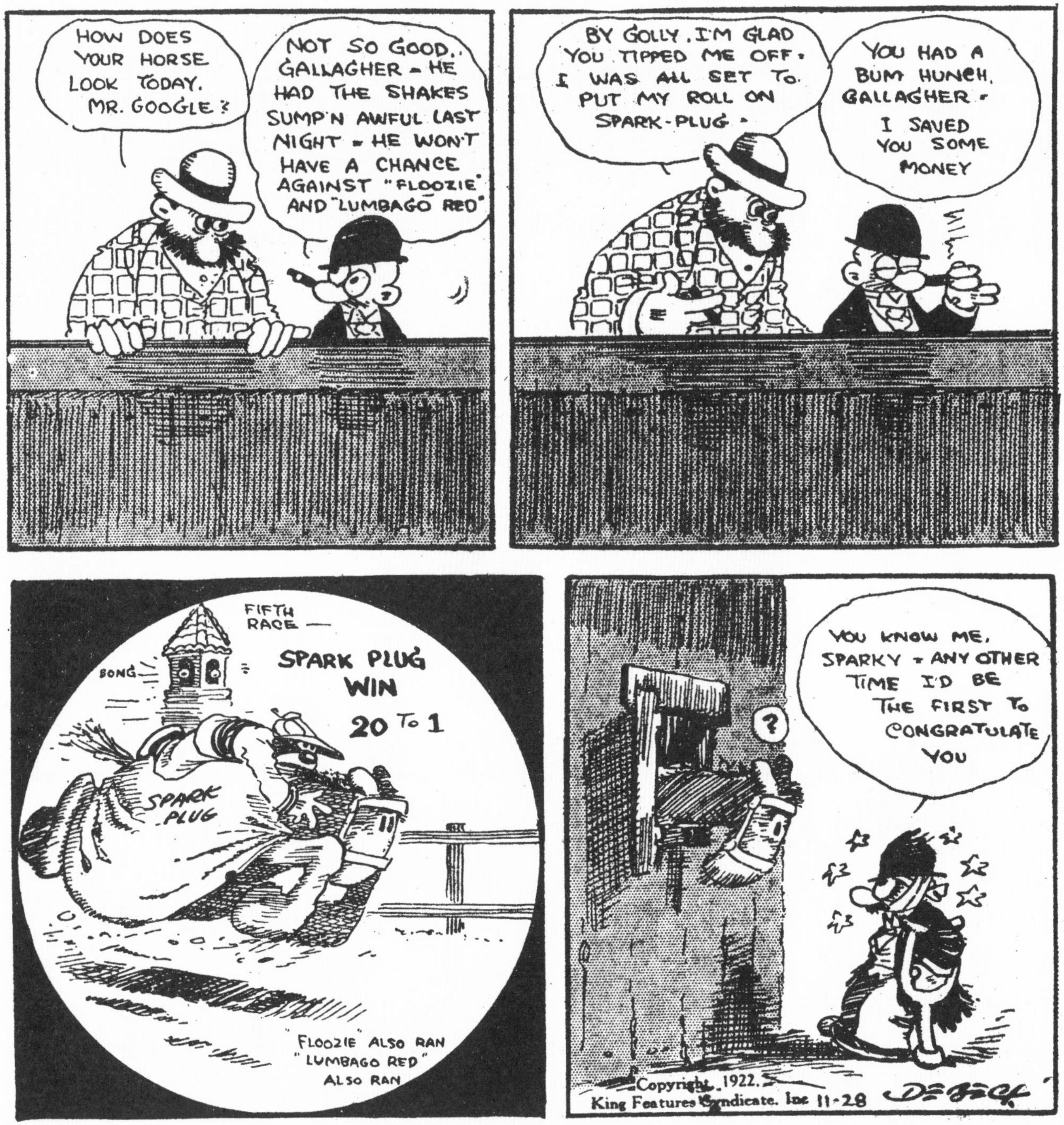
HOW DOES YOUR HORSE LOOK TODAY, MR. GOOGLE?
NOT SO GOOD, GALLAGHER - HE HAD THE SHAKES SUMP'N AWFUL LAST NIGHT - HE WON'T HAVE A CHANCE AGAINST "FLOOZIE" AND "LUMBAGO RED"
BY GOLLY, I'M GLAD YOU TIPPED ME OFF - I WAS ALL SET TO PUT MY ROLL ON SPARK-PLUG -
YOU HAD A BUM HUNCH, GALLAGHER - I SAVED YOU SOME MONEY
FIFTH RACE —
BONG
SPARK PLUG WIN 20 TO 1
SPARK PLUG
"FLOOZIE" ALSO RAN
"LUMBAGO RED" ALSO RAN
?
YOU KNOW ME, SPARKY - ANY OTHER TIME I'D BE THE FIRST TO CONGRATULATE YOU
Copyright, 1922, King Features Syndicate, Inc 11-28
De Beck

This Is the Pace That Kills

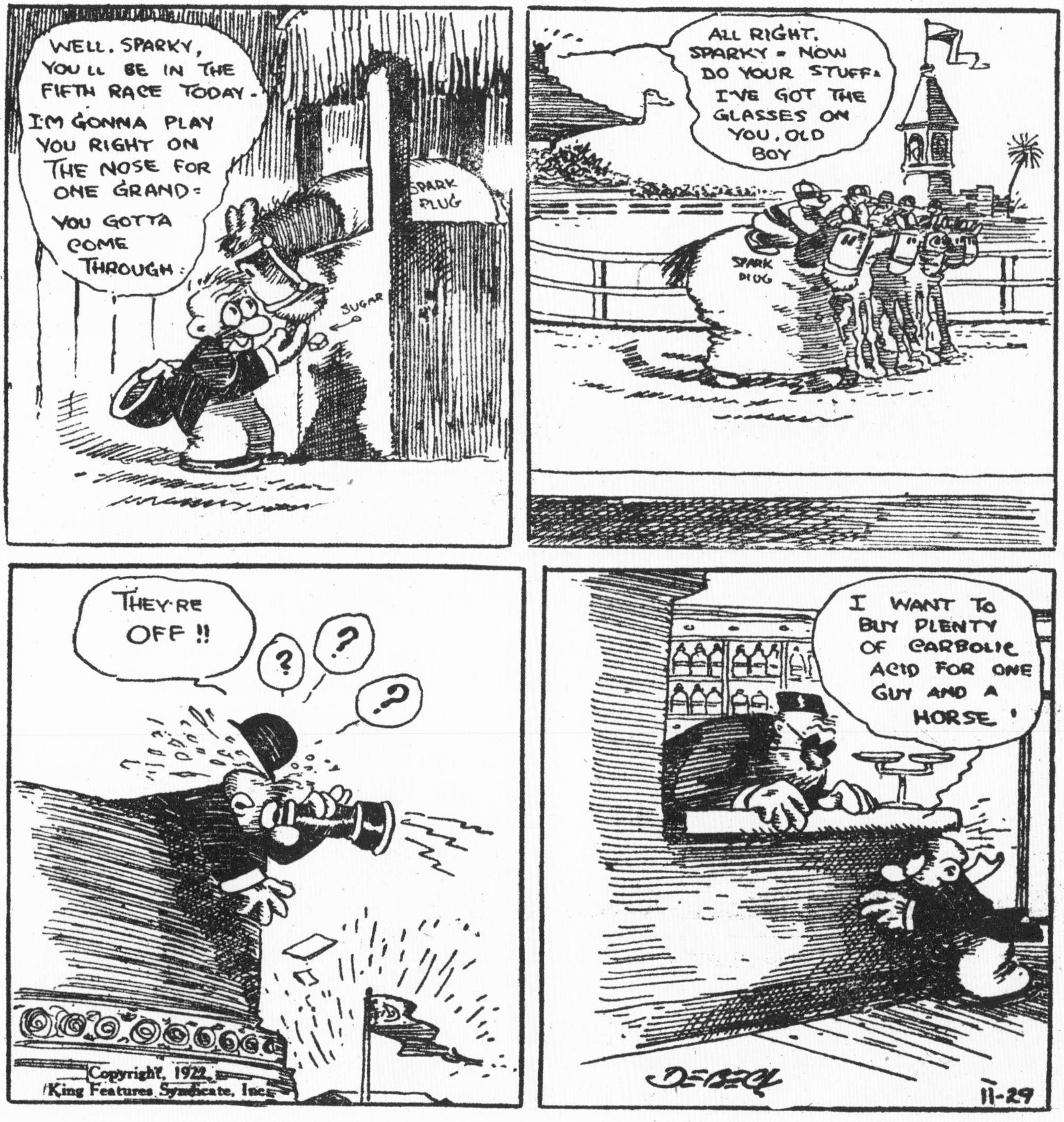
WELL. SPARKY, YOU'LL BE IN THE FIFTH RACE TODAY - I'M GONNA PLAY YOU RIGHT ON THE NOSE FOR ONE GRAND - YOU GOTTA COME THROUGH -
SPARK PLUG
SUGAR
ALL RIGHT, SPARKY - NOW DO YOUR STUFF - I'VE GOT THE GLASSES ON YOU, OLD BOY
SPARK PLUG
THEY'RE OFF !!
?
?
?
Copyright, 1922, King Features Syndicate, Inc.
I WANT TO BUY PLENTY OF CARBOLIC ACID FOR ONE GUY AND A HORSE!
DE BECK
11-29

Thanksgiving Day Is "Fast" Day for Sparky

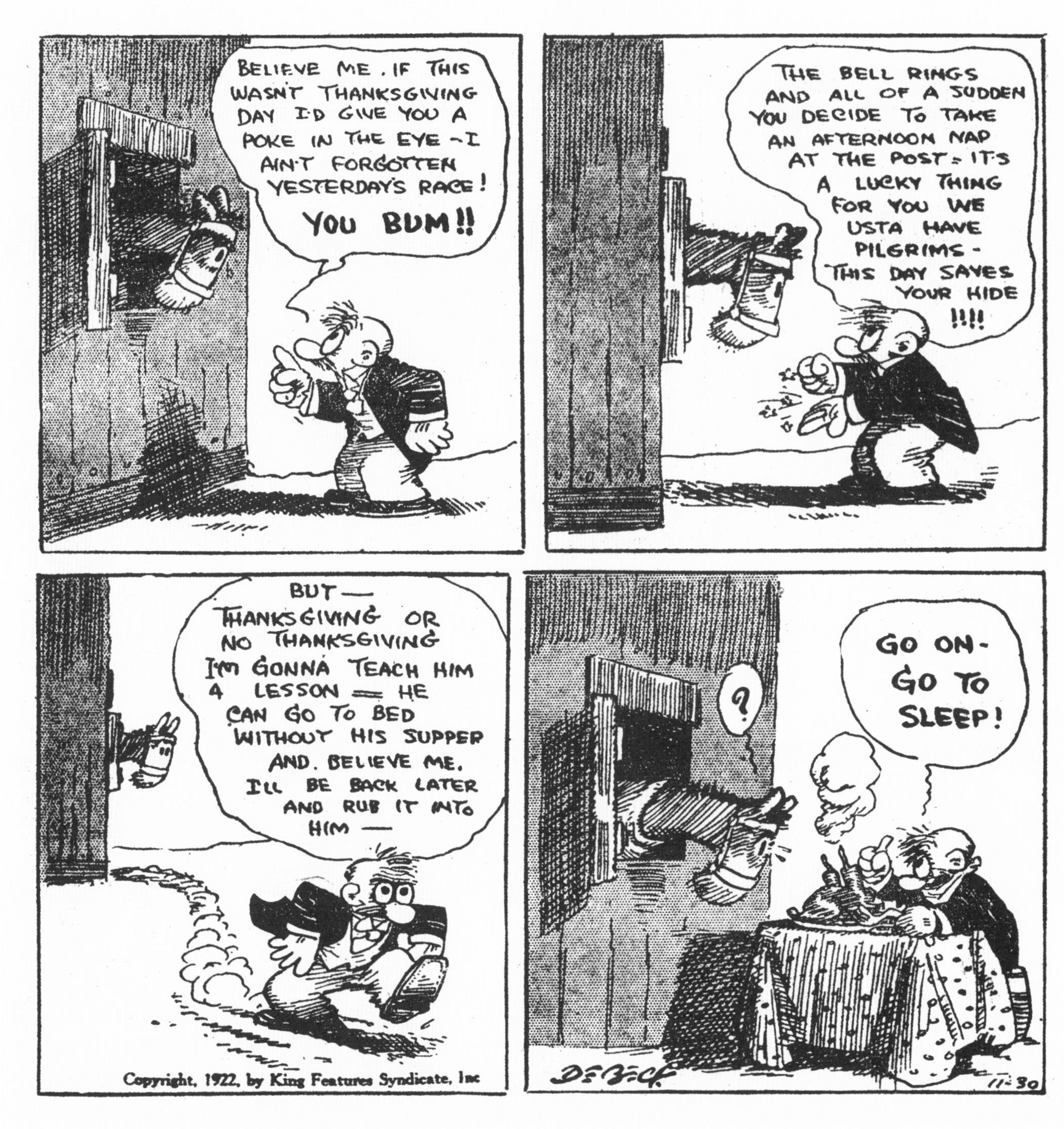
BELIEVE ME. IF THIS WASN'T THANKSGIVING DAY I·D GIVE YOU A POKE IN THE EYE - I AIN·T FORGOTTEN YESTERDAY'S RACE! YOU BUM!!
THE BELL RINGS AND ALL OF A SUDDEN YOU DECIDE TO TAKE AN AFTERNOON NAP AT THE POST - IT'S A LUCKY THING FOR YOU WE USTA HAVE PILGRIMS - THIS DAY SAVES YOUR HIDE !!!!
BUT — THANKSGIVING OR NO THANKSGIVING I'M GONNA TEACH HIM A LESSON = HE CAN GO TO BED WITHOUT HIS SUPPER AND. BELIEVE ME. I'LL BE BACK LATER AND RUB IT INTO HIM —
?
GO ON - GO TO SLEEP!
Copyright, 1922, by King Features Syndicate, Inc
DE BECK
11-30

Barney Wasn't Sure, but He Thought Somebody Was All to the "Co-Co"

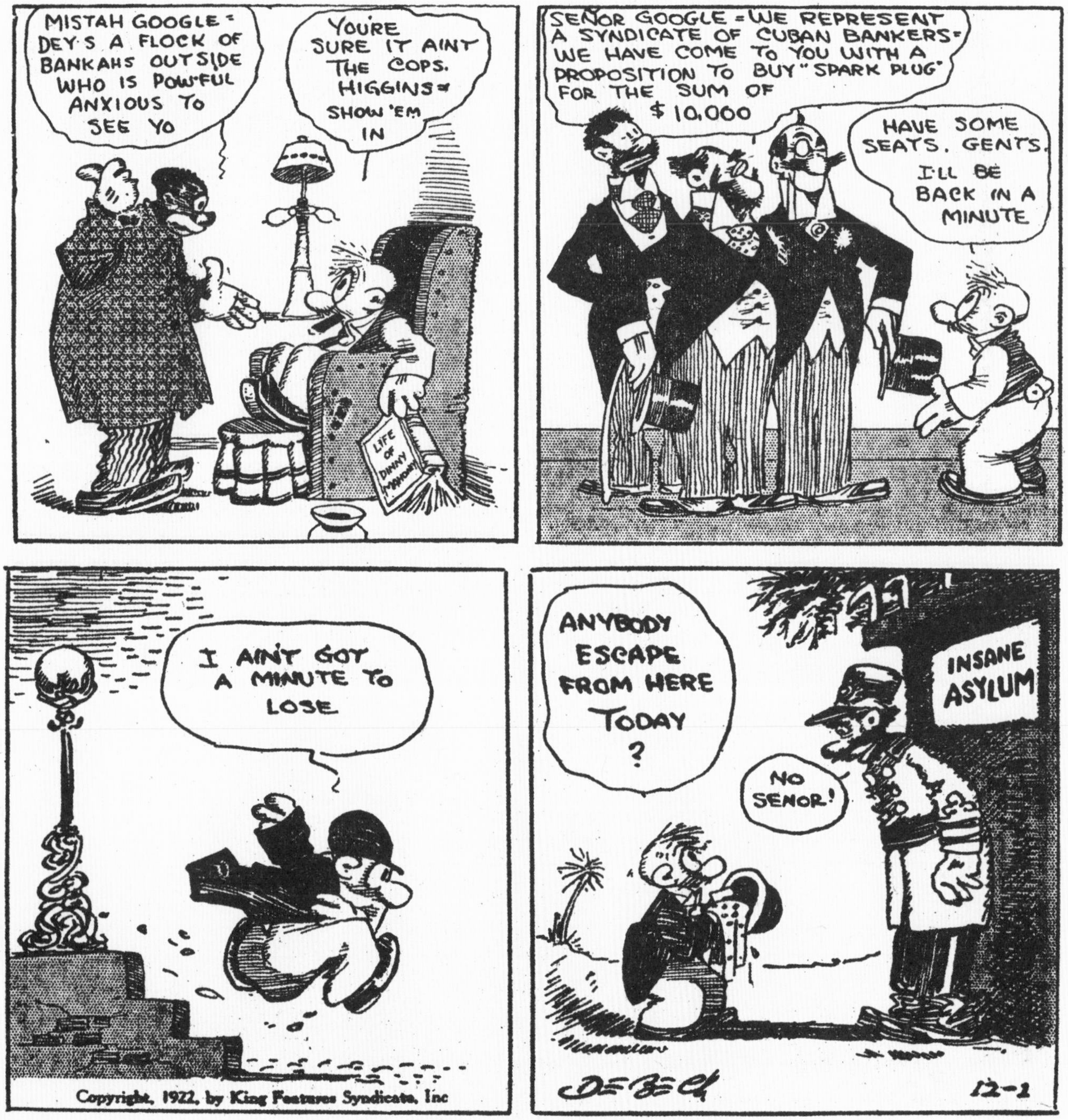
MISTAH GOOGLE = DEY'S A FLOCK OF BANKAHS OUTSIDE WHO IS POW'FUL ANXIOUS TO SEE YO
YOU'RE SURE IT AINT THE COPS. HIGGINS = SHOW 'EM IN
LIFE OF DINNY
SEÑOR GOOGLE = WE REPRESENT A SYNDICATE OF CUBAN BANKERS = WE HAVE COME TO YOU WITH A PROPOSITION TO BUY "SPARK PLUG" FOR THE SUM OF $10,000
HAVE SOME SEATS, GENTS. I'LL BE BACK IN A MINUTE
I AIN'T GOT A MINUTE TO LOSE
Copyright, 1922, by King Features Syndicate, Inc
ANYBODY ESCAPE FROM HERE TODAY ?
NO SENOR!
INSANE ASYLUM
DE BECK
12-1

This Is the Saddest Day in Barney's Life

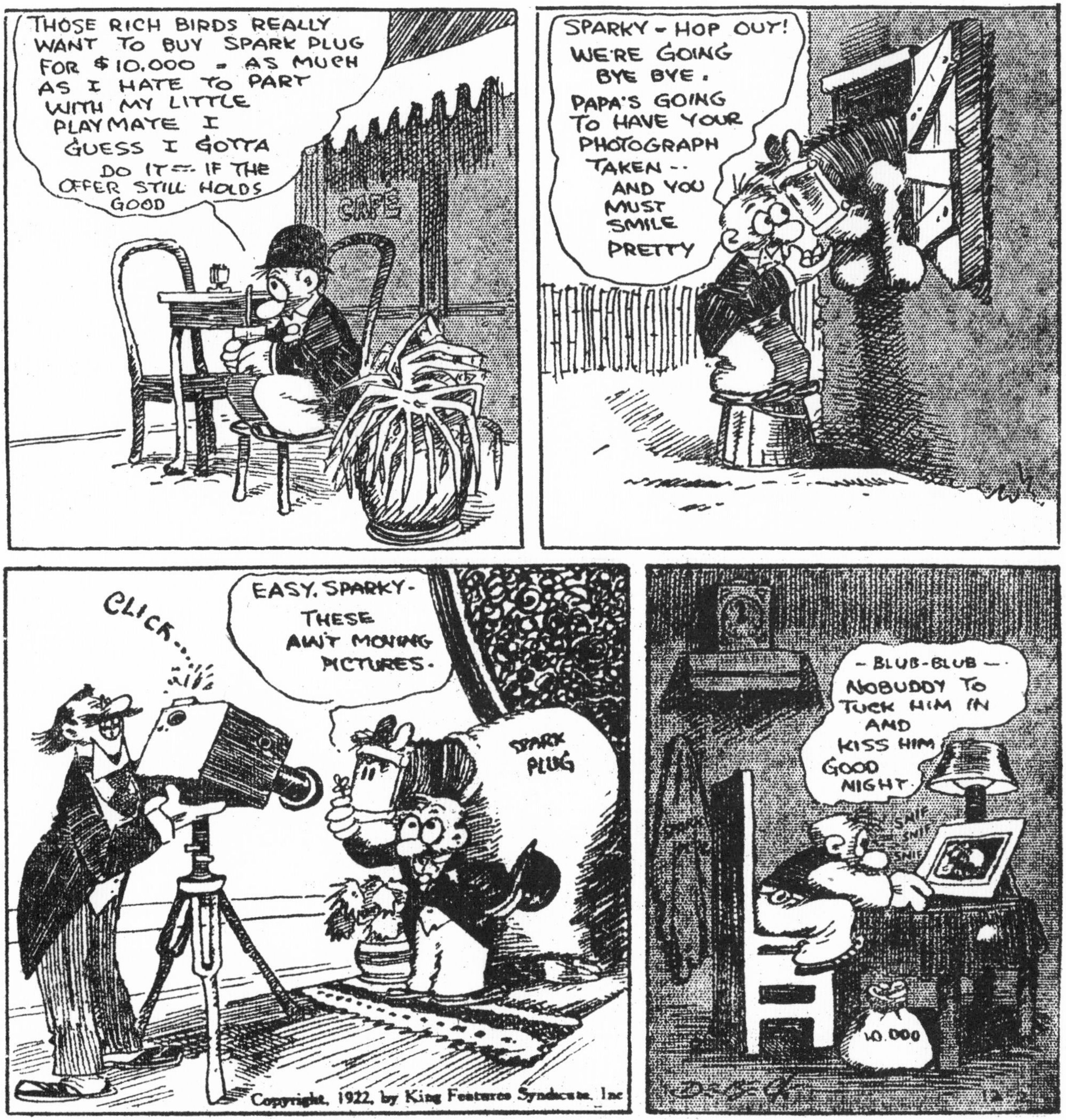
THOSE RICH BIRDS REALLY WANT TO BUY SPARK PLUG FOR $10,000 - AS MUCH AS I HATE TO PART WITH MY LITTLE PLAYMATE I GUESS I GOTTA DO IT -- IF THE OFFER STILL HOLDS GOOD
CAFE
SPARKY - HOP OUT! WE'RE GOING BYE BYE. PAPA'S GOING TO HAVE YOUR PHOTOGRAPH TAKEN -- AND YOU MUST SMILE PRETTY
CLICK....
EASY, SPARKY - THESE AIN'T MOVING PICTURES.
SPARK PLUG
Copyright, 1922, by King Features Syndicate, Inc
- BLUB-BLUB - NOBUDDY TO TUCK HIM IN AND KISS HIM GOOD NIGHT.
10,000

Barney May Be Crazy, But Not That Crazy

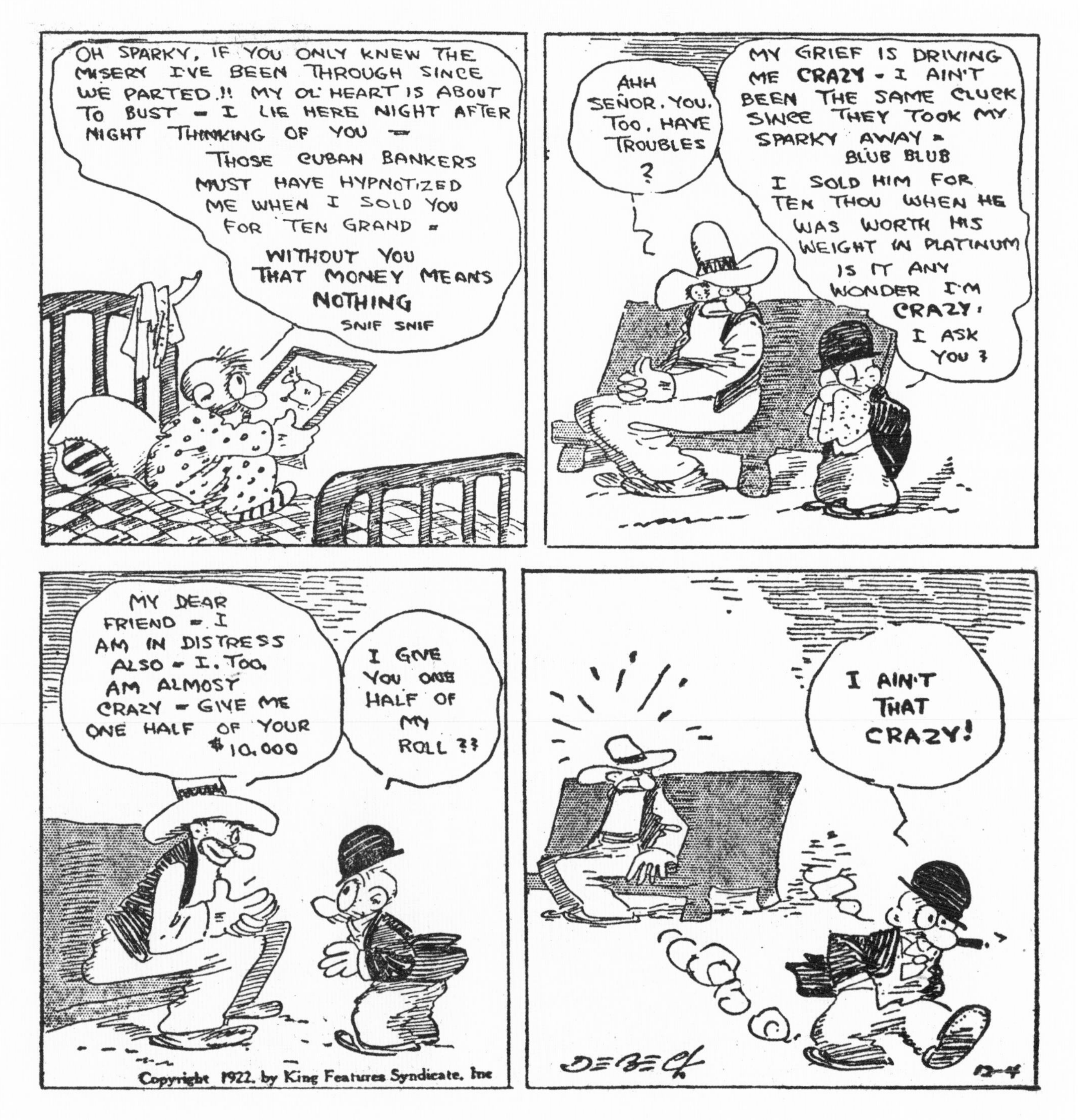

OH SPARKY, IF YOU ONLY KNEW THE MISERY I'VE BEEN THROUGH SINCE WE PARTED!! MY OL' HEART IS ABOUT TO BUST - I LIE HERE NIGHT AFTER NIGHT THINKING OF YOU - THOSE CUBAN BANKERS MUST HAVE HYPNOTIZED ME WHEN I SOLD YOU FOR TEN GRAND - WITHOUT YOU THAT MONEY MEANS NOTHING SNIF SNIF
AHH SEÑOR, YOU, TOO, HAVE TROUBLES ?
MY GRIEF IS DRIVING ME CRAZY - I AIN'T BEEN THE SAME CLUCK SINCE THEY TOOK MY SPARKY AWAY - BLUB BLUB I SOLD HIM FOR TEN THOU WHEN HE WAS WORTH HIS WEIGHT IN PLATINUM IS IT ANY WONDER I'M CRAZY: I ASK YOU ?
MY DEAR FRIEND - I AM IN DISTRESS ALSO - I, TOO, AM ALMOST CRAZY - GIVE ME ONE HALF OF YOUR ONE HALF OF $10,000
I GIVE YOU ONE HALF OF MY ROLL ??
I AIN'T THAT CRAZY!
Copyright 1922, by King Features Syndicate, Inc
DEBECK
12-4

Sparky Has An Apartment De Luxe Now

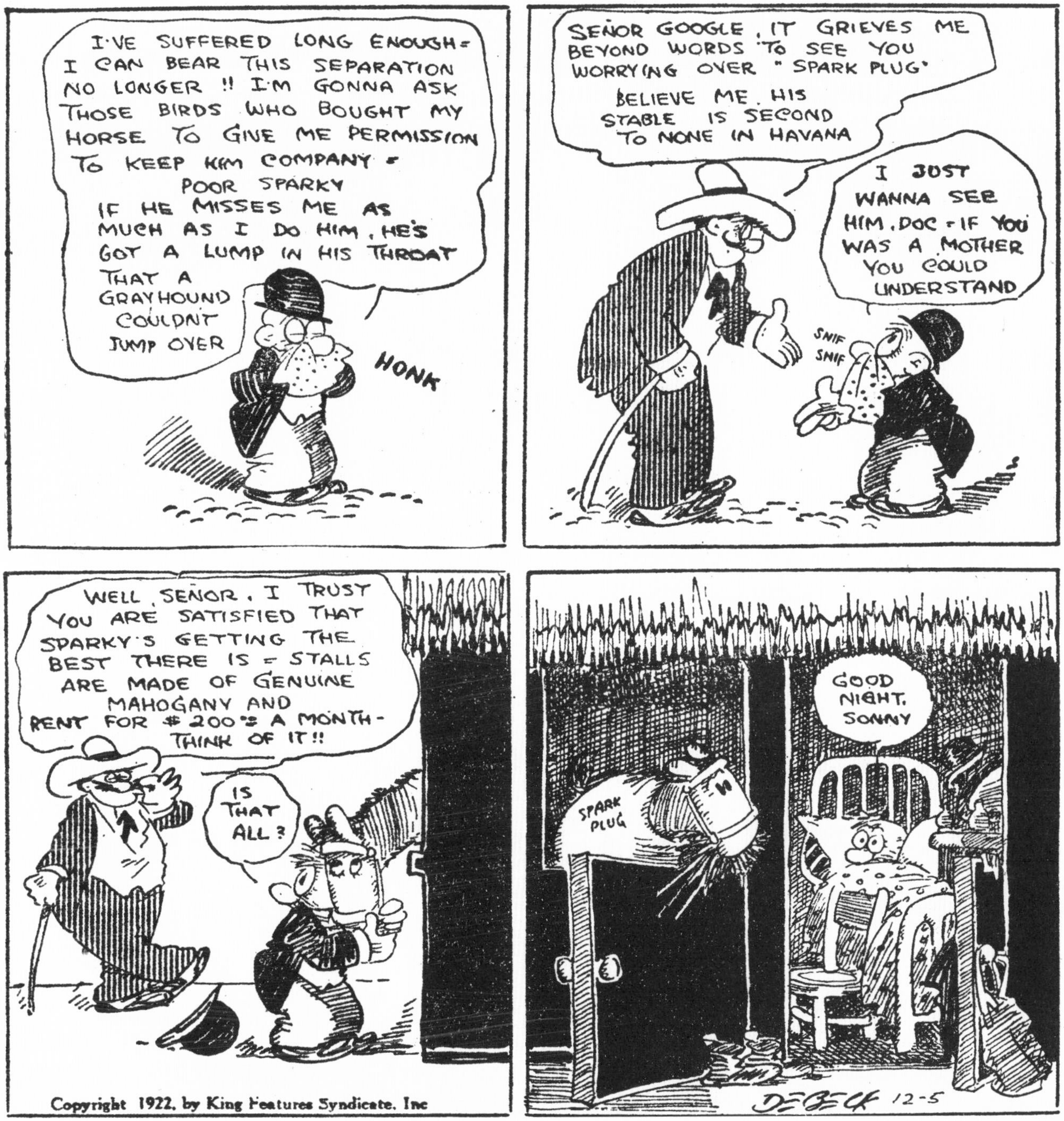
I'VE SUFFERED LONG ENOUGH = I CAN BEAR THIS SEPARATION NO LONGER !! I'M GONNA ASK THOSE BIRDS WHO BOUGHT MY HORSE TO GIVE ME PERMISSION TO KEEP HIM COMPANY = POOR SPARKY IF HE MISSES ME AS MUCH AS I DO HIM, HE'S GOT A LUMP IN HIS THROAT THAT A GRAYHOUND COULDN'T JUMP OVER
HONK
SEÑOR GOOGLE, IT GRIEVES ME BEYOND WORDS TO SEE YOU WORRYING OVER "SPARK PLUG" BELIEVE ME, HIS STABLE IS SECOND TO NONE IN HAVANA
I JUST WANNA SEE HIM, DOC = IF YOU WAS A MOTHER YOU COULD UNDERSTAND
SNIF SNIF
WELL, SEÑOR, I TRUST YOU ARE SATISFIED THAT SPARKY'S GETTING THE BEST THERE IS = STALLS ARE MADE OF GENUINE MAHOGANY AND RENT FOR $200 A MONTH - THINK OF IT !!
IS THAT ALL ?
SPARK PLUG
GOOD NIGHT, SONNY
Copyright 1922, by King Features Syndicate, Inc
DE BECK 12-5

Barney Has Had Some Sad Days, but None to Equal This!

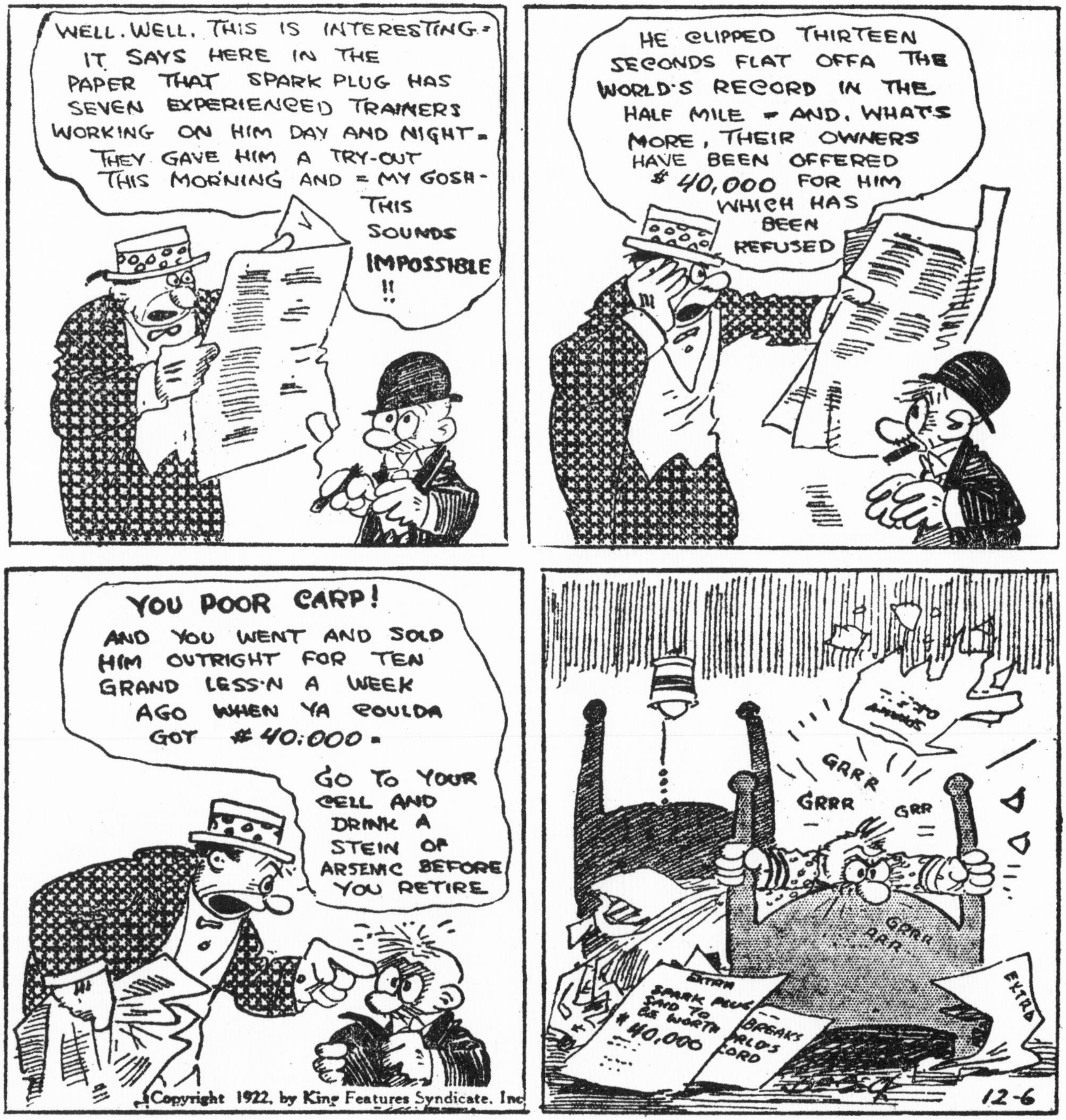
WELL. WELL. THIS IS INTERESTING - IT SAYS HERE IN THE PAPER THAT SPARK PLUG HAS SEVEN EXPERIENCED TRAINERS WORKING ON HIM DAY AND NIGHT - THEY GAVE HIM A TRY-OUT THIS MORNING AND - MY GOSH - THIS SOUNDS IMPOSSIBLE !!
HE CLIPPED THIRTEEN SECONDS FLAT OFFA THE WORLD'S RECORD IN THE HALF MILE - AND, WHAT'S MORE, THEIR OWNERS HAVE BEEN OFFERED $40,000 FOR HIM WHICH HAS BEEN REFUSED
YOU POOR CARP! AND YOU WENT AND SOLD HIM OUTRIGHT FOR TEN GRAND LESS'N A WEEK AGO WHEN YA COULDA GOT $40,000 -
GO TO YOUR CELL AND DRINK A STEIN OF ARSENIC BEFORE YOU RETIRE
Copyright 1922, by King Features Syndicate, Inc
GRRR
GRRR
GRR
GRRR
EXTRA
SPARK PLUG SAID TO BE WORTH $40,000
EXTRA
12-6

And They Say Love Is Blind!

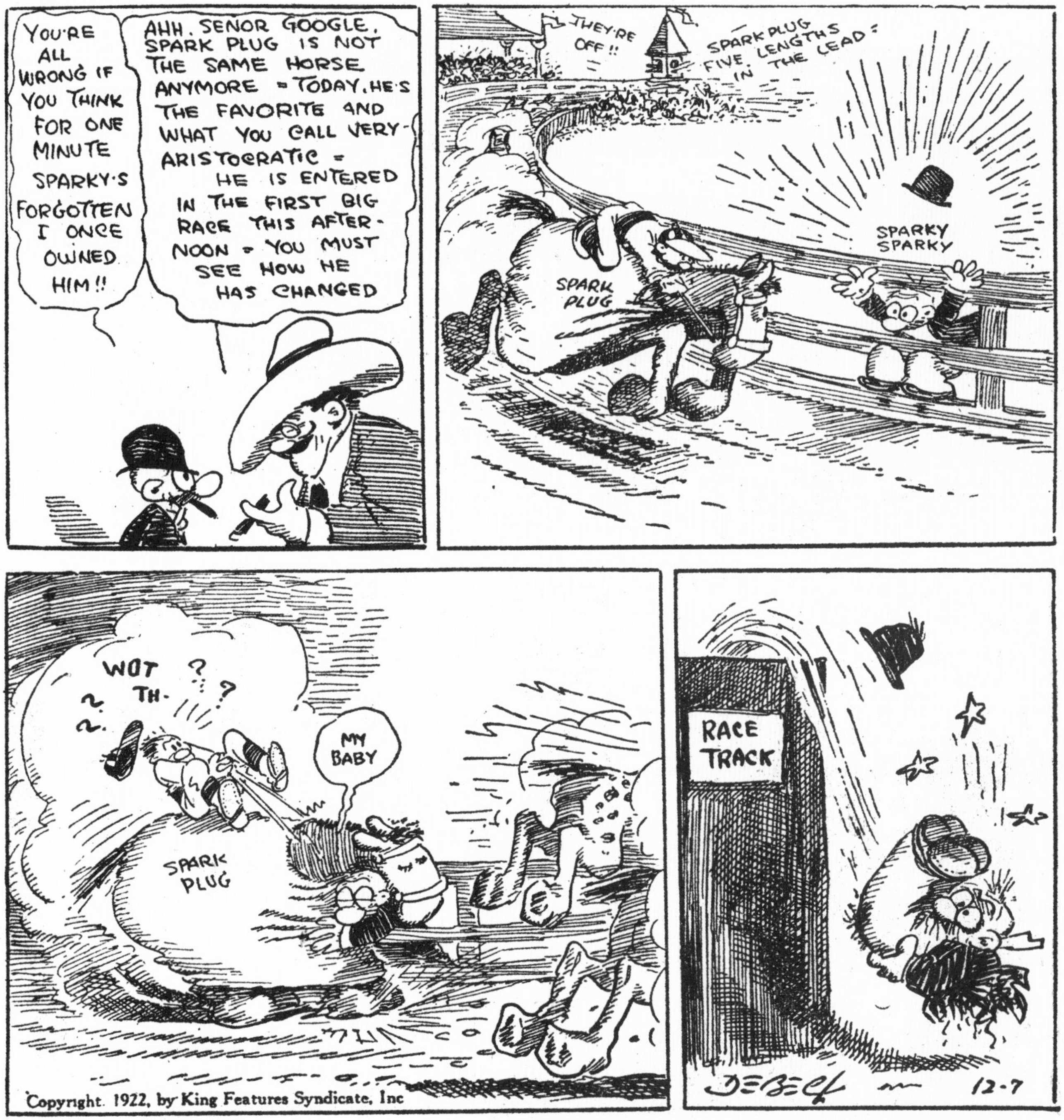

YOU'RE ALL WRONG IF YOU THINK FOR ONE MINUTE SPARKY'S FORGOTTEN I ONCE OWNED HIM!!
AHH, SENOR GOOGLE, SPARK PLUG IS NOT THE SAME HORSE ANYMORE = TODAY, HE'S THE FAVORITE AND WHAT YOU CALL VERY-ARISTOCRATIC = HE IS ENTERED IN THE FIRST BIG RACE THIS AFTER-NOON = YOU MUST SEE HOW HE HAS CHANGED
THEY'RE OFF!!
SPARK PLUG FIVE LENGTHS IN THE LEAD =
SPARKY SPARKY
SPARK PLUG
WOT TH- ? ? ?
MY BABY
SPARK PLUG
RACE TRACK
DE BECK
12-7
Copyright. 1922, by King Features Syndicate, Inc

Well, Well! This Tickles Barney's Scalp Pink

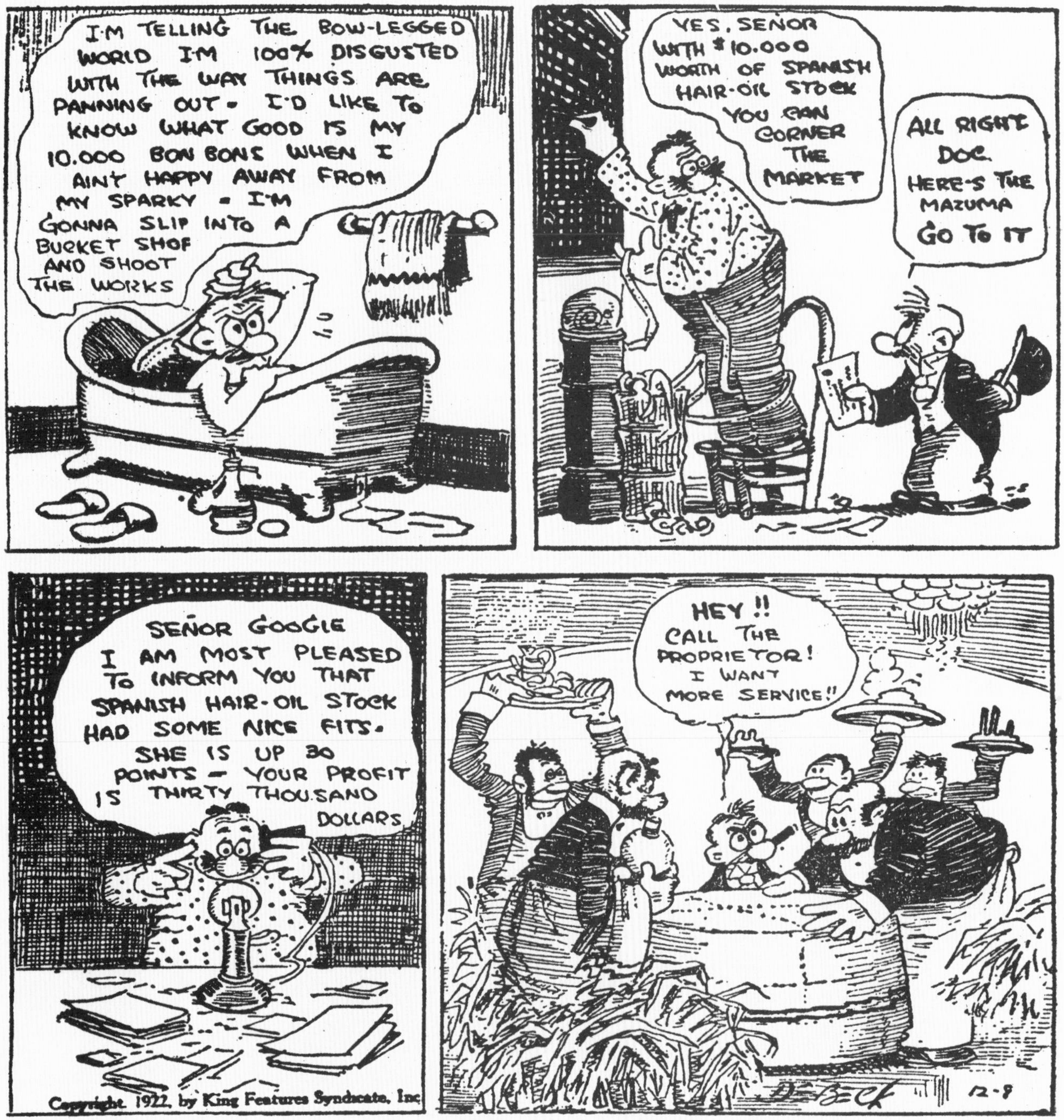
I'M TELLING THE BOW-LEGGED WORLD I'M 100% DISGUSTED WITH THE WAY THINGS ARE PANNING OUT - I'D LIKE TO KNOW WHAT GOOD IS MY 10.000 BON BONS WHEN I AIN'T HAPPY AWAY FROM MY SPARKY - I'M GONNA SLIP INTO A BUCKET SHOP AND SHOOT THE WORKS
YES, SENOR WITH $10.000 WORTH OF SPANISH HAIR-OIL STOCK YOU CAN CORNER THE MARKET
ALL RIGHT DOC. HERE'S THE MAZUMA GO TO IT
SEÑOR GOOGLE I AM MOST PLEASED TO INFORM YOU THAT SPANISH HAIR-OIL STOCK HAD SOME NICE FITS. SHE IS UP 30 POINTS - YOUR PROFIT IS THIRTY THOUSAND DOLLARS
HEY !! CALL THE PROPRIETOR! I WANT MORE SERVICE!!
Copyright 1922, by King Features Syndicate, Inc
12-9

Barney Goes Broke for Sparky—Almost

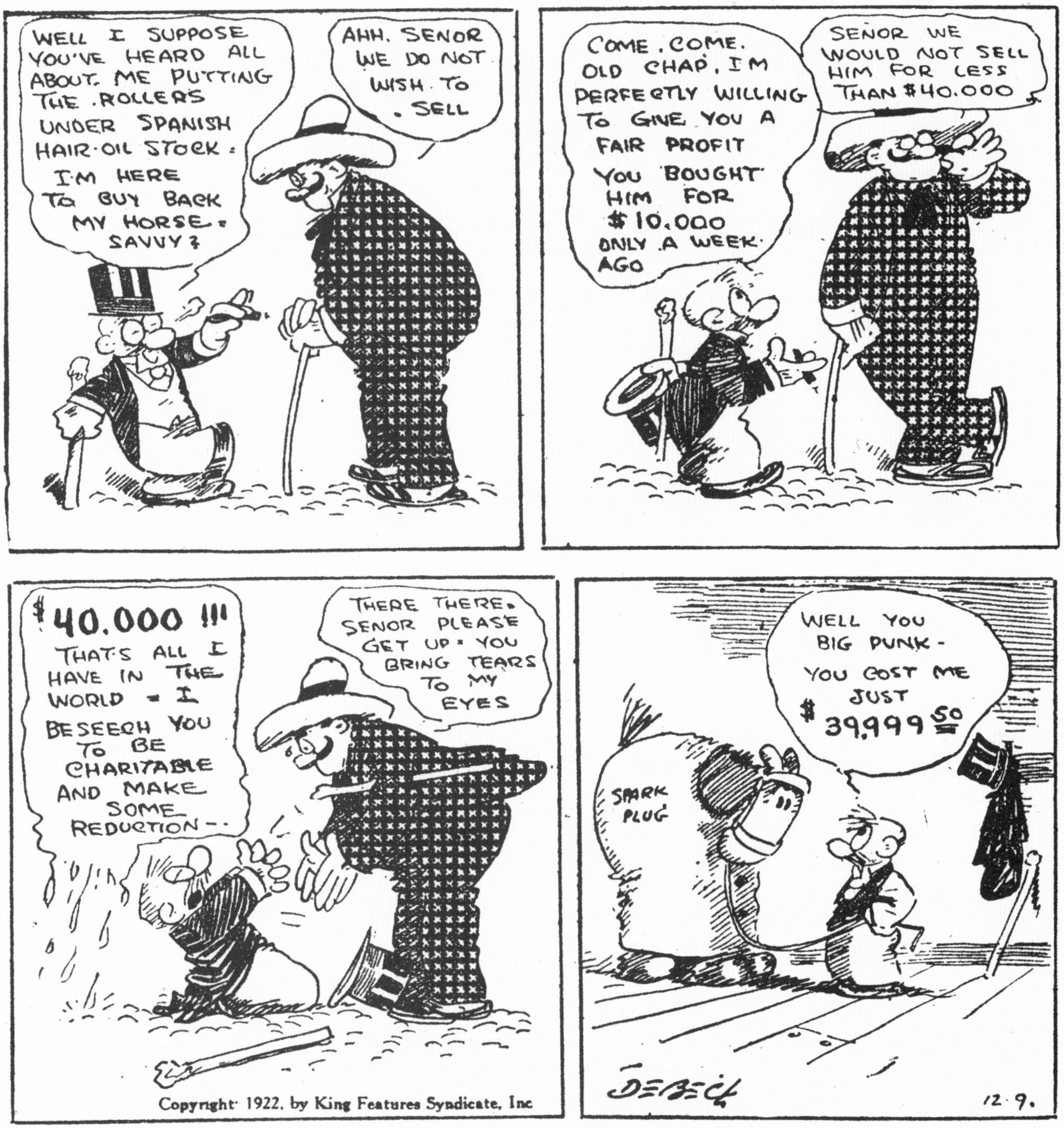
WELL I SUPPOSE YOU'VE HEARD ALL ABOUT ME PUTTING THE ROLLERS UNDER SPANISH HAIR-OIL STOCK = I'M HERE TO BUY BACK MY HORSE = SAVVY?
AHH. SENOR WE DO NOT WISH TO SELL
COME. COME. OLD CHAP. I'M PERFECTLY WILLING TO GIVE YOU A FAIR PROFIT YOU BOUGHT HIM FOR $10.000 ONLY A WEEK AGO
SENOR WE WOULD NOT SELL HIM FOR LESS THAN $40.000
$40.000 !!! THAT'S ALL I HAVE IN THE WORLD = I BESEECH YOU TO BE CHARITABLE AND MAKE SOME REDUCTION --
THERE THERE. SENOR PLEASE GET UP = YOU BRING TEARS TO MY EYES
WELL YOU BIG PUNK - YOU COST ME JUST $39,999 50
SPARK PLUG
Copyright 1922, by King Features Syndicate, Inc
DEBECK
12-9.

Barney Decides to Stay a Little Longer in Havana

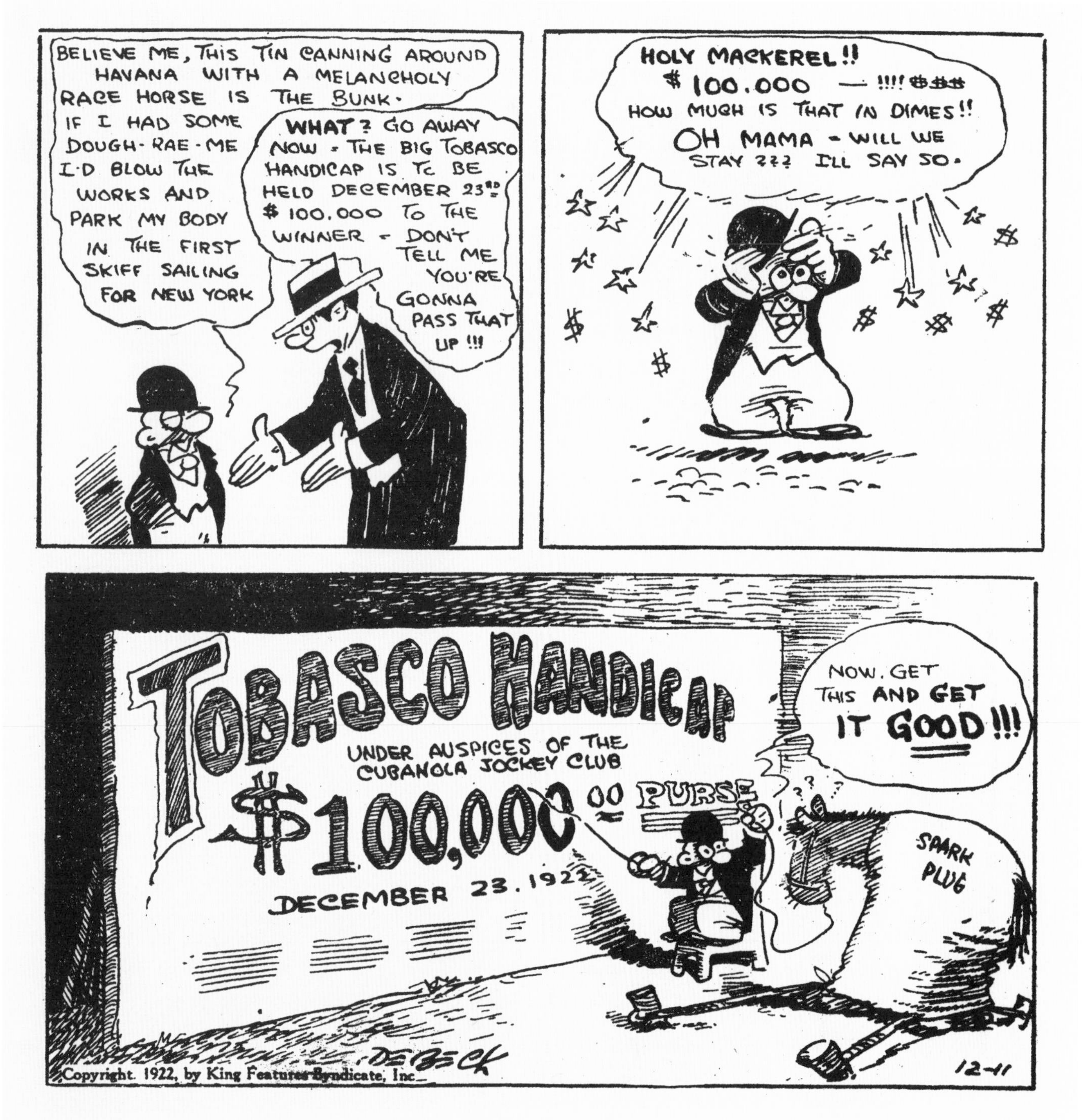

BELIEVE ME, THIS TIN CANNING AROUND HAVANA WITH A MELANCHOLY RACE HORSE IS THE BUNK. IF I HAD SOME DOUGH-RAE-ME I'D BLOW THE WORKS AND PARK MY BODY IN THE FIRST SKIFF SAILING FOR NEW YORK
WHAT? GO AWAY NOW - THE BIG TOBASCO HANDICAP IS TO BE HELD DECEMBER 23RD - $100,000 TO THE WINNER - DON'T TELL ME YOU'RE GONNA PASS THAT UP !!!
HOLY MACKEREL!! $100.000 — !!!! $$$ HOW MUCH IS THAT IN DIMES!! OH MAMA - WILL WE STAY ??? I'LL SAY SO.
TOBASCO HANDICAP
UNDER AUSPICES OF THE CUBANOLA JOCKEY CLUB
$100,000.00 PURSE
DECEMBER 23. 1922
NOW, GET THIS AND GET IT GOOD!!!
SPARK PLUG
DE BECK
12-11

This Makes Sparky Feel His Oats

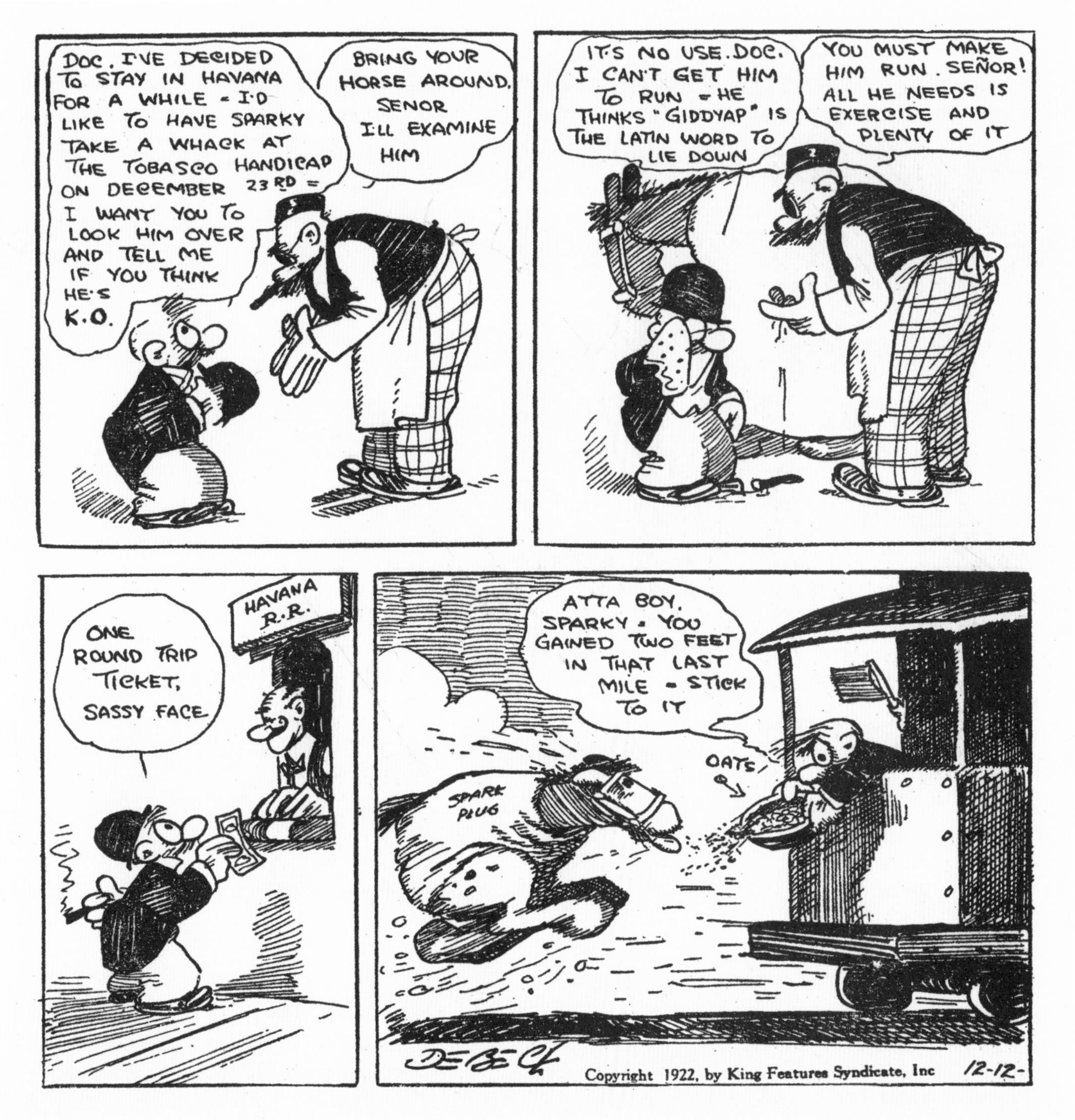

DOC, I'VE DECIDED TO STAY IN HAVANA FOR A WHILE - I'D LIKE TO HAVE SPARKY TAKE A WHACK AT THE TOBASCO HANDICAP ON DECEMBER 23RD - I WANT YOU TO LOOK HIM OVER AND TELL ME IF YOU THINK HE'S K.O.
BRING YOUR HORSE AROUND, SENOR I'LL EXAMINE HIM
IT'S NO USE, DOC. I CAN'T GET HIM TO RUN - HE THINKS "GIDDYAP" IS THE LATIN WORD TO LIE DOWN
YOU MUST MAKE HIM RUN, SEÑOR! ALL HE NEEDS IS EXERCISE AND PLENTY OF IT
HAVANA R.R.
ONE ROUND TRIP TICKET, SASSY FACE
ATTA BOY, SPARKY - YOU GAINED TWO FEET IN THAT LAST MILE - STICK TO IT
OATS
SPARK PLUG
DE BECK
Copyright 1922, by King Features Syndicate, Inc
12-12-

Sparky's Deaf to Everything—Almost

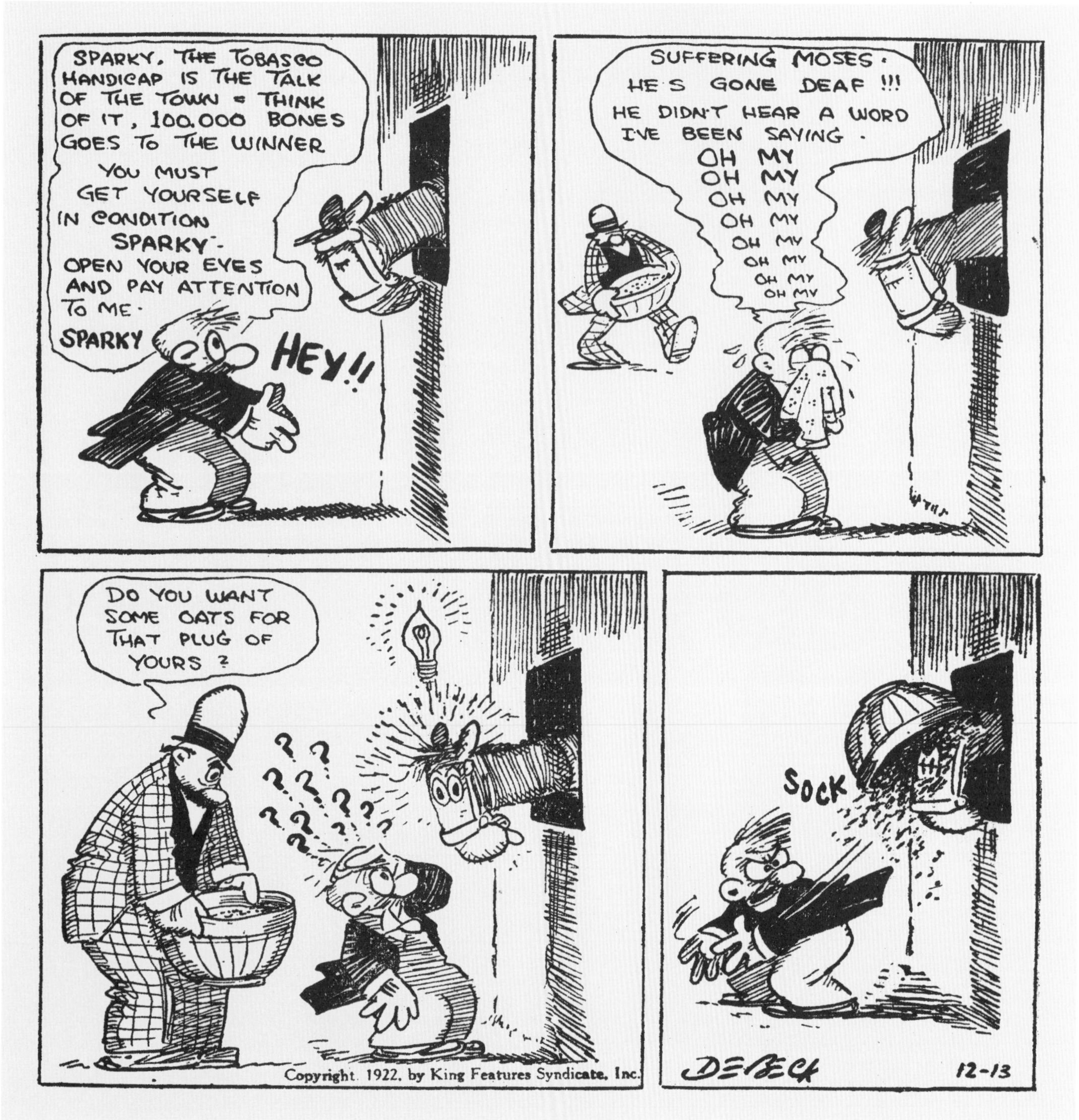
SPARKY, THE TOBASCO HANDICAP IS THE TALK OF THE TOWN = THINK OF IT, 100,000 BONES GOES TO THE WINNER
YOU MUST GET YOURSELF IN CONDITION SPARKY- OPEN YOUR EYES AND PAY ATTENTION TO ME. SPARKY
HEY!!
SUFFERING MOSES. HE'S GONE DEAF !!! HE DIDN'T HEAR A WORD I'VE BEEN SAYING. OH MY OH MY OH MY OH MY OH MY OH MY OH MY OH MY
DO YOU WANT SOME OATS FOR THAT PLUG OF YOURS ?
SOCK
Copyright. 1922, by King Features Syndicate, Inc.
DEBECK
12-13

Well, You Know How It Is in a Tropical Climate

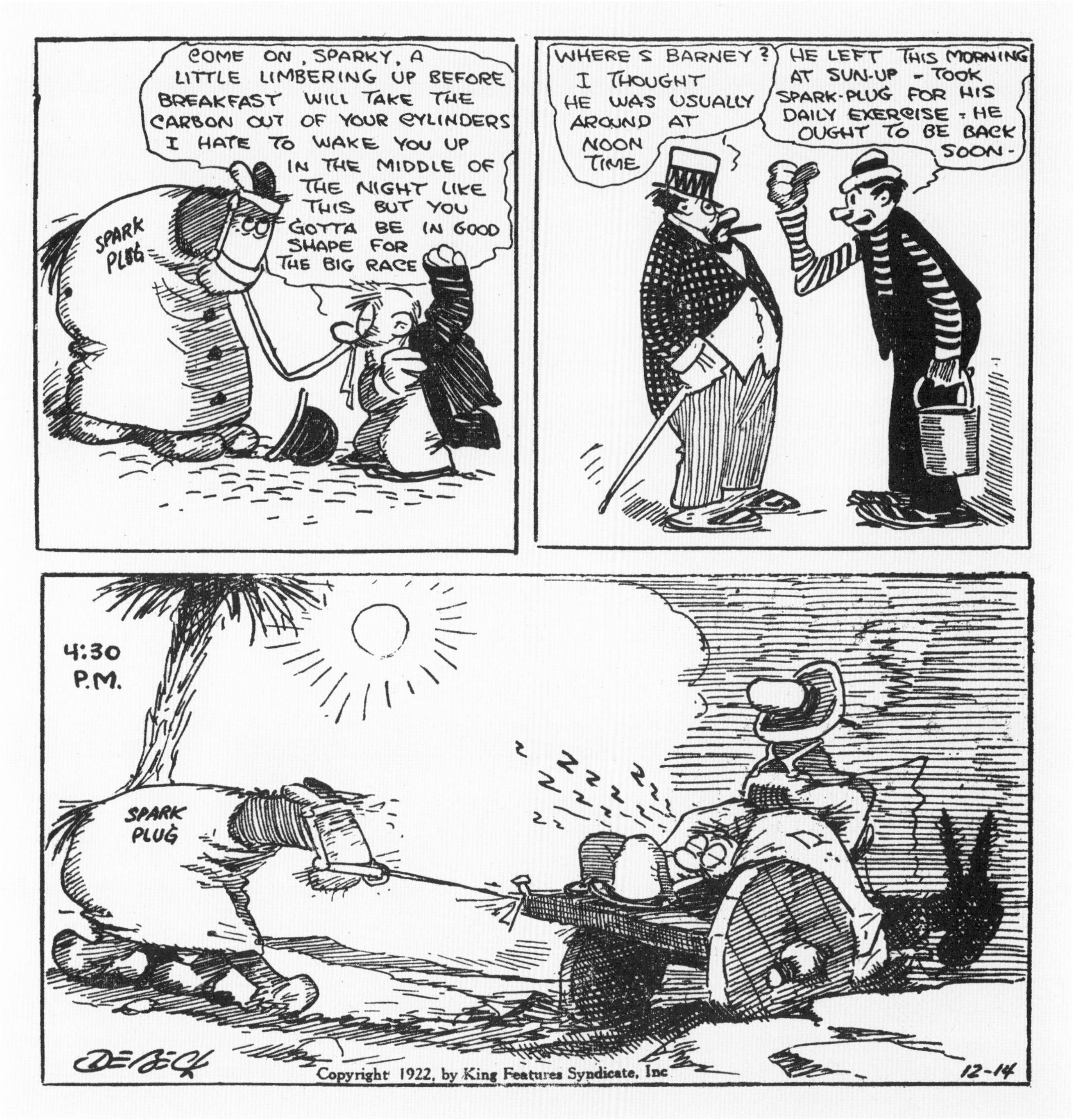
COME ON, SPARKY, A LITTLE LIMBERING UP BEFORE BREAKFAST WILL TAKE THE CARBON OUT OF YOUR CYLINDERS I HATE TO WAKE YOU UP IN THE MIDDLE OF THE NIGHT LIKE THIS BUT YOU GOTTA BE IN GOOD SHAPE FOR THE BIG RACE
SPARK PLUG
WHERE'S BARNEY? I THOUGHT HE WAS USUALLY AROUND AT NOON TIME
HE LEFT THIS MORNING AT SUN-UP - TOOK SPARK-PLUG FOR HIS DAILY EXERCISE - HE OUGHT TO BE BACK SOON -
4:30 P.M.
SPARK PLUG
Z Z Z Z Z
DE BECK
Copyright 1922, by King Features Syndicate, Inc
12-14

"He Who Reads May Run"

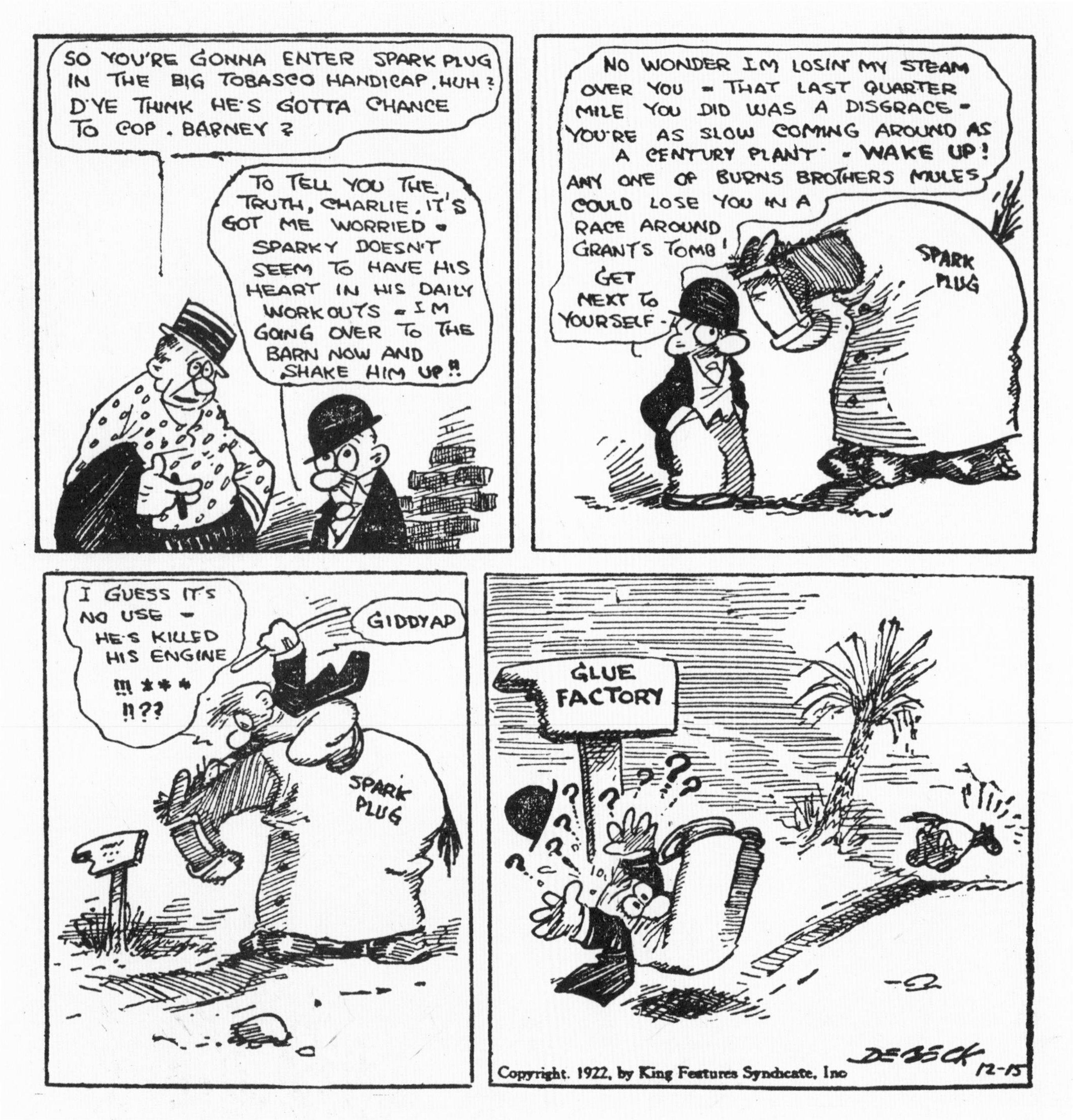
SO YOU'RE GONNA ENTER SPARK PLUG IN THE BIG TOBASCO HANDICAP, HUH? D'YE THINK HE'S GOTTA CHANCE TO COP, BARNEY?
TO TELL YOU THE TRUTH, CHARLIE, IT'S GOT ME WORRIED - SPARKY DOESN'T SEEM TO HAVE HIS HEART IN HIS DAILY WORKOUTS - I'M GOING OVER TO THE BARN NOW AND SHAKE HIM UP!!
NO WONDER I'M LOSIN' MY STEAM OVER YOU - THAT LAST QUARTER MILE YOU DID WAS A DISGRACE - YOU'RE AS SLOW COMING AROUND AS A CENTURY PLANT - WAKE UP! ANY ONE OF BURNS BROTHERS MULES COULD LOSE YOU IN A RACE AROUND GRANT'S TOMB! GET NEXT TO YOURSELF -
SPARK PLUG
I GUESS IT'S NO USE - HE'S KILLED HIS ENGINE
!!! *** !!??
GIDDYAP
SPARK PLUG
GLUE FACTORY
Copyright. 1922, by King Features Syndicate, Inc
DEBECK 12-15

Barney's Affection Is Reciprocated

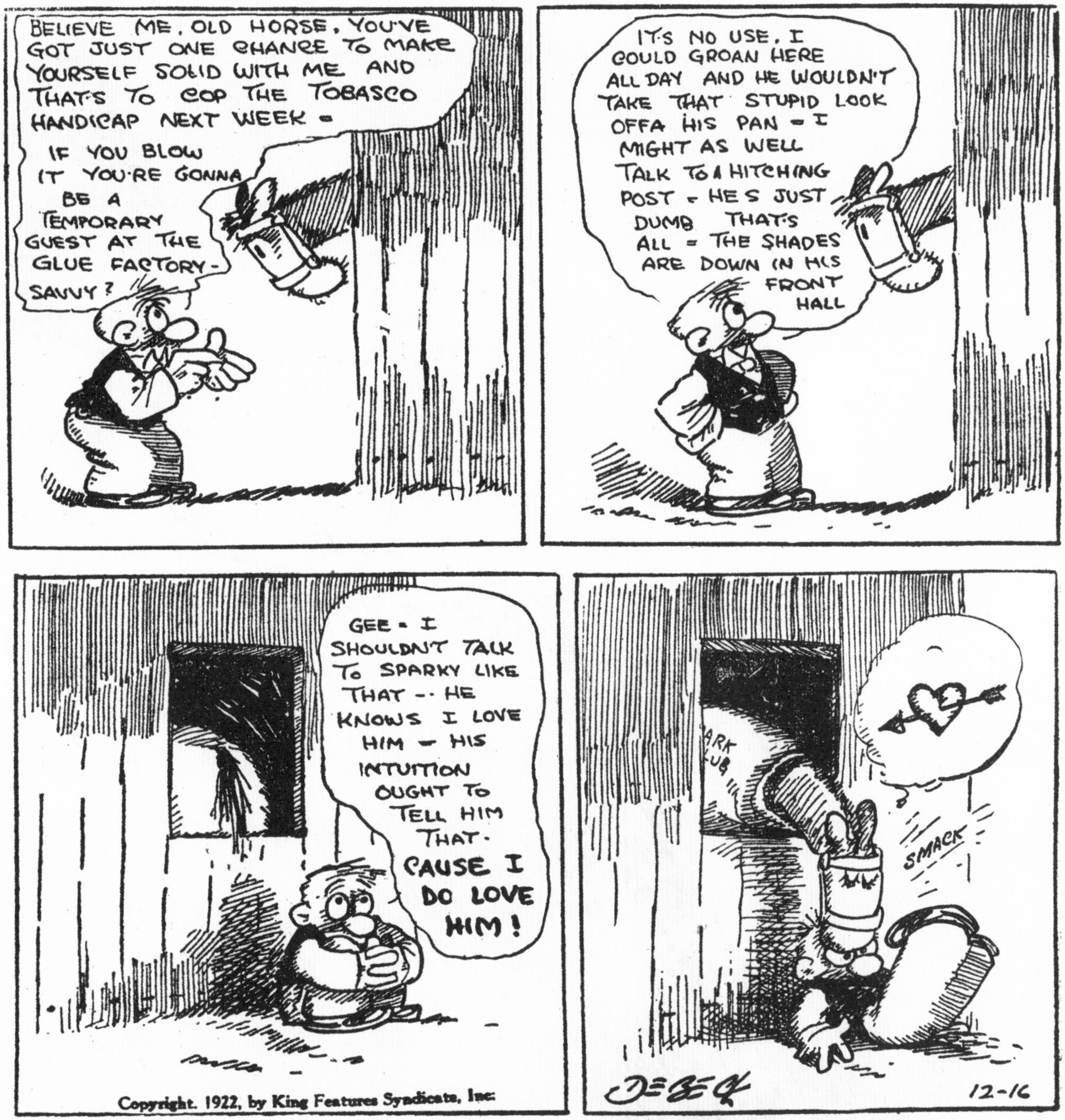

BELIEVE ME, OLD HORSE, YOU'VE GOT JUST ONE CHANCE TO MAKE YOURSELF SOLID WITH ME AND THAT'S TO COP THE TOBASCO HANDICAP NEXT WEEK -
IF YOU BLOW IT YOU'RE GONNA BE A TEMPORARY GUEST AT THE GLUE FACTORY - SAVVY?
IT'S NO USE, I COULD GROAN HERE ALL DAY AND HE WOULDN'T TAKE THAT STUPID LOOK OFFA HIS PAN - I MIGHT AS WELL TALK TO A HITCHING POST - HE'S JUST DUMB THAT'S ALL - THE SHADES ARE DOWN IN HIS FRONT HALL
GEE - I SHOULDN'T TALK TO SPARKY LIKE THAT -- HE KNOWS I LOVE HIM - HIS INTUITION OUGHT TO TELL HIM THAT.
'CAUSE I DO LOVE HIM!
Copyright. 1922, by King Features Syndicate, Inc.
SMACK
DeBECK
12-16

Easy Money for Barney

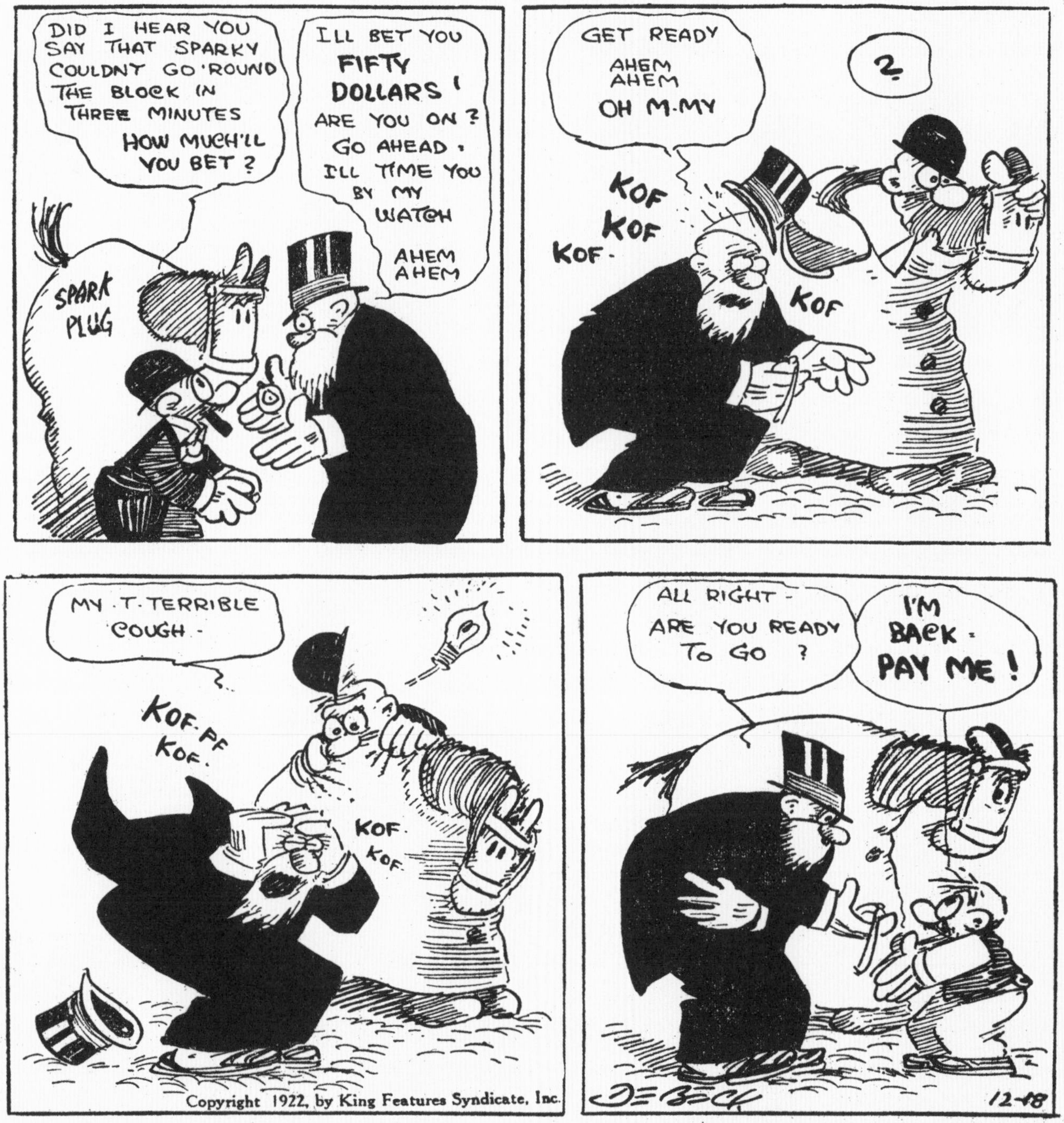
DID I HEAR YOU SAY THAT SPARKY COULDN'T GO 'ROUND THE BLOCK IN THREE MINUTES
HOW MUCH'LL YOU BET ?
I'LL BET YOU FIFTY DOLLARS ! ARE YOU ON ? GO AHEAD - I'LL TIME YOU BY MY WATCH
AHEM AHEM
SPARK PLUG
GET READY
AHEM AHEM
OH M-MY
?
KOF KOF KOF-
KOF
MY T-TERRIBLE COUGH -
KOF-PF KOF-
KOF KOF-
ALL RIGHT - ARE YOU READY TO GO ?
I'M BACK - PAY ME !
DE BECK
12-18

Copyright 1922, by King Features Syndicate, Inc.

And the Great Tobasco Handicap Only Four Days Off

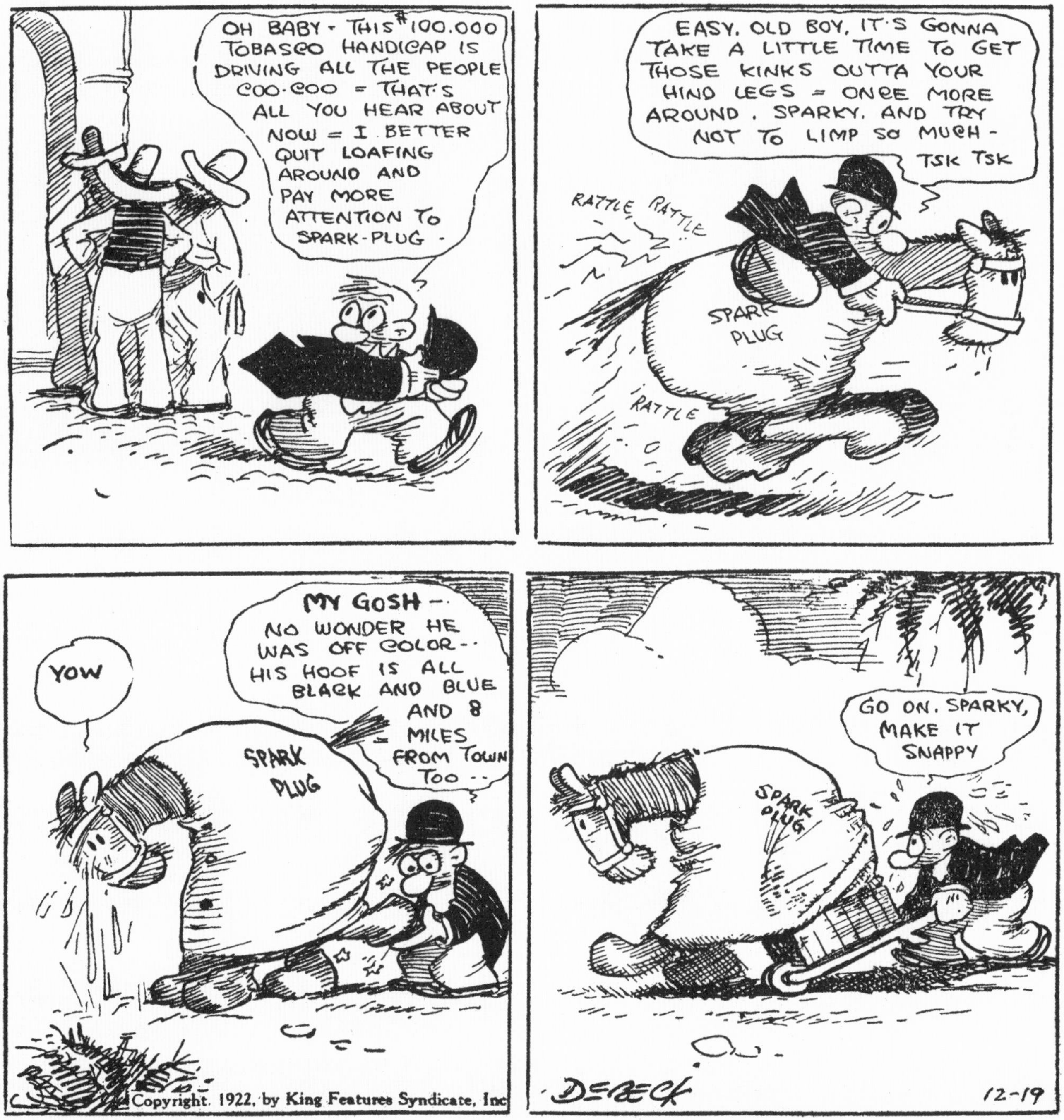
OH BABY - THIS #100.000 TOBASCO HANDICAP IS DRIVING ALL THE PEOPLE COO-COO = THAT'S ALL YOU HEAR ABOUT NOW = I BETTER QUIT LOAFING AROUND AND PAY MORE ATTENTION TO SPARK-PLUG -
EASY, OLD BOY, IT'S GONNA TAKE A LITTLE TIME TO GET THOSE KINKS OUTTA YOUR HIND LEGS = ONCE MORE AROUND, SPARKY, AND TRY NOT TO LIMP SO MUCH - TSK TSK
RATTLE RATTLE
SPARK PLUG
RATTLE
YOW
MY GOSH - NO WONDER HE WAS OFF COLOR - HIS HOOF IS ALL BLACK AND BLUE AND 8 MILES FROM TOWN TOO -
SPARK PLUG
GO ON, SPARKY, MAKE IT SNAPPY
SPARK PLUG
Copyright, 1922, by King Features Syndicate, Inc
DEBECK
12-19

A K.O. for Barney's Appetite

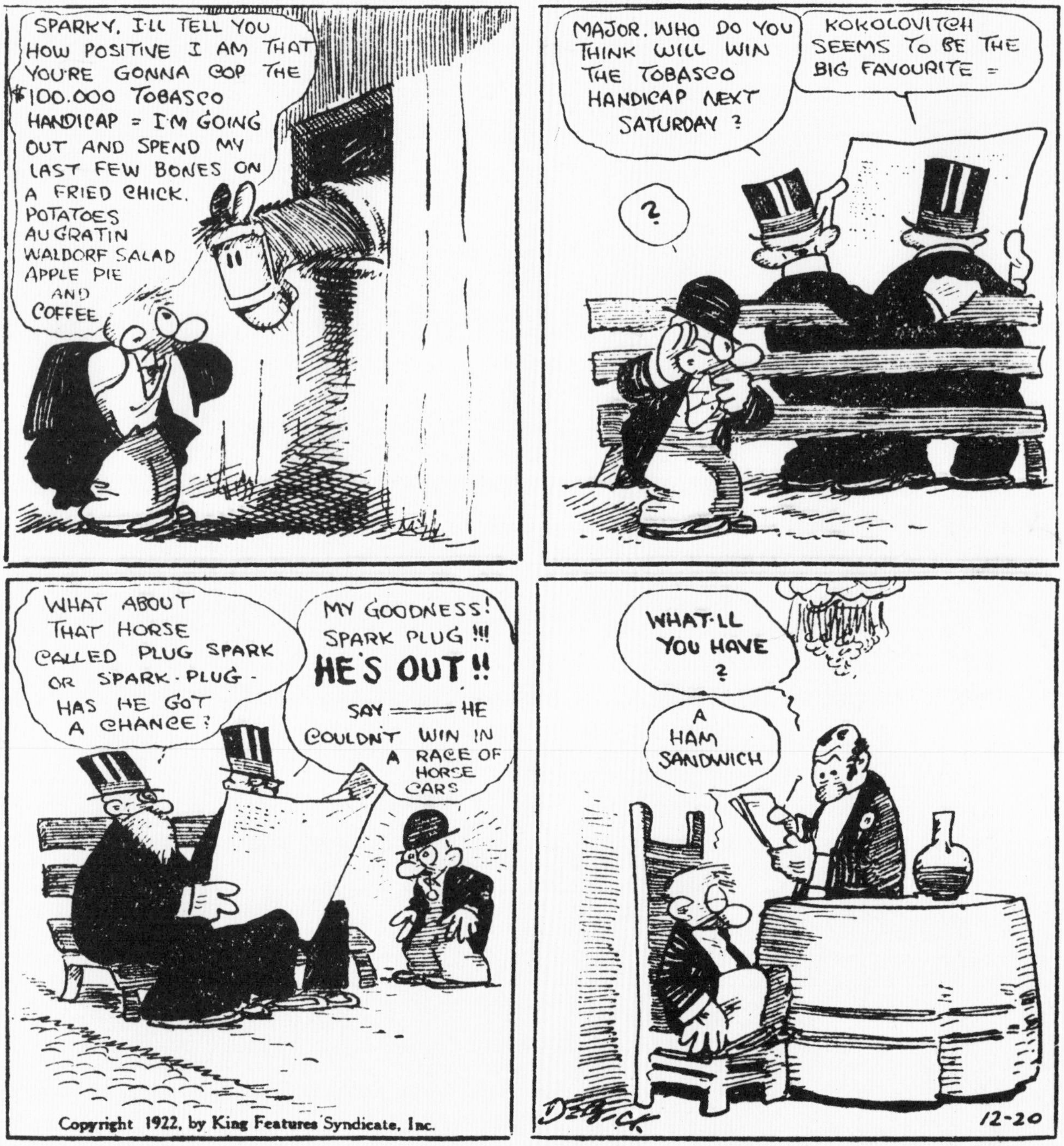
SPARKY, I'LL TELL YOU HOW POSITIVE I AM THAT YOU'RE GONNA COP THE $100,000 TOBASCO HANDICAP = I'M GOING OUT AND SPEND MY LAST FEW BONES ON A FRIED CHICK, POTATOES AU GRATIN WALDORF SALAD APPLE PIE AND COFFEE
MAJOR, WHO DO YOU THINK WILL WIN THE TOBASCO HANDICAP NEXT SATURDAY ?
KOKOLOVITCH SEEMS TO BE THE BIG FAVOURITE =
?
WHAT ABOUT THAT HORSE CALLED PLUG SPARK OR SPARK-PLUG - HAS HE GOT A CHANCE ?
MY GOODNESS! SPARK PLUG !!! HE'S OUT !! SAY —— HE COULDN'T WIN IN A RACE OF HORSE CARS
WHAT'LL YOU HAVE ?
A HAM SANDWICH
12-20

Read the Life of Spark Plug—A Thrill on Each Page!

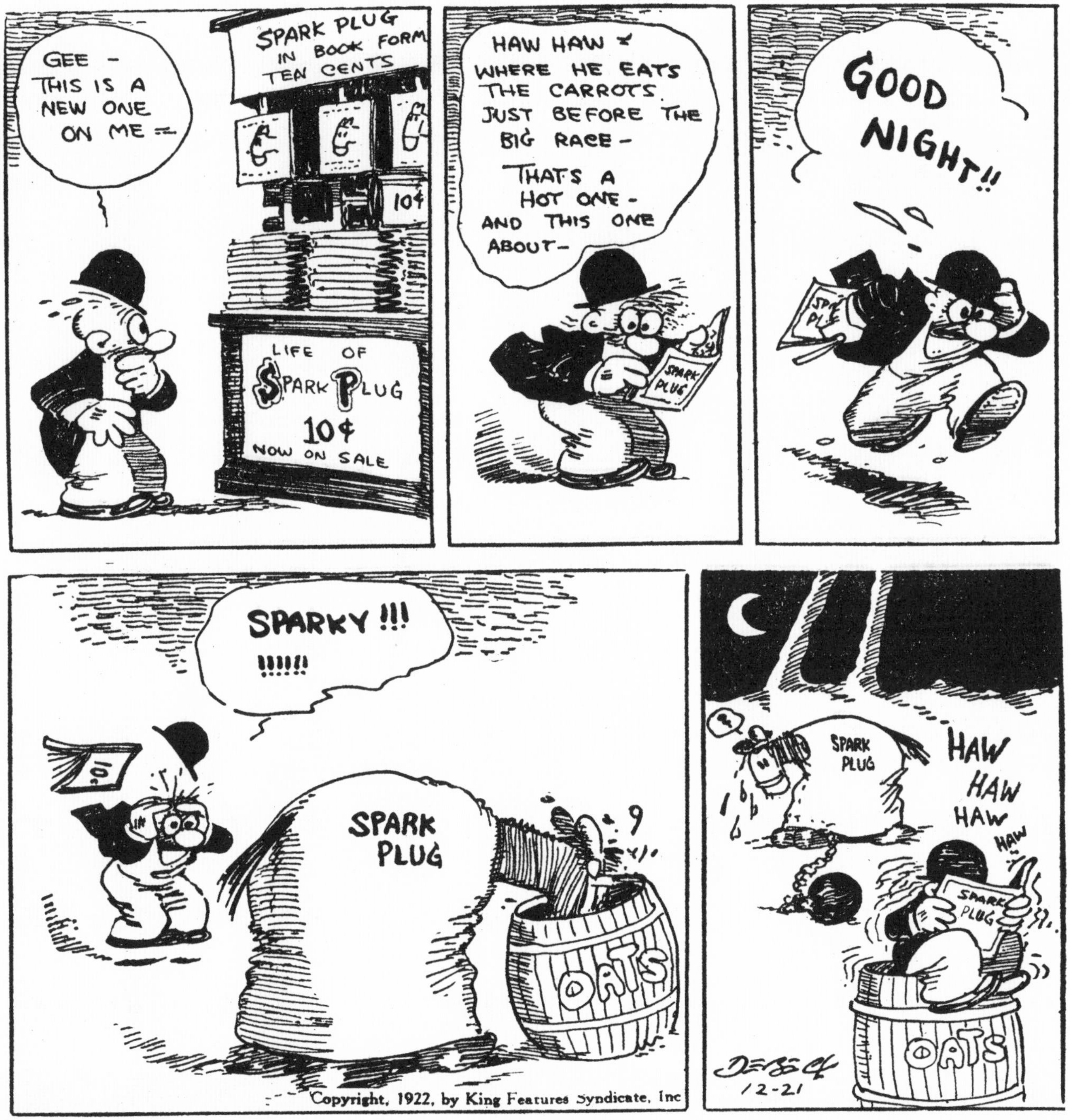
SPARK PLUG IN BOOK FORM TEN CENTS
GEE - THIS IS A NEW ONE ON ME
10¢
LIFE OF SPARK PLUG 10¢ NOW ON SALE
HAW HAW - WHERE HE EATS THE CARROTS JUST BEFORE THE BIG RACE - THAT'S A HOT ONE - AND THIS ONE ABOUT -
SPARK PLUG
GOOD NIGHT!!
SPARKY!!! !!!!!!
10¢
SPARK PLUG
OATS
Copyright, 1922, by King Features Syndicate, Inc
SPARK PLUG
HAW HAW HAW HAW
SPARK PLUG
OATS

Will Barney Be in Clover Tomorrow?

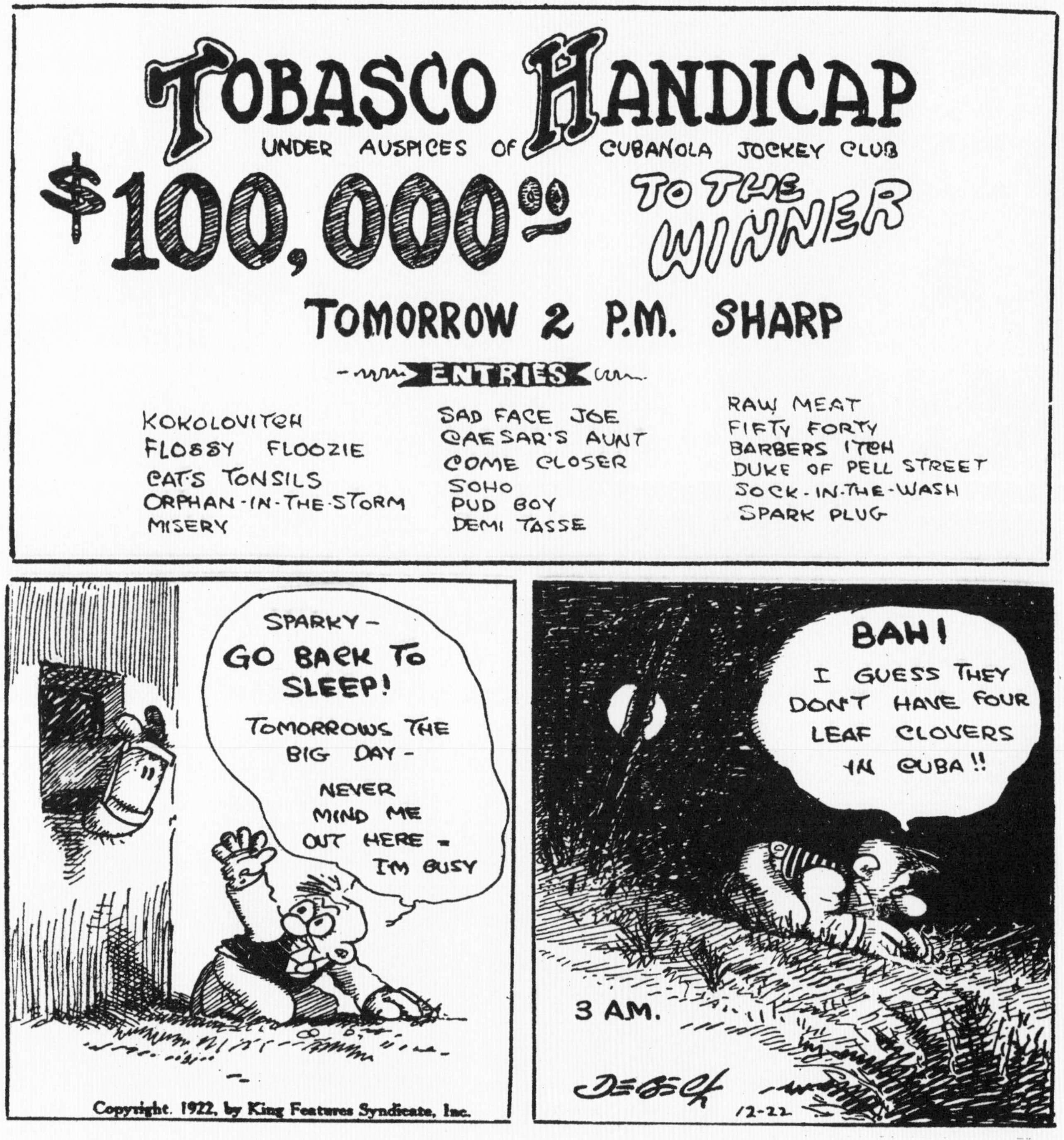
TOBASCO HANDICAP
UNDER AUSPICES OF CUBANOLA JOCKEY CLUB
$100,000.00 TO THE WINNER
TOMORROW 2 P.M. SHARP
ENTRIES
KOKOLOVITCH
FLOSSY FLOOZIE
CAT'S TONSILS
ORPHAN-IN-THE-STORM
MISERY
SAD FACE JOE
CAESAR'S AUNT
COME CLOSER
SOHO
PUD BOY
DEMI TASSE
RAW MEAT
FIFTY FORTY
BARBERS ITCH
DUKE OF PELL STREET
SOCK-IN-THE-WASH
SPARK PLUG
SPARKY - GO BACK TO SLEEP! TOMORROWS THE BIG DAY - NEVER MIND ME OUT HERE - I'M BUSY
Copyright. 1922, by King Features Syndicate, Inc.
BAH! I GUESS THEY DON'T HAVE FOUR LEAF CLOVERS IN CUBA!!
3 AM.
12-22

Pearls? Barney Can Afford to Feed 'Em to Sparky!

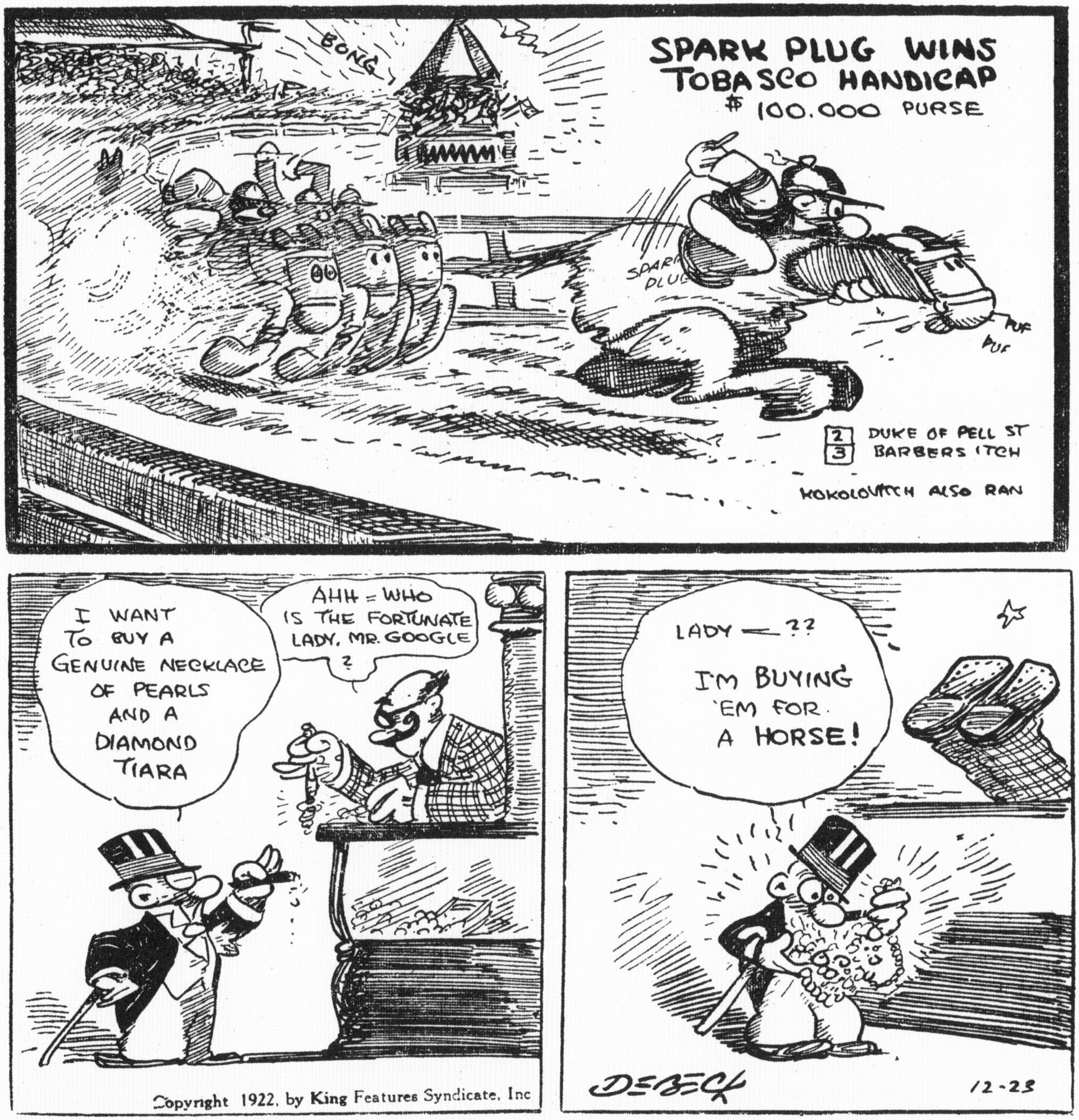
BONG
SPARK PLUG WINS TOBASCO HANDICAP
$ 100.000 PURSE
SPARK PLUG
PUF
PUF
2 DUKE OF PELL ST
3 BARBERS ITCH
KOKOLOVITCH ALSO RAN
I WANT TO BUY A GENUINE NECKLACE OF PEARLS AND A DIAMOND TIARA
AHH = WHO IS THE FORTUNATE LADY, MR. GOOGLE ?
LADY — ??
I'M BUYING 'EM FOR A HORSE!
Copyright 1922, by King Features Syndicate, Inc
DEBECK
12-23

Merry Christmas! Barney Feels at Home Again

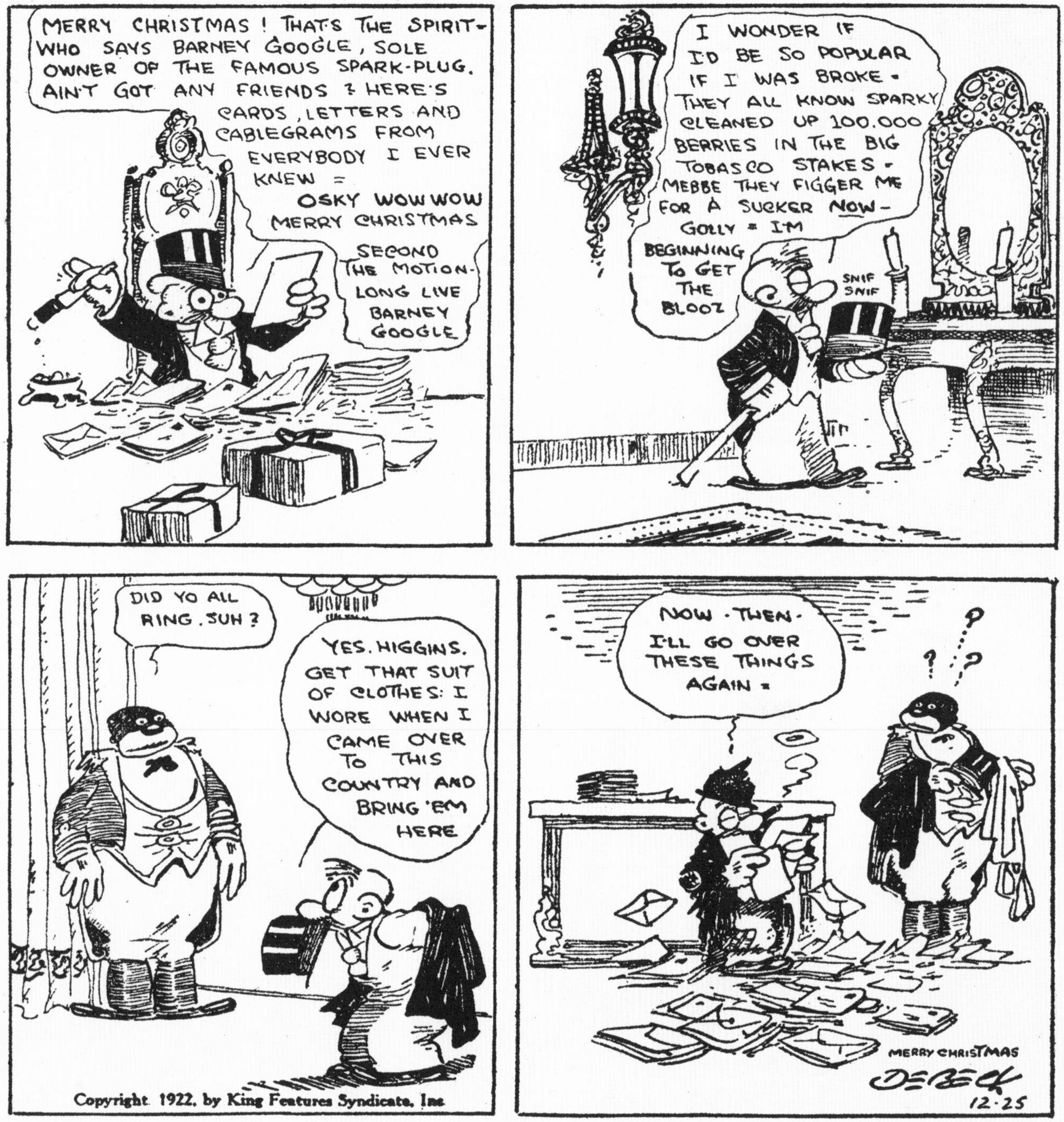
MERRY CHRISTMAS! THAT'S THE SPIRIT- WHO SAYS BARNEY GOOGLE, SOLE OWNER OF THE FAMOUS SPARK-PLUG. AIN'T GOT ANY FRIENDS? HERE'S CARDS, LETTERS AND CABLEGRAMS FROM EVERYBODY I EVER KNEW = OSKY WOW WOW MERRY CHRISTMAS
SECOND THE MOTION- LONG LIVE BARNEY GOOGLE
I WONDER IF I'D BE SO POPULAR IF I WAS BROKE- THEY ALL KNOW SPARKY CLEANED UP 100.000 BERRIES IN THE BIG TOBASCO STAKES- MEBBE THEY FIGGER ME FOR A SUCKER NOW- GOLLY = I'M BEGINNING TO GET THE BLOOZ
SNIF SNIF
DID YO ALL RING, SUH?
YES, HIGGINS. GET THAT SUIT OF CLOTHES: I WORE WHEN I CAME OVER TO THIS COUNTRY AND BRING 'EM HERE
NOW-THEN- I'LL GO OVER THESE THINGS AGAIN =
? ? ?
Copyright 1922, by King Features Syndicate, Inc
MERRY CHRISTMAS
DEBECK
12-25

Well! Well! There's Nothing Slow About Sparky

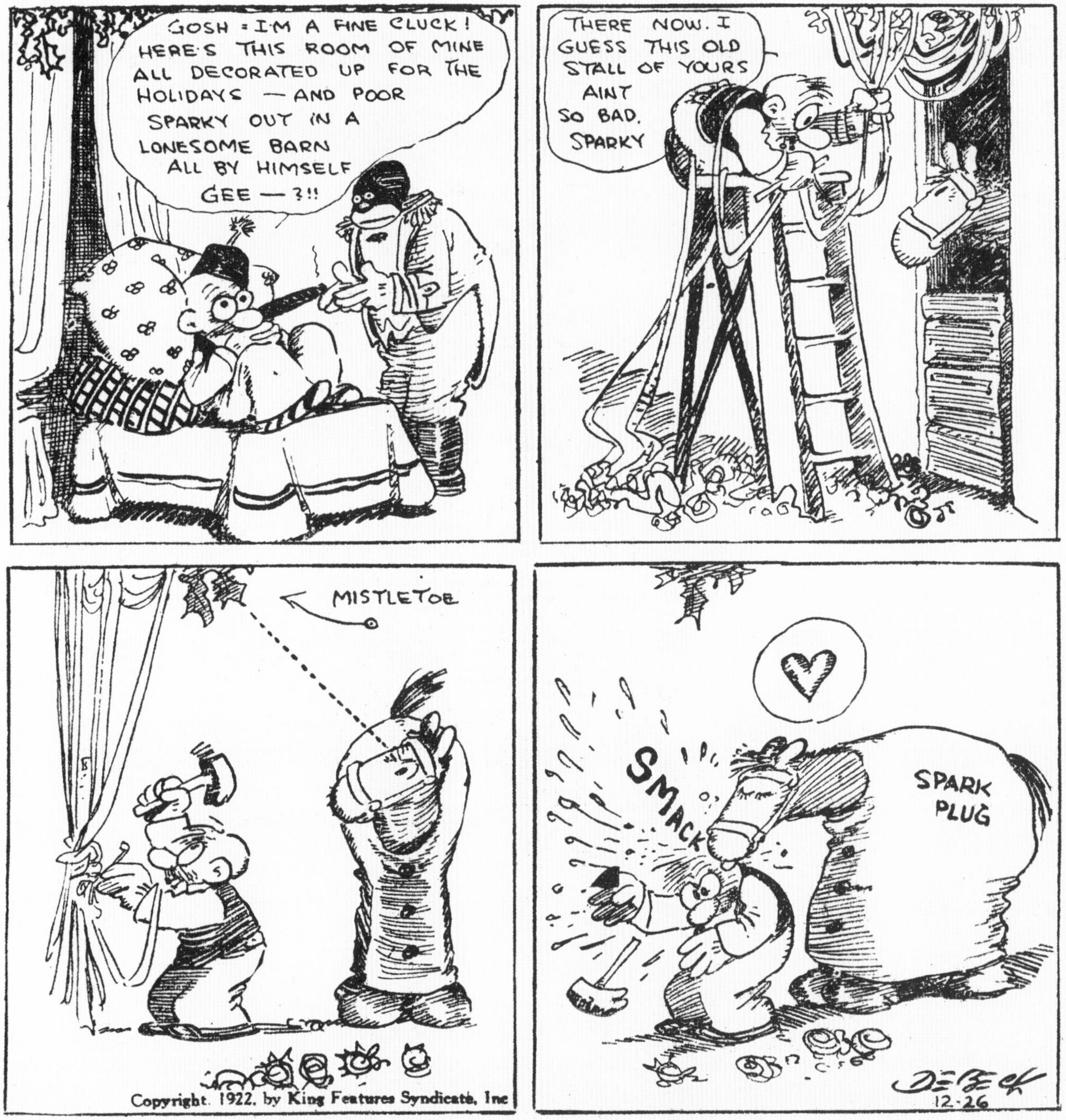
GOSH = I'M A FINE CLUCK! HERE'S THIS ROOM OF MINE ALL DECORATED UP FOR THE HOLIDAYS — AND POOR SPARKY OUT IN A LONESOME BARN ALL BY HIMSELF GEE — ?!!
THERE NOW. I GUESS THIS OLD STALL OF YOURS AINT SO BAD, SPARKY
MISTLETOE
Copyright. 1922, by King Features Syndicate, Inc
SMACK
SPARK PLUG
DE BECK
12-26

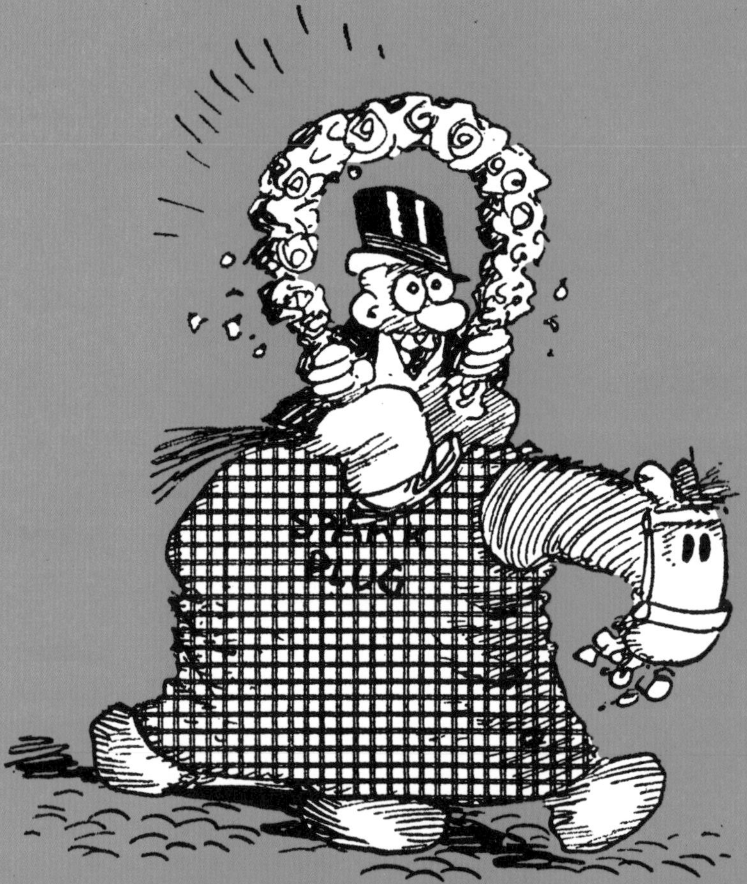
SPARK
PLUG